JACK DEMPSEY

DATE			

Jack Dempsey, Heavyweight Champion of the World, 1921

Culver

Jack Dempsey

The
Manassa Mauler

Randy Roberts

LOUISIANA STATE UNIVERSITY PRESS
Baton Rouge and London

Copyright © 1979 by Louisiana State University Press
All rights reserved
Manufactured in the United States of America

Design: Dwight Agner
Typeface: VIP Goudy
Composition: The Composing Room of Michigan, Inc.

Louisiana Paperback Edition, 1984

95 94 93 92 91 90   5 4 3 2

LIBRARY OF CONGRESS CATALOGING IN PUBLICATION DATA

Roberts, Randy, 1951–
  Jack Dempsey, the Manassa mauler.

  Bibliography: p.
  Includes index.
  1. Dempsey, Jack, 1895– 2. Boxers (Sports)—
United States—Biography. I. Title
GV1132.D4R62 1984   796.8'3'0924 [B]   83-27514
ISBN 0-8071-0588-0 (cloth)
ISBN 0-8071-1161-9 (paper)

For my mother
and to the memory
of my father

Contents

Illustrations

Acknowledgments

I T IS with a sense of pleasure that I acknowledge the debts I incurred while writing this book. I owe the largest debt to Burl Noggle who was always generous with his time, advice, criticism, and friendship. John Loos, Tom Carleton, Stan Hilton, and Karl Roider were equally kind, and all helped to improve the book. Paul O'Rourke was particularly valuable in helping me to organize my ideas about Dempsey and the 1920s in the earliest stage of my work, and Lou Vyhnanek went beyond friendship in reading the entire manuscript version and typing large portions of it. Ronda Cabot Tentarelli was kind enough to help me with proofreading and indexing, and she deserves a special thanks. I thank Beverly Jarrett, Martha Hall, and Les Phillabaum of the Louisiana State University Press for the help, warmth, and kindness they extended to me.

I wish to acknowledge two people who, without reading a page of this book, improved it. My brother, Craig Roberts, provided a knowledge of boxing that was indispensable, and his determined prodding forced me to finish the study. I may be able to repay his timely gifts of money—though I doubt if I ever will—but I will never be able to repay him for his knowledge and character. Similarly, I will always be grateful to my wife Ilsa for her loving nature. In her place, I could never have acted as kindly as she did. She never allowed my spirit to falter.

Acknowledgment

JACK DEMPSEY

Prologue:
Toledo,
1919

OUTSIDE Jack Dempsey's Restaurant, for years a Broadway landmark, snow was beginning to blanket the ground. It was the day after Christmas, 1973, and the snowfall was one of the first of the season. Inside the restaurant, sitting at his usual table just to the left of the front doors, Jack Dempsey looked out the large plate-glass windows as if he were contemplating the snow. His features showed signs of age. His hair was turning gray and thinning on the top. By his chair a heavy mahogany cane rested against his leg. He no longer remembered the exact details of his long career, a career that had been filled to the brim with action. But there was still so much life in this man. His eyes seemed to capture electricity from the overhead lights as he talked about a recent fight he had become entangled in with several New York City youths. His gravel-tinged voice sputtered occasionally, but his laugh was warm and rich.

Menus were passed around the table, and, taking out his glasses with extreme care, Dempsey commenced what his wife called his dinner ritual. He seemed to weigh each alternative, giving judicial consideration to fish and fowl as well as the different steaks. But in the end he went with his usual meal—tossed salad, steak, and baked potato.

The meal was not a quiet one. As Dempsey ate, his restaurant filled and he was constantly interrupted by out-of-town visitors. A man whose father saw Dempsey fight Tommy Gibbons in Shelby, Montana; a family from South Africa, who linked the name of Dempsey with the American Dream; and an elderly gentleman from some

1

town near Dallas who remembered listening to the first Tunney fight on the radio. On and on they came. Dempsey smiled, shook hands, laughed, and asked everyone where they came from. He did not tire of the hands and pictures and people.

After dinner, as he ate cheesecake and drank coffee, he recalled the major events in his career. With his wife filling in some details, Dempsey talked about the twenties and his years as heavyweight champion, about his childhood in Colorado and his fights in the western mining towns, about Tex Rickard and Doc Kearns and Estelle Taylor. "I was champion for—what was it, honey—eight years. That's a long time. I'm proud of that." Pausing for a moment, he considered his statement as if he had never thought of it before.

Another interruption. "My father saw the Willard fight and it will make him happy that I met you." As the middle-aged man from Toledo spoke, his eyes reflected his hero worship. "Thank you, son. Here's a picture of that fight, the one that's on the wall over there," Dempsey said, pointing to a mural on the far wall. Dempsey remembered the Willard fight. "God, it was a long time ago. I was a hard kid from the West and it was my chance. God, he was so big. But it was my one chance. Doc said I could win and (laugh) he was the Doctor. I knocked him out in—what was it, honey—three rounds. No, he never came out of his corner for the fourth round. God, it was a long time ago." His eyes left 1973.

CHAPTER I

The Son
of a
Pipe Dream [1]

A S ALMOST every frontier historian since Frederick Jackson Turner has proclaimed, the western frontier was the spawning ground for that nebulous figure of the late nineteenth century, the American hero. In the early 1890s Colorado was one of the newest frontier states. The majesty of its mountains, the golden wealth of its luckiest citizens, and the tales of half-civilized modes of life were powerful magnets, drawing men who had failed to find a place in the more stable eastern society.

In his letters written during a tour of the United States, Oscar Wilde left a vivid picture of Colorado. He found a rough beauty in the Rockies, "shining like shields of polished silver in that vault of blue flame we call the sky," and in the red-shirted, blond-bearded miners. Writing to Fanny Whitehead Beere, an English actress, Wilde described the noble miners who slept through his lecture on the early Florentines and who only awoke at the mention of Botticelli, which sounded to them like a new drink. [1]

Wilde's letters from this period imply that every man in Colorado carried a Colt .45 on his hip, mined gold, and drank whiskey until his nose turned red. Everyone, of course, was not so colorful, and many men never attained the vague or undefined goal that brought them there. Such a man was Hyrum Dempsey. While Oscar Wilde was celebrating with the miners in Leadville, Hyrum Dempsey, his wife, and their two children were attempting to put down new roots in the town of Manassa about a hundred miles south of Leadville.

Situated in the rugged San Luis Valley, Manassa is a town where the forces of nature seem to conspire against comfort. In summer it is hot and dry. In winter the frigid air and huge snowfalls make any excursion outdoors an ordeal. In addition to its bad weather, the valley is surrounded by mountains—some in excess of fourteen thousand feet—that seriously hinder commerce with the outside world. It was into these forbidding circumstances that Hyrum, brimming with optimism, brought his small family in the early 1880s.

Optimism was indeed the hallmark of the men who founded Manassa several years prior to Hyrum's arrival. In 1878 a group of Mormons from Alabama and Georgia ventured into the San Luis Valley. Behind them lay a society that, if it did not persecute them, certainly scorned their beliefs. Believing that the Spanish-Indian inhabitants of the valley were direct descendants of Manasseh, eldest son of Joseph, the Mormons named their settlement Manassa. Although the Indians proved to be friendly, the Mormons were ill-treated by the climate, and through the first harsh Colorado winter they shivered in clothing more appropriate to the temperate climate of the South. But most survived that first winter, and though their population did not grow, it did remain constant at about one hundred people.[2]

Two years later, Hyrum Dempsey and his family wandered into Manassa. Hyrum was a strange man, but among the people attracted by the lure of the West he did not stand out as especially unusual. He was tall, wiry—a shade over six feet—with a wizened face and ears too large for his head, and arms too long for his body. For enjoyment, he played the fiddle, sired eleven children, and told stories of his Uncle Devil Anse Hatfield. Something of a philosopher, he liked to say, "Boys, never kick a cripple or go to bed with a fool."[3] He never explained this remarkable admonition, but the sense of well-being that such oft-repeated axioms provided helped him to survive for well over eighty years without losing his zest for life.

Nevertheless, Hyrum, like his Irish ancestors, had a black as well as a carefree side. Years later Jack Dempsey described his father as a dreamer, a confused man seeking a better life. Born into a family of moderate means in Logan County, West Virginia, Hyrum had been afforded the luxury of one year in college. This bit of education admirably equipped him to be a complete misfit in the rough timber and

coal region of Logan County. After trying and failing at several occupations, he accepted a job as schoolteacher in Mud Fork, West
Virginia. He learned, like Ichabod Crane, that teaching children
who care little about the declension of a Latin verb can produce a
sense of personal frustration. Hyrum Dempsey hated teaching and
found no value in a community that regarded him as an infringer in
an exclusively feminine domain. Only a "fool" or a "dreamer" spent
his valuable time reading in Mud Fork or Logan County in those
days, his son later recalled.[4] And since Hyrum was more than a little
of both of these, he sold all his worldly possessions, bought a wagon,
packed up his wife and children, and headed toward the frontier.

True, hundreds of thousands of people were doing the same
thing, but one might still wonder why Hyrum left everything he
knew as stable to chase a pipe dream. He left no letters, kept no di-
ary, and even in later years never talked much about why he went
west. But the main ingredient of restlessness is everywhere apparent—that visceral feeling that life promised much more than it
was producing. For the remainder of his life he reenacted the American odyssey, moving from a mining camp, to a farm, to a ranch, and
then to another mining camp, as one season gave way to another,
one job gave way to the next. Ever seeking another season, another
job, he never found the right occupation. His son best summed up
his father's quest by recalling that Hyrum's "face was turned toward
the West, I think, all his life."[5]

Hyrum's initial move was undoubtedly spurred by his religious
impulses. In the late 1870s a Mormon missionary converted him to
the Church of the Latter-day Saints and told him about the Mormon
settlements in the West. Religious conversion came easy in Logan
County, and Hyrum's lasted long enough to lure him westward where
Mormonism flourished. Selling his valuable coal and timberland for
one dollar an acre, he accrued three hundred dollars, enough to buy a
prairie wagon and finance his trip. He attributed the ridiculous price
for his land to the will of heaven. Had he not, Hyrum said to his
wife, Celia, prayed only the night before for an offer? So with his
business settled and his heart fired with religious fervor, he packed
Celia and their two children, Bernie and Effie, into the wagon and
headed west. It was about 1880.

5

Although religion lay behind Hyrum's migration, he was not the sort of man to remain very religious very long. He accepted all the laws of the Mormon faith on principle, but his body was not as strong as his faith. He enjoyed worldly pleasures too much to remain faithful to any strict religion. He drank whiskey and coffee, smoked, and indulged in other vices. He became a Jack Mormon, one who does not live by the book. When confronted with this paradox he would grin and drawl, "I'm just too weak to live up to those rules."[6]

Before he realized he could not live up to those rules, however, he started west. Hyrum's journey stopped when he, hungry and penniless, came to the community of Manassa. There he worked at a number of jobs, trying his luck at painting, cooking, farming, ranch work, and more; but since he worked only a few months at any one job and since he was essentially a lazy man, he was never able to earn enough money to feed and clothe his family properly. On a small plot of land he built an undistinguished stucco and frame home, surrounding it with a tattered picket fence, but the dwelling was always in a state of decay. During the times when Hyrum could find no job, the Mormon sense of community provided some relief. When a bishop heard of Hyrum's problems, the church doled out food to the Dempsey household.[7] The Dempseys frequently received this form of charity, because even if Hyrum managed to hold on to a job for more than a month or two, his ever-increasing family made it impossible to pay all his bills.

Even for a western clan, Hyrum's family was exceptional. Celia had the two children when she left West Virginia, but after arriving in Colorado the sons and daughters came with almost perfect biannual regularity. Florence, the first to be born in the West, was followed by Stella and Joe. All three survived to adulthood. The next two, Alice and Robert, were not so fortunate. Johnny, William, Elsie, and Bruce concluded the list of Dempsey children. Between 1875 and 1900 Hyrum and Celia had eleven children, and the deaths of five of them give some indication of the physical and mental hardships of frontier life. Alice and Robert died in infancy; Johnny committed suicide after shooting his estranged wife; Bruce was stabbed to death while peddling newspapers in Salt Lake City; and Bernie died of "miners' tuberculosis," a common enough end in Colorado mining

6

towns. Five children grew into what would be statistically labeled normal lives, although there was always an abnormally high incidence of sickness in the family. One of the eleven children, William Harrison, became famous and made the family name synonymous with heavyweight champion.[8]

The birth of William Harrison Dempsey on June 24, 1895, is surrounded by a mythology that is similar to the birth of famous mythical heroes. The common denominator in all stories of the births of mythological supermen is, of course, a mother who correctly prophesies her son's future. In William's case his mother had given an itinerant salesman a glass of cold milk in return for which he gave her a book about John L. Sullivan, *The Modern Gladiator*. This book is a curious specimen of moral platitudes thinly disguised as facts, and facts openly translated into moral platitudes. "The lessons taught by the career of John L. Sullivan," the anonymous author writes, "are lessons that every man will be better for learning. The experiences of this magnificent machine of flesh and blood, are valuable in showing things that should certainly be avoided, as well as things that may profitably be copied. . . . Who is there from the parson in his pulpit to the student burning the midnight oil, who would not, if he could, have Sullivan's girth of chest and strength of back, his grim power of taking punishment and his skill in sparring?" The answer, the author believes, would include the most "fastidious moralist," as well as the most "reckless free liver."[9]

During her pregnancy Celia read this morally uplifting book; she was attracted by its doctrines of abstention as well as by the heroic figure of the legendary John L. So when her son was born, strong and healthy, she said, "William is going to grow up to be the world's champion fighter. Just like John L. Sullivan."[10] It is interesting that Celia Dempsey was influenced by the popular image of Sullivan, for during her son's career his life would be viewed more as a medieval morality play than as the life of a mortal man. Just as John L. Sullivan emerged from the pages of *The Modern Gladiator* as a machine of force and power, somehow above the average man, so Jack Dempsey was viewed in the 1920s as a figure of moral instruction.

Within four or five years after William's birth, Hyrum Dempsey felt that Manassa had not satisfied his need. He had not prospered materially or psychologically, so he decided to move on. With the exception of having fewer worldly goods to sell and more children to pack into the wagon, his departure from Manassa was governed by the same haphazard rules that were employed in his move from Logan County. Nothing was planned or thought out in advance. Later Jack Dempsey said that although he was young he remembered the move as sudden: "One day we were in Manassa and the next day we were gone." With the hope that if Manassa did not hold what he was looking for, perhaps the next town would, Hyrum moved farther west.[11]

He followed the rumor of opportunity, through the San Luis Valley north, first to Creede and then to Antonito and Alamosa. When he found no work in the valley, he started the climb toward the Great Divide, settling for a time in Leadville. Situated almost two miles above sea level, Leadville was still largely a rough frontier mining town in the early years of the twentieth century. Settled only a quarter of a century before the Dempseys arrived, the town was renowned for lawlessness, wealth, and an infamous red-light district.[12]

In Leadville, Hyrum and his sons earned as much as $4.00 a day in mining and railroad jobs, but the money did not go far. In 1896 miners were earning $3.00 a day but were spending $63.00 a month for food, rent, fuel, water, and clothing, which left almost no money to meet other expenses. A strike in the late nineties failed, and the men had to return to the mines on the owners' terms. When Hyrum reached Leadville a few years later, economic conditions had not improved much.

During the winter, temperatures often dipped to thirty degrees below zero, and the lack of oxygen in the air made outdoor jobs dangerous. At one time the toll of pneumonia deaths resulting from breathing the freezing air became so alarming that dozens of victims were buried secretly in the night to prevent the truth from affecting the growth of Leadville.[13]

Other ills were ready to claim their victims. Today's tourists who ski in the Colorado mountains know that the reflection of the sun on the snow can give them beautiful tans. The miners cared nothing for tans, but the same combination of sun and snow caused their skin to peel off in great flakes. The sun and snow also turned streets into impassable quagmires by ten o'clock in the morning. Waste was thrown onto the streets, sewers were either inadequate or nonexistent, housing was deplorable, and most food and liquor were barely consumable. There were other hazards: periodic epidemics of smallpox and typhoid fever, mining accidents, and the generally violent character of local nightlife. Leadville offered employment to Hyrum Dempsey and his family, but life was so threatened by dangers and violence that Hyrum soon decided to move on. He continued his ramblings, staying a month in one town and several weeks in the next.[14] A few months after leaving Leadville, Celia became ill, possibly from disease or possibly from life with Hyrum. Their marriage was not always stable. Celia was a quiet woman, but as lean and strong as a mountain fir. Where Hyrum tended toward dreaming and laziness, she was a bastion of practical sense and industry. Often they fought, and occasionally they would separate. Finally, after many years, they divorced. But during their first separation Celia ascribed her illness to the altitude, and along with several of her children she went to visit her daughter Florence in Denver. "Mile-high" Denver seems hardly the best site to cure altitude sickness, but the quiet visit with her daughter did restore Celia's battered spirits, and soon she rejoined Hyrum's meandering Colorado voyage through Wolcott, Steamboat Springs, Mt. Harris, Craig, Meeker, Rifle, and Delta. Finally, in Uncompahgre, near Montrose, Hyrum found a job on a ranch and the family was allowed to rest. Traveling ten or fifteen miles a day, the 175 miles between Manassa and Montrose could easily have been covered in two weeks. With stops, it took Hyrum Dempsey two years.

The western slope where Uncompahgre lies was less settled in the first decade of the twentieth century than the eastern slope. The Brunot Treaty of 1873 had done little to ease the tension between the settlers and the Utes, the major Indian tribe in the area. Finally in 1879 the constant friction between the two groups erupted into open warfare, culminating with the Meeker Massacre. After the massacre the Indians were resettled, and though sporadic fighting continued until the middle of the 1880s, Indian troubles had subsided by the turn of the century. Montrose became one of the major stations for the Denver and Rio Grande Railroad, and with the railroad to market ranch and farm goods, the area soon became one of the richest food-producing regions of the state. Fruit, sugar beets, and cattle thrived on the fertile soil and favorable climate of the western slope.[15]

The name Montrose was taken from Sir Walter Scott's "Legend of Montrose" because the beautiful countryside resembled the rolling fields of Scotland where Montrose fought. The land became a source of wealth for many of the farmers and ranchers who were fortunate enough to obtain a section of it. Hyrum, Celia, and the children worked hard to make their ranch as profitable as the rest, but again things just did not work out. Among small farmers financial survival demanded meticulous management of land and cattle, and, as Jack Dempsey later remembered, his father "just wasn't up to it." As a rancher and later as a sharecropper he was a failure.[16]

The Dempseys left their lonely two-story wooden house on the Albrush Ranch and moved into Montrose. Hyrum and the older boys worked as day laborers on the neighboring farms, and Celia opened a cheap restaurant called the Rio Grande Eating House. The time for such a venture seemed ripe, since less than nine miles southeast of Montrose workers for the federal government were digging the Gunnison tunnel. Started by the Denver and Rio Grande Railroad, the project was soon taken over by the federal government, and when completed the 5.8-mile excavation through solid granite was one of the world's great tunnels.[17] Workers on the project provided a ready-made clientele for Celia's establishment, and the future restaurateur William Dempsey, still less than eleven years old, washed dishes, waited on tables, and served tough railroad construction workers hearty meals.

During the two years he lived in Montrose, William began to fight. When he was not working at the restaurant, shining shoes, or peddling newspapers, he was brawling with other youngsters. To kids bred in the dusty poverty of western towns, nurtured on desire to escape one's fate, and conditioned by the casual violence of frontier life, prize fighting came naturally. Years after he retired from boxing, Dempsey told a House of Representatives investigating committee that he started to box at age ten. Along with the Dempseys, the boys from the Woods and Pitts families fought on every possible occasion. Nobody was angry; it was just a way of life, an entertainment for poor boys. It taught Dempsey the skills that were to make him famous.[18]

The older brother Bernie taught William, along with Johnny, the finer aspects of the trade—to jab and hook, feint and counter. On Saturday nights, William and Johnny would tag along with Bernie to local mining or railroad camps. There Bernie would battle the local tough, and from his seat on a floor of sawdust or dirt, William would watch and listen to the cheers. It was all part of a fighter's education, as was learning to condition his body. At eleven he was bathing his face and hands in beef brine, giving them a leatherlike texture. Chewing resin from pine trees added strength to his jaw. He later recalled that the beef brine smelled like something dead and the pine gum tasted worse, but he never missed a day. Bernie told him it would make him a fighter, and he "loved to fight."[19]

When the Gunnison tunnel was complete, the Dempseys moved again, this time to Provo, Utah. Then they moved to Lakeview, Utah, where they bought a little red brick house overlooking the Utah Lake and surrounded by mountains. There William divided his time between school—a new and unpleasant experience—work, and fighting. His family was starting to split up, and as his older brothers and sisters left to start families of their own, William began to feel the impulse to leave. He had never enjoyed the luxury of a carefree adolescence. So, like millions of other boys from poor families, he ventured out on his own as soon as he was able. In 1911, at the age of sixteen, William left Lakeview.[20]

Pictures from this period show William Dempsey as a beetle-browed, dark-haired youth with dirty hands and long, taut muscles, all combined on a large-boned but thin frame. One's attention, however, is immediately focused on his face, which might bring to mind second-rate detective novels. The nose, broken in several places, the expressionless mouth, and the cold, haunting eyes suggest a childhood that had been something less than kind.[21] The reasons for leaving home are written everywhere on that hungry face. Turning his back on the past, he symbolically broke the ties with his former life by changing his name; William Dempsey, or Harry as all his family save his mother called him, became Kid Blackie. With no real trade and little education he turned to the only thing he could do to scrounge a livelihood—fighting.

From 1911 until 1916 Dempsey was a hobo. There was no romance in the life; he lived in mining camps and hobo jungles, begged

11

for work and food. He also risked his life every time he rode the rods, the two narrow steel beams on the belly of a Pullman car. Unlike the men who climbed into the freight cars, those who rode the rods were seldom in fear of being brutalized by a sadistic railway watchman. However, the rods held their own dangers. The one- or two-inch-wide lines of steel were only inches above the tracks and roadbed; if the rider fell asleep or slipped off his rods, death was almost certain. On a summer afternoon the ride was relatively hazardless, but on a stark winter's night in the Rocky Mountains the rider literally bet his life that the train would stop before he shivered his way down to the roadbed. A popular biography of Dempsey observes, "You have to be desperate to gamble like that, but if you weren't desperate you wouldn't be on the rods."[22]

Transportation was only one of the many dangers the hobo faced. Illness was a constant problem, if early statistics are any indication. Alice W. Solenberger studied one thousand homeless men and found that two-thirds suffered from physical or mental disabilities, the most prominent of which were tuberculosis, rheumatism, and venereal disease. Of 627 men who suffered from physical ailments, 168 were either crippled, maimed, or deformed.[23] Constant exposure to hot summers and freezing winters, as well as the hazards of travel and violence, left the hobo an enormous chance to die young.

The problem of hobo homosexuals was a constant and plaguing one. To hear of a boy traveling with an older man referred to as the "wife" or "woman" was common, and rape, according to Josiah Flynt, who was familiar with hobo life, was practiced by older hoboes with alarming frequency.[24] A young hobo's best defense was either to travel in groups or to be a capable fighter. Dempsey, who preferred to travel alone, chose the second defense.

Although Dempsey spent time in hobo jungles, rode the rods, and more than once begged for food, he essentially lived on the periphery of the hobo community. What separated him was his willingness, even eagerness, to work. He accepted any type of employment from washing dishes, cutting lawns, and scrubbing floors to the harder work of mining coal, digging ditches, and picking fruit. However, these jobs were always temporary; his most enjoyable source of income was fighting, and from the time he left home in 1911 he fought to earn money whenever and wherever he could.[25]

Today, long since the popular image of Jack Dempsey was formed, one tends to view the man through stained-glass eyes. He is the kind, genial ex-champ with the affable manner. There is nothing hard or cruel about Dempsey today. But in the days when he rode the rods and ate with his hands in hobo jungles he was a different man. He was then literally and metaphorically hungry. And he was comfortable in his violent world. Not complacent; he wanted desperately to leave the world of poverty, but he was at ease amidst violence. He was certainly not afraid of being hurt or of injuring other men. Even after he became champion, he evinced a quite casual attitude toward punishing sparring partners. Trained in a world of broken and cut faces, where the loser in a barroom fight was more likely to get a beer poured on him than to receive sympathy, Dempsey learned to fight all-out, all the time. The only thing people respected was a winner; the niceties of the rules were something a loser complained about as he held a steak up to his eye.[26]

In his early fights, Dempsey acted as promoter, boxer, and money collector. He battled in barrooms, mining camps, wherever men gathered. His method was simple but effective: swaggering into a western saloon he would boldly announce, "I can lick any sonofabitch in the house." In his prime John L. Sullivan used to do the same thing, but the burly, two-hundred-pound Sullivan received few takers. However, Dempsey looked like a hungry teenager, and he sounded like a girl. When the saloon customers saw that the challenger with the high-pitched, screechy voice weighed only about 130 pounds, they laughed and prepared to slaughter him. Usually Dempsey easily defeated his overconfident foe with a devastating left hook that seemed to roll off his shoulder like a smoothly released baseball. Sometimes he was beaten, for in the world of miners, cowboys, railroad workers, and lumberjacks there was frequently someone who could maul a 130-pound, sixteen-year-old. There were also times when even the brash Dempsey saw that he was overmatched, and he would "run like hell."[27]

Occasionally Dempsey would first ask a bartender if there was anyone whom he would enjoy seeing a skinny kid knock out. Usually the bartender knew at least one bully who was a constant source of irritation to himself and his customers, and the thought of that bully suffering an ignominious defeat was all the bartender needed to accept Dempsey's plan. A match was easy to arrange. Today the broken-nosed, half-shaven, scared teenager would look formidable, but in a western saloon where nearly everybody looked tough, Dempsey inspired little awe. Just as the match was easily arranged, the result was usually predictable. With the bully stretched out on the sawdust floor, the hat was passed around, and depending on the hatred for the bully and the size of the crowd, the purse could be as large as fifty dollars, half going to Dempsey and half to the bartender.[28]

From 1911 until 1914 Dempsey had hundreds of barroom fights. But the three years of almost constant travel through Utah, Colorado, and Nevada made Dempsey long for something more permanent. The trouble with saloon fighting was that with one fight he gained a reputation that excluded him from other fights in that town. More than anything else, it was this continuous need to leave town after each fight that influenced his decision to enter profession boxing on a more organized basis. The bouts would be harder, but at least there would be no need to disguise his occupation.[29]

Salt Lake City, specifically Commercial Street, became his base. Commercial Street was the vice center, the part of town where the Mormons let the "Gentiles" do as they wished. By the Woodruff Manifesto of 1890 the Mormon Church yielded to the power of the "Gentile" Liberal party which had gained political control of Salt Lake City in 1889. This document set the pattern for the rapprochement between the two communities.[30] So by the second decade of the twentieth century, prostitution, gambling, and boxing had become blatant in Salt Lake City. Although the Mormons openly abhorred the activities of Commercial Street, they did not attempt to close the saloons, pool halls, whorehouses, or boxing clubs.

Dempsey sampled all the vices that Commercial Street offered, but he specialized in boxing. An older fighter from Baltimore, "Young" Peter Jackson, owned the gym where Dempsey trained and performed odd jobs. Occasionally, when Jackson ran short of boxers, he allowed Dempsey to fight in a preliminary bout for the standard fee of $2.50. Other times Dempsey would box on one of the Monday night cards staged by another local promoter named Hardy Downing. A pleasant man, with a ruddy face and an easy smile, Downing was, nevertheless, not averse to allowing the inexperienced Dempsey to fight the best boxers in the area. Matched against older and wiser fighters like Jack Downey and Andy Malloy, Dempsey began to practice his trade at a professional level. To be sure, he lost some of his early fights, but from the first he was a crowd pleaser. In the parlance of the sport, Dempsey came to fight. If he looked foolish before a fight, with his closely cropped hair, skinny legs, and American flag strung through his beltloops, he was all business once the bell sounded. Then, his arms flailing like a broken windmill in a strong breeze, Dempsey would go straight at his opponent.[31]

He learned fast. He had to. Fighters who were not quick learners did not long remain fighters. By the end of 1915, his second year of professional boxing on an organized level, Dempsey was able to defeat the fighters who had beaten him less than a year before. Eventually, he knocked out both Downey and Malloy. And there were others. At times, Dempsey received even more work than he anticipated. One night he fought a boxer called "One-Punch" Hancock. Living up to his name, One-Punch lasted exactly one punch. As Dempsey's hand was being raised, One-Punch's brother, upset by the outcome of the bout and emboldened by alcohol, jumped into the ring and challenged Jack. His name might have been "Two-Punch," commented Rex Lardner, for that was the number of blows it took to put him out of the fight.[32] Fighting for Downing was good for Dempsey. Downing, who was known to withhold a purse from a timid or "scientific" boxer, liked Dempsey. Yet Downing never paid a fighter over twenty dollars for an evening's work, a sum that never covered Dempsey's bills for the long interfight periods. In order to augment his Salt Lake City purses and to fill in the empty spaces between the Downing cards, Dempsey accepted professional fights in other western towns. The rough mining towns of Nevada were particularly fruitful. In 1915 and 1916 he often fought in towns like Reno, Goldfield, and Ely. Any match, even an interracial bout, was welcomed in the Nevada towns; after all, it had not been too long before that Jack Johnson and James J. Jeffries battled for the heavyweight crown in Reno. At this stage in his career, Dempsey felt no compunction against boxing black fighters, for on April 26, 1915, he easily knocked out a black, Anamas Campbell, in three rounds.[33]

Most of his fights in 1915 ended in a similar fashion. Indeed, it appears that the majority of his adversaries had two things in common. First, almost to a man, they had colorful names—Two Round Gilhan, Kid Hancock, One-Punch Hancock, Chief Gordon, Joe Lions, Battling Johnson, and the Boston Bearcat. Second, most of Dempsey's opponents were on their backs when the bout ended. Of the seventeen fights listed on Dempsey's record for 1915, he won thirteen, twelve by knockout; he lost only one, the other three were draws.[34] If he fought more times, the records have been lost. He possibly fought under several names, a fairly common practice for that era in boxing. However, with few exceptions, Dempsey had every reason to be optimistic about his future in the ring.

Two of those exceptions were his fights with Johnny Sudenberg. Like Dempsey, Sudenberg was a young, hungry fighter with a lot of heart. Trained in the same type no-fight–no-pay atmosphere as Dempsey, Sudenberg had gained a following in the Reno area. Their first fight, staged in Goldfield, in June, 1915, was a grueling affair. The altitude and dust combined with the heat sorely tested Dempsey, and when it was over Sudenberg was given the decision. A few weeks later, they met again, this time in the backroom of a saloon in Tonapah, Nevada. Before a crowded room of miners, both fighters, as if by some mutual decision, eschewed defense and concentrated their efforts on the other's face. Knockdown followed knockdown, and in each round the fight seemed sure to end. But it did not end until the final bell, at which time the referee judged the fight to be a draw. Afterwards Dempsey and Sudenberg collected their money—about $100 each—and went to a bar where they drank free beers for the rest of the night. Later Dempsey remembered the fight as one of the toughest of his life.[35]

It was about this time, when his reputation was increasing with each fight, that he dropped the name of Kid Blackie and became Jack Dempsey. In a way it was a family legacy; his older brothers Bernie and Johnny had both used the name in their short-lived ring careers. But more than a family heirloom, it was a name with a rich tradition behind it. The great middleweight of the late nineteenth century had used the name Jack Dempsey. Dubbed the Nonpareil, he was consid-

16

ered one of the greatest boxers of all time, so it was natural that any Irishman named Dempsey should attach Jack as a first name.

As the newly christened Jack Dempsey continued his winning ways, he also found matches more difficult to obtain, so he acquired a manager, Jack Price of Salt Lake City. Price quickly arranged for Dempsey to fight the Boston Bearcat, a black eastern boxer who carried clippings to prove he had lasted twenty rounds with Sam Langford. As Dempsey told the story to Nat Fleischer, he knocked the Bearcat down in the first round, and as the referee's count reached three the Bearcat raised his head and moaned, "That's nuff, white boy. I'se got sufficient. I'se tru for de night. No moh fighting for me." Although the eloquent surrender might be apocryphal, the result of the bout is correct. And more knockouts followed. Rematched with Sudenberg in Ely, Nevada, Dempsey won in two rounds. Next he disposed of his old rival Jack Downey in Salt Lake City. The fighters got better and the purses larger but still Dempsey won. After a few more quick knockouts he defeated Joe Bonds and Terry Keller, boxers who had substantial reputations in the West. Finally in June of 1916 he knocked out a good fighter named Bob York in Price, Utah.[36]

Suddenly there was only one direction to go. Boxing in the West held no further opportunities for Dempsey. The days of riding the rods, mining gold, and loading beets were over. Boxing had ended all that. But after the York fight there was no one as good as Dempsey in the mountain states, or at least that was how it seemed to Dempsey and Price in the summer of 1916. Therefore the fighter and the manager decided to move to where the real fighters were—New York City. At the symbolic age of twenty-one, Dempsey believed his future would be found in the East. Roughly thirty-five years earlier Hyrum Dempsey had believed the same thing about the West.

CHAPTER II

A Trade
for the
Hungry

ARRIVING in New York City with less than thirty dollars between them, Dempsey and Price quickly discovered that fame was not there waiting for them. Price, a heavyset, pleasant man who had sometime before abandoned dreams of becoming a Broadway dancer, determined now to help make Dempsey a known fighter.[1] Dempsey, however, was not encouraged when a taxi driver shrugged off his newspaper clippings and said he had never heard of Johnny Sudenberg, George Copelin, Bob York, or even the Boston Bearcat.[2] If a New York taxi driver did not know a boxer, no one else did. So, Dempsey and Price began making rounds among newspaper writers and boxing promoters to correct this appalling ignorance.

Dempsey and Price had not realized that the popularity of boxing was at low ebb. It, more than other sports, is subject to sudden and marked changes, and the gauge for boxing is the heavyweight champion. If his charisma is equal to his boxing, the sport as a whole will usually be popular. Of course, boxers must always contend with critics. Moral reformers, who view boxing as a manifestation of the sins of the cities, and religious zealots, who maintain that the sport is a perversion of the Golden Rule, have continually been in the forefront of antiboxing crusades. But they go unheeded, if not unnoticed, during the reign of a popular heavyweight champion. During the careers of such men as John L. Sullivan, James J. Corbett, Robert Fitzsimmons, and James J. Jeffries, boxing had enjoyed widespread popularity. Although it was illegal in most states, it was tacitly accepted, and matches were permitted regardless of laws. Interest in boxing began to decline when Jeffries decided to retire after his match with Jack Munroe in San Francisco on August 26, 1904. The decline soon became sharp, during which time the antiboxing crusade reached its height. If this process had escaped Dempsey's attention while he fought in the Rocky Mountain cities, it could not be overlooked in the more cultivated eastern cities.

Sullivan, Corbett, and Fitzsimmons, the three heavyweight champions who preceded Jeffries, had all lost the championship in the ring, thereby providing a successor to their crown. Jeffries' break with this tradition introduced an element of chaos into the sport. There were no such things as official rankings, boxing organizations, or a boxing commission, therefore no set procedure for handling the unprecedented move. How would a new champion be crowned? If crowned, would he be accepted? These were only two problematic questions facing promoters and boxing enthusiasts.

Jeffries tried to settle the problem himself.. Encouraged by Lou Houseman, a writer for the Chicago *Inter-Ocean* and the manager of Jack Root, Jeffries agreed to referee a contest between Root and Marvin Hart and then to name the winner the heavyweight champion. Although both men were respectable fighters, neither seemed qualified to hold the same championship that Sullivan, Corbett, and Jeffries had held. Root was a clever boxer but certainly not a heavyweight. Boxing expert Nat Fleischer ranked Root as the fifth-best light heavyweight of all time, but Root rarely weighed more than 165 pounds. Hart was similarly handicapped. And though his opponents did not realize it, he was totally blind in his right eye.[3] For eleven rounds Hart charged Root, hoping to land one of his wild swings. Root sidestepped, parried Hart's punches, and effectively scored with counterblows. However, the 96° temperature had its effect on Root, and in the twelfth round Hart knocked him out.

Awkward in the ring, Hart was also unexciting outside the ropes, and interest in boxing declined further. It was becoming a western sport, a mining-town and cowboy sport, and very few fights were held east of the Mississippi River. The major fights of the day were staged in such towns as Reno, Butte, San Francisco, and Los Angeles. Between 1901 and 1915 not one heavyweight championship fight was held in the eastern United States. With western promoters and fighters dominating boxing, the sport seemed on the verge of becoming simply an amusement for the western miners.

Hart's reign as heavyweight champion came to an end on February 23, 1906, when he fought Tommy Burns, a five-foot–seven-inch French-Canadian, in Los Angeles. The dull twenty-round contest reflected the public's disinterest in boxing. After defending his title several times in California, Burns realized that if he was to make any money in the sport he would have to venture outside of the United States. In Europe he was at least a novelty. For over a year he fought boxers of little or no ability in Europe. From London to Dublin to Paris, he traveled and fought. When interest declined in Europe, Burns once again packed up, this time taking his championship to Australia. There he successfully defended his title twice; he knocked out Bill Squires in thirteen rounds in Sydney and disposed of Bill Land in six rounds in Melbourne. Then he was persuaded to meet one of the few Americans who cared about the championship. The bout changed the complexion of the heavyweight division.[4]

On the day after Christmas, 1908, Burns shattered one of the heavyweight division's most sacred traditions. In a wooden amphitheatre in Ruschcutter's Bay, near Sydney, Burns broke the "color line." This line had originated with John L. Sullivan's famous 1892 challenge to fight contenders: "In this challenge I include all fighters—first come, first served—who are white. I will not fight a Negro. I never have and I never shall."[5] True to his word, the Boston Strong Boy never did. His precedent was followed by Corbett, Fitzsimmons, Jeffries, and Hart. By going against this tradition, Burns opened the door for the first black heavyweight champion.

The man he fought, Jack Johnson, has in recent years become a myth. His life has been the subject of a major play, a popular movie, several biographies, and a historical study. Why did Burns risk his title? In 1908 Johnson was not yet considered to be a superman. Certainly, he had an impressive record, but he had been defeated; Marvin Hart, before he became champion, had won a twenty-round decision over him, and Joe Choynski, a great fighter at the turn of the century, had knocked out Johnson in three rounds. Burns needed the money. Guided by Hugh D. "Huge Deal" McIntosh, an enterprising entrepreneur whose checkered career included such occupations as bicycle racer, boxer, newspaper owner, member of Parliament, and theatrical producer, Burns agreed to fight Johnson at the time when the United States goodwill fleet was scheduled to be harbored at Sydney. For the bout Burns was promised the unprecedented sum of thirty-five thousand dollars. [6]

The fight was completely one-sided. Johnson floored Burns in the first round, toyed with him and taunted him for the next twelve, and then finished him in the fourteenth round. In evaluating Burns, Johnson said, "He is the easiest man I ever met. I could have put him away quicker, but I wanted to punish him. I had my revenge." Suddenly the heavyweight championship, the very symbol of physical superiority, was held by Jack Johnson, a swaggering, smiling, gold-toothed black man. As a New York newspaper reported, "Never before in the history of the prize ring has such a crisis arisen as that which faces the followers of the game tonight." [7]

Others believed that Johnson was not the true champion. Jeffries had never been beaten, many said, and, therefore, Johnson could not become the heavyweight champion until he defeated "Old Jeff." After watching Johnson humiliate Burns, novelist-turned-sportswriter Jack London sounded the battle cry: "One thing remains. Jeffries must emerge from his alfalfa farm and remove that smile from Johnson's face. Jeff, it's up to you!" Even after Johnson defeated Stanley Ketchel, the middleweight champion, white partisans still counted on Jeffries to regain the championship. Indeed, it was the opinion of many students of the game that Johnson would prove no match for Jeffries; the boxing oracles believed that if Jeffries had "one-half his old-time form, [he would] clean up the negro in jig time." [8]

Jeffries' western idyll ended. Urged on for psychological, patriotic, and even genetic reasons, he started the long, arduous process of getting his 320-pound body into condition to do battle for his race. All arrangements were handled by George Lewis "Tex" Rickard, a fight promoter whose cold, even gaze was attributed to his hitch as a faro dealer in the Klondike. As Jeffries trained and Johnson attended

21

parties and Rickard searched for a site to stage the bout, millions of Americans began watching the sports pages of newspapers for news about the upcoming fight.[9]

The bout soon outgrew the boxing ring. Much more than a mere athletic contest, it became a focal point for racism. From the political stumps of backwater Louisiana towns to the pulpits of midwestern churches, the Johnson-Jeffries match elicited seething emotion. Below the Mason and Dixon line, local public officials and even congressmen talked freely of the "danger of the negroes having their heads turned by a victory for Johnson" and of young blacks "crowding white women off the sidewalks." A southern congressman justified a Johnson victory according to the iron precepts of Jim Crow: "I think that a white man who would deliberately get in a ring to fight a negro deserves to be beaten to death. If Jeffries is defeated, most southerners will see he got what was coming to him."[10]

Above the Mason and Dixon line, many citizens agreed with California's Governor James Gillette that whites in America would simply not allow a Johnson victory. Hinting that the fight was just a scheme to make money, Gillette added that anyone with "the least sense knows the whites of this country won't allow Johnson or any other negro to win the world's championship from Jeffries. They simply won't stand for it." Of course, Gillette continued, Johnson was cognizant of his position. "He's no fool. He knows that to win that fight he would have to whip every white man at the ringside. . . . Why, he would no more think of trying to knock Jeffries out than he would of trying to stop a bolt of lightning."[11]

Stop a bolt of lightning—no, Johnson would not think of it. But beat a white man? Soft spoken with a deep Texas accent, this large, ever-smiling black man had begun to haunt the race consciousness of white America. Educated blacks did their best to soothe the emotions that Johnson stirred. The Reverend Reverdy C. Ransom of the Bethel African Methodist Church in New York City claimed, "We do not think that Jack Johnson thinks or has ever thought of holding the championship for the 'black race.'" Johnson's actions were hardly calculated to calm white fears. Whatever he did, Johnson seemed to have the ability to view himself as a symbol, if not a god, of his race. Arrested for speeding, several months before the fight, in

22

his scarlet racing car in Chicago, Johnson was quoted in Farr's *Black Champion* as goading a white policeman, "Stand back, Mr. White Offisah, and let dem colored peoples hab a look at me."[12]

As the fight drew closer, tensions grew tauter. Two Americans, one white and one black, evoked God to their cause as they faced this early twentieth-century Armageddon. The Colored Holiness Church of Hutchinson, Kansas, was one of many black churches that conducted special services to pray for Johnson. And in Omaha the Reverend H. E. Traile, pastor of the white First Baptist Church, chose the white man to win. Traile used the moral sanction of his pulpit to affirm that "every man with red blood in his veins should see Jim Jeffries regain the heavyweight championship from Jack Johnson at Reno, July 4."[13]

By Independence Day, Reno had been temporarily transformed from a dusty desert town into a resort city. The gaudiest circus could not compare with Reno on the days before the bout. Indians, cowboys, bankers, industrialists, gamblers, pickpockets, hustlers, and fighters mingled. Cincinnati Slim, the famous bank robber, was there, as was Hip Sing Tong, the number-one executioner of the San Francisco Chinatown hatchet wars. Presided over by toastmaster Rickard, who in addition to promoting the bout also had named himself referee, Reno rocked with trumpets and tubas playing "There'll Be a Hot Time in the Old Town Tonight" and men singing "All Coons Look Alike to Me."[14]

The mood became deadly serious when the two boxers entered the ring. Jeffries, who even during his prime had not been a polished fighter, looked awkward and foolish beside the vastly superior Johnson. His crouching, rushing, wild-swinging style that had made him famous was ineffective against Johnson's cold, cruel, precise jabs and right-hand leads that repeatedly found their mark. As Johnson cut open Jeffries' face, he verbally assaulted him: "I can go on like this all afternoon, Mr. Jeff." Taunting, feinting, jabbing, moving— Johnson had never been better. In the fifteenth round as the spectators yelled, "Stop it! Don't let him be knocked out!" Rickard counted ten over Jeffries' bruised and bleeding body. Johnson was indeed the champion of the world.[15]

Almost as soon as his gloves were cut off, a wave of interracial

23

rioting and violence swept the country. In Little Rock two blacks were killed by whites; in Houston a white cut a black to death; in Roanoke six blacks were critically beaten; in Wilmington, Delaware, a group of blacks attacked a white, and whites retaliated with a "lynching bee"; in Atlanta a black ran "amuck" with a knife; in Washington, D.C., two whites were fatally stabbed by blacks; in New York, one black was beaten to death and scores were injured; in Pueblo, Colorado, thirty people were injured in a race riot; and in Shreveport, Louisiana, three blacks were killed by white assailants. Every section of the country experienced the racial violence and the Johnson-Jeffries fight was named as the catalyst.[16]

Some of the violence was provoked by individual acts. In New York City, for example, Nelson Turner, a young black, was almost lynched for yelling to a crowd of whites: "We blacks put one over on you whites, and we're going to do more." Yet by far the more usual scenario saw groups of whites attacking blacks in revenge for the beating Johnson had inflicted upon Jeffries. White gangs, such as New York City's Hounds of Hell and Pearl Button Gang, moved through black sections assaulting blacks on no provocation save skin color.[17] Never before had a single event caused such widespread rioting. Not until the assassination of Martin Luther King would another event elicit a similar reaction.

The fight and its aftermath led reform groups to intensify their efforts to push for legislation that would abolish boxing. Encouraged by the work of the Reverend H. R. Jamison and Congressman William S. Bennett, who, with the General Assembly of the Presbyterian Church, led an earlier campaign to stop the fight from being staged in California, reformers nourished hopes that the disgraceful affair in Reno would ignite public sentiment against boxing. Angered by the fight, William Shaw, general secretary of the United Society of Christian Endeavor, declared that "Independence Day had been dishonored and disgraced by a brutal prizefight; that the moral sense of the nation had been outraged."[18]

Members of the influential Anti-Saloon League of America viewed Johnson as a friend of publicans, a frequenter of saloons, and the epitome of every type of sleazy and licentious sinner. His bragging manner and ostentatious lifestyle provoked the London *Times* to describe him as a "flash nigger" whose "golden teeth" and "multitude of diamonds" resembled "a starry night." Such organs of middle-class indignation as the law and order leagues, committees of public decency, and protective societies were unanimous in their condemnation of Johnson. [19]

Armed with the power of righteous indignation, the United Society of Christian Endeavor launched its attack on boxing: William Shaw, the general secretary of the organization, which boasted 71,000 societies and over 4,000,000 members, called for governors to bar showing film of the fight in their states. Southern and northern governors wholeheartedly endorsed Shaw's request, and the news of prohibition came from Texas, Virginia, Pennsylvania, Kentucky, Missouri, Maine, South Carolina, West Virginia, Illinois, Arkansas, Michigan, Utah, Montana, Iowa, Washington, D.C., South Dakota, England, and South Africa. Within three days after the fight, almost every major city in the United States had enacted local legislation prohibiting the showing of the film. [20]

Reasons for banning the film ran the gamut from noble to ignoble. Christian Endeavor members, following a doctrine remarkably similar to Thomas Arnold's exaltation of Muscular Christianity, claimed that games were to be played, not watched. The spectator who sat passively on the sideline or in the movie theater completely undermined the spiritual and moral benefits of a sport. Mrs. James Crawford, vice-president of the California Women's Clubs, declared that her organization had only the welfare of the black man in mind: "The negroes are to some extent a childlike race, needing guidance, schooling and encouragement. We deny them this by encouraging them to believe that they have gained anything by having one of their race as a champion fighter." Yet for all the Christian nobility and humanitarian virtue of Mrs. Crawford and the Christian Endeavor society, perhaps Mayor E. S. Meals of Harrisburg, Pennsylvania, had his finger on his country's pulse when he said, "Harrisburg has many colored people and . . . could not take any chances of disturbances." [21] Indeed, by 1910 blacks in America had been indoctrinated in the belief that they were in all ways inferior to whites. Fear rendered it essential that this belief remain unchallenged.

Although the Johnson-Jeffries fight film was successfully suppressed in 1910, there remained the possibility that Johnson would again fight a white boxer in front of the movie cameras. With this in mind, Representative Seaborn A. Roddenberry of Georgia and Senator Furnifold Simmons of North Carolina, in late May and early June, 1912, introduced bills in Congress calling for a prohibition of the interstate transportation of fight films. Advocates of Roddenberry's bill tried to hurry the legislation through Congress before Johnson fought "Fireman" Jim Flynn on July 4, 1912. Lacking a quorum, Congress failed to meet the deadline, but Johnson's victory over Flynn served to strengthen Roddenberry's determination to see his bill into law. "No man descended from the old Saxon race can look upon that kind of contest without abhorrence and disgust," Roddenberry said shortly before the House passed his bill. The Senate followed the House's lead, and on July 31, 1912, the law was passed.[22]

If Johnson's activities within the ring upset white Americans to the extent that they called for laws to prohibit the showing of fight films, his behavior outside the ring enraged whites. Uneducated though he was, Johnson understood what whites hated. Folklorist William H. Wiggins, Jr., claims that Johnson's personality fits into the tradition of the "bad nigger." If, as Wiggins asserts, the "bad nigger" is the black who has an utter disregard for death and danger, an insatiable love of a good time, a desire for fast cars and fine clothes, and an unquenchable sexual appetite, then certainly Johnson was a "bad nigger" of the highest order. Johnson knew that whites hated the "bad nigger" because such a man was beyond control. He was the black who lived on the border between sanity and insanity, with no fear of death and, therefore, no fear of life. Johnson reveled in this lifestyle. The stories of the night life at his Café de Champion in Chicago, the tale of his fast cars and silk suits, and the accounts of his brushes with "the man" disgusted whites in direct proportion to which they amused blacks.[23]

But Johnson did not stop with fast cars and flashy clothes. Like a dentist with a high-powered drill, he probed deep into the pulp of the great American fear; he touched the nerve of miscegenation. He married one white woman, Etta Duryea, and after she shot herself in the head, he took a second white wife, Lucille Cameron. The long and tempestuous story of Johnson's relationships with white women reads like a nineteenth-century melodrama, replete with deathbed vigils, flights from the law, and amorous adventures.[24] In an age when blacks were occasionally lynched for brazenly looking at white women, Johnson loved to be seen in public with a white woman on each arm.

Of course, his practice drew heated and protracted criticism. Ministers abhorred it, newspapers condemned it, and politicians tried to legislate against it, but nobody could forget it. While the Fort Worth *Citizen Star* commented, "We bet we know one person that isn't singing 'I Wish I Was in Dixie,'" Congressman Roddenberry was again mounting his Washington stage.[25] In a lengthy speech the representative from Georgia denounced Johnson in particular, blacks in general, white women who would have anything to do with blacks, and the American Constitution since it did not prohibit blacks from marrying whites:

> "No brutality, no infamy, no degredation in all the years of southern slavery possessed such a villainous character and such atrocious qualities as the provisions of the laws of Illinois, New York, Massachusetts, and other states which allow the marriage of the negro Jack Johnson to a woman of the Caucasian strain. (Applause.) . . . Intermarriage between whites and blacks is repulsive and averse to every sentiment of pure American spirit. It is abhorrent and repugnant to the very principles of a pure Saxon government. . . . Let us uproot and exterminate now this debasing, ultrademoralizing, un-American, and inhuman leprosy."[26]

Roddenberry predicted that if a constitutional amendment prohibiting marriage between "fallen white women" and the "sombre-hued, black-skinned, thick-lipped, bull-necked, brutal-hearted African" were not passed, the Johnson precedent would lead to other such unions and eventually to war more bloody than the conflict between the North and South. Thus when less than two months later a forty-two-year-old black married a fifteen-year-old "feeble minded white girl," Roddenberry again reminded his fellow members in Congress that there was no time to delay.[27] Much to his dismay, the amendment was never passed.

The trauma of Johnson's eight years as champion led to a swifter decline in the popularity of boxing. It is true that during these years the search for the Great White Hope generated some interest. But when each Great White Hope turned into a Great White Joke, interest in boxing suffered drastically. When Johnson was forced to flee the country to escape prosecution for a violation of the Mann

JACK DEMPSEY: THE MANASSA MAULER

Act, the American public breathed a collective sigh of relief. Johnson was now the concern of Europeans or South Americans. Americans wanted to forget the Johnson experience and boxing. A cartoon in a New York newspaper that pictured Johnson as a world problem best summed up white America's feelings toward him. Its caption read: "There is only one place we know of where Jack might establish popularity—Mars!"[28]

Eventually, of course, Johnson was defeated. On April 5, 1915, some sixteen thousand spectators braved the blistering sun to watch Jess Willard knock out Johnson in an arena in Havana, Cuba. Was the fight fixed? For years everyone connected with boxing believed so. In recent years, however, a large portion of the boxing community has begun to claim that Willard won the heavyweight title in a fair match.[29] Regardless of whether the bout was or was not fixed, the status of boxing had suffered a severe decline during the Johnson years. The new champion was neither mentally nor physically able to change the state of affairs. By 1916, the year Jack Dempsey traveled to New York, boxing was a thoroughly unpopular and disreputable sport.

Moving from one newspaper to the next, from one promoter to another, Dempsey became increasingly aware of the status of the sport. It was a hard, competitive business. In New York City hundreds of boxers competed for a place on a very limited number of boxing cards. The best fought at Madison Square Garden. Ruled by Jimmy Johnston, a leathery-faced London cockney of Irish descent, the Garden was considered the castle of eastern boxing. Rich in tradition, richer still in low-hanging smoke and the smell of tobacco and sweat, the Garden was chosen as the site for Willard's first title defense in the spring of 1916. When Dempsey's name was mentioned to Johnston as a possible Garden fighter, Johnston ignored the suggestion. The new crop of eastern boxers was more than enough to keep him busy; he had no desire to take a chance on a skinny western fighter with a high-pitched voice.[30]

Unable to attract the attention of the major promoters, Dempsey and Price lowered their sights. They needed a payday, any kind of payday. Their limited funds were gone, and they were sleeping on park benches and eating the free meals that came with a nickel beer.

This pickled diet was disastrous. Dempsey lost weight, weakened, and argued with Price. New York, which seemed to offer so much a few weeks before, was obviously not going to be an easy town in which to earn a reputation.[31]

Eventually Dempsey's chance appeared. Jim Price of the New York *Press* took pity on Dempsey and assigned Nat Fleischer, then a young sportswriter for the paper, to do a story on the western fighter. Another sportswriter, Damon Runyon, extended his sympathy and influence. Finally, Jim Price and Runyon convinced Tom McArdle, a matchmaker with considerable influence, that Dempsey was worthy of a New York fight. Matched against André Anderson, a 215-pound fighter from the West, Dempsey fought his first New York fight on June 24, 1916, at the Fairmont Club.[32]

Anderson, known by the fighting name of "Agile," was anything but agile in his fight with Dempsey. The New York *Tribune's* leading boxing writer, W. O. McGeehan, noted that Anderson had grown circumferentially to the size of a "young barrel," and Jimmy Johnston added that Anderson might well be "the greatest diver that ever entered the ring." Fleischer believed that Dempsey's ability, more than Anderson's inability, was the deciding factor in the fight.[33] Everyone agreed that Dempsey was the clear victor. New York laws prohibited a decision in any fight; the bout is officially listed as a "no decision." However, the newspapers gave the decision to Dempsey, and in the age of no-decision fights, all bets were paid off according to newspaper "decisions."

For the Anderson fight, Dempsey was paid sixteen dollars. But it got his name into the newspapers. His aggressive fighting style was popular with the audience at the Fairmont Club, and within a few weeks he received another chance. This time he was matched with a tough Irish heavyweight named Wild Bert Kenny. In a fight punctuated by late knockdowns and early bells, Dempsey again won the newspaper decision. And the Fairmont, never noted as a club where a fighter might become rich, paid him forty-three dollars.[34]

Both Anderson and Kenny were respected fighters. When a 160-pound kid was able to defeat them, the New York City sporting public took note. Unfortunately for Dempsey, notoriety ushered in the unctuous figure of John "the Barber" Reisler. A former Broadway

29

barber, Reisler was a boisterous, obnoxious parasite. Ostensibly a fight manager, he was noted for his heartless use of boxers. If he believed he could make a few dollars at the expense of one of his fighter's careers, he did so. He overmatched his fighters with alarming regularity, and, not content to see them broken and bloody, just as often cheated them on their purses. He left the greatest fighter he managed, Sam Langford, to live blind and penniless in the cellar of a Boston tenement.[35]

Looking at Dempsey, Reisler saw an easy payday. First he got rid of Price, Dempsey's unofficial manager. One morning Price awoke to find a telegram that his mother was sick and dying back in Utah. He had no choice; he had to return home. With Price successfully maneuvered out of the way, Reisler moved in on Dempsey with piranhic intent. He told Dempsey that not only had he bought his contract for fifty dollars, but that he had lent Price fifty dollars against Dempsey's next fight. It little mattered that Dempsey and Price had no written contract, Reisler informed his new boxer; Dempsey would fight for John the Barber or not at all.[36]

With Dempsey finally under his control, Reisler began to search for a fight. It was clear from the start that he was willing to sacrifice Dempsey's career for one payday. He arranged for Dempsey to fight Sam Langford, possibly the greatest fighter of the first quarter of the twentieth century. Dempsey wisely refused. Next, John the Barber proposed that Dempsey fight Gunboat Smith, one of the leading white boxers during the White Hope years. Again Dempsey sensed a mismatch and refused. Reisler became angry; he was not willing to submit to Dempsey's decisions. Several days later, he told his fighter that he believed he could get a match with Frank Moran, a good Pittsburgh heavyweight who had fought Willard for the title only a few months before. Once again Dempsey refused.

Finally Reisler's constant pressure forced Dempsey to agree to fight John Lester Johnson, a sinewy black boxer who had fought the likes of Langford, Smith, Joe Jeanette, Harry Wills, and Sam McVey. Even the circumstances of the fight insured that Dempsey would be humiliated. Scheduled for Friday night, July 14, 1916, the fight was held at the Harlem Sporting Club. The card featured a series of mixed bouts, and the promoters hoped that the Johnson-

Dempsey fight would end the night on a pleasant note for the residents of Harlem. The promoters were not disappointed. Although Dempsey fought with great courage, he was no match for Johnson. In the second round Johnson broke three of Dempsey's ribs. For the rest of the fight Dempsey was in constant pain. He survived the ten rounds, but as he later confessed, "I was never hurt so bad."[37]

Reisler had promised Dempsey a good payday, but, typically, he cheated his fighter. John the Barber pocketed four hundred of a five-hundred-dollar purse, and then left Dempsey to find a way to mend his injuries.[38] Disillusioned with New York, boxing, and managers, Dempsey headed home. Back in Salt Lake City he spent several months resting. When he needed money he either worked in the mines or fought other western fighters. In the East he would have had to fight for Reisler, and that would have meant he would have more ribs broken by fighters like Johnson, Langford, and Moran. For the moment, Dempsey was content with the West.

If there was anything fortunate about his Reisler experience, it was that Dempsey learned a lesson about managers. Never again would he trust his career to a heartless parasite. Crude socially, uneducated, and unworldly, Dempsey nevertheless had an intuitive understanding of his own ability. He knew exactly what he was capable of doing, and, more important, he had a remarkable ability for assessing the talents of other fighters. No manager would ever again match him against an opponent who he believed was too good for him.

By the end of 1916 Dempsey had no more illusions about his trade. Boxing was a hard, dirty business. Littered with characters like Reisler, it was a sport that had no room for the uninitiated. If he was going to succeed in the game, Dempsey realized, he would need a manager who could be depended upon to look out for Dempsey's interests as well as work with the unsavory characters who controlled boxing. In 1917 Dempsey found such a manager.

CHAPTER III

Marriages of Different Kinds

W HEN Dempsey left New York in 1916, he was forced to ride the rods to get back to Salt Lake City. The unseasonably cold weather and the sight of the wet iron rails vanishing into the misty darkness gave external expression to his feelings. He was depressed. Behind him lay failure. He had traveled to New York in search of success, or, at least, the rewards of success—fame and fortune. But nothing had turned out as he had planned. All that New York now held was Reisler's vituperative insults. After their final dispute, Reisler had told him to leave boxing if he was afraid to fight. Dempsey curbed his desire to hit Reisler, but he was unable to articulate his feelings. Instead, he reacted much as his father had years before: he fled the scene of unhappiness. He needed time to rethink his plans. In fact, he needed a new set of plans.[1]

The dilemma of the existential world is life without values. Man instinctively needs an anchor; he fears being set free in a valueless sea. He moves away from void and toward human warmth. In a limited sense, when Dempsey left New York in 1916, he confronted this horrifying existential dilemma. His career was in shambles, he lacked strong personal ties, and his life no longer had a direction. Confronted with massive change, he began to search for something stable, anything warm. Although he had never developed any intense romantic relationships, he was now very receptive to feminine kindness. Once settled again in Salt Lake City, he soon fell prey to this sort of kindness. He was certainly not the first or last person to marry during one of the lowest emotional periods in his life.

32

Almost from the first, it was a mistake. Dempsey had met Maxine Cates in the spring of 1916 before he left for New York. She was a common prostitute of the dancehall variety who worked in the red-light district of Salt Lake City along Commercial Street. Before he left for New York he had displayed only minor interest in the woman, who was at least fifteen years older than he was. However, he returned from New York a defeated man; his confidence had been severely shaken and he was now vulnerable to Maxine's well-worn charms. In late September and early October of 1916, Dempsey passed his idle hours in the company of the brunette veteran of the western saloon. In some ways they had much in common. Dempsey had learned to box in the mining towns and bars of the West, and Maxine had refined her skills in the same areas. Toward the end of the first week in October, she suggested that they make the relationship more binding. Dempsey, thinking of no real objection, agreed and on October 9, 1916, in Farmington, Utah, they were married by a justice of the peace.[2]

After a brief honeymoon in a cheap hotel, the couple returned to Salt Lake City. Instability marked their marriage from its first weeks. To begin with, Dempsey's parents deeply resented Maxine's sordid past and, in return, Maxine was disgusted by the quasi-respectability of the Dempsey household. Sometimes when Dempsey left Salt Lake City to fight in another town, Maxine would stay with his parents. Such visits were usually brief and riddled with emotional friction. Dempsey's mother, Celia, would try to interest Maxine in home-life—cooking, sewing, and similar domestic tasks. But Maxine would soon become restless and complain that her hands were becoming rough from work. On one of these occasions she told Celia, "I'd rather go back to my old life and smoke hop than stay in any slow place like this."[3]

Furthermore, Dempsey's trade required him to spend extended periods away from Maxine. One month he would fight in Ely, Nevada, and the next he might have to travel to Murry, Utah. In between there were the training periods, mine work, or some other odd job. Dempsey often asked Maxine to accompany him, but she almost always refused, choosing instead to stay in Salt Lake City and keep in touch with her profession and friends. Maxine was unable or unwilling to sever her ties with her past. She continued to work in western dancehalls as a prostitute and a piano player. After only a few months of marriage, their life together reverted to their premarital relationship. Dempsey traveled and fought. Maxine worked at her trade. When they were both in Salt Lake City at the same time they lived together; otherwise, they lived separate lives linked only by the money Dempsey sent Maxine whenever he could.[4]

As bad as their marriage was, Dempsey's mind was nevertheless occupied by the considerations of making a living. The only thing he really knew how to do was to fight, so in late 1916 he returned to the ring. Against average competition he was successful. In his last three fights of 1916 he defeated Young Hector, Terry Keller, and Dick Gilbert. When he could not find a fight, Dempsey acted as a sparring partner for some of the better western fighters. Working for less than one dollar per day, he sparred with, and learned to hate, Carl Morris, a big heavyweight who was considered one of the best fighters of the period. On one occasion, early in 1917, he was even matched against one of the best heavyweights of the White Hope era, "Fireman" Jim Flynn. A short but thick-boned man who had begun boxing professionally in 1901, Flynn had boxed the best fighters of the first twenty years of the century. He had battled Tommy Burns, Jack Twin Sullivan, Sam Langford, Billy Papke, Philadelphia Jack O'Brien, Luther McCarthy, Carl Morris, Gunboat Smith, Jack Dillon, and Battling Levinsky. In 1912 Flynn had even fought Jack Johnson for the heavyweight crown. For a man of Dempsey's experience to agree to fight Flynn bespoke courage and financial desperation. The fight did not take long: Flynn knocked Dempsey down several times and before the bell rang to end the first round, Dempsey's brother Bernie, who was acting as his manager, wisely threw in the towel. For the first and only time in his life, Dempsey suffered a technical knockout.[5]

Several weeks later to Dempsey's surprise, he received a telegram from Fred Windsor, the promoter of his bout with Flynn, indicating that he might find more matches in the San Francisco-Oakland area. Windsor also said that he would be willing to manage Dempsey. Actually, Dempsey did not have much of a choice; if he hoped to advance in his sport, he had to go to either San Francisco or New York, the two centers of boxing in the United States. The specter of John "the Barber" Reisler eliminated New York from consideration; San Francisco was the only alternative. He told Maxine of his plans, and again he was surprised. She told him that she intended to go along. Toward the end of February they made the trip to the Bay City area.[6]

They traveled together, but they did not remain together long. Early in May, 1917, Dr. Joseph Fife was called to the Gibson Hotel on Jackson Street, a rough section of San Francisco bordering the Barbary Coast to administer to Maxine, who had dislocated her jaw when she tripped over the raised door sill and fell on her chin. Later Maxine testified that Dempsey had dislocated her jaw with a right-hand punch. Her story, which Dempsey firmly denied, was told during moments of desperation and in all likelihood was a fabrication. Regardless of the truth, however, Maxine left Dempsey several days later to visit her mother in Yakima, Washington. She never returned. Months later Dempsey learned that she was working as a prostitute in Cairo, Illinois. Dempsey continued to send her money whenever he could, but they never again lived as husband and wife. When they did meet once more, years later, Maxine made a concerted effort to ruin Dempsey's career.[7]

At the time of Maxine's departure, though, her husband was in the process of building that career. Under the management of Windsor, he was introduced to West Coast boxing on the fight card at Tommy Simpson's West Oakland Club. Located in the poverty-stricken black section of West Oakland, Tommy Simpson's club nevertheless attracted some the best West Coast fighters. In structure, all the bouts were the same. California boxing legislation allowed no fight to be scheduled for more than four rounds, so boxers were expected to fight each second at full speed. There was no room for the slow starter or the particularly timid, defensive-minded boxer. Dempsey's later reputation as a quick starter undoubtedly owes something to his California training. On March 22, 1917, he made his debut against Al Norton, a handsome heavyweight who had earned a good reputation. Although the bout was called a draw, the San Francisco *Chronicle* reported the next day that "Dempsey looks to be a good boy and went through the four rounds unscratched." In contrast, Norton had been badly cut.[8]

35

During April and May, Dempsey might have had other fights in the Bay City area. He might have fought Norton again, and he possibly lost a decision to Willie Meehan. But his activities for the early months of 1917 are difficult to verify. The most that is known is that he did not prosper under Windsor's management. Forced to supplement his ring earnings with other jobs, he worked for a time in the shipyards of Tacoma, Washington. But even this job was cut short by news from Salt Lake City. In a telegram from his mother, he learned that his brother Bruce, the youngest child of the family, had been stabbed to death while selling newspapers. Dempsey returned home at once but was too late for the funeral. It had been a senseless murder, one in which neither the motive nor the killer was ever discovered. The tragedy was compounded; in his efforts to return to Salt Lake City, he had lost his job at the shipyard.[9]

During the past year Dempsey twice had failed in his efforts to become a successful boxer—in New York and in San Francisco. He had been involved in an unsuccessful marriage, he had lost several jobs, and his brother had been stabbed to death. His father was unemployed and crippled with rheumatism, absentmindedness, and melancholy; his mother suffered from periodic bouts of illness; and one of his sisters and two of his brothers were seriously ill. Perhaps, at this time in his life what Dempsey needed most was a bit of simple good luck. It came from an unlikely source: John Leo McKernan, known to his friends, enemies, and history as Doc Kearns. Dempsey's previous encounters with Kearns had been brief. In 1916 Dempsey had fought Joe Bond, a fighter Kearns managed, and before Dempsey left San Francisco he had helped Kearns to survive a barroom fight. For some reason, Kearns had been impressed with the fighter, and while Dempsey was in Salt Lake City he received a letter from Kearns. It was short: if Dempsey needed a manager, Kearns needed a fighter. Dempsey wrote back to Kearns expressing his willingness to form a partnership. Less than one week later, Dempsey received a one-way ticket to San Francisco and a five-dollar bill. The most famous manager-fighter relationship in boxing's history had begun.[10]

Kearns's career had been even more spotty than Dempsey's. Before he met Dempsey, he had exhausted a number of careers. He had been a fair welterweight boxer who often boasted about his losses to two welterweight champions, Honey Mellody and Mysterious Billy Smith. Of Smith, Kearns said, "He was always doing something mysterious. Like he would step on your foot, and when you looked down, he would bite you in the ear." For a season he had played baseball with Seattle in the Pacific Coast League. After his athletic careers ended, he had gone to the Klondike, where he weighed gold in saloons, promoted fights, and managed boxers. Traveling back to the United States, he had been a taxi driver in Seattle, a bouncer in a dive on the Barbary Coast, a dealer in a gambling house, a saloonkeeper, and a manufacturer of fire extinguishers. By the time he met Dempsey, however, Kearns had settled comfortably into the business of managing prizefighters.[11]

Two factors made Kearns a remarkable manager. First, he had great courage and no ethics or morality; if he believed he could cheat, push, or connive his fighter to the top of the division, he would not hesitate to do so. During their partnership, Kearns was to engage in any number of highly unethical—and even illegal—practices to advance Dempsey's position. Second, Kearns had a wide array of friends and acquaintances who were influential in boxing. He knew promoters of every level from Tommy Simpson to Tex Rickard, and he had met scores of boxers, sports writers, trainers, and other managers. Although very few people trusted Kearns, they respected his ability to build up fighters, matches, and gates.

As a team, Dempsey and Kearns formed a study in contrasts. Dempsey was simple in tastes and subdued in manners. He wore his poverty like a badge, dressing modestly, eating at barroom lunch tables, and riding the rods. He was quiet and not given to expressing any emotions. In his later years this personal reserve would evolve into an air of graceful modesty, but in 1917 it was more likely to be mistaken for morose insolence. Kearns was the exact opposite. He was loud—in speech, in dress, and in manners. He was the first fight manager to use the first person singular when referring to one of his fighters, and he was a master of the verbal ballyhoo. After he became rich, he changed clothes three times a day, wore large diamond rings and tie pins, and covered himself with expensive perfume. A pushing, forceful type of man, he tended to be as insensitive to others as he was irresponsible with his fighter's money. Although Dempsey and Kearns never really became close friends, they were able to trust each other enough to stay together for eight years without a formal contract, and it is doubtful whether either would have advanced to the top of his profession without the aid of the other.[12]

Under Kearns's guidance Dempsey once again entered the ring. Because Dempsey had no reputation, Kearns was forced to accept any match, with the result that Dempsey was pitted against Willie Meehan. In the language of boxing, Meehan was a "spoiler," that breed of fighter who was not of championship caliber but who was very difficult to fight and often made a better opponent look bad. Meehan was hard to fight because he did everything wrong; indeed, he was nicknamed the "Whirling Dervish" because of his penchant for throwing wild punches from odd angles as he pivoted about the ring. Furthermore, Meehan did not look like a boxer. Fleshy to the point of being fat, he had a baby-fat face that made him look like a pugilistic Porky Pig. Therefore, audiences usually expected Meehan to be soundly defeated even though he rarely was. In his fight against Meehan, Dempsey looked very good. He was not able to hurt the rotund boxer, but he did win the decision. It was an impressive start.[13]

More fights followed. On August 1, 1917, Dempsey knocked out Al Norton in the first round. He followed this victory with two slow fights with Meehan, both of which ended in draws. Between fights he trained. Instead of seeking another job, he worked in the gyms to improve his technique. Kearns liked to credit himself with developing Dempsey's left hand. Perhaps Kearns gave himself too much credit, for even in his early days as a fighter Dempsey could use his left. Yet it is true that Dempsey improved under Kearns's instruction. After several months of training, Dempsey began to be recognized as a gifted heavyweight. He was matched against Charley Miller, who had "long been noted for his gameness as well as his ability to . . . give his opponent much trouble," and knocked out the more experienced boxer in one round. One week later he easily decisioned Bob McAllister, one of the best of the West Coast heavyweights.[14] In two months, Dempsey had built a solid reputation for himself in the San Francisco area and had attracted national attention.

Any doubts about Dempsey's ability were settled during his fight with Gunboat Smith. During the White Hope era, Smith had been the best white heavyweight, holding victories over Jess Willard, Sam Langford, Frank Moran, and many other leading heavyweights. When the White Heavyweight Championship of the World was created in an attempt to ignore or detract from Jack Johnson's title, Smith had been its most logical claimant. Even though Smith was thirty years old when he fought Dempsey, he was still recognized as one of the four or five best heavyweights of the period. Promoted by Harry Sullivan, a baseball park and fight magnate in the San Francisco area, the bout attracted considerable interest. The sports section of the San Francisco *Chronicle* ran a banner headline announcing the day the bout was to be held. The fight proved worthy of the attention. Held outdoors at the Mission Baseball Park on a beautiful October night before a large crowd, the match lasted four brutal rounds. In the second round Dempsey was hit by what he later said was the hardest punch he ever took. But he survived the blow and fought back savagely in the next two rounds. When the fight ended, Dempsey was given the decision. The fight marked the end of Smith as a viable contender. As Harry B. Smith, the leading sports columnist for the San Francisco *Chronicle* noted, Smith had lost the "punching power, stamina to resist the other fellow's onslaught and judgment of distance" of his youth.[15] What the writer did not immediately recognize was that a new force had stepped onto the heavyweight stage.

Dempsey ended his fighting for 1917 by boxing another of the holdovers from the White Hope era, his former employer Carl Morris. A tall Oklahoman who weighed about 235 pounds, Morris had the unenviable ability to attract the hatred of other people. When Dempsey worked as a sparring partner for Morris, the heavyweight would constantly remind Dempsey of his poverty. In addition, audiences hated Morris' fighting tactics of stalling and fouling. Harry B. Smith believed that Morris had done "more to kill the boxing game than to help it" by his unethical methods of boxing. But Morris was no match for Dempsey when they met at the Dreamland Rink in San Francisco. Dempsey easily won a four-round decision, and Morris, who hoped to fight other bouts on the West Coast, was forced to head back east.[16] In less than half a year together, Dempsey and Kearns had climbed to the top of their trade; by the end of 1917 Dempsey was considered one of the three best heavyweights in America.

In early 1918 Dempsey and Kearns decided that the time was ripe for leaving the Bay City area. If Dempsey was to contend for the title, Kearns believed, he had to fight in different cities and construct a web of boxing connections that would exert their influence in favor of a Willard-Dempsey bout. His reasoning was sound. Together the manager and fighter traveled east, and while Dempsey fought, Kearns lobbied for a championship match. Of course, Willard had no thoughts of fighting Dempsey, who was still practically unknown east of California. But to hear Kearns talk throughout 1918, the match was only months away. [17]

Fortunately for Kearns, Dempsey was extremely impressive during the swing east. On January 24 he knocked out Homer Smith, "a tough bird from Benton Harbor," in one round. Rematched against Carl Morris, Dempsey was soundly drubbing the Oklahoman when Morris deliberately hit Dempsey in the groin and was disqualified in the sixth round. In Fort Sheridan, Illinois, Dempsey once again fought Fireman Jim Flynn, the man who had knocked him out in one round almost exactly one year before. This time around, Flynn was no match, and Dempsey scored an impressive two-round knockout. In just twenty days Dempsey had defeated three of the best heavyweights in America. For the first time, the New York newspapers took note of his performances, and Willard mentioned Dempsey's name as one of the top two contenders. [18] Kearns was quickly achieving his wish: Dempsey was attracting a following.

Dempsey's prestige was further enhanced in his next fight. In Bill Brennan, an excellent New York boxer who was later to give Dempsey one of his toughest fights, Dempsey was matched against a young, rising heavyweight like himself. Unlike Gunboat Smith, Fireman Jim Flynn, and Carl Morris, Brennan was not a leftover from the White Hope years. Instead, Brennan looked upon the fight with Dempsey as a prelude to a match for the title. Similarly, Leo P. Flynn, Brennan's able manager, believed his fighter would have little trouble with Dempsey. Both fighter and manager made a grave miscalculation. Dempsey floored Brennan four times in the second round, landed repeated body blows for the next two rounds, and again knocked him down in the sixth round. As Brennan fell he broke his ankle and a loud "crack" was heard by men in the ringside seats. Mercifully, the referee stopped the bout as Brennan struggled to stand on one foot.[19]

As well as Dempsey was fighting, however, Kearns was determined to make his fighter's record even more impressive. On March 16, Dempsey fought a good heavyweight named Jack Smith and won by a first-round knockout. After the bout, it was discovered that Jack Smith was actually Fred Soddy, a common sparring partner, who was being passed off as Smith to make Dempsey's victory look more impressive. When questioned about the affair, Kearns acted offended and said he had no knowledge of the "set up." It is probable, though, that sports columnist Harry B. Smith was closer to the truth when he commented that "you can write your own ticket that he [Kearns] knew the real name of these soft spots picked for his heavy." On the day when Smith's observation was printed in the *Chronicle*, Dempsey knocked out another "soft spot," Tom Riley, in the first round. Unconscious for ten minutes after the fight, Riley paid the price of acting as a stepping-stone.[20]

Dempsey's first setback after forming his partnership with Kearns occurred in early May, 1918, when he fought Bill Miske, a good heavyweight from St. Paul. From start to finish, Dempsey fought without his usual recklessness. In fact, both fighters were overly cautious, and very few solid punches were landed during their uninspired ten-round match. Although the bout was officially listed as a no-contest decision, the sports writers present agreed that the fight was a "poor draw."[21] Perhaps Dempsey's friendship with Miske accounts for his poor performance, or it may have been that Dempsey was just stale. Certainly, when Dempsey fought Miske in 1920 he extended very little friendship.

In either case, Dempsey soon returned to his proper fighting form. Within a period of seven days at the end of May, he knocked out both Dan Ketchell and Arthur Pelky, the former in two rounds and the latter in less than two minutes. In the Ketchall fight, Dempsey defeated a boxer who was a virtual unknown. However, Arthur Pelky was another of the famous Great White Hopes. A Canadian boxer, he had burst upon the heavyweight scene when he killed the previously undefeated and highly respected Luther McCarthy in their match at Calgary, Canada, in 1913. Since the McCarthy bout, Pelky had sadly declined. Indeed, in his thirteen bouts between the McCarthy and Dempsey fights, Pelky had fought one no-decision, lost two bouts by decision, and had been knocked out ten times. Hence Dempsey could gain little satisfaction from his victory over Pelky. The *Stars and Stripes,* American military newspaper, correctly assessed the situation when it suggested that it was time for Pelky to retire.

As well as Dempsey's career was going inside the ring, by July, problems of an unpugilistic nature began to plague him outside of the ring. One irritation was John "the Barber" J. Reisler, Dempsey's former manager. Reisler bitterly resented his former fighter's success, and he continually did everything within his power to make life difficult for Dempsey. His expressed intent was to prohibit Dempsey from fighting under any management other than his own. However, beneath the stated objective lay an ugly mass of bitterness, twisted thinking, and malice. From state to state, Reisler followed Dempsey and attempted to gain injunctions that would prevent Dempsey from boxing or earning any money from his reputation. Usually Reisler's court actions failed, but they always created problems, either by delaying bouts or forcing Dempsey to reply to his charges. Reisler never did produce the contract he said Dempsey had signed, yet his countless lawsuits against Dempsey and Kearns followed the pair throughout most of the 1920s.[22]

Of a more serious and immediate concern by the middle of 1918 was the war in Europe. Contrary to the general belief in 1914, the conflict was proving to be a long and bloody affair rather than a short war of position and tactical finesse. After America was pulled into the war in early April, 1917, the United States government was forced to resort to a military draft in order to fill the army. This Selective Service Law, promulgated on May 16, 1917, was expanded one year later by Major General E. H. Crowder's famous "work-or-fight" orders. Essentially, under Crowder's system, two types of physically fit men of military age were exempt from serving in the army or navy. The first type comprised those working for a "productive industry," that is, an industry essential to the war effort. The second group were those who supported a family. "The deferred classes," Crowder wrote, "were meant to protect domestic relations and also economic interests." [23]

During a time of war, an athlete is placed in a unique position. Most men who return safely after serving in the military during their twenties can resume their normal occupation when they are discharged. But if an athlete is forced from his occupation for two or three years during his prime, the result can be disastrous. Therefore, most professional athletes try to circumvent their military duty to their country. If they cannot find a legitimate reason for deferment, they often join the National Guard or some other reserve unit. During World War I, for example, Babe Ruth enlisted in the Massachusetts Home Guard, a reserve unit formed to replace the federalized National Guard. Ruth was then able to serve both his country and the Boston Red Sox. Bill Tilden literally served out his stint in the Signal Corps giving tennis lessons to his commanding officer in Pittsburgh. [24] Hundreds of professional athletes followed this path, technically doing their duty but not missing a single season of athletic competition.

Boxers were no exception. When Crowder issued his orders to "work or fight" a New York *Tribune* columnist predicted that the command would "kick the bottom clean out of the pugilistic bucket." The writer noted that heavyweights such as Dempsey, Fred Fulton, Billy Miske, Harry Wills, Sam McVey, and Gunboat Smith would undoubtedly be doing more fighting in the trenches of France than in Madison Square Garden. The assumption was naïve to the point of being ludicrous. Actually, most of the famous boxers skirted their military duty by acting as boxing instructors at various training camps and military posts in the United States. In an article about boxing and the military, Thomas Forster noted that the list of famous boxers to serve their country in the capacity of boxing instructors included Mike Gibbons, Johnny Kilbane, Benny Leonard, Packy McFarland, Battling Levinsky, and Frank Moran. Service as boxing instructors soon proved to be a windfall for the fighters and their sport. The boxers were applauded for being patriotic while practicing their trade and maintaining their good physical condition.

43

Whenever they required a leave to engage in a real match, they were always granted a pass. In addition, their service was good public relations work for their sport. The editor of the *Ring*, Nat Fleischer, went so far as to credit the revival of interest in boxing to the World War I experience.[25]

Like his fellow boxers, Jack Dempsey was not so patriotic that he wanted to leave his profession to fight for a better world, and Kearns was determined to prevent Dempsey's eligibility to be drafted. The draft worry was successfully eliminated when Dempsey applied for exemption on the grounds that his wife, father, mother, widowed sister, and her children were dependent upon him for support. Essentially the statement was true, except for the part that claimed that his wife was "sickly" and had never been employed. On the basis of the questionnaire, Dempsey was granted a 4-A exemption by John S. Hogan, chairman of the local draft board in the San Francisco area.[26]

Exempt from the draft, Dempsey nevertheless helped the war effort in numerous ways. Many of the bouts in which he fought during 1918 were sponsored by charitable organizations. His bout with Dan Ketchell raised $3,500 for the Salvation Army; $26,000 was gathered for the Knights of Columbus from the proceeds of his match with Clay Turner; a tournament he participated in at Madison Square Garden collected $130,000 for the Army and Navy War Activities Fund; and one of the bouts he fought with Willie Meehan resulted in a donation of $17,000 to the Army and Navy War Activities Fund. In fact, before the Meehan fight, a writer for the San Francisco *Chronicle* commended Dempsey for establishing the precedent of a boxer paying his own expenses to a charity bout. Beyond fighting matches to aid different war-related charities, Dempsey aided in recruiting between three hundred to four hundred workers for Philadelphia shipyards. And, as Lieutenant John F. Kennedy of the United States Navy would later testify, Dempsey had been in the process of enlisting in the navy when the war ended.[27]

Regardless of his attempts to aid the American war effort, and Dempsey's war-related activities were far greater than those of many other famous athletes, he was criticized. The sports section of *Stars and Stripes* admitted that Dempsey was a "real scrapper," a "natural

44

fighter," who if not big was "awfully fast" and could "hit like a mule's kick." However, the newspaper questioned if Dempsey was an American as his solid Irish name implied. His swarthy complexion and rugged body, said a writer for the military newspaper, reminded one of a Slav. Was there truth, the author concluded, to the rumor that Dempsey's real name was "Shinsky"? The *Stars and Stripes* made a more serious comment about Dempsey and professional athletes on July 26, 1918. On that day the newspaper suspended the publication of its sports section, stating the staff's opinion that such stories as "Dempsey and Fulton fighting over the size of a purse" were demoralizing to American doughboys battling for their lives in French forests and trenches. "The glorified, the commercialized, the spectatorial sport of the past," read the obituary to the sports page, "has been burnt out by gun fire." Not until the end of the war did the sports section return to *Stars and Stripes.* [28]

Dempsey's war record is significant only in retrospect: had the issue not surfaced again in 1920 it might justifiably have been relegated to an unimportant aspect of his career. For in the middle of 1918, Dempsey was far more concerned with his boxing career than with the war in Europe, During July, the month that the staff of *Stars and Stripes* suspended publication of its sports section, Dempsey had four fights. The first two bouts were of little importance. His two-round knockout victory over Tommy McCarthy in Tulsa and his one-round knockout of Bob Devere were little more than tune-up fights, preparation for what was to come later.[29] His next two fights, though, were of more interest: one is interesting as a footnote to the social history of the South, and the other made Dempsey the number one contender in the heavyweight division.

After the Devere bout, Dempsey and Kearns took a train to Atlanta, where Dempsey was scheduled to box Dan "Porky" Flynn, a Boston heavyweight who had been another of the Great White Hopes several years before. In public Kearns expressed anxiety about the match. "You fellows," he told representatives of the Atlanta press, "picked up a real tough bird for Dempsey to battle, the toughest in the game." Regardless of what Kearns said, Flynn was not a good fighter. Against Dempsey the Bostonian lasted less than two minutes. Quick victories over Flynn and other heavyweights led an

Atlanta *Constitution* sports writer to compare Dempsey's success to that of the American marines: "Dempsey has been wading through the heavies of late as the American marines have been tearing through the ranks of the Boches."[30] Pugilistically, then, the Flynn match was of only slightly more interest than the McCarthy and Devere fights.

On the same card as the Dempsey-Flynn bout was a Battle Royal, an example of diseased race relations in the South. Its format was simple: usually between ten and twenty black youths would enter the ring at the same time; occasionally they were blindfolded, but usually they were not; and the winner was the last person standing in the ring. There were, of course, no limits on time or method of fighting. At the end of the bout the spectators would pay the winner by throwing nickels, dimes, and quarters into the ring. The Battle Royal before the Dempsey-Flynn match engaged nine young blacks who, according to one reporter, "fought like little black demons" until only one "little son of Ham" was left standing. Veteran fans who witnessed the affair called it "the greatest battle royal ever held in Atlanta, if not in the south."[31]

Dempsey's last fight in July, 1918, was the most important bout he fought before winning the championship. He was matched against Fred Fulton, who was considered the number-one contender for Jess Willard's crown. Another fight involved finding a city that would stage the bout; although boxing was achieving a respectable status in army camps and naval stations, the sport was still criticized by many Americans. A New York *Times* editorialist, for example, found nothing wrong with boxing "as a sport, as a form of exercise, and as a means both of self-defense and of righteous aggression," but when boxing was transformed into a source of profit it showed a "lamentable, and seemingly irremediable, tendency to degenerate at once and wholly into fraud, corruption, and brutality." A similar bias was voiced by Americans who believed that it was immoral for men to box for money while thousands of Americans were fighting for their lives in Europe. Added to this was the fear that the epidemic Spanish influenza would spread in a crowded arena.[32] Any would-be promoter of a major prizefight, therefore, was faced with a host of difficulties.

As the major boxing match of 1918, the Dempsey-Fulton fight

proved to be a promotion nightmare. One promoter scheduled the bout for Danbury, Connecticut, but several weeks later Governor Thomas Holcomb and the leaders of the Connecticut State Police barred the bout in their state. Next, a Baltimore promoter announced that he had obtained permission from the Maryland State Police to hold the bout in his city; a week later the Board of Police Commissioners said that no more boxing permits would be granted until the war was over. New Jersey promoters became the next bidders. A Newark promoter promised that the proceeds of the bout would be donated to the Clark C. Griffith Bat and Ball Fund for soldiers in Europe, but city officials vetoed the patriotic suggestion. Finally, Jack Curley, who had promoted the racially sensitive Johnson-Willard bout, received a firm guarantee from officials in Harrison, New Jersey, that the bout could be staged in their town.[33] After almost half a year of negotiations and press publicity, the bout had found a home.

A long time in promotion, the bout itself was amazingly short. Staged at the old Federal League Ball Park, it drew only about ten thousand spectators, and few of those purchased the high-priced ringside tickets. But the gate did not affect Dempsey, who was determined to win. As he looked across the ring at the bigger Fulton before the fight, "there was the cold, sneering look of a primitive man on [Dempsey's] face." When the bell rang, Dempsey rushed to the center of the ring. Fulton threw a weak left jab, and Dempsey countered with a left hook to the stomach and a straight right to the jaw. Fulton sank to the canvas, and although his manager pleaded with him to rise, he did not move. Eighteen seconds after the opening bell, Fulton was counted out by referee Johnny Eckhardt. Dempsey was now the number-one contender. At his home in Lawrence, Kansas, heavyweight champion Jess Willard told reporters, "I'd like to fight Dempsey. . . . He is not going to win the championship in twenty-three seconds. No, not in one hour and twenty-three seconds."[34] Less than one year later Willard was proven wrong.

But Dempsey's chance to win the title was still one year away, and during the interval Kearns made certain that his boxer remained visible to the followers of the sport. In August he knocked out his friend from his Colorado days, Terry Keller, in five rounds. His one setback during 1918 occurred several weeks later. He lost a four-round exhibition match against Willie Meehan in a bout staged for a charity drive. But the loss did not hinder Dempsey's career, for no-body could consider a four-round loss to the comical Meehan as any-thing but a fluke. Indeed, the next night in Reno, Dempsey showed his true form in a one-round knockout victory over Jack Moran.[35]

Kearns and Dempsey worked their way back east toward the end of September. During November, Dempsey recruited workers for the Sun Shipyard in Chester, Pennsylvania. He even posed for a public-ity photograph in which he appeared to be a shipyard worker himself. The next day the picture was published in a local newspaper and completely misunderstood. Dempsey's well-creased trousers could be discerned beneath his work overalls, and his spats and patent leather suede-topped shoes seemed incongruous with the riveter's trade. Eventually, the photograph was published in other newspapers, and Dempsey was roundly criticized, especially by the American Legion. But the incident was soon forgotten and would have remained so had it not been revived under the more sensational circumstances in 1920.[36]

While in Philadelphia, Dempsey continued to fight. He knocked out the World Lightheavyweight Champion, Battling Levinsky, in three rounds. After the fight, agents from the Department of Justice surrounded the arena and would not let anyone out until they showed their draft registration card. Problems also arose in Demp-sey's next scheduled fight. Matched against Joe Bonds in a bout sponsored by the War Fund Boxing Committee, Dempsey traveled to New York City only to discover that instead of fighting Bonds he was to battle Joe Jeannette, the noted black heavyweight. As reported by Dan Daniel of the New York *Sun*, it was a plot to get Dempsey to fight Jeannette. If Dempsey refused, Jeannette was to insult him and, if needed, hit him. Dempsey did refuse to fight Jeannette, and al-though the black fighter said something to him, no punches were thrown. Disgusted by the affair, Dempsey went back to Philadelphia. Later Jimmy Coffroth, the chairman of the War Fund Boxing Com-mittee, publicly apologized to Dempsey.[37]

Dempsey and Kearns stayed in Philadelphia until the end of November. During that time the fighter improved his record. Re-

48

matched with Porky Flynn, Dempsey again knocked out the Boston fighter in one round. In another rematch, this time with Billy Miske, Dempsey improved upon his previous performance. Although the two boxers fought a dull and slow fight, Dempsey won the popular decision.[38] Both rematches were symptomatic of Dempsey's position in the heavyweight ranks. He had fought and defeated all the best white heavyweights from the leading Great White Hopes of the Johnson years to the best of the young fighters. Kearns refused to let Dempsey fight the black heavyweights. The manager correctly assumed that such a match could do his fighter no good but much harm. Willard had promised to fight when the war ended, so Kearns and Dempsey decided to take no chances and fight only boxers of known—and usually low—quality.

Between the second Miske fight and his bout with Willard, Dempsey entered the ring nine times. Two of the matches were exhibitions, and the other seven fights he won by knockouts, six in one round and one in two rounds. Amidst cries of "fake," "police," and "jail the big tramp," he knocked out Carl Morris in ten seconds of the first round of a match promoted by Dominick Tortorich in New Orleans. The outcome of the bout, noted one local sports writer, gave "a blackeye to the boxing game" in the New Orleans area. The only other noted boxer he fought was Gunboat Smith, whom Dempsey knocked out in the second round. The other knockout victims were completely unknown boxers.[39] Indeed, after the Fulton fight there was really only one more heavyweight for Dempsey to fight—Jess Willard. Dempsey's rise to the top of the division had been swift, but it also had been complete.

CHAPTER IV

Crucible
Under
the Sun

B Y THE end of 1918 Dempsey was clearly the leading contender in the heavyweight division, but by then his elevated
status did not seem to matter. The division was slowly dying
from its champion's lethargy. Jess Willard, who had won the title
from Jack Johnson on April 5, 1915, defended his crown once in
1916 and then, except for several exhibitions, fought no more. The
personality of the champion sets the temper for the entire division.
Electing to stay on his farm in Kansas rather than defend his title or
even stage boxing exhibitions for war fund drives, Willard became as
hated as Leach Cross, perhaps the dirtiest fighter of the period. The
Bridgehead Sentinel, a newspaper published by the First Division of
the U.S. Army of Occupation at Montabaum, Germany, said in an
editorial, "The only proper treatment for this great, hulking, money
grabbing slacker is tar and feathers," and Dan Daniel, the leading
boxing columnist for the New York *Sun,* agreed. In addition, his
general unfriendliness and reluctance to part with even a nickel made
him unpopular with the press.[1]

To Tex Rickard, Willard's unattractiveness made a fight all the
more desirable. The Great War was over, the troops were coming
home, and Rickard was willing to bet his own money that the public
would pay a great deal to boo the heavyweight champion who had
ignored America's war effort.[2] Thus convinced, Rickard began to
lure Willard out of his semiretirement.

Willard was tempted by one one thing—money. Although he
had a farm, and his appearances in a movie here and a circus there

brought in a comfortable income, he was not a rich man. In addition, his years as a public attraction were drawing to a close. After he had defeated Johnson in 1915, he had been a hero. Crowds watched his every public move, Hammerstein's New York theater paid him $10,000 for a two-week engagement, and he earned many more thousands of dollars in Buffalo Bill's Wild West Show.[3] With one more big payday he would be able to retire to his farm.

Rickard offered Willard that payday, and the heavyweight champion eagerly signed a contract calling for him to fight anyone Rickard chose for a maximum of forty rounds. Willard was guaranteed $100,000. Fighter and promoter followed the usual procedure for a major bout. Willard deposited $10,000, and Rickard deposited $15,000 in a fund that would be forfeited if either party reneged on the contract. The choice of whom Willard fought, and when and where, was left up to Tex. After all, Rickard had established himself as a capable and honest promoter, and even Willard, who could never trust a manager, let alone a promoter, seemed satisfied that Rickard would settle affairs to everyone's satisfaction.[4]

In 1919 there were few good heavyweight fighters. Of the best Europeans, Georges Carpentier of France and Joe Beckett of England, the first was too small and the second was unproven. The American picture was equally dismal. Perhaps the best boxer was the aging Sam Langford, but he was black, and after the Jeffries-Johnson catastrophe in Reno, Rickard had sworn he would never again promote an interracial match.[5] Sam McVey, Harry Wills, Bill Tate, and Joe Jeannette were also eliminated because of their color. This left Rickard with a handful of white fighters, most of whom could also be crossed out because of age, size, or lack of ability. Fireman Jim Flynn was at least forty years old, and Gunboat Smith was no longer the puncher he once was. Carl Morris, although almost as big as Willard, had lost both of his fights in 1918. As for the rest—Fred Fulton, Willie Meehan, Billy Miske, Terry Keller, Tommy Gibbons, and Bill Brennan—they lacked the popular appeal as well as the ability to challenge the champion.

Jack Dempsey was the only logical contender. But Dempsey's size made Rickard hesitate. "Everytime I see you," he said to Dempsey in early 1919, "you look smaller to me." But finally, after a talk with

Kearns at the Hotel Claridge in New York City, Rickard was convinced that Dempsey might not be killed by Willard. A few days later in an out-of-the-way corner of the Weehauken, New Jersey, terminal of the West Shore Railroad, Jack Dempsey signed a contract to fight Willard. Since boxing was illegal in New York, the New Jersey site was chosen to make the contract official. The event saw no popping of corks or flourishings of huge sums of money; everyone was businesslike. Dempsey signed a contract that guaranteed him $27,500, and then he left for Uniontown, Pennsylvania, where he was scheduled to open in a play. Rickard left, unusually quiet, for now he had other problems.[6]

Since prizefighting was illegal in almost every state, finding a city to stage the event would be difficult. Politically, the legalization of prizefighting was a delicate issue. On the one hand, returning war veterans wholeheartedly endorsed boxing. Many had been instructed in the sport, for the army used boxing both as training for warfare and a means to dispel camp tensions. Major Anthony Drexel Biddle, of the prominent Philadelphia family, supported boxing throughout his lifetime. Even General John J. Pershing encouraged boxing for his troops in Europe. According to Jimmy Bronson, after Pershing saw Sergeant Bob Martin win the Inter-Allied Heavyweight Championship, he told Martin, "This game of yours is a game that makes the American Army the greatest in the world."[7] Such praise from the men who led America's armies lent prestige to boxing in the postwar years.

On the other hand, forces just as powerful stood inexorably opposed to the rise of boxing. As early as 1918 ministers and reformers were dismayed by the growing interest in pugilism in America. Remembering the long, bitter struggle to suppress prizefighting in the late nineteenth century, the *Northwestern Christian Advocate* noted that, unfortunately, the war had caused the revival and that professional boxers were "working overtime." The Methodist newspaper instructed its readers to exercise Christian perseverance until the Huns were defeated and then close the evil inroads that the wartime atmosphere had opened.[8]

This moral opposition everywhere confronted Rickard as he searched for a city that would permit the championship bout. Before the war he had staged several major championship fights in the West, but in 1919 western states were, for one reason or another, unreceptive. Two days after Willard signed to defend his title, Governor W. P. Hobley of Rickard's native state of Texas announced that the Lone Star State would not sanction the match. A month later, the governor of Nevada vetoed a bill to permit a twenty-five-round boxing match there. Although Shreveport, Louisiana, and Pocatello, Idaho, offered large sums of money for the right to stage the bout, by April, Rickard had abandoned his plans to hold the match west of the Mississippi River.[9]

As the weeks passed, Rickard seriously considered New Jersey, where boxing was legal and which, as a population center, should draw a large crowd. However, Willard's apathy toward wartime charities caused John S. Smith, chairman of the New Jersey Boxing Commission, to prohibit the title fight in his jurisdiction. Actually Rickard favored New York as the site for the match, but New York was deeply involved in a legal battle over boxing, and legalization in that state was still one year away.[10] By the end of March, Rickard was beginning to fear he might not find a city that would permit the contest. Earlier he had threatened to hold it in Europe, but most sports writers realized that such talk was a bluff. Yet Rickard was an optimist; experience had taught him that money could buy anything, especially a politician. With purchase on his mind, he approached Governor James M. Cox of Ohio. Rickard was not a subtle man. He went to Cox's hotel room when the latter was visiting New York City and, announcing his firm belief that Cox would be nominated by the Democratic party for president in the 1920 convention, offered Cox $25,000 to facilitate his nomination. Cox easily saw through Rickard's undisguised bribe and replied that he could not be bought, but he added, since boxing was legal in Ohio and since his state had a "sport-loving public," he saw no reason why the attorney general would prohibit the bout.[11]

The attorney general did not object, and Mayor Cornell Schrieber of Toledo welcomed the fight. On May 5, 1919, the arrangements were concluded: the bout was scheduled for twelve rounds, with 7 percent of the gate pledged to the poor in Toledo. Rickard was pleased. There had not been a major outdoor prizefight

in the United States since 1910, when Jack Johnson defeated Jim Jeffries, and Toledo, situated amidst the major eastern and midwestern
cities, seemed in a perfect location to draw a large crowd. Rickard
said he expected the match to yield approximately $400,000.[12]

Not everyone was as pleased as Rickard was. The progressive
movement in Toledo was still strong in 1919, and, influenced by
their religious beliefs, hundreds of people greeted the odious prospect
of a heavyweight championship fight with an outburst of protest.

Less than two weeks after Toledo was chosen as the site for the
match, the local ministers lodged their complaint. First, the Toledo
Ministerial Union sent a petition to Mayor Schrieber calling for him
to cancel the bout. The Reverend Frank M. Silsbly of Oakland,
California, introduced a resolution before the General Assembly of
Presbyterian Churches meeting in St. Louis, which proposed that the
bout should be prohibited because "one of the participants failed to
answer the call of patriotic duty."[13] The petition of the Toledo
ministers and the Reverend Silsbly resolution failed to prompt Toledo officials to cancel the match.

Where God's ordained failed, politicians, both state and national, hoped to succeed. Representative Robert Dunn of Wood
County, Ohio, introduced a bill before the state house of representatives to prevent public boxing exhibitions. Although the Dunn bill
was later defeated, the lower house did adopt a resolution calling
upon Governor Cox to uphold the "fair name of the State of Ohio"
and prohibit a bout not "conducive to good morals." Sick in bed,
Cox refused even to acknowledge the Pearson resolution, which leading Democrats in Ohio believed was passed on purely political
grounds to embarrass the Cox administration.[14]

The last serious effort to block the Willard-Dempsey match was
made on the floor of the House of Representatives in Washington.
On June 26, 1919, Representative Charles H. Randall of California
implored Congress to adopt a resolution "to protect the Nation's
birthday against desecration by a prize fight." Randall asked the
press, "Why should a fight between bruiser slackers, who were not
brave enough to join the war against German murderers, be permitted in this country?" The next day Randall wired Cox to inform the
governor that "the enlightened public sentiment of this nation is

against this proposed disgraceful exhibition and looks to you to prevent it." [15]

Throughout the month of protest Cox remained silent. Undoubtedly this was wise politically, for although many ministers and politicians were vigorous in their opposition to the match, many more, if less vocal, citizens were just as adamant in their support of the fight. This larger voice was articulated in an open letter to Edward R. Wright, the secretary of the national organization of ministers. Written by the Army, Navy, and Civilian Board of Boxing Control, the letter suggested that the revival of boxing was a positive result of the war, and that for every one person opposed to the fight one thousand believed the match would be a source of "innocent and pleasurable entertainment." The letter concluded by adding that the ministers of America were "a half a century behind the times." [16] The public did not well up against the Willard-Dempsey bout; a sport which had caused angry controversies during the first fifteen years of the twentieth century was now on the verge of complete acceptance. Times were changing.

As the June days became hotter and hotter, religious and progressive protest melted like a spring snow. The important public issues inadvertently benefited the Dempsey-Willard bout by completely overshadowing it. Religious zealots, moral reformers, and progressive crusaders were by the summer of 1919 on the verge of a far greater triumph—the National Prohibition Amendment. And while the battle for the Volstead Act (to implement prohibition) overshadowed the Willard-Dempsey contest in the moral sphere, interest in the Versailles Treaty obscured the Toledo affair in the political realm. But neither the dreams of teetotalers nor President Wilson could remove the Willard-Dempsey bout from the sports pages of the American newspapers or the minds of millions of people throughout the United States.

Willard himself aroused little excitement. Although his secretary, Ray Archer, insisted that Willard did not weigh over three hundred pounds, visitors to his camp were not so sure. During training sessions, which he directed himself, Willard lacked discipline and appeared dull and slow to even the uninitiated in the mysteries of training. The listless atmosphere of Willard's camp is best indicated by the one event which caused excitement. On June 18, 1919, several hundred miles away from Toledo, the champion's latest movie opened at the Park Theater. Like his other acting adventures, *The Challenge of Chance* was a melodramatic, mock-heroic affair that featured big Jess "as popular ranch foreman, representative *pro tem* of the SPCA, and innocent buyer of horses for a crooked dealer in El Paso." However, through no fault of Willard's heroic actions, the film became jumbled toward the end, and the reviewer was not exactly sure how Jess lost the sweet young girl he loved to another man. Thus Willard, accused as unpatriotic by the press and uninspiring in training camp, could not win even in the dream world of the cinema. The champion's major problem was that he hated everyone and everything connected with boxing. As Nat Fleischer remarked, "His heart had never been in the fighting game, and had finances permitted" he would undoubtedly have retired after his fight with Jack Johnson.[17]

Dempsey was another matter. The challenger's camp at the Overland Club was organized, and he worked every day with exuberance. Dempsey's camp was a circus; thousands of men and hundreds of women braved the mud, mosquitoes, and sweltering heat to watch.[18] No one objected to paying a quarter to watch him work, because Dempsey fought each sparring partner as though he were fighting Willard. So vicious was he that W. O. McGeehan, a leading sports columnist, said the challenger would have to get "another pair of coons" before his next fight.

The carnival atmosphere of Dempsey's camp was contagious. During the weeks before the fight the character of Toledo drastically altered. The staid, respectable town, which had grown in prosperity and population during the war, became a hectic parade ground for every sort of hustler, crook, and flimflam man. Following the typical order of events in boxing, the parasites arrived first. From New York City, Dempsey's old manager, John the Barber Reisler, strolled into town accompanied by five lawyers and flourishing a document that he claimed made him Dempsey's manager until December, 1919. His attempt to regain Dempsey's contract met with failure, however.[19]

Next to arrive were the get-rich-quick schemers. When these hustlers died out in the 1920s as boxing became more organized, they were replaced by respectable entertainment syndicates. But whatever sport gained in organization and efficiency, it lost in stories and atmosphere. Two of the greatest "prefight businessmen," Professor Billy McCarney and Thomas V. Bodkin, were present in Toledo in the weeks before the fight.

McCarney and Bodkin helped out at Dempsey's training grounds by entertaining the press, but they also managed to corner the concession market for the fight. Ice cream, sandwiches, near beer, cigarettes, seat cushions, lemonade, glims (opera glasses), and other concessions were handed over to them on the authority of Dempsey's manager, Doc Kearns. Of course, McCarney and Bodkin, each of whom had the ethics of a shell-game operator, did not plan actually to handle the concessions themselves. "Prizefight men," observed John Lardner, "enjoy the romance of business—i.e., the profits—but do not care for the sordid details of bookkeeping." McCarney and Bodkin were not exceptions; as soon as they were granted the concessions they started to sell them; this was to prove the wisest decision that the two men made.[20]

The next arrivals in the overcrowded city were the numerous champions, ex-champions, near-champions; the now-ares, the has-beens, and the never-weres who form the rank and file of the boxing community. Some of the fighters and ex-fighters came on the pretext of covering the bout for a major newspaper. The Washington *Post* and the San Francisco *Chronicle* printed columns by dapper lightweight champion Benny Leonard, and the Chicago *Daily News* sent the notorious Battling Nelson to keep their readers informed about events in Toledo. Other boxers simply came to watch, talk, and possibly do a bit of business on the side. Along with Leonard and Nelson, former champions Jack McAuliffe, Freddie Welsh, Jim Corbett, Jack Dillon, and Philadelphia Jack O'Brien added a festive charm. Everyone missed John L. Sullivan, the first modern heavyweight champion who had died on February 2, 1918, but mourning did not dampen the Toledo holiday.[21]

The eccentric Nelson caused the most controversy. During his years as lightweight champion the Durable Dane established an unshakable reputation as an aggressive, unstoppable, and notoriously unhygienic fighter. Short of funds, he was forced to camp out at Dempsey's training quarters. The night before the fight was so hot and humid that Nelson appropriated a bathing suit from Jack Kearns and started toward Lake Erie in search of a bath. Unfortunately for the lemonade concessionist he came upon six galvanized tubs containing a lemon syrup and melting ice mixture before he reached the lake. Afterwards, his underwear had to be torn off him in strips, and Kearns, who wisely burned his bathing suit, ordered Nelson to leave Dempsey's camp.[22]

By the time of Nelson's midnight lemonade dip most of the reporters, politicians, and spectators had arrived in Toledo. Their behavior was only slightly more respectable than Nelson's. During the day congressmen, jurists, intellectuals, and businessmen rubbed elbows with pickpockets, bank robbers, and the "unemployed sons of chance." It seemed as if all the nation was interested in the fight. Amidst conditions that resembled the Black Hole of Calcutta, Toledo's population climbed from 225,000 to approximately 400,000 in only a few weeks.[23]

Of course everyone had an opinion about who would win the fight. According to a *Police Gazette* poll of 336 experts, Dempsey was favored by 172, Willard received 144 votes, and 20 admitted that they were stumped. Even the politicians offered a guess. Judge Joseph W. Wescott, who knew how to pick a winner when he nominated Wilson for president, said Willard would win. Former Tammany Hall leader Richard Croker, stopping in New York City en route from his home in Palm Beach to his Irish estate at Glencairn, counseled reporters to place their money on Dempsey. Finally, women, who for the first time showed an interest in boxing, ventured opinions. When a sweet-faced, gray-haired old lady was asked by R. L. Goldberg, a columnist for the Chicago *Daily News,* who she believed would win the match, she replied, "I think the big guy packs a mean kick in either ham and will stick Dempsey for his roll on the Fourth."[24]

Celebration increased in the few days before the Fourth. Long years of moral reform and war had taken their toll; Americans were now ready to relax. Reaction from the war, a New York *Times* editorialist noted, had brought about the greatest sporting season in the history of the country. Boxing became a salve to heal the scars of war and an opiate to help America forget it. Toledo, the stories, and the holiday atmosphere symbolized this attempt to forget the Argonne Forest and the Americans buried in French soil. Grantland Rice, who could or would not forget, noted with a touch of remorse in the New York *Tribune* that in September, 1918, when the First Army struck St. Mihiel, the twenty correspondents present sent back about 50,000 words chronicling the downfall of Mont Sec. Now, in Toledo, four hundred correspondents would write over 600,000 words about the Dempsey-Willard fight. The thirty thousand ghosts in the Argonne Woods, Rice concluded, must be wondering what they died for.[25]

The irony of two slackers receiving the nation's attention only a few months after men had been dying in the Great War moved Rice to lodge his protest in doggerel:

> Here they come—nut and bum,
> Banker, Yeggman—all the nation,
> File by File of varied style
> In one vast conglomeration;
> Picking Jess or backing Jack,
> Doping out the bloke who'll win it
> Where the atmosphere is black
> With a million words a minute.
> . . . .
>
> If Tex promotes another bout
> (Here boy—I'll take another rickey)
> I hope they'll call the army out
> And treat him as a Bolsheviki;
> Though Willard fade and Dempsey fret—
> Let us forget—let us forget.

The final chorus of the verse is addressed to Tex Rickard and contains a note of self, and by extension, national, shame: "You made me what I am to-day—I hope you're satisfied."[26] Rice's lamentations, however, were sung to deaf ears. When the Fourth came, America's attention was focused on the shores of Maumee Bay. Constructed by Jim McLaughlin, the same architect who had built the arena for the Johnson-Jeffries bout, the Bay View Park Arena was designed to hold a crowd of 97,000 people and had not one stairway. To prevent freeloaders from gaining illegal access to the arena, a problem that plagued him in Reno, the builder surrounded the stadium with a wooden and barbed wire fence. The most uncomfortable part of the arena, however, was the seating. In the over one hundred-degree temperature the unpolished pine benches left the spectators' trousers full of splinters and white pine sap. Unfortunately for the local merchant who bought the seat-cushion concession from McCarney and Bodkin, almost everyone who came to the fight had purchased cushions before reaching the arena.[27]

Dan Daniel, the only member of the press box alive today, remembered that the "terrible, hot, cloudless day with heat beating down on your head" made men pay any price for something cold and wet. As he recalled, Henry Young, an enterprising youth from New York City, made a modest fortune selling ice water for fifty cents a glass. Other concessions did not fare as well. On Friday, the day of the fight, the fire commissioner barred smoking in the stadium; the ham and cheese rotted under the blazing sun, much to the delight of the Jewish and Catholic customers; and the ice cream degenerated into "a lake of milk." A question posed by McCarney best described the fate of the lemonade concession: "Did you ever see the Battler?"[28]

But the Fourth's activities pushed on toward the climax. At 11:00 A.M. the preliminary bouts began, but attracted little attention. By 1:00 P.M. it was obvious that heat and overcrowding would preclude Rickard's million-dollar gate. Around two-thirty the wealthy, who had purchased their ringside seats months before, started to filter into the arena. Many of them had arrived only that morning on the two New York Central charter trains, or by the extra cars detailed by the Pennsylvania Railroad. For the first time a number of women attended a major bout. Arriving at various times during the morning, they were quickly ushered up into a "Jenny Wren" section reserved especially for them by Rickard. The fear that raised parasols would block their view caused a number of men behind the female section prefight anxiety. At three-thirty Major Anthony Drexel Biddle, one of the judges for the fight, led his marines through a drill exhibition which ruined the canvas. Finally, after a fresh canvas was installed, the spectators began to look toward the dressing rooms.[29]

Dempsey was first to step into the ring. Although he weighed only about 180 pounds, his physical appearance was awesome. The leatherlike quality of his skin was accentuated by a deep purplish tan. The sides of his head had been shaved, giving the impression that it was too narrow for his heavily muscled body. Lastly, instead of the normal boxing robe, Dempsey wore an old black, wool cardigan, a left-over from his mining days. As he waited for Willard to enter the ring, Dempsey later remembered, he became irritated. Yet when Willard did arrive, and Dempsey saw how large the champion really was, the challenger's only thoughts were, "Oh my God I'm not fighting for the title, I'm fighting for my life."[30]

The first minute of the fight was slow, with Dempsey cautiously bobbing and weaving and Willard just as cautiously watching. Then, as John Lardner wrote, "the air turned red."[31] After a minute of showing Willard the utmost respect, Dempsey suddenly hit the champion with a five punch combination. The first four blows—two lefts and two rights—landed solidly to Willard's body; the last punch—a devastating left hook—connected with the right side of the champion's face. As the crowd of white-shirted, straw-hat-wearing men jumped to their feet, Willard fell to the canvas. As soon as Willard stood upright, Dempsey was upon him aiming every punch to the champion's head. Pinned against the ropes, Willard was helpless. Another left hook knocked Willard to the canvas for a second time. Only with the aid of the ropes was he able to stand, and while he held on there, turning away from the challenger, Dempsey hit him from behind with more punches. Finally, another left hook sent Willard sprawling to the canvas for a third time.

A more humane referee might have stopped the bout; Ollie Pecord merely tried to prevent Dempsey from circling behind Willard. This was one of Dempsey's favorite tactics: whenever he knocked down an opponent, he tried to get behind the unfortunate foe so that his next punches would be unseen by the victim. Although Pecord prevented this tactic after the third knock down, he could do nothing to help Willard once the champion regained his feet. Therefore, Dempsey easily floored Willard again. And this time the challenger did circle behind Willard. Back on his feet, Willard was subjected to a rear attack, knocked across the ring, and hit from every conceivable angle. Again Willard sought help from the ropes, but with the same result. As the champion gripped the middle rope,

Dempsey hit him time after time on the right side of his face. For the sixth time Willard sank to the canvas. By some insane instinct, Willard once more pulled himself upright with the aid of the ropes. Showing no pity, Dempsey punched Willard's face and kidneys, finally scoring another knockdown. As Pecord counted, the end of the round was signified in military fashion by a whistle; however, the whistle was inaudible both to the crowd and the officials, and Willard was counted out.

But the confusion was only starting. Kearns, dressed in a red and white striped shirt and white shoes and looking every inch a carnival shell man, knew the round had ended before Willard had been officially counted out, but he also remembered that several days before he had bet $10,000 at ten to one odds that Dempsey would knock out Willard in the first round. Kearns gave about one second of serious thought before he jumped into the ring and started to usher Dempsey toward the challenger's dressing room. Sitting in the press box, Ring Lardner reported that he saw a fat man climb into the ring and kiss Dempsey on the cheek, "so you can't say [Dempsey] didn't take no punishment."[32] But by the time Dempsey realized that the fight was not over, he was almost into his dressing room. At Kearns's frantic call, Dempsey returned to the ring.

Compared to the first round, the next two rounds were slow. There were no knockdowns, but Willard nevertheless absorbed an excessive amount of punishment. His eyes were dull, he was cut above and below both eyes, and he was bleeding from inside his mouth. Six of his teeth had been knocked out. His jaw had been broken. But most unsightly of all was the right side of the champion's face. Swollen, bloodstained, and cut, the right side of Willard's face looked like a peach that had been repeatedly dropped onto concrete. Willard was in no condition to go on. Even when he landed a punch it had no effect. He was physically and mentally destroyed. When Dempsey answered the whistle for round four he found Willard was still sitting in his corner. The fight was over. Jack Dempsey was the new heavyweight champion.

The controversy that still surrounds this bout equals the debate over Babe Ruth's "called" home run. Were Dempsey's gloves loaded? Jerry McKernan, Kearns's second son, said his father often told the story of how he put plaster of paris on the bandages covering Dempsey's hands before the Toledo fight. Kearns was confident that Dempsey would win; the plaster of paris was to guarantee that he would win in the first round and win $100,000 for Kearns.[33]

Kearns's story doesn't hold up in the light of known facts. Jimmy DeForest, who taped Dempsey's hands, admitted that he used a hard but perfectly legal adhesive tape. The plaster of paris story, he said, was unfounded. Such boxing experts as Dan Daniel, Nat Fleischer, and Nat Loubet also emphasize the apocryphal nature of the story. Loubet did not doubt that the tape was watered, a fairly common practice at that time, but he completely discounted the plaster of paris story. Daniel, who was at the fight, bluntly claimed that one could not believe anything that Kearns said. Lastly, an attempt to duplicate the method Kearns said he used proved to be an utter failure. The plaster of paris did not dry in the prescribed time and it crumbled as soon as it hit another object.[34]

Regardless of how hard the tape was during the fight, Dempsey was champion. A New York *Times* reporter wrote the fight gave "no satisfaction." However, the amount of newspaper space devoted to the fight and the reactions of many people illustrate that the fight gave considerable satisfaction. Throughout the country men had gathered below the windows of local newspaper offices to hear the results of the fight. Dempsey's victory was well received. Not since John L. Sullivan had there been a champion who so obviously loved to fight. John E. Wray, columnist for the St. Louis *Post-Dispatch,* stressed Dempsey's "young and pleasing" good looks and his "frank and affable" manner that compared favorably with Willard's dull, clumsy character.[35] This theme was reiterated in paper after paper. Although he was a slacker, unpolished socially, and rough in his habits, Dempsey was on the verge of becoming a hero.

After the fight it was reasoned that any man who could inflict such damage must be in some way superhuman. And in America superhuman performances did not go unrewarded. With the Great War concluded in an uncertain treaty, and with insecurity growing like a virile cancer in American cities and villages, Dempsey became a token of stability, a symbol of heroism. Social commentators of the time were fully aware of this phenomenon. "If man is weak," a New

York *Times* editorialist wrote, "with the spirit of an armadillo, there may be no limit to his idolatry for a champion of the world."[36]

In order to make Dempsey the symbol of all-American masculinity, his rough, hungry features were touched up by the writer's pen. The same fighter who as a boy rode the rods, struggled with poverty, and fought miners in saloons was transformed into a "modest" man "with boyish simplicity" who "refuses to indulge in braggadocio." Several hours after Dempsey ruthlessly butchered Willard he appeared to one writer as "a model of clean living," who "reflects the disposition of a gentleman from head to heels." And stories of how he loved children and animals added to his new image. It was reported that his first official act after he became champion was to dash off a wire to his mother: "Dear Mother: Won in third round. Received your wire. Will be home as soon as possible. Love and Kisses, Jack."[37]

Everything about his new image bespoke stability and tradition. Following the example of John L. Sullivan, Dempsey issued a statement the day after he won the title asserting that he would under no circumstances pay any attention to a "Negro Challenger." The thought of Jack Johnson, "gloating over the fact that he was the big rooster of the world," was still horrifying to many white Americans who gained a cozy sense of security from Dempsey's refusal not to enter the ring with such black fighters as Harry Wills, Kid Norfolk, Sam Langford, or Joe Jeannette.[38]

Women, who for the first time attended a title fight in substantial numbers, sensed that Dempsey was larger than life. Compared to Dempsey, Ethel Barrymore exclaimed, the gigantic Willard seemed like a little boy throwing out his chest and "trying to imitate a strong man in front of a mirror."[39] His brutal treatment of Willard did not send women in search of smelling salts, as many men predicted; rather, it induced a sense of admiration.

Not all observers were so enthusiastic about Dempsey's victory. To many religious leaders and concerned Americans, the fight was interpreted as a clear indication of the moral corrosion present in American society. One would have imagined, a New Orleans *Times-Picayune* editorialist lamented, that after five years of war Americans would have had enough. Americans seemed to have grown calloused to fighting and bloodshed. Richard Gottheil, in a letter to the New York *Times,* wondered if mankind was ready for Wilson's noble peace. It seemed to him that the interest in the Dempsey-Willard bout suggested that Americans did not deserve Wilson's efforts. Even the American Medical Association, whose annual convention was overshadowed by the match, scolded the American public for lavishing so much attention on the Toledo affair.[40]

American ministers were much quicker to note that the contest demonstrated that law and order in America were in dire jeopardy. Looking at Toledo on the eve of the big fight, they saw immedicable evil—prostitution, gambling, and worse. The Reverend L. H. Gressley noted that, in order to protect the health standards and morals of Toledo, more than sixty "bad women" were arrested and jailed after the fight. The redundant Reverend M. Macleod sadly confessed, in the article reprinted in *Literary Digest,* "As I view the aftermath of the fight, it seems to me that there is a decided drop in the moral temperament, a misplacing of standards, and a coarsening of the moral fiber." There can be no doubt, he concluded, "that the recent fight has made the maintenance of a mental and moral standard appreciably more difficult."[41]

As ministers pondered the moral decline in the country, newspaper editorialists dolefully noted the rise in commercialism. In prewar days there was never a thought of making a spectator pay to see a boxer train. The Dempsey-Willard fight put those open-to-the-public days behind. Willard charged fifty cents for the privilege of watching his light workouts, and Dempsey, after a brief period of free admittance, began to require a quarter fee. However, Grantland Rice sarcastically commented, "neither charged the city of Toledo a cent for walking along the streets. Both graciously and amiably refused to collect any revenues from acquaintances who spoke to them." Indeed, the greed that writers saw everywhere in boxing caused as much comment as the moral aspect of the bout.[42]

Eventually talk of moralism and commercialism subsided, but the fight had taken up so much press space that Rice opined in his poem "The Day After":

> O jab and upper cut and punch
> O Jess and Jack—O phrases dreary—
> I've had them now for breakfast, lunch

And dinner till I'm overweary;
I've heard them stand around and guess
Until my brain began to caper;
Who knows where there's a game of chess
That I can cover for the paper?[43]

Rice did not know that it was only beginning. The year 1919 only saw the tip of the iceberg of words that would be devoted to Jack Dempsey in the years and decades to come. However, the importance of the year Dempsey won the crown cannot be minimized. It was a year of change—prohibition, women's suffrage, and the Treaty of Versailles. And it was a year of uncertainty—race riots and the red scare. Sociologists maintain that the forces of change and uncertainty create a need for some visible symbol of stability.[44] In the 1920s a number of movements and persons would attempt to fill this cultural vacuum. From old-time religion and Billy Sunday to Gene Stratton Porter and Charles Lindbergh, solutions and heroes were advanced, each in its own way trying to provide an anchor during a time of flux. As a cultural symbol Jack Dempsey is interesting because his career spans the decade. His popular image would mirror the different cultural shifts and schisms of the 1920s, just as his personal life and boxing career would exemplify the age of heroes and the rise of modern, commercialized sports.

CHAPTER V

Champion: Roses and Thorns

T HE YEAR 1920 ushered in a decade that historians steadfastly refuse to discuss in anything less than superlative terms. The decade brings to mind Dickens' discussion of the revolutionary years of the eighteenth century: "It was the best of times, it was worst of times . . . it was the season of Light, it was the season of Darkness, it was the spring of hope, it was the winter of despair, we had everything before us, we had nothing before us." It was a decade that glittered like a diamond held in a strong light, emitting countless combinations of kaleidoscopic patterns of colors. If a decade, or, for that matter, any span of years, may be said to have a personality, then the 1920s was a child, sometimes laughing and playful but at other times brooding and brutal and ugly. Whenever one thinks that he can capture the childlike personality of the 1920s in a cute phrase or a convenient thesis, something surfaces to disrupt the too easily chosen label.

After Dempsey won the heavyweight championship the doors of the twenties opened wide for him. To be sure he was champion, and as such something of a demigod, but—more than this—Dempsey became a product: his handshake converted into dollars and cents, and his appearance on stage, screen, or circus floor became a commodity for which promoters and producers would bid high. In the social arena Dempsey became just as desirable. The sociological phenomenon whereby a crude prizefighter is transformed into a celebrity perfectly acceptable to the upper classes is best described by the French phrase *nostalgie de la boue.* If Dempsey was not the first boxer to experience this peculiar form of instant social elevation, it can be said that few other fighters were accepted as cordially as he was into every stratum of society. American blue bloods as well as the nouveau riches stood in line, invitations in hand, hoping that Dempsey would favor them with a personal visit. If he came finally to feel more comfortable with the most select Hollywood coterie, it was only to be expected, for like himself the men and women involved with the motion picture industry of the twenties were wealthy and famous because they offered something unique, not because they were unique. Thus, after winning the championship Dempsey found himself in an idyllic world. Once married to the title everything came easy—money, friends, and good times. But the honeymoon would not last long.

Unlike many professions where a successful man never has the time to enjoy the fruits of his labor, Dempsey found himself with unlimited time. Leisure time is part of the sport, and far more boxers' careers have been ruined by free time than by punches. Normally, a champion defends his title roughly every six months, with the usual training period prior to each contest ranging from three to six weeks. Therefore, it is likely that a heavyweight champion will devote only two months of every year to boxing. In Dempsey's case there was even more leisure time. In seven years as champion he defended his title a mere six times. Yet in those seven years he was seldom far from the public spotlight. His face—scar tissue, broken nose, white-wall haircut, and all—became as familiar on stage and screen as it was in the ring.

No sooner had Dempsey humiliated Willard in Toledo than he climbed into a ring of a different sort. Induced by the Sells-Floto Circus to join their troop, Dempsey found himself working alongside a high-wire act that performed without a net, trapeze acrobats who had mastered the double flip, and a portly baby elephant named after the popular evangelist Billy Sunday. In short, the Sells-Floto Circus had everything in the way of wholesome entertainment, and when Dempsey's name was added to the existing cavalcade of stars it was, as former president Theodore Roosevelt enthusiastically exclaimed, a "bully circus throughout." [1]

Dempsey's job was simple. Moving about the circus ring with the grace of a caged lion, he flexed his muscles, looked ferocious, told how he defeated Willard, and ended the night by sparring several light rounds with Bill Tate. No punches were actually landed. The sparring session was staged to stimulate the imagination, not the spectators' lust for blood; only the more cerebrally inclined of the audience could watch Dempsey dance with Tate and understand how he destroyed Willard. But the audience was not disappointed. In an age when physical mobility more resembled the 1870s than the 1970s, just to see a heavyweight champion was a treat.

When he was not performing, Dempsey's job was equally simple. Smiling and impish, Dempsey shook an endless stream of hands and delivered timeless lectures on the virtues and benefits of the clean life. If he did not always follow his own advice he might be forgiven, for much of his shy, sincere persona contained elements of truth. And the public loved him. When the circus moved into Baton Rouge, Louisiana, the champion granted one of his typical interviews to the *State Times*, a local newspaper. Did he drink? No; didn't even know what beer or whisky tasted like. Did he smoke? No; bad for the lungs. He lived, he claimed, according to two principles: first, he always tried to be himself; and second, he tried to learn "something new every day if possible." Although the reporter admitted a certain reserve about boxing, he had to confess that any sport that could produce a Jack Dempsey must have some good aspects. Another story about Dempsey in the same paper several days later labeled the champion as everything a man should be—temperate, clean, and sincere: "It goes without saying," the editorial concluded, "that morally he must be clean."[2]

Controversy, however, was not totally absent. As long as the circus performed in the upper Mississippi Valley everything was fine. But as the show moved south down the Mississippi River toward the delta region, problems surfaced. It started with grumblings in Natchez, Mississippi; a few days later, in Mobile, Alabama, the grumblings became more focused and erupted into a wave of protest. As editorials suspected, Dempsey's trouble stemmed from his ignorance of southern mores and customs. His staccato western accent, the way he bit off his words almost before they were out of his mouth, could be politely forgiven, but his sparring sessions with a black fight-

er, Bill Tate, were a matter beyond toleration. Baton Rouge newspapers, even as they extolled the virtues of the new champion,
joined the press of Mobile and other southern cities in condemning
the interracial contests. "Every thinking white man," commented
the Baton Rouge *State Times*, "knows the importance of absolute
separation of the races in everything approaching social contact."[3]

Perhaps some older Louisianians' memories stretched back to the
first week in September, 1892, when the Olympic Club of New Orleans staged three championship bouts in a three-day period. In the
second championship contest a black fighter, George "Kid Choco-
late" Dixon, caused white fans to wince as he brutally defeated a
white fighter, Jack Skelly. At the time, the New Orleans *Times-
Democrat* observed that it was "a mistake to match a negro and a
white, a mistake to bring the races together on any terms of equality,
even in the prize ring." Maybe some southerners recalled the time
that Henry Long, "a loyal Southerner," halted a match between a
black boxer, Joe Green, and a white fighter known only as "the
Sweed." Long's rationale was simple southern logic: "The idea of
niggers fighting white men. Why if that darned scoundrel would beat
that white boy the niggers would never stop gloating over it and, as it
is, we have enough trouble with them."[4]

Regardless of the reason, however, Baton Rouge reporters maintained that they spoke for the majority when they called on Dempsey
to end his sparring bouts with Tate. True, there was no fear that Tate
would defeat the white champion in their nonviolent exhibitions,
but why take even the smallest risk? After all, Tate was a big man
who might accidentally trip Dempsey or make the champion look
bad. Then, too, for the two boxers to enter the ring on equal terms
was a symbol of integration, however small. It was far more desirable,
one editorial concluded, to watch Dempsey hit air rather than a
black man.[5]

The fear that Dempsey might trip was not completely groundless.
As he entered the ring in Baton Rouge he did stumble over one of
the stakes for the guy ropes. In athletics freak accidents are usually
viewed in the bleakest light. The New York *Times*, for instance, reported that the injury would force the champion to use crutches for
at least several weeks. Actually, although the fall tore his trousers

and slightly scratched his leg, he recovered in time to make another appearance in the customary parade that ended all circus performances.[6]

Shortly after his accident in Baton Rouge, Dempsey retired from the circus business. After taking his final bows in Hot Springs, Arkansas, he left the South for the sun and motion picture industry of southern California.[7] He had been in the far West before; the excitement and streamlined pace of life in California attracted him. It was a land not yet steeped in tradition, a land of new money and new names and new businesses.

Dempsey had visited California several weeks after he defeated Willard. During this visit he had shed his all-American persona as so much useless baggage and enjoyed the frivolities. Charles H. Bliss, after watching Dempsey "unwind" with several of his friends, speculated that wine, women, and song might well lead to a short reign for the new champion. As the San Francisco *Chronicle* columnist told the story, Dempsey and his friends—a liberal sprinkling of ex-fighters, hangers-on, and flashy women—made the rounds of the bars and cafés in San Francisco. Drinking 4.5 percent beer and harder beverages when they could be found, Dempsey proved to be both a convivial champion and an easy touch. Toward the early hours of morning the mood turned raw when one of the ladies present began to twit the champion about the need to save money for his wife. Eyeing the right fist that destroyed Willard, Dempsey hinted that possibly the woman would be wise to shut up, at which point the lady threw her drink in the champion's face.[8]

To be sure, this less than chivalric scene was uncharacteristic of the champion, but in the California of the early twenties the proper scenario was yet to be written. Just as the famed forty-niners had chiseled their way into American mythology, a new group of gold miners were in the process of leaving their mark on the American social landscape. The motion picture industry was in full swing. Men and women with obscure backgrounds but fortified by business savvy or beautiful faces had created a new industry. Not that they did it alone; the war helped. Hollywood's major prewar competitors—France, Italy, Germany, Sweden, Norway, and England—had been forced by the hardships of war to halt the production of films. But even with the elimination of foreign competition, American film-makers were never for a second complacent. Among themselves they battled ruthlessly and bitterly for control of their industry.[9]

The film industry of 1920 had reached its own Gilded Age. Nothing was stable. Fortunes were being made and lost literally every week. There was nothing approaching uniformity in the quality of films, cost of production, method of distribution, or knowledge of the market. During the twenties all this was to change. Consolidation and uniformity began when Paramount introduced the revolutionary feature-length film. After its appearance, the companies that emphasized the "shorts," such as the influential General Film Company, faded into the background or went out of business. Just as Paramount began to standardize the industry, the tough-minded leaders of that studio introduced other innovations to help bring order to the chaotic film world. From block-booking and chain theaters to formula pictures and a clearly defined method of manufacturing a star, the film industry, just as other industries had done in the Gilded Age, moved toward monopoly and order. If, finally, complete order and monopoly were never obtained, the leaders of the major studios were certainly not to blame.[10]

The Gilded Age analogy can be extended to the sleazy morality of Hollywood in the early 1920s. In part, it was a time of careless rumors. What really happened in that San Francisco hotel room between Roscoe "Fatty" Arbuckle and the unfortunate Virginia Rappe? What, if any, role did Mabel Normand and Mary Minter Miles play in the murder of the English-born director? Such questions, and a host of similar ones, convinced most of America that just to look at the word *Hollywood* was to risk being turned into a pillar of salt. And if rumors were not enough, what of the true stories? Wallace Reid, the clean-cut, all-American boy in many of the features of the early twenties, died in January of 1923 as a result of narcotic addiction. The man everyone loved to hate, Eric von Stroheim, went to excessive lengths to capture the realism of his orgy scenes. Finally, after several major trials, scores of scandals, and mounting public pressure, the industry was forced to look outside of Hollywood for regulation. In 1923 Will Hays, President Harding's friend and postmaster general, was chosen to head a new organization called the Motion Picture Producers and Distributors Board.[11]

Into this formless and, to a large extent, lawless, industry Dempsey ventured in 1920. Doc Kearns, who had billed Dempsey as a circus performer and himself as a vaudevillian in the wake of the Willard fight, was always on the lookout for ways to fill in the "empty spaces," as he called the periods between fights. Therefore, when Fred C. Quimby of Pathé in New York City approached Kearns about the possibility of putting Dempsey into the movies, Doc only asked how much. The contract Quimby offered reflected Dempsey's new status as an American hero, calling for a large advance and about $1,000 each week.[12] During the 1920s whenever Dempsey worked in Hollywood, he was never paid less than $1,000 each week, and he was usually paid much more.

Pathé Studios was ideally suited to Dempsey's abilities. Originally a French company, it had been one of the nine film companies to organize the Motion Picture Patents Company on January 1, 1909. By 1920 Pathé had sprouted an American branch and had become a successful member of the New York Stock Exchange.[13] Specializing in shorts and serials, they planned to introduce Dempsey into the trade in a low-budget, speedily filmed, fifteen-episode serial entitled *Daredevil Jack*. With no thought of art or message, the filmmakers wanted strictly a formula picture: Dempsey, who was cast as a sports star, was required in each episode to save the heroine's life or property, or both.

Dempsey was no actor. As he laughingly confessed in later years, "When I started I was really bad and I never got any better." Fortunately, nobody involved with Pathé expected him to be any better. The motion picture industry was simply following an old tradition: put the heavyweight champion on stage or screen and the public would pay to see him. In the days before the turn of the century, when they battled wearing long tights and using nothing but their bare fists, men such as Gentleman Jim Jackson, John Morrissey, John Heenan, and John L. Sullivan used their talent in the ring as a basis for lucrative stage careers. The Great John L., in fact, had been a very successful actor. In one melodramatic stage production, *Honest*

Hearts and Willing Hands, Sullivan played a poor but honest blacksmith, and though the sophisticates sneered and scoffed at his performance, scores of thousands of people saw the play, which ran for two years. Furthermore, Sullivan earned more than $100,000, far more than he might have earned from boxing. After 1900, fighters began to wear boxing trunks and gloves, but they still continued to go on stage. James J. Corbett, perhaps the best actor of them all, made $150,000 in one season in the play *Gentleman Jim,* and in later years he acted in several movies. Even Jess Willard had starred in the movie *A Fighting Chance,* which was released the week before the Dempsey-Willard bout and withdrawn the day after.[14]

With this tradition behind them, Pathé felt no anxiety about the success of *Daredevil Jack.* Even when Dempsey informed the studio that he had only twelve weeks free, Pathé was not troubled. The producer, Robert C. Brunton, told W. S. "Woody" Van Dyke, who had been hired to direct the film, that a five-hundred-dollar bonus would be paid for each episode completed within one week. This suited Van Dyke perfectly; with his reputation for shooting only one take and working long hours, he rose to the challenge of completing in twelve weeks what under normal swift conditions would take about twenty-five weeks. After hiring Josie Sedgwick to play the heroine and Bull Montana and Spike Robinson, both ex-fighters, to make Dempsey feel comfortable, Van Dyke started shooting.[15]

First, Van Dyke altered Dempsey's appearance. It was not an easy task, for the champion's face was constructed for fighting, not movies. Dempsey's hair, always cut so that his natural widow's peak was prominent, was wiry and unmanageable; his eyebrows and facial hair were thick; his ears were small; his eyes never seemed to open more than one-eighth of an inch; his nose formed an irregular pattern in the center of his face; his lips were wafer thin; and his chin was muscular but rounded. To make matters worse, his skin had the texture of dried leather and was lined with ridges of scar tissue. Although he was ruggedly handsome, in its natural state his face could never withstand the relentless scrutiny of a movie camera.[16]

Hollywood, at least superficially, changed all this. Lon Chaney, today as legendary as a makeup artist as an actor, was called upon to transform Dempsey into the all-American hero type. Chaney used putty to recast Dempsey's nose and ears, pencil to reshape the scarred eyebrows, liner to round the narrow eyes, lipstick to give body to the mouth, and large quantities of pancake makeup and rouge to give the face a smoother, gentler texture. The result was a joke. Chaney's makeup job made Dempsey look more suitable for a coffin than the silver screen. However, there was not time to start again.[17]

Dempsey enjoyed working on *Daredevil Jack*. Besides Bull Montana and Spike Robinson, Kearns recruited a gang of ex-fighters, whom he called his plug-uglies, and they were joined by more regular actors such as Edgar Kennedy, Carl Stockdale, and Eddie Hearn. With these men together, the chemistry was both dangerous and amusing. Sets were broken, putty noses and toupees were knocked off, and the fight scenes—which made up most of the movie—saw an uneasy blend of pulled and real punches.[18] The only constant throughout the weeks of shooting was that Dempsey would be the hero when the final cutting was completed. Van Dyke was wise enough to know that the public would applaud even a bad picture if Dempsey's all-American persona remained fixed. In *Daredevil Jack* the champion was destined to make sure that the forces of good defeated the legions of evil.

The scenario of the film emphasized the Horatio Alger nature of the hero. As the movie opens, Jack and his father are cheated out of their gold mine in Nevada, but, undaunted, the hero begins to work his way through college. Of course, the college's football coach soon recognizes that Jack is all the team needs to secure an undefeated season. Complications arise, however, when Jack falls in love with the campus sweetheart, who also happens to be the daughter of the man who cheated Jack's father out of his mine. By the time the hero works his way through college, he has earned the respect of his haughty future father-in-law, won the love of the cute campus sweetheart, defeated a gang of five thugs (who appear in the movie for no apparent reason), out-fought nineteen smart-aleck college lads, and somehow accumulated enough money to go into business for himself. By the picture's conclusion, the Dempsey persona was well established. Not a bad year's work, or so the *National Police Gazette* reasoned.[19]

Off the set Dempsey dropped his stage persona. This is not to say that he entered wholeheartedly into Hollywood's subculture. He did not. But he did drift about the edges, sometimes dipping into the festivities but usually quietly watching from a safe distance. His picture was snapped as he sipped drinks with starlets at the Montmartre Café. He was invited to the most exclusive Hollywood parties. The biggest stars befriended him—Tom Mix, William S. Hart, Will Rogers, Rudolph Valentino, and Charlie Chaplin. Douglas Fairbanks and Wally Reid were even closer friends. It was Reid and his circle of friends who undoubtedly introduced Dempsey's handsome younger brother Johnny into the Hollywood drug world. Johnny's addiction ended several days before Dempsey fought Jack Sharkey in 1927, when the younger brother killed his wife and then shot himself. As for Dempsey's friendship with Fairbanks, there were no tragic memories. Fairbanks enjoyed the manner in which Dempsey accepted a practical joke, and the champion was struck by the kindness of Hollywood's leading star, especially Fairbanks' policy of keeping ex-fighters on his regular payroll.[20]

Actually Dempsey fit in well with the stars. They moved on common ground and had essentially the same outlook on life. Their lives were built around illusions and titles—the world's greatest fighter, the world's greatest lover, the world's most beautiful woman. With transitory titles and illusions that might shatter any day, they lived on the borders, seldom venturing outside their fragile pleasure domes. Although their earning power was nearly unlimited, they never knew when it would end. They lived a dream and their lives depended on selling that dream to the public. If the public did not buy, then it was all over.

About the time Dempsey finished *Daredevil Jack,* his world teetered toward destruction. From the time of the Willard fight, newspapers sniped at his war record and questioned his patriotism. Dempsey overheard cocktail party whispers and read the papers, and it hurt. Maybe he had been wrong not to enlist; possibly he should not have listened to Kearns. Now there was no escape from the criticism, and the press would not let the issue die. Dempsey, with his fur coats, fat movie contracts, and a large bank account, had stayed at home during America's greatest fight. The *Home Sector,* a magazine for former soldiers published by the former editorial council of *Stars and Stripes,* questioned how great a fighter Dempsey really was: "Is he as great a fighter as Scotty, the seventeen-year-old boy who, put to hold a path in the woods north of Chateau-Thierry, killed thirty charging Germans before he died on his chauchat? . . . Is he as great a fighter

76

as the smallest, weakest, humblest of the men who put on O-D or blue or forest green when their country called?"[21] The questions are obviously rhetorical. The answer of "no" echoed and reechoed in Dempsey's mind until he questioned his own motives for not enlisting.

Then the whispers and snipes erupted into a loud series of accusations. On January 23, 1920, the San Francisco *Chronicle* published a bitter letter calling Dempsey a draft dodger. The letter, written by his former wife who had retained his name, systematically refuted every reason for which Dempsey had been granted a 4-A status. First, according to Maxine, not only had her husband not supported her during the war, but she had actually supported him with the money she earned working in a dancehall. Next, she said that Dempsey did not qualify as even a "shipyard slacker," for he had never been employed by any shipbuilding firm. She saved her coup de grace for the end: "I have positive proofs of a letter in his own handwriting, naming his manager, Jack Kearns, and two others, and telling me how they succeeded in having him put in class 4-A." It was Maxine's plan to give Dempsey time to refute her claims—give him enough rope to hang himself—before she published her evidence. In her mind, however, there was no doubt that Dempsey illegally conspired to evade the draft.[22]

In the days that followed, an acrimonious battle raged between Kearns and Maxine. From the moment he read her letter, he suspected that there was someone behind her, prodding her on with threats or bribes or both. Within twenty-four hours Kearns made his thoughts public. Maxine's letter, he told the *Chronicle*, was "a gigantic and malicious effort," undoubtedly engineered by some person with legal experience, to defame the champion and sabotage his future earning power. Maxine was a prostitute, a fact that was hardly a guarded secret, and Kearns reasoned that someone was using her background to exact revenge on Dempsey; years of prostitution in western mining towns would hardly have equipped her to write a detailed legal letter that read like a lawyer's brief.[23]

Maxine, not content to let the matter rest, kept the pressure on. The day after her damning letter, she wired the *Chronicle*: "Have letters in Jack Dempsey's own handwriting. Will send you affidavits to prove every charge that I made and more." The following day she responded to Kearns's letter with yet another telegram to the news-paper: "I am having affidavits made, together with copies of original letters from Jack Dempsey, attested to by a notary. No one got me to send the first letter to you. Mr. Kearns can have proofs any time he wants them."[24] These telegrams indicated that Maxine had a strong case and that she was ready to nail Dempsey to the wall.

Then without warning on the night of January 26, as the snow was falling on the foothills of the Ruby Mountains, Maxine and three other women left Wells, Nevada, on a train heading east. Maxine's three friends were in gay spirits; they laughingly remarked to report-ers that they would protect their litigious friend. Maxine, however, was unusually quiet. Refusing to comment on her charges, she looked straight ahead and clutched the incriminating letters in her hand. Her mission was a mystery to the reporters, who did not even know where she was going. Likewise, the federal government, which by this time had become interested in the case, was in the dark, and four days later it was reported that federal agents were looking for Maxine, who had disappeared.[25]

By the time Maxine disappeared, Americans were arguing Demp-sey's culpability—on one level, in an open controversy between former soldiers. As early as January 13, the Meuse-Rhine Post of the American Legion unanimously adopted a resolution condemning Dempsey's war record. Other posts followed suit, but not all. In Mil-waukee the local post voted Dempsey an honorary membership, al-though later the national organization disallowed it because of con-stitutional irregularities. At a federal military hospital in Fox Hills, Staten Island, Lieutenant Arthur Robinson wrote a letter endorsing Dempsey's stand. According to Robinson, the entire hospital was behind the champion. Finally, Dempsey requested that the Army, Navy, and Civilian Board of Boxing Control investigate his case; "Am I to be crucified and condemned because I followed the orders as given to me by the Government?" Dempsey asked the board. They agreed to hear Dempsey's case.[26]

On the question that caused disagreement in military circles, the press found itself in surprising unanimity. W. O. McGeehan, the leading sports writer for the New York *Tribune,* saw an ethical ques-tion at the root of the Dempsey affair. The Great War, he said, was "a fight where no body was barred, where all holds went, and a fight where the so-called manly art would have been vindicated gloriously." McGeehan did not quarrel with Dempsey's alibi, but he did question the champion's actions. Did not Dempsey, as the world's greatest fighter, have an ethical obligation to enlist?[27]

An editorial in the New York *Times* made the larger moral issue dramatically clear:

> Dempsey says that he is not a draft dodger. Technical facts sustain him. His adherents assert that his negative patriotism, negative actions, brings him forth from the slacker shadows and put him, head up and dauntless, in the clear light of noble duty, nobly done. . . . Dempsey, whose profession is fighting, whose living is combat, whose fame is battle; Dempsey, six feet one of strength, in the glowing splendor of youth, a man fashioned by nature as an athlete and a warrior—Dempsey did not go to the war, while weak-armed, strong-hearted clerks reeled under pack and rifle; while middle-aged men with families volunteered; while America asked for its manhood. . . . There rests the reason for the Dempsey chorus of dispraise.[28]

It was this moral issue that disturbed such sports writers as Grantland Rice and McGeehan, and inspired scores of editorials. Kearns might claim that Dempsey had been under "work or fight" orders and chose to work in the shipyards of Chester, Pennsylvania, rather than fight in the trenches of France; Dempsey might repeat that he was supporting a wife, father, mother, sister, and several invalid brothers; and the government might even point to Dempsey's wartime benefits— but the fact remained, Dempsey never left the United States.[29]

The editorialists were in earnest; but their conception of warfare was more appropriate to *La Morte d'Arthur*. The draft-dodging episode is a remarkable picture of a society that had failed to grasp the grisly truth about modern warfare. World War I was a war of numbers, not individuals, a war where Dempsey would have meant no more than the weak clerks and near-sighted boys he might have fought alongside. Europeans recognized this fact. They saw that the war transformed active heroism into impotency. It was a war not for the Dempseys of the world, but, ironically, for the Prufrocks, Jake Barneses, Malones, and Charlie Chaplins. Therefore, the writers criticized Dempsey with the subconscious vigor of a moral voice that was no longer applicable.[30]

As American Legion posts quarreled and sports writers carped the search for Maxine continued. Then, as suddenly as she had disappeared, she surfaced. The venom was reported to be gone. Pathé's Frank Spellman, who had been in contact with Maxine, voiced his belief that she "was used as a catspaw" to get at Dempsey. He denied that Pathé was in any way involved in the case. To be sure, Pathé had invested some $300,000 in the *Daredevil Jack* serial, but, he noted, his company would gladly throw away that money if Dempsey was proved to be a "slacker." However, after talking with Maxine, Spellman believed there was no proof.[31]

On February 4, 1920, Maxine met with Charles W. Thomas, the assistant U.S. attorney in charge of the case. Demurely clothed in a long flowing dress and a fox stole, the puppy-eyed Maxine told Thomas that everything she had said or written about her former husband was untrue. After she and Dempsey had divorced, in February, 1919, she went to work for Mrs. Tommy Wilson, proprietress of a dancehall in Wells. It was there that she heard rumors that Tommy had gone back east with Dempsey prior to the divorce. She became jealous. Added to this was the constant ribbing and twitting she took from the other dancehall girls. In a moment of rage she wrote the letter to the San Francisco *Chronicle*. When later she discovered that Dempsey had not gone east with Tommy, Maxine began to feel sorry. In truth, she said, Jack had been "a wonderful man and husband." He had supported her, as well as his mother, father, sister, and brothers. As for the letters, she reported that there simply were none. Everything she had said was a lie. Her only hope was that the whole matter might be forgotten. In later interviews reporters noted that it was obvious that she still loved Dempsey and wished to remarry him.[32]

As much as Maxine may have wished it, the affair was not forgotten. Too far entangled to extricate itself without embarrassment, the government, under the direction of Charles Thomas, began to carefully build its case. By the end of February, Thomas was prepared to move, and on the twenty-fourth a grand jury voted unanimously to indict Dempsey and Kearns on conspiracy to avoid the draft. The indictment was largely based on thirty-five letters from Dempsey to Maxine and other western friends, which had been uncovered by

federal agent O. O. Orr. After the grand jury's vote, Orr told reporters that the government's case was sound, and, hinting of things
to come, that many of the letters Dempsey wrote were of a "salacious
nature." Three days later Dempsey and Kearns were arrested by U.S.
Marshall James R. Holohan, then quickly released on $1,000 bail.[33]

Publicly the government was confident, but behind the scenes
the action more closely resembled a Keystone Cops movie. In the
center of the closed-door maneuvering, shuffling the cards of justice,
slick as a Reno blackjack dealer, was the former casino owner Doc
Kearns. He was in his element. Kearns's concept of the law being
essentially that the side with the best lawyer won, he obtained the
services of the best lawyer he could find. Gavin McNab, who was
then handling Mary Pickford's divorce from Owen Moore, agreed to
take the Dempsey case for $50,000. Not content to hand the entire
case over to McNab, Kearns took a train to Washington, D.C., in an
effort to secure political support. Two things worried him: first, the
probable judge, Annette Adams, according to Kearns, believed "every man should do ten years in the can just for the hell of it"; and
second, the obscenities in the letters Dempsey wrote. However, after
talking with several men in Wilson's administration, Kearns left for
the West Coast in a better frame of mind.[34]

The government's case began to disintegrate. Although the trial
was scheduled for early April, a series of delays forced the trial date to
be moved back.[35] Nobody was certain what was happening. Maxine
was an unknown quantity who had equivocated to such a degree that
neither the government nor Kearns placed any faith in her. As for
the letters, all that was known was that they had been found by Orr,
read by the grand jury, and supposedly contained enough evidence to
brand Dempsey as a sexual beast and put him behind bars. On this
note of suspense, the case went to court.

On Tuesday, June 8, 1920, the trial began. By this time the
female judge whom Kearns feared, Annette Adams, had been promoted to a higher position, and in her place sat Judge Maurice T.
Dooling, who proved much more sympathetic to Dempsey's case.
Prosecutor Thomas spent most of the first day attempting to convince
the jury that Dempsey was not the sole support for his family.
Thomas had prepared his case well; in the best traditions of the law,

81

he planned to present a mass of material that taken as a whole would suggest that Dempsey and Kearns had falsified the questionnaire, which was the basis for the champion's military exemption. First, Thomas had John S. Hogan, chairman of the local draft board that passed Dempsey's questionnaire, and Rudolph Goodman, a Chicago notary who witnessed the champion's signature on the questionnaire, testify that Dempsey had sworn that his parents and wife were dependent upon him for support. With this done, Thomas proceeded to show that Dempsey's family was not dependent upon him: Hiram Dempsey had earned over $400 in 1917; Mrs. Effie Clarkson, a sister whom Dempsey claimed he supported, worked from time to time; and both the pugilist's brothers, who were also listed as dependents, had been employed for a time in 1917. When the trial adjourned for the day, Dempsey's case looked bad.[36]

Maxine had rested in her hotel room during the first day of the trial. She wanted to first appear in the courtroom as a witness. On June 9, the second day of the trial, she took the stand. Dressed in a fashionable outfit, highlighted by a plunging neckline, she appeared self-possessed and calm as she ignored the gaze of the crowded courtroom and walked to the stand. She stood for a moment within a few feet of Dempsey, whose fingers were nervously toying with the fur collar of his mother's coat that lay on the table beside him, and looked at him "without recognition and apparently without interest." As a court reporter noted, "To a spectator who did not know their relation, it would have seemed that the big man sprawled in a chair scarcely large enough for him meant no more to her than anyone of the crowd of lookers-on."[37]

With Maxine sworn in, Thomas came directly to the point: holding Dempsey's questionnaire so Maxine could see it, he asked, "Do you recognize the signature?" Before she could answer, Dempsey's lawyer, McNab, sprang to his feet. Any communication, verbal or written, between husband and wife is confidential and, therefore, could not be used as testimony under the common-law rule. Thomas argued that once Dempsey and Maxine were divorced the common-law rule was invalid. Judge Dooling, after listening to both sides, admitted that "the question was beyond his knowledge"; he would continue with the trial and leave the "confidential communications" matter and Maxine's testimony in limbo for another day.[38]

The remainder of the testimony for the day focused on the question of whether Dempsey supported Maxine during 1917. The stories disgusted some, amused others, and shocked many of the people in the courtroom. Several of Maxine's friends structured a rambling odyssey that ranged from one shabby whorehouse to the next. Traveling under the name Bobby Stewart, Maxine worked as a prostitute in towns from San Francisco to Cairo, Illinois. In 1917 she settled for several months in Cairo in a house run by Mrs. Nannie Coffey. Mrs. Coffey, an aggressive, hard-mouthed woman who freely admitted that she ran the house, remembered Maxine as a "delicate looking" girl who left Cairo with a number of unpaid debts. Helen Goodrich, who worked with Maxine in 1917, spoke in a low voice infused with shame, confessing that she too was a prostitute. Although each of the women spent an hour or more in recounting events that had no bearing on the case, both agreed on one important thing: Jack Dempsey had never sent his wife a penny.[39]

In a trial that was becoming noted for surprises and about-faces, the third day proved no exception. In the morning Thomas tried to introduce a letter that he believed would prove Dempsey had been involved in a conspiracy to evade the draft. As the "courtroom hovered on the edge of sensation," Judge Dooling read the letter, then, without emotion, refused to admit it as evidence. If the letters could not be read—and the judge said they could not—then at least they could be discussed. And discussed they were. In a cross-examination punctuated by disgust and structured on cynicism, McNab worked Maxine into an unenviable position. Why had she saved certain letters and thrown others away? Why did she speak up only after Dempsey became famous? What did she hope to gain by threatening to publish the letters? With such questions McNab exposed her motives. Although Maxine reiterated that she was "thinking only of the Government," McNab made it clear that dreams of personal gain motivated her actions.[40]

As McNab pressured, Maxine turned bitter. With "apparent enjoyment" she told of her adventures as a prostitute: "So eager was she to dwell on the sordid details of her life in one city after another that she ran ahead of the questions." Dempsey sat silent as Maxine made it "unmistakably clear" that she tired of marriage after several months. For her the "underworld" life of prostitution and crime was preferable to holy wedlock. If she confessed that Dempsey did send her some money—the only part of her testimony germane to the case—she also accused him of being stingy and hard to live with. As the boxer "gazed steadily at the floor," Maxine delivered her own blow. The champion of the world, she said, had dislocated her jaw with one of his famed punches.[41]

Next, McNab established that Maxine had received money from her husband, and considerably more than she cared to admit. J. B. McCloud, manager of the Western Union office in Salt Lake City, produced records of money sent by Dempsey to his wife. A cashier in the office, R. W. Burton, remembered that after the Fulton fight Dempsey had sent Maxine two hundred dollars; he recalled the instance because Maxine had remarked "that Fulton must have hit Jack hard to jar him loose from $200." The night manager of the office, E. B. Thompson, supplied added evidence of Dempsey's support of his wife and family. He told of how Maxine proudly remarked that "Jack always sends plenty of money when he has it." By the time the court adjourned for the day, McNab had exposed Maxine and proved that Dempsey had been a good provider.[42]

If there was any doubt of the eventual outcome of the trial after the third day, it was resolved the next afternoon. Maxine had been the last government witness. Now McNab took the offensive. He called Celia Dempsey, "a little white-haired, wrinkled woman with hands gnarled by hard work and shoulders bent by years." Her story might well have won Dempsey's nomination for sainthood. She told of her hard-luck family: a husband crippled by rheumatism and plagued by absentmindedness and melancholia; a daughter, Effie Clarkson, weakened by an unsuccessful operation; two sons, Johnny and Joseph, exempted from the draft because of their ill health; another son, Bruce, stabbed to death while selling newspapers in Salt Lake City; and herself often sick in bed. Through it all, she said, Jack had been her only support. Without him, she quietly added, "We wouldn't have had anything." Celia recounted her son's rise in boxing; after each fight he would send her money, adding only that she should buy some clothes for herself. When Jack defeated Willard, he bought a $20,000 house for the family. After Celia's testimony there was no doubt that Dempsey supported his family.[43]

On Monday, June 15, Dempsey took the stand. In a simple and unaffected manner he refuted everything that Maxine had claimed. When he had the money and knew where Maxine was, Dempsey said, he had always supported her. Furthermore, he denied that he ever struck a woman, let alone his wife; denied that she had ever worked as a prostitute while living with him; and denied that he had ever attempted to evade the draft. Maintaining that his only reason for not enlisting was to support his family, Dempsey also spoke of his war-related services. Fighting for war benefit drives, he had earned over $330,000 for the government. Working as a recruiting officer in Philadelphia, he had convinced three to four hundred men to work in the shipyards. By the time that Dempsey stepped down from the witness stand, few people could have doubted that he served both his family and his country.[44]

If there were even a few doubters, they must have come over to the Dempsey camp by the end of the day, for McNab had witnesses to confirm everything Dempsey said. The most important was Lieutenant John F. Kennedy, a naval officer attached to the Great Lakes Training Station during the war, who told the court that Dempsey had been in the process of enlisting when the war ended. He recounted a talk with Dempsey when the fighter said, "If there is any way for me to get into the service and have my people looked out for, I want to do it." After this talk Kennedy had taken the necessary steps to enlist Dempsey; but several days before the boxer was to be inducted, Secretary of the Navy Josephus Daniels ordered enlistments stopped.[45]

Dempsey left the courtroom a confident man. The following day vindicated his optimism. After being given their instructions by Judge Dooling, the jury adjourned for only ten minutes and then returned a verdict of not guilty. No demonstration followed, but the orderly crowd waited, almost to a man, to congratulate Dempsey. Simply, boyishly, the champion expressed this emotion: "I'm the happiest boy in the world." As for Maxine, she left the courtroom in a bitter rage. When asked her plans, she replied that she was going to publish the letters; otherwise, "I have no plans for the future." She then walked out of the courtroom and out of Dempsey's life. The letters were never published. In 1924, as she was sleeping in an upstairs room, a Juarez dancehall was destroyed by fire, and Maxine was burned to death.[46]

The press greeted the decision with mixed feelings. "We believe the majority," a New Orleans *Times-Picayune* editorial began, "the vast majority, of American followers of sports will be pleased with the decision." The editorial continued with an unusual amount of logic and justice. It argued that pugilistic prowess no more qualified Dempsey as a soldier than the ability to ride a horse qualified a man as a tank commander. Neither did the championship belt elevate Dempsey to an unequaled moral plane: "Certainly the business of battering another man into insensibility is, whatever the skill required, not ipso facto an indication of moral grandeur, and frankly we are asking too much to expect it."[47]

Other papers continued to ponder unanswered questions. What, for example, did the letters say? Did they prove, as Colonel Thomas had maintained, that Dempsey was guilty? And what really happened on that night in San Francisco when Maxine dislocated her jaw? These questions, and more, were raised by Cliff Wheatley, sports editorialist for the Atlanta *Constitution*. He indicated that a cloud would always follow Dempsey and that the champion was "unworthy of holding the honor" of being the world's greatest fighter. Wheatley could only pray, along with millions of other Americans, that Georges Carpentier, "idol of the French nation, fighter in the ring and battlefield, [would] snatch the world's championship" from Dempsey.[48]

Logic might have been with the *Times-Picayune* editorialist, but emotion, usually the stronger of the senses, was on the side of Wheatley. Dempsey's trial raised questions which till this day remain unanswered, or, at best, only partially answered. There is no doubt that the letters would have been explosive. The government's case, as Thomas had maintained, rested on them. Throughout the trial, Thomas had a handwriting expert, Edward O. Heinrich, waiting in the wings to testify that Dempsey had written the documents. According to McNab, Maxine had attempted to blackmail Dempsey with the letters. As the trial revealed, Kearns had sent Tommy Fitzgerald to talk to Maxine at Wells before Dempsey was indicted. At that meeting, Maxine had told Fitzgerald that for $40,000 Dempsey could have the letters and "to hell with the Government." Even the wily Kearns confessed toward the end of his life that if the letters had been made public Dempsey would have suffered.[49]

Another unanswered question centers on who set the trial in motion. McNab put the blame on Maxine, Beulah Taylor, and several other prostitutes who worked at Tommy Wilson's establishment in Wells. However, Dempsey and Kearns do not agree with McNab. The fighter and manager would certainly not put blackmail beyond Maxine, but they believed she was too simple to conceive such a plan. They maintained that the final culpability rested with a San Francisco *Chronicle* sportwriter. As Dempsey tells the story, during the war years the writer approached him about boxing in an event for charity sponsored by the paper. Because he disliked the man, Dempsey refused. The champion believed that the letter published in the *Chronicle,* which set the scandal in motion, was the work of the same writer.

The draft issue did not end in 1920. Throughout the rest of his career Dempsey heard the word *slacker* often attached to his name. While walking down the streets of New York, boxing in exhibitions, or even acting on the Broadway stage, he would inevitably encounter questions about the patent-leather shoes he wore in the famous picture of him "working" in the shipyards of Chester, Pennsylvania. Always sensitive on the subject, he suffered psychologically from the cheap insults. A friend, Dan Daniel, said that one of Dempsey's happiest days was when he enlisted for World War II. Only then could Dempsey let the issue sleep in his own mind.[50]

So the pain remained so much scar tissue on his psyche. Otherwise, life went back to normal. Pathé released *Daredevil Jack* to an American public curious to see the champion on the silver screen. The movie was successful, but Kearns knew that movie contracts would vanish like a morning mist if Dempsey remained out of the ring for too long. Except for a three-round exhibition fight with an old friend, Terry Keller, in Los Angeles in early March, Dempsey had not even stepped into the ring. Therefore, Kearns began to do what he did best—talk fight. It was not easy, for in 1920 there were few heavyweights, and no white heavyweights, who could hope to challenge the champion.

If no boxer could challenge Dempsey's ring ability, there was one fighter who rivaled the champion's aptitude for attracting attention. Georges Carpentier in the winter of 1920 was poised at the height of his career, eagerly requesting a match with Dempsey. After his sensational one-round knockout of the best English heavyweight, Joe Beckett, in London just before the end of 1919, Carpentier and his flamboyant manager, François Descamps, had sailed for America. Georges' urbanity and François' mysticism, both mixed with incomprehensible French accents, captured the fancy of the press. Almost to a man, sports writers joined the two Frenchmen in their attempt to promote a bout with Dempsey. Eventually, the champion would succumb to the lure of promised gold—but not in 1920. The Dempsey-Carpentier bout, like a good wine, needed time to ferment properly.

Wine lacking, Dempsey turned to a hardy brew for satisfaction. In late July a Chicago promoter, Floyd Fitzsimmons, signed Dempsey to fight Billy Miske. In a match scheduled for Labor Day in Benton Harbor, Michigan, Dempsey was guaranteed $50,000 and a percentage of the gate, and Miske was promised a flat $25,000. Why the match was made is something of a mystery, for Miske was far from championship caliber. Like many fighters known as "ham-and-eggers," Miske's face carried a reminder of nearly every boxer he fought. There were more gaps than teeth in the front of his mouth, his ears were horizontal to his head, his nose followed a line from his left eye to the right corner of his mouth, and the scar tissue above his eyes formed sagging eyelids.[51] The best that could be said of Miske was that in his two previous meetings with Dempsey he had been a game battler who could take a punch as well as throw one.

Also, Dempsey liked Miske. When Dempsey had been training for the Willard fight, Miske had been a good sparring partner and friend. Therefore, when Miske approached the champion and told him how much he needed the fight, Dempsey agreed without any reservations. Miske needed money, of this Dempsey was certain. Dempsey, if not certain, at least suspected why his friend needed money. Miske had in recent years become more susceptible to illness. Working with Dempsey in Toledo, Miske had to take several days off because he was sick; back pains had forced him into the hospital in early 1920; and in training for his fight with Dempsey he appeared listless and ill to many who watched.[52] The sad truth was that Miske was a sick man who desperately needed a big payday to pay his hospital bills and to insure that his family would not be left in poverty.

Dempsey might have known Miske's condition, but as a professional he prepared for the fight with utmost seriousness. Kearns realized that for Dempsey to be his best he had to train against good fighters. With this in mind, Kearns hired Bill Tate, Panama Joe Gans, Marty Farrell, and Harry Greb. Tate was an excellent boxer, and Greb is still considered one of the great fighters of all time. How hard Dempsey trained was amusingly illustrated when a local army heavyweight, Soldier Jack Riley, applied for a job as one of the champion's sparring partners. In the second round of their first session Dempsey hit Riley with a double left hook and then mercifully caught him under the armpits and walked him over to his corner.[53] The soldier was never seen around Dempsey's camp again.

As Dempsey prepared himself physically for the contest, Kearns took care of his end of the business—making sure that the referee would be sympathetic to Dempsey. In a close fight the referee often spells the difference between winning and losing. Arthur Donovan, for example, refereed twelve heavyweight championship bouts involving Joe Louis and may well have saved Louis' crown on at least one occasion. Kearns's choice for referee for the Miske fight was James F. Daugherty, the Leiperville, Pennsylvania, fight promoter who had been responsible for the Sun Shipbuilding Company in Chester hiring Dempsey in 1917. Kearns's rationale was simple: Daugherty had helped keep Dempsey out of the war, and he would protect the champion as much as possible within the ring.[54]

Problems arose when Chairman Thomas Bigger of the Michigan State Athletic Commission refused to grant Daugherty a referee's license. Instead, several days before the fight Bigger named Al A. Day of Detroit the referee. Kearns was outraged and informed Bigger, Fitzsimmons, and the general public that either Daugherty refereed the bout or the contest was off. On the day before the fight, Dempsey's ballpark fight headquarters was besieged by anxious fans demanding to know the status of the bout; Fitzsimmons, whose reputation was in jeopardy, pleaded with Bigger to change his decision; and even Day indicated that he would withdraw in favor of Daugherty. Finally, after hours of discussion, Bigger relented and granted Daugherty a license. Satisfied, Kearns smiled as he predicted a good fight.[55]

The anxiety aroused by Kearns's battle of nerves with Bigger undoubtedly hurt the gate for the fight. Also, on the night before the fight, sheets of rain covered the Benton Harbor ballpark, and although the rain slacked up to drizzle by early morning, many would-be spectators chose to remain in their homes. Shortly after noon the drizzle stopped and the sun shooed away the clouds. The day became hot and uncomfortable as the moisture from the night before rose in waves from the soaked sand floor of the arena. At one o'clock, as spectators started to arrive at the ballpark, the saucer-shaped stadium looked like a mosquito-breeding ground. Some fans became rowdy and tried to cross the high barbed wire fences that separated the ringside seats from the less desirable seats—a ploy that had worked in Toledo—but uniformed soldiers from Camp Custer, Benton Harbor police, and husky guards were on hand to preserve the sanctity of the high-priced seats.[56]

The crowd continued to move into the arena as the preliminary bouts got under way. Two of Dempsey's sparring partners looked good in winning six-round decisions. Bill Tate defeated the venerable Sam Langford, and Harry Greb won the nod over Chuck Wiggins. But few people watched these bouts. Most of the high-priced ticket holders were still downtown, jamming the streets, clamoring for sandwiches and coffee, listening to members of the House of David warn about the evils of prizefighting, and attempting to secure some whiskey for less than the going price of fifteen dollars per pint. Yet by five o'clock, when Dempsey stepped into the ring which was padded by old-fashioned bed quilts, some fifteen thousand bodies had crowded into the arena.[57]

Instructions were given, Dempsey removed his worn red sweater, and the bell rang. Miske lunged at the champion at the opening bell, hoping to catch him off his guard; but Dempsey quickly stepped inside the bull-like rush and landed a right and left to the head. After ten seconds the outcome was no longer in doubt. Dempsey had been out of the ring for over a year; yet he boxed with as cruel a precision

90

as he ever achieved. He was a master of the combination. A right to the body and a left to the head and a right to the body, two left hooks to the chin, a left hook and a right cross, a left to the jaw and a dozen rights to the body—and the challenger went down. After one minute and thirty-one seconds of the third round, Miske, a fighter who had never before been knocked off his feet, sagged unconscious against the ropes in his corner.[58]

There is no question that Miske was not in the best condition. In the clinches Dempsey felt that Miske was a far weaker fighter than when they had last fought in Philadelphia in November of 1918. But then again, Dempsey had greatly improved since 1918. He had learned his craft well, and his style was beginning to demonstrate more maturity and control. In short, it is too simple to join the chorus of Dempsey biographers and say that in Benton Harbor the champion looked great because he was fighting a corpse. Miske was ill but his career was still far from over. The game challenger lived until January 1, 1924; and between the day he fought Dempsey and the day he died, he had twenty-four more fights, winning all of them and defeating such notables as Bill Brennan, Homer Smith, Willie Meehan, Fred Fulton, and Tommy Gibbons.[59] Dempsey looked great in Benton Harbor because he was great.

Not only was Dempsey superb within the ring, outside the squared circle he was portrayed as being warm and gentle and kind. With an awkward shift of metaphors, which somehow succeeded, the press-box transformed Dempsey's large destructive hands into instruments of infinite tenderness. The fighter was absorbed by the persona. As quickly as he knocked out Miske, Dempsey rushed over to try to revive the unconscious challenger. Next, in the locker room, the champion thought of mom back home in Salt Lake City and sent off a telegram: "Everything is O.K. Love to Effie." Then his ruminations settled on children. Before the fight, so the story goes, a cute dimple-faced little girl had presented Dempsey with a four-leaf clover, and as the champion removed the glove that contained the good luck charm he remembered the lass. In later years this image was further buttressed when Miske's illness became public knowledge. Then Dempsey was viewed as the consummate humanitarian who mercifully ended the fight fast and provided Miske with the largest payday of his life. On his deathbed Miske was reported to have gasped: "Tell Jack thanks. Tell him thanks from Billy." [60] From such stories the Dempsey image of the all-American, even old-American, boy—was molded. The draft trial had shaken this process for a moment, but after the Miske bout the persona was again being aired.

Financially the fight had been a success for Dempsey and Kearns. The two men split a purse of fifty-five thousand dollars, or slightly less than one half of the total receipts for the fight. But the fight lacked the glamour of a contest promoted by Tex Rickard. Kearns, who harbored ambitions to be more than just a manager, resented Rickard's influence over Dempsey just as he envied Rickard's promotional acumen. The Benton Harbor fight was an attempt to escape Rickard's domination, and as such it failed. [61] After the bout Dempsey and Kearns boarded a train for New York City to meet with Rickard, the new head of Madison Square Garden. Legal developments in 1920 had made it essential to do business with the czar of the Garden.

In 1920 boxing entered a new age. Although many people clamored for its legalization, some loudly in newspaper editorials and some less demonstratively by attending fights, the pressures that were so obvious in Toledo before and after the Dempsey-Willard bout influenced politicians. One prominent example was Major Anthony Drexel Biddle, a straightforward speaker who enunciated an enthusiasm for boxing and the Bible with his thick Main Line Philadelphia accent. Biddle was the prime mover of the Army, Navy and Civilian Board of Boxing Control, which, in turn, was the leading proboxing voice. Certainly, he and his board gained many converts among influential politicians, but none of the converts had enough faith to risk his political neck by introducing proboxing legislation. [62]

One member of the New York State senate, however, was not afraid. James J. Walker, whose roots were embedded in the tough Irish district of Greenwich Village and whose politics reflected the morals of Tammany Hall, cared little for middle-class morality. Therefore, when he was approached by William Gavin, organizer of the National Sports Club in London, about the possibility of sponsoring a bill for the complete legalization of boxing in New York City,

Jimmy Walker naturally and wholeheartedly embraced the scheme. Gavin hoped to establish an International Sporting Club in New York City along the lines of his London club; Walker recognized that such a club would be popular with his constituency. Furthermore, he enjoyed boxing and numbered the likes of James A. Farley, Caleb Baumes, Battling Marty McCue, and Anthony Biddle as his close friends.[63]

On January 14, 1920, Walker confidently introduced his boxing bill in the Albany senate. There were those who criticized the boxing bill, but far more men stood publicly in favor of passage. Anthony Biddle, the Army, Navy and Civilian Board of Boxing Control, and the Military Athletic League lobbied for it. Finally the senate capitulated; on March 24, by a vote of thirty-one to nineteen, the bill passed the upper house of the New York legislature. Although many upstate Republicans and former soldiers voiced concern over the possibility of Dempsey boxing in New York and although there was a general concern about commercialism, Walker was able to soothe enough fears to win the battle.[64]

In the lower house the bill faced stronger, more organized, opposition. Many New Yorkers recalled the days when the Horton Law had been in effect and boxing had been controlled by gamblers, corrupt officials, and crooked fight managers with weak-minded boxers. At the nadir in 1900 Governor Theodore Roosevelt, himself a firm believer in the beneficial aspects of pugilism, had been forced to call for the repeal of the Horton Law. And the years after the passage of the Frawley Law had done little to sanitize the image of the sport. Nevertheless, shortly after midnight on April 25, the assembly passed the Walker boxing bill by a vote of ninety-one to forty-six. While Assemblyman John J. Slacer bemoaned the brutalities of the ring and Assemblyman J. T. Carroll hoped that no fighter who had evaded the war would be licensed to box in New York, Walker turned his attention to the governor.[65]

Serving his first term in the Executive Mansion, Governor Alfred E. Smith was acutely sensitive to the position in which the boxing bill placed him. As a machine politician and an Irish Catholic, he was forced to battle a bad national press all his life. To sign the Walker bill would only confirm the suspicions of his enemies: elect an Irish Catholic to the Executive Mansion, the theory went, and his first act would be to revive boxing and end Prohibition. Fear for his public image was intensified by several other concerns. Smith bitterly resented the alliance between Tammany Hall's ward heelers and the unsavory elements who controlled boxing. Also, earlier in the year Franklin Delano Roosevelt had promised to present Smith's name as New York's favorite son at the coming Democratic National Convention. Reviving boxing would not enhance his chances to move into the White House.[66]

Through public debate, political examination, and mounting interest, the bill sat unsigned and unwanted on Smith's desk. Canon Chase, an influential political and moral leader, mustered the anti-boxing legion behind his cause at the same time that Biddle rallied his troops in favor of the bill. But Smith remained mute. Finally, on Friday, May 22, Walker took his case before the governor, whom he always called "Algie." As Smith puffed on his cigar and looked out the window, Walker pleaded his case. The bill, Walker said, had every safeguard: unsalaried commissioners, mandatory licensing for everyone from the promoter down to the boxer's seconds, punishment for anyone who violated the rules, and a guarantee that a spectator would be given the seat for which he had paid. Smith refused to budge. Exasperated, Walker rose from his seat and started for the door.[67]

Walker may have been a gadfly, but Smith liked him and did not want him to leave without any hope. With some sympathy and a touch of irony, Smith told Walker that if one hundred clergymen wrote to him in favor of the bill before nine o'clock Monday morning, he would sign it into law. He added another demand: all the writers had to be Protestant clergymen; no Irish priests who fondly remembered the days of Sullivan, Corbett, and Jeffries, or rabbis who supported Benny Leonard. On Monday morning over one thousand telegrams, all from bona fide religious leaders, littered Smith's desk.[68]

As much as the dapper Jimmy might have liked to credit himself with the weekend miracle, ultimate responsibility lay with Anthony Biddle. He had recently contributed one-half million dollars to the Protestant Bible Society and the result of his generosity was what covered Smith's desk on Monday. At a press conference later on that

94

day, Smith signed the Walker boxing bill into law, along with the Walker beer bill, which legalized 2.75 percent beer. "The stress of the time," Smith told the reporters, "demands healthy and wholesome amusement for the men of the state." Acknowledging the "small group" that opposed the boxing bill, Smith quickly added that it had been "almost unanimously approved by the Legislature, the American Legion and over 1,000 clergymen of all denominations." In the final analysis, the governor concluded, boxing would financially and morally aid the state of New York.[69]

Not everyone agreed with Smith's decision. Wilber Crafts, the superintendent and treasurer of a Washington religious lobby, wrote the attorney general that "while no religious people were present, by a dirty trick and undoubtedly through bribery, the law legalizing prize fights in New York was passed." To Crafts's organization, which attempted "to destroy the work of the devil," the passage of the bill was lamentable. He closed his letter by proposing that the government use the motto, "Let no guilty man escape."[70]

Other voices were more moderate. Several weeks before Smith signed the bill a New York *Times* editorialist remarked that legalized boxing was favored by the majority of New Yorkers. After the bill became law others came to its defense. A New York *Tribune* editorial claimed the Walker Boxing Law to be a positive result of the "health, stamina and courage" that had been nourished by the Great War. As long as the newly formed boxing commission remained vigilant, the sport had nothing to fear from nefarious racketeers and evil-minded managers. W. O. McGeehan concurred with this opinion. He added that boxing had been killed in New York earlier because it was crooked.[71] The consensus was clear: keep boxing clean and it will not have to worry about moral reforms.

Now New York City became the mecca of the pugilistic world. For over a generation boxing had been a western sport, financed and dominated by westerners. The shift eastward marked a significant change in the sport. Tex Rickard, who remained the single most important man in boxing, realized that if the sport was to thrive in the East it would have to attract the rich. With this foremost in his mind, he beckoned Dempsey to the city of lights. Rickard's goal was to make boxing a thoroughly respectable sport, a sport that would toss together wealthy heiresses, rich businessmen, stable members of the middle class, and strong-armed laborers in arenas, capturing the salad-bowl nature of American society. Within a year his goal was achieved.

Step one of his plan was to book Dempsey into Madison Square Garden. Less than two months after boxing became fully legal in New York, Rickard became the proprietor of the Garden, which stood on the square for which it was named. Designed by Stanford White and completed in 1889, the old Garden was a magnificent structure which had been the scene of not only many athletic contests but also the most sensational love murder in America, the shooting of White by Harry K. Thaw. Impressive in form, steeped in tradition, and loved by New Yorkers, the Garden was nevertheless a white elephant. Realizing that the building was miserably in debt, Rickard hoped that a Dempsey fight would start it on the road to solvency.[72]

In a secret conversation with Dempsey before the Miske bout, Rickard had convinced the champion that Kearns was incapable of promoting a big money fight. It was agreed that Rickard would handle the promotional duties for the championship match with Bill Brennan. In mid-November, Joseph Johnson, chairman of the New York Boxing Commission, and Larry McGuire, chairman of the New York License Committee, agreed to lift the state ban on heavyweight championship bouts and the match was scheduled for December 14.[73]

A great town to fight in, New York was not a great city for training. But Dempsey tried. In the early morning he ran over the frozen paths of Central Park. During the afternoon he trained on board the old battleship *Granite State,* moored off Ninety-Sixth Street in the North River. As always, he worked hard, sparring with Irish Patsy Cline, Marty Farrell, Bill Tate, and Sam McVea. For laughs he even boxed several rounds with a New York fighter named Al Reich, who was locally known as the "diving Adonis" of the heavyweight division. Everything taken into consideration, during the day Dempsey trained as seriously as possible.[74]

But the night was a different matter. The nightclubs and speakeasies of the twenties gave New York City its well-deserved reputation as a city that never slept. Dempsey moved with the

Broadway crowd, today memorialized in *Guys and Dolls*. He ate dinner at LaHiff's, picked up women at the Follies and the Scandals, and enjoyed the night life of Perona's, George LaMaze's, and Jerry Docker's. He and Kearns became regular customers at the Silver Slipper, Texas Guinan's Club Richman, and Barney Gallant's. Harlem was not off limits in the twenties. On any given night Connie's Inn, Small's, or the Cotton Club had as many white customers as black. In short, if Dempsey trained during the day, he untrained after nightfall.[75]

Why not enjoy himself, Dempsey reasoned. When he had fought Brennan in 1918, Dempsey had hit him so hard that Brennan broke his ankle as he fell. Even after Brennan's manager, the colorful Leo P. Flynn, announced that the challenger would bandage both ankles to prevent the recurrence of such an accident, few believed that the Chicago fighter had any chance. That Brennan was the best of a "poor crop" of white heavyweights, no one doubted. That the Irish challenger trained hard in Grupp's gymnasium was certain. But Dempsey was considered too good, too much for any other heavyweight. As W. O. McGeehan commented, Dempsey was now "involved in demonstrations instead of contests."[76]

Fourteen thousand fans jammed Madison Square Garden on the night of the fight, most hoping that Brennan would upset Dempsey just as Ed Strangler Lewis had upset Joe Stecher the night before, in the World's Heavyweight Wrestling Championship. Wild cheers penetrated the thick smoke haze when the handsome Irishman from Chicago entered the ring, clad in green tights and a red sweater. With a look of complete bewilderment, Brennan grinned nervously at the celebrities in the ring. To W. O. McGeehan, Brennan "suggested the rabbit, blinking around, after being thrown into the snake den to act as a dinner." Dempsey's entrance was another matter. Booed from the twenty-five dollar seats to the two-fifty seats, the champion stepped through the ropes at ten-thirty. He scowled at Brennan, sneered at the audience, and moved about like a pent-up tiger in long white boxing trunks.[77]

Sitting at ringside, McGeehan started to write his scenario. It was intended to be a farce. Like many at ringside, he believed that the challenger survived the first round because Dempsey was "letting

Brennan stay for the sake of the motion pictures." Then, with dramatic suddenness, the farce ended in the second round when Brennan nailed Dempsey with a perfectly timed uppercut. Dempsey was dazed; somewhat surprised himself, Brennan did not snap up his opportunity. One thing was certain, however; what had started as a farce was transformed into a serious melodrama.[78]

Drama increased as the bout progressed. Brennan fought like a classic heavyweight, flicking out his jab, keeping Dempsey off balance, and bringing across a right hand whenever he saw a chance. As a stunned but cheering crowd watched, Brennan won round after round. Dempsey was fighting in a fog. His punches lacked authority, and he was roundly booed when he tried to hit Brennan in the clinches or hold-and-hit the challenger. In the tenth round, Dempsey paid for his wildness when Brennan hit him with a right hook behind the left ear. The punch split open his ear at the base and warm blood cascaded over his shoulders. In boxing such an injury meant only one thing—a cauliflower ear. McGeehan reported that "Dempsey was white and ghastly with rage as he glared at Brennan from his stool."[79]

After the eleventh round Kearns informed Dempsey that only a knockout would save the title. Although hurt and tired, Dempsey was determined not to lose the title. Years later he remembered that after the second round "everything was blank" except the possibility of losing the title, something he would not let happen. In the twelfth round Dempsey intensified his body attack. Two hard rights to the stomach and Brennan began to fall, but before he could do so Dempsey stepped inside, lifted him up with a left to the chest, and sent him sprawling onto the ropes with a right to the head. Referee Johnny Haukaup held Dempsey away from Brennan with one hand as he counted with the other. An instant before Brennan regained a standing position the count reached ten. With an ear that "looked like a cross between a veal cutlet breaded and a sponge dipped in gore," Grantland Rice wrote, Dempsey returned to his corner. He had retained the title.[80]

"Dempsey is no superman," John E. Wray commented after the fight. In the St. Louis *Post-Dispatch* he noted that hero worship for Dempsey "had been over-played to the point of near-infallibility."[81]

Yet millions of Americans had made Dempsey into such a hero after his fight with Willard, and the circus and the movie industries had helped. But Dempsey had floundered in the public spotlight, and by the end of 1920 many observers reasoned that if Dempsey could not be their complete hero, then possibly America needed a new man for the job. Brennan obviously was not such a man; after the Dempsey fight he opened a speakeasy in New York City, where, several years later, he was shot to death. There was one man, however, who fit the specifications. In 1921 he and Dempsey battled for the right to be the world's hero.

CHAPTER VI

The Battle
of the
Century

I DON'T know nothing that you don't know, but if you want to
hear it again, all right." [1] In 1921 when Ring Lardner began a
thinly disguised fictional work about the Dempsey-Carpentier
fight with this sentence, most Americans either knew the real story
or at least suspected the truth. It was in that year that the "battle of
the century" took place, a fight that Lardner characterized as the
seedy embodiment of American greed. If the outcome of the bout
was never in doubt—and it was not—Lardner nevertheless understood the deep symbolic importance of the fight as a cultural event.
Rhetoric does not have to be believed by the speaker to be of importance; it is what the listener feels and thinks that matters. So
it was with the web of words, images, and attitudes surrounding the
Dempsey-Carpentier affair. What may have started as a ruthless attempt to separate thousands of people from an insignificant portion
of their money, soon grew into something far larger and much more
significant. In 1921 a boxing contest became a cultural rostrum.

Perhaps one should not place too much faith in Lardner's account of the Dempsey-Carpentier fight. Although he wrote with a
Twainesque, down-home style, Lardner never viewed man as a noble
creature. For him, man was a highly complex schemer, an animal
who naturally preferred to conspire, plot, and cheat. His son, Ring
Jr., who knew of the distrustful side of his father wrote: "Ring was
reserved, laconic, uneasy in crowds, with a mask over his emotions
and a deep-seated mistrust of face values, a cynic who felt that if
something could be faked it probably was." [2] So one might ask: Why
believe Lardner's fictional account of the fight?

100

The plot of "The Battle of the Century" does seem a bit far-fetched. The opening scene introduces Jim Dugan, the heavyweight champion who has just won the title from Big Wheeler. Dugan's manager, Larry Moon is bemoaning their plight; Jim, because he is better than the other heavyweights, is forced to work in circuses and the movies to earn money. "They's just one chance for us," Larry informs the storyteller, "and that's to have some young fella spring up from nowheres and knock five or six of these 'contenders' for a gool, then we'll have to stall a w'ile and pretend like we're scared of him till we've got the bugs thinking that maybe he has a look-in." No sooner had Moon made his wish than the idol of the French nation, Goulet, knocks out the best English heavyweight in one round. Immediately Moon devises a plan; he decides to capitalize on Goulet's good looks and outstanding war record. Dugan, of course, realizes that Goulet is no match for him, but he agrees to Moon's plan only adding, "But I don't see how you come to overlook Benny Leonard."[3]

In the months that follow, Moon's plan begins to take form. First, he convinces Goulet's manager, LaChance, not to let his fighter engage in any serious boxing contests. In return for keeping Goulet inactive, Moon promises LaChance "Two hundred thousand [dollars] . . . draw, lose, or get killed." Next, Moon tricks a group of promoters into staging the bout. The movie *The Sting* is reminiscent of Moon at his Machiavellian best. Playing one promoter off against the next—and them all off against several Cuban waiters disguised as boxing promoters—Moon connives a one-half-million-dollar guarantee for Dugan and Goulet. Finally, after the fight is scheduled, Moon and the trio of promoters launch a crusade to convince the public that the pale, frail Frenchman might just possibly not get killed by Dugan. If Barnum was right when he said that there was a fool born every minute, then several million days' worth believed Moon's story. The tale ends, of course, with Dugan easily knocking out Goulet: "Well the way I've got it figured out," said a Goulet fan on the way home from the fight, "he [Goulet] wasn't big enough." The storyteller is forced to agree: "By gosh! I believe you've hit the nail right on the head!"[4]

The true story of the "fight of the century" began in Holborn Stadium, London, about one year after the signing of the armistice that ended the Great War. Writer and essayist Arnold Bennett was one of thousands who pushed and shoved their way along the dark, narrow, crowded streets that led to the stadium. He went to the fight to see a clash between two civilizations, one French and the other English, and captured by the electric ambiance of the night, Bennett felt that "the subject of the reconstruction of Europe lacked actuality." In this sentiment he was joined by other ringside millionaires, resplendent in smoking jackets, swallowtails, and tuxedoes; he was joined, also, by thousands more who shuffled toward the ten-guinea seats with only their tickets in their pockets. They had all gathered at Holborn Stadium to watch the pride of England, Joe Beckett, fight Georges Carpentier, the idol of the French nation.[5]

Unlike earlier fights, the Carpentier-Beckett bout was attended by the outstanding members of society and the literati in England. Joining Bennet at ringside were George Bernard Shaw and H. G. Wells, both of whom had been commissioned to write magazine articles about the night's event. Bluebloods, such as Robert Loraine, Granville Barker, and Maurice Baring, sat comfortably discussing the aesthetics of boxing and the course of the Empire. The Prince of Wales, puffing on a cigar in the manner of his grandfather, Edward VII, lent royal sanction by his presence. And women were present. Shaw noted the phenomenon: "Not any particular sort of a lady: just an ordinary lady. The one who happens to be sitting by me is one next [to] whom I might find myself in the stall of any theatre, or in church. The girl at the end of the next row would be perfectly in place in any west-end drawing room."[6] They had all assembled to watch a sport that had been considered vulgar before the war.

Veteran sports reporters picked the rugged, well-built Englishman to win. Beckett was a strapping two-hundred-pounder who, if not exactly a good fighter, certainly "looks a bruiser," and he held an impressive knockout victory over Bombardier Wells. By contrast, Carpentier looked anything but a bruiser. Watching the Frenchman slip gracefully through the ring ropes, Bennett wrote, "He might have been a barrister, a poet, a musician, a Foreign Office attaché, a Fellow of All Souls; but not a boxer." Shaw, too, was stirred by Carpentier's frail appearance. He was moved by the ease with which Carpentier ignited the passions of the crowd: "He was at home with it; he dominated it and picked out his friends and kissed hands to

102

them in his debonair way quite naturally, without swank or much modesty, as one born to move assemblies."[7] Indeed, Shaw's concept of the superman seemed to be molded to Carpentier's form.

In this rarefied atmosphere of adulation the fight began. At the bell both men moved out of their corners and approached the center of the ring. For a minute or so they watched each other, then there was a brief flurry of punches and Beckett fell to the canvas as if he had been shot. And there he stayed for ten seconds. The men who had so confidently predicted a Beckett victory were stunned. Carpentier's backers rushed into the ring and lifted their champion to their shoulders; a French woman embraced Carpentier and they kissed "passionately" within a few feet of the Prince of Wales; and the Englishmen watching the bout spontaneously adopted the handsome fighter from across the channel. Bennett was as moved as the rest of his countrymen: "Nothing less than winning the greatest war could have interested and moved it ['the English race'] more profoundly. This emotion was no product of a press campaign, but the press campaign was a correct symptom of it. It was as genuine as British fundamental decency."[8]

Carpentier became the idol of Europe. Shaw, describing the boxer as a "jubilant spring in the air," perfectly captured Carpentier's impact on Europe. After four years of war, after millions of deaths, after countless pictures of and stories about twisted, broken bodies and shattered lives—Europe found a hero who embodied both the romantic expectations of the war and the zest for life and peace. During the Great War, Carpentier had served with distinction in France's air force. Twice he had been wounded by shrapnel, once in the right foot and once in the head. Twice he had been decorated for heroism, once with the *Croix de Guerre* and once with the *Médaille Militaire.* [9] No sooner had the war ended than he distinguished himself in the ring. Handsome, urbane, slender, and debonair—Carpentier, Europeans believed, would be the perfect man to hold the World Heavyweight boxing title.

Promoters were quick to match the Frenchman with Dempsey. As early as December 6, 1919, there was talk of staging the bout either in Paris or London. Charles B. Cochran, the dapper Englishman who had promoted the Carpentier-Beckett bout and who held the Frenchman under a first refusal contract, sailed to America to talk with Dempsey.[10] He spoke in quiet tones about the possibility of a million dollar gate, a feat that had never even been approached. Of course, most of this early talk was just that—talk. It was one thing for a promoter to say he would guarantee a fighter $200,000; it was another thing to sign the contracts and post the bonds.

But the talk influenced men who were willing to take action. Most importantly, Doc Kearns took note. Kearns understood what the fight would symbolize, especially after the San Francisco draft-dodging trial. He also knew that a bout surrounded by black-white symbolism would draw a large gate. It was during the early part of 1920 that he decided to match Dempsey against Carpentier, but he was determined to dictate terms. His first move was to encourage more talk and to wait, giving the public time to warm to the fight. Throughout 1920 Kearns had talks with many promoters about sites, figures, and dates, all carefully noted by the newspapers. Long before the fight was scheduled, the names Dempsey and Carpentier became as familiar as Laurel and Hardy.

After a year of talk Kearns was ready for the second stage of his plan—promotion. He knew that only Tex Rickard could promote a bout of the magnitude that he planned; he did not want Rickard to know it. The way to intrigue Rickard was to ignore him. Earlier in the year Kearns had told reporters that several rich Cubans had offered Dempsey $100,000 to fight the Cuban bullfighting hero John B. Sanchez in Havana. In November of 1920 two Cuban sugar and tobacco barons appeared in New York City. They first were seen at the Hotel Claridge at noon, where Rickard customarily ate lunch. The Cubans, later introduced to Rickard as Marcos Gonzalez and Rafael Passo, were sitting at a corner table intently speaking with Kearns. When Kearns saw Rickard, he invited the promoter over to meet the Cubans who were now offering $500,000 to stage the Dempsey-Carpentier fight in Havana. Unsettled, Rickard excused himself, telling Kearns not to sign anything for several days. He then left, but Kearns continued to rub his hands together, nod, and chat with the Cubans.[11]

Fearing that the big match might slip past him, Rickard frantically went to work. He spoke with Charles B. Cochran, the English sports and theatrical promoter who held Carpentier under contract; then he had a conference with William H. Brady, a Broadway play producer who had expressed serious interest in the fight. Both Cochran and Brady agreed to back Rickard to the limit. Both consented to risk their professional and financial reputations on the fight.[12]

Once the three promoters were in agreement, the action moved into high speed. Rickard had not forgotten the Cuban millionaires, but he was more concerned that Carpentier and his manager, who had been visiting America, were due to sail for France in less than a week. Finally, on the day before Carpentier was to leave for France, all parties concerned gathered at the Hotel Claridge to sign the contract. Except for the absence of the champagne that had accompanied such occasions in the days before Prohibition, the ceremony was a notable affair. The hotel ballroom was crowded with sports writers and sports celebrities; motion picture cameras recorded the historic event and flashlight discharges boomed through the room; and master of ceremonies, attorney Nathan Vidauer, called the participants to the stage, one at a time, to be introduced to the press. After the introductions, everyone shook hands, and Dempsey and Carpentier sat together on a couch chatting about the upcoming fight, Carpentier in French and Dempsey in English. Everyone left happy with the exception of the Cuban team of promoters, who waited in the wings eating lunch, and Abe Attell, the gambler and former boxer who never missed a signing, who was whisked away by police to Chicago to answer questions about the 1919 World Series scandal.[13]

Weeks later Rickard learned that the two Cubans at the Claridge were actually a couple of waiters from the hotel whom Kearns had dressed in tailor-made suits, fortified with five-dollar cigars, and promised a free meal and twenty-five dollars each to pretend they were Cuban millionaires.

Commercially, the contract marked the advent of a new age in sports. For the fight Dempsey was guaranteed $300,000 and 25 percent of the motion picture rights; Carpentier was guaranteed the same percentage of the motion picture rights and $200,000. The money, the sheer mass of dollars and cents, worried many people. As early as the Willard-Dempsey bout, writers like Grantland Rice and

Dan Daniel had noted that commercialism was beginning to erode the good-time atmosphere of the game. Why "if anybody had offered $100,000 to John L. Sullivan to fight for his title," Daniel wrote in the *Sun* in 1919, "he would have expired on the spot."[14]

Fears that were raised in 1919 were intensified and multiplied in 1920 and 1921. A New York *Times* editorialist predicted that commercialism would kill boxing. We live in a world that overpays its heroes, the editorialist began. It was bad enough that Caruso, John McCormack (the leading ballad singer of the day), and movie stars earned fortunes at their trade, but for a boxer to accumulate such sums was positively disgraceful. The editorialist pointed out that Dempsey's guaranteed purse of $300,000 was more than the president made in four years in office, more than a vice-president would make in twenty-five years in office, more than the chief justice would make in over twenty years, and three times more than America paid all ten of its cabinet members each year. The London *Times* commented, "No man, whatever may be his position which he has reached in his own profession, is worth such wages. . . . From the financial point of view of Carpentier and Dempsey, the enormous purses which are being offered may be satisfactory, but a bubble, when it is blown sufficiently large, is certain to burst."[15]

Actually, the bubble almost burst before the two boxers went into training. The contract stipulated that the promoters were to deposit $100,000 with the Central Union Trust Company of New York, which amount was to be equally divided between the fighters if the promoters failed to carry out their pledge. Likewise, Kearns and Descamps were to deposit $50,000 each as a guarantee that their fighters would show up for the bout. All deposits were to be posted by November 20, 1920. That date came and passed, but Central Union Trust Company did not see any money.

Behind the confident smiles of promoters and managers lay a web of confusion, doubts, and difficulties. Kearns deposited his forfeit money in the wrong bank, a bank that remains a mystery to this day; Descamps was prohibited by the French government from sending so large a sum of money out of the war-battered, economically destroyed country, or so the French manager claimed; and Rickard, Brady, and Cochran failed to meet their financial obligations. Part of the problem was the fear that Governor-elect Nathan L. Miller of New York would follow through with his threat to have the Walker Boxing Law repealed. The promoters had planned to stage the bout in one of New York City's ballparks, thereby eliminating the cost of building an arena. But Miller's unreceptive attitude spelled added expenses for the increasingly cautious promoters. By the end of November, Brady withdrew from the promotional triumvirate, using the excuse that the fighters' forfeit money had not been posted on time. Shortly afterwards, Cochran used the same excuse to bow gracefully out of the picture. Rickard was left alone.[16]

Unlike Brady and Cochran, Rickard was far from cautious or financially timid. He built a fortune and a career on risk. Orphaned at the age of ten, he had grown up on the bloody strip of land in Missouri along the Kansas border that comprised Clay County during the years when the James brothers ruled that section of the country. Later he moved to Cambridge, Texas, where he worked as a cowboy and a horse wrangler, and eventually he became the marshal of Henrietta, Texas. After his wife and baby died—the same year Dempsey was born—Rickard drifted north to Alaska. This was during the gold rush days, and Rickard tended bar, panned for the valued yellow ore, and gambled. He managed the Northern Saloon in Nome, but everything he earned he lost at poker or the roulette table. After he lost a fortune in Alaska he drifted south, later settling in the gold fields of South Africa. Next he wandered back to the United States and opened the famous Northern Saloon in Goldfield, Nevada, where there was another gold rush in progress. It was there in the hot, dirty-rich town of Goldfield that Rickard started promoting boxing bouts. He matched Joe Gans, the black lightweight champion from Baltimore, against the rugged Battling Nelson, and for forty-two rounds the two men butted and kicked, sweated and bled, and occasionally punched until Nelson sank a left hook in Gans's groin and lost on a foul. But Rickard had found his niche. Many promotions followed, including the Jeffries-Johnson and the Willard-Dempsey contests. By the end of 1920 Rickard was considered the best in the business. By the end of 1921 he would be judged the greatest promoter who ever lived. For a man who had made and lost millions of dollars, risk was not something to keep one up at night.[17]

Rickard decided to promote the fight on his own. Yet with all his willingness to risk his reputation, he was still woefully short of funds. The desertion by Cochran and Brady meant that Rickard would have to post the $100,000 out of his own pocket as well as pay for the construction of a stadium. Seeking money, he approached Mike Jacobs, the leading ticket speculator. In the twenties the business of ticket speculation was carried on in a more or less public fashion, although Jacobs was known to charge $7,500 for a $250 box, and he would inflate the tickets he sold by at least 15 or 20 percent. The prospect of the Dempsey-Carpentier bout excited Jacobs, who believed the fight would draw over $1,000,000; he therefore advanced Rickard between $160,000 and $200,000. In return, Rickard promised to give $200,000 worth of choice tickets to Jacobs as well as good tickets for every other bout he promoted.[18]

With this money Rickard posted his forfeit bond and began to search for a place to build the arena. He raised extra money in the months before the bout by the advance sale of tickets. As the money orders and checks poured into Rickard's Madison Square Garden offices, he paid off building contractors, ticket engravers, bodyguards, ushers, and a whole range of other people involved with the promotion of a million-dollar event. He insured both Dempsey and Carpentier for $50,000, but if anything had happened to either of the two boxers, Rickard's reputation and personal wealth would have been destroyed. If ever an event was promoted on sheer personal courage and grit, the Dempsey-Carpentier fight was such an event.[19]

Rickard in his eventful past had learned the secret to modern promotional techniques: money breeds money. As Paul Gallico put it, Rickard understood the psychological effect of money: "He knew how to exhibit it, use it, ballyhoo it, spend it, and make it work for him." Before the Gans-Nelson fight, Rickard had displayed the winner's prize of 20,000 gold dollars in a store window.[20] He used the same psychology in the promotion of the Dempsey-Carpentier bout. Everything about the fight was underlined by Rickard's gaudy sense of class. The oversized, beautifully engraved tickets with their embossed gold backs told the tale far better than any advertising campaign: boxing was entering a new age.

By paying a boxer a fortune to fight another man, Rickard elevated that prizefighter from the rank of a common pug to the status of a wealthy man. A fighter who could earn $500,000 for ten minutes of boxing was certainly different from the cheap ham-and-egger who ate with his hands, associated with lowlife criminals, spoke in slurred sentences, and sprang out of his chair whenever a bell rang. Rickard made Dempsey and the men he fought into "somebodies," that is, people who were important. Rickard planted the seed of a ring aristocracy ideal in the minds of the public, and then he cultivated that seed. A Rickard boxer drove high-priced cars, ate in the best restaurants, lived in palatial mansions, and accumulated fat bank accounts. The epitome of this idea, Dempsey became a demigod, larger than life, a symbol of the entertainment aristocracy. The public would pay any price to see such a man perform. More important, at least for Rickard, men of wealth would gladly patronize a sport which clothed itself in such regal garments.[21]

Not only did Rickard understand the psychology of the use of money, he also was a master of dramatic symbolism. The people he sought to attract to boxing were not particularly lovers of a good fight, but, rather, men and women, especially wealthy ones, who were interested in the drama inherent in a battle of contrasts. For Rickard, a good fight did not entail matching a clever boxer against a punishing puncher as much as it did pitting a hero against a villian. Rickard realized quite correctly that this would capture the public's imagination to an extent that no purely athletic matchup could rival. Give the masses of people some rosy-cheeked, clear-complectioned Lancelot to cheer and some thick-bearded, scowling Simon Legree to boo and jeer, and the money would roll in in waves and people of both sexes and all classes would perk up and take notice. On a smaller scale, Rickard used this formula to promote the Dempsey-Willard contest. However, its most classic development was in the promotion of the Dempsey-Carpentier fight. Never would a Rickard hero be so white and a villain so black. Never would the issue and symbols be so simple and so devastating.

Carpentier, from his French accent to his frail, almost ethereal, features, was the ideal Lancelot for Rickard's medieval morality play promotional formula. Shaw had noted Carpentier's aristocratic bearing the night of the Beckett bout, only the French boxer appeared more like a king than a mere knight. Drawing from his knowledge of Scandinavian history, Shaw described Carpentier's entry into the ring as "nothing less than Charles XII, 'the madman of the North,' striding along the gangway in a Japanese silk dressing gown as gallantly as if he had not been killed almost exactly 201 years before." Other writers, possibly less knowledgeable about Scandinavian history, agreed that Carpentier was, if not a god, certainly a rank above mortal man. Heywood Broun compared the Frenchman to a Greek statue, so perfectly symmetrical was Carpentier's build. A female reporter for the *Morning Telegram* literally quivered with emotion when she described Carpentier as "a Greek athlete statue of Parian marble warmed to life." Neysa McMein, a famous magazine illustrator, said that from an artistic standpoint "Michael Angelo [sic] would have fainted for joy with the beauty of his profile, which is almost pure Greek." And, finally, New York *Tribune* columnist James Hopper observed that Carpentier "looked like a priestess of the white Attic times come forth to some harmonious sacrifice."[22]

Scandinavian king, Greek statue, Attic priestess—by the time Carpentier came to America to train for the fight, he was certainly the most glamorous boxer ever to step into the ring. When Carpentier landed on American shores on May 16, 1921, he was greeted with royal splendor. The Gallic flavor of his name was anglicized to read either "Gorgeous Car-painter" or George S. Carpenter," and, at least according to the American press, he was the perfect embodiment of the ideal man. Somehow Carpentier's prewar years were forgotten, except for the fact that he was born into a humble family in Liévin, a coal-mining area near Lens, in 1894. Popular memory failed to revive his habit of falling to the canvas clutching his groin with his face disfigured by a feigned anguish whenever he was losing a bout; or, if that tactic failed, his unattractive penchant for hitting below the belt if he believed a fight was lost. During the early years of the war he had defeated two very good American boxers, Gunboat Smith and Kid Jackson, by using the first tactic; and several years before the war he had been defeated by two equally fine American fighters, Frank Klaus and Billy Papke, for resorting to the second one.[23] Fortunately for Carpentier, Rickard, Dempsey and everyone involved in the promotion of the bout, the American press did not revive Carpentier's prewar record.

What the press did note was the Frenchman's savoir-faire. R. L. Goldberg of the New York *Evening Mail* wrote, "The thing that impresses you most about Carpentier is his quiet grace. . . . His smile is more the smile of embarrassment than boyish exultation." Goldberg goes on to note that the look in Carpentier's eyes says only, "I just want to be natural and to do things that other people do." Another journalist, Marguerite Marshall of the New York *Evening World,* was impressed by Carpentier's clean-cut features, unblemished by scar tissue. Because of his good looks, Old World charm, and impeccable manners, "he is an unmistakeable exponent of French gallantry and grace, as well as of French valor, intelligence, and endurance."[24]

Next to Carpentier, Dempsey appeared to be deficient in both charm and valor. In every way he was Carpentier's opposite. Carpentier was the light-skinned, cosmopolitan, ever-smiling war hero. Dempsey was dark-complexioned; his beard was coarse, his eyebrows were thick, and his face seemed to be cast in a permanent iron scowl. In the latter part of his career, Dempsey's reserve in public would be recognized for what it was—an indication of his basic shyness. But in 1920 and 1921 his reserve and awkwardness around people were interpreted as the characteristics of a mean, conceited man. There was still too much of the hungry hobo about him for the public to regard the champion with love. Far too much of the animal viciousness, the reason for Dempsey's success in the ring, could be seen in his actions outside of the squared circle.

If Dempsey's looks and mannerisms cast him as a villain, his war record solidified him in that role in the minds of millions of Americans. He was the fighter who did not fight when his country most needed his services, reasoned Herbert Reed of the New York *Evening Journal.* "There is a great host of followers of sport," wrote Reed, "that believes that in time of war such a man should not wait for a draft, but should volunteer." For Reed and others of like mind no excuse could justify Dempsey's absence from the trenches of France. Branded as a slacker, Dempsey thus became a villain to the most patriotic of American groups. In typical protest, a Chicago chapter of the American Legion appropriated money to wager on Carpentier.[25]

As central as the war issue was, there were other matters that further complicated the affair. Dempsey, for the most part, was a known quantity. Except for his amorphous stand on the war, he seemed

111

quintessentially American. His love of children, animals, and his family had been given maximum press coverage in 1919 and 1920. Carpentier, on the other hand, was both physically and symbolically foreign. A Frenchman through and through, he spoke no English and showed no desire to learn the language. Everything about him was somehow flashy, foreign. The Old World charm and manners he wore so naturally were alien to many Americans. In shades of Valentino, he was described as being a "tall, slender, urbane, and debonair young exquisite." His tastes were portrayed as being strictly aristocratic. Owning over two hundred suits and changing clothes six or eight times a day, Carpentier was a fashion plate. In his leisure hours, he enjoyed fast cars, billiards, bridge, serious plays, highbrow literature, opera, and at dancing he was said to be unsurpassed. Although he liked movies and Charlie Chaplin—proving that he was "not too bright or good for nature's daily food"—Carpentier was most assuredly not representative of the traditional values that Dempsey was.[26]

Viewing the two boxers, the American public was faced with a perplexing dilemma: Carpentier was a war hero but he was also a foreigner; the American, Dempsey, was labeled as a draft dodger. Obviously, this was no easy choice to make. Intellectuals on both sides of the Atlantic overwhelmingly favored the dapper Frenchman.[27] If the intellectuals were astute enough to realize that Carpentier stood no chance against the champion, this dismal knowledge only served to further endear the Frenchman to them. He was the underdog with no chance whatsoever; he was the existential man fighting to maintain his dignity in the face of a losing cause. He appealed to the artistic impulse in painters, playwrights, and poets; he was so handsome and valiant. Here was no common pugilist with a broken nose and cauliflowered ears.

On the other hand, Dempsey's followers earned their livings working with their hands. In the champion they recognized something familiar. As one commentator observed, "Why, if he weren't a prize-fighter, he'd be a teamster." Heywood Broun, who visited Dempsey before the fight, found the champion to be a timid, gentle man who enjoyed romantic literature and was highly sensitive to the controversy over his draft record. The Veterans of Foreign Wars of

Atlantic City sounded a sympathetic chord when they pledged their support for him: "We look on Dempsey as the American champion going into the ring to uphold America's title of supremacy in a game at which it has excelled for generations."[28]

Thus both Carpentier and Dempsey were converted into cultural heroes, each representing a constituency with a set pattern of beliefs. Both fighters became symbols of something that transcended the ring, or even sports in general. This process was clearly recognized at the time. In "an orgy of sentimentality," wrote an editorialist for the *New Republic*, Carpentier had been twisted "into a figure which the realities of this attractive prize-fighter do not support." And Dempsey was made the symbol of muscular, big-limbed youths who have "a small verbal repertory but a large stock of scowls and blows." Rickard and Kearns may have started the symbolism to increase the financial attractiveness of the mismatch, but as the bout grew nearer the symbolism surrounding the fight gained impetus from its own momentum. No longer mere ballyhoo, it became a firmly believed credo, a web of words and images that was taken quite seriously. Looking at the process of symbol-making from across the Atlantic Ocean, a Manchester *Guardian* editorialist remarked that Americans had lost their "sense of proportion." The London *Times* agreed. Some future day, one of the *Times's* columnists wrote, a professor of history will use the Dempsey-Carpentier fight as proof that "the age lacked a sense of proportion."[29]

The lack of a sense of proportion was what Rickard had hoped for. It meant money in the bank. But in the months before the bout his mind was occupied by more immediate concerns, most prominent of which was a place to stage the fight. Governor Nathan L. Miller of New York stood firmly against professional boxing, and even though the Walker Boxing Law had legalized the sport in the Empire State, he was opposed to an outdoor heavyweight championship fight. Throughout the early months of 1921, Rickard searched for a suitable location. Offers as far apart as Fallon, Nevada; Cumberland, Maryland; and London, England, greeted Rickard, but none of the offers were considered very seriously. Rickard wanted the fight staged as close to New York City as possible. In early April, Governor Edward I. Edwards of New Jersey offered his state to Rickard. The choice was thus narrowed to the leading New Jersey cities—Newark, Atlantic City, and Jersey City. Political infighting followed, but just how much and by whom is not known. The fight would certainly be a boon to the chosen city, and the person who owned the land that was picked for the site of the arena would stand to make a small fortune. In mid-April, the nod went to Jersey City, a town blessed by its proximity to New York City and the support of Governor Edwards. For the actual site of the fight, Rickard chose Boyle's Thirty Acres, a fen on the outskirts of Jersey City which was owned by an influential local citizen.[30]

Workers at once started to build the all-pine arena which cost $250,000 to construct. For its time, it was a magnificent structure. It was built to hold a crowd of 91,613 persons. Oval in shape, the arena looked like a gigantic saucer in the middle of the New Jersey marsh. And it was egalitarian; ticket prices offered something for everyone. There were the fifty-dollar ringside seats for the rich patrons Rickard hoped to attract; the "inner circle" of thirty- and forty-dollar seats for the men and women of solid income; the "outer circle" of twenty-five dollar seats for respectable members of society; the reserve seats priced at fifteen dollars for the gainfully employed; and the general admission seats which were close to the New Jersey-New York border and cost only five dollars and fifty cents.[31] As it turned out, customers got what they paid for. In the best seats the match would be watched without fear of life or limb; but the wooden outskirts of the arena shook frightfully from any commotion initiated by the holders of the expensive seats. It was truly a democratic arrangement.

On the same day that the construction of the arena began, protest against the bout was voiced. In the political arena, Governor Miller of New York led the forces that opposed the fight. Miller, entrenched in the nineteenth-century world of amateurism, was quick to draw the distinction between boxing for exercise and professional prizefighting. For the former, he expressed the wholesome fondness of a normal, masculine person, even recalling that as a youth he had engaged in a bout or two. But for the "commercial enterprise" of professional boxing he held only disgust. Applauding Miller's stand, a New York *Times* editorialist emphasized that the governor was not opposed so much to a sport as to "a particularly sorry business."[32]

Politically, the bout was also opposed on the floor of Congress. James A. Gallivan, a Democratic representative from Massachusetts, believed that the attention lavished upon the upcoming fight was a slap in the face of every veteran of the Great War. After calling Dempsey a "big bum," Gallivan introduced a resolution that, if adopted, would have prohibited the heavyweight title contest until every World War I veteran received a bonus. Why, Gallivan reasoned, should the Wall Street brokers, Pittsburgh industrialists, and the Chicago bankers be permitted to enjoy "their greatest thrill" while millions of men who risked their lives for America went hungry and were forced to live without the basic necessities of existence?[33] Gallivan's resolution was sent to the Committee on Ways and Means, and there it was promptly forgotten.

Far more numerous but no more effective than the political opposition to the fight were the protests voiced by moralistic reformers and religious leaders. After Jersey City was announced as the site for the fight, the Clergymen's Community Club of that city sent an official protest to Mayor Hague. The organization of pastors carefully listed the reasons for their opposition: the bout would attract "bruisers" rather than the "finer types" of citizens; the fight would serve to "brutalize" the youth and foster juvenile delinquency; and the entire standards of Jersey City would be corrupted by allowing the match to be staged. Other morally motivated societies followed the example established by the Jersey City organization. The General Assembly of the Presbyterian Church voiced its "hearty condemnation" of the affair at their annual meeting in Winona Lake, Indiana. The Board of Temperance and Public Morals of the Methodist Episcopal Church labeled the contest an impediment to public morality. Dr. Wilber F. Crafts of the International Reform Bureau in Washington, D.C., even tried to get an injunction to prohibit the fight. The Secretary of the IRB, Clifton W. Howard, said the injunction was based on the fact that the bout would be a "fight to the finish for financial profit" and not simply an exhibition of boxing. Like Gallivan's resolution, the proposed injunction failed to interrupt the contest.[34]

Throughout the month before the fight, Carpentier and Dempsey remained in their training camps, deaf to the voices of protest that wished to prevent their title fight. In Carpentier's case, he was deaf to almost all human voices other than those of the men in his entourage. From the time that the European champion set foot on American shores, accompanied by his manager François Descamps, a sparring partner, a French chef, and his dog, he was surrounded with mystery. His training camp was set up on the Matthews farm in Manhasset, Long Island, near the Louis Sherry and Payne Whitney estates. For neighbors and visitors who hoped to watch Carpentier train, the Frenchman's quarters most closely resembled the Castle of Udolpho. The public was most emphatically not welcome. Barbed wire surrounded the farmhouse and barn where Carpentier trained, and when it was discovered that young boys were looking over the fence from an adjoining field, a board enclosure was added to the barbed wire fence. A Belgian police dog and a deputy sheriff, in addition, patrolled the grounds and shooed away would-be spectators. Only during the rare and uneventful press days was it possible to gain entrance to Carpentier's camp.[35]

The mystery and secrecy invited speculation, and much of the guessing centered on François Descamps. The swarthy manager supervised the camp's activity habitually dressed in a purple sweater, fawn slacks, and embroidered red Persian slippers. If he was oddly dressed, his slanted eyes were even more unusual. In late May a Parisian daily, La Petit Parisien, published a story that claimed that Descamps had occult power. According to the paper, Descamps used the "projection of personality," or hypnotism, to aid Carpentier in the Joe Beckett and Bombardier Billy Wells fights. Before the Beckett fight, for example, it was said that Descamps' stealthy assault on Beckett's brain filled the Englishman with "one vast, uncontrollable, irresistible, all pervading, supremely passionate, overwhelming desire to lie down and quit." Stuart Martin, of the London Mail, cautioned Dempsey to be alert for Descamps' "evil eye" as well as Carpentier's right hand. Properly warned, Dempsey said that he would insist that Descamps wear opaque motor goggles "through which the malevolent emanation [would be] unable to pass."[36]

Evil eye considered, however, Ring Lardner believed there were other motives for the secrecy that hung over the Manhasset training grounds. Lardner, who owned a home close to Carpentier's camp, suspected that the mystery was maintained to hide the truth of the situation. Carpentier, wrote Lardner, "realized what a fat chance he had and that it was silly to go through a rigorous grind of preparation for inevitable defeat." Lardner's cynical observation was probably true, for although Carpentier sparred with such good fighters as Italian Joe Gans and Joe Jeannette (who had defeated the Frenchman in 1914), the contests were largely lackluster affairs in which the sparring partners fell to the canvas on the slightest provocation.[37] Carpentier undoubtedly reasoned that he would be paid $200,000 whether he trained hard or not, and there was no reason to overprepare for a losing cause.

No mystery clung to Dempsey's Atlantic City training camp. Upon Dempsey's arrival horns blared and whistles shrieked as if to signify the start of an extended and rowdy holiday. Even the rain and "young gale" failed to dampen the spirits of the thousands of people who turned out to greet the champion. The mood stayed. It was a loose and easy camp, and everyone was invited to watch the champion train. As always, Dempsey worked hard in camp, sparring daily with a number of respectable fighters. On one day, in fact, Jack Renault ripped open Dempsey's left eye with a solid right hook. When not training, Dempsey good-naturedly talked with reporters and even made a publicity film, *A Day with Jack Dempsey.* His manner was increasingly more considerate and humble. In a moment of candor, he came as close to a prediction of victory as he ever did in his career. When asked if he would defeat Carpentier, Dempsey replied, "Why, he's kind of small, isn't he?"[38]

Thousands of people visited Dempsey's Atlantic City camp. Although the temperatures were often in the nineties, a cool ocean breeze and midsummer rain provided relief. When rain canceled his workouts, Dempsey read western novels or surveyed the mysteries of French. Heywood Broun, who visited the champion, reported that the champion enjoyed escapist literature. If the public was surprised to discover that the world's heavyweight boxing champion was a closet Walter Mitty, it was amused by Dempsey's adventures with the French language. Hoping to understand the chatter between Carpentier and Descamps, Dempsey announced that he would learn French while he trained.[39] But as the day of the fight grew nearer, he decided to rely upon his fists instead of his French.

117

Except for his name being mentioned as a corespondent in a divorce suit—an Osage Indian mistakenly believed that his wife and Dempsey were writing letters to each other—the champion passed the weeks before the fight with unusual tranquility. Not so for Kearns. Choosing a sleazy hotel on the Atlantic City Boardwalk for his headquarters, Kearns did his best to make sure that the prohibition laws were broken every day and night. Sports writers, show business people, members of the fight business, and every sort of footloose rowdy frequented Kearns's rooms. More than once the police were summoned to the hotel to quiet the all-night celebrations. Two men claiming to be part of Dempsey's camp forced their way into the Moulin Rouge, a Broadway cabaret, with the use of switchblade knives. Although Kearns denied that the two men were officially part of the camp, he confessed to being their friend.[40]

By the end of June, the Dempsey-Carpentier fight was the biggest story in the world. Newspapers, both American and foreign, detailed each day's activity of both fighters. Important prefight developments were announced on the front pages of every newspaper in the country, with the exception of journals like the *Christian Science Monitor*. A liberal Swiss daily, the *Neue Zürcher Zeitung*, speculated that one-tenth of the "press-power concentrated upon [the fight] would have easily put the United States into the League of Nations. . . . America [is] more engaged by this even than by the Versailles peace or by the greatest European revolution." The Manchester *Guardian* and London *Times* agreed, the former even suggesting that the clever Clemenceau was encouraging interest in the fight to divert attention from France's grave economic and social problems. Half way around the world, in Japan, the fight generated interest. In fact, the *Japan Times* registered a complaint against the inconsiderate promoters of the bout who scheduled the match for Saturday which, of course, was Sunday for half the world; it was time that "the sensibilities of persons living here [Japan] were accorded recognition by the fight promoter."[41]

Every scrap of information about the bout, each prophecy and speculation, was greedily consumed by the news-starved public. Every writer, it seemed, tried to outguess the next. The majority of experts wisely picked Dempsey to win, but a remarkable number

118

Although Jack Dempsey earned thousands of dollars for the war effort, he was called a draftdodger because of his 4-A status during World War I. This obviously posed picture of him as a shipyard worker drew harsh criticism.

Jack Dempsey won the World's Heavyweight Championship from Jess Willard at Toledo, on July 4, 1919. Dempsey knocked the heavier, taller Willard down seven times before knocking him out in the fourth round. The lower photograph shows spectators in the "broiling sun."

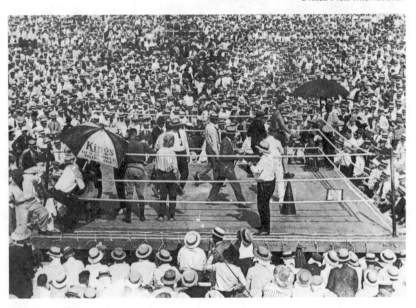

Tex Rickard, who promoted the Dempsey-Willard fight, purchased Madison Square Garden and became boxing's most colorful entrepreneur.

Culver

Beginning in 1920, Jack Dempsey appeared in such movies as the melodramas *The Health Farm Wallop* (left) and *The Winning Way.*

The Manassa Mauler with his parents in 1920. After they became Mormons, Celia and Hyrum Dempsey headed west about 1880. They were living in Manassa, Colorado, when Jack was born on June 24, 1895.

United Press International

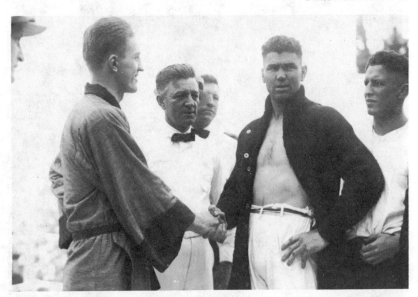

The fight between Jack Dempsey and the Frenchman Georges Carpentier, held in Jersey City on July 2, 1921, was called the Battle of the Century. H. L. Mencken wrote, "Dempsey was never in any more danger of being knocked out than I was."

Culver

Jack Dempsey during his training for the fight with Tommy Gibbons.

Culver

Jack Dempsey successfully defended his title against Tommy Gibbons at Shelby, Montana, on July 4, 1923. The mayor of Shelby said, "Well, we saw a fight, didn't we?" But the fight cost the mayor at least $140,000.

When Jack Dempsey fought Luis Firpo at the Polo Grounds, New York City, on September 14, 1923, the Argentine knocked the champion out of the ring, but Dempsey was immediately helped back to the canvas by sportswriters sitting at ringside. *Culver*

In 1925 Jack Dempsey married an actress, Estelle Taylor. On their European honeymoon Dempsey bought Estelle a boisterous blue boarhound named Castor. Castor cost the champion $10,000 in fines, court costs, and damages.

On a fishing trip in Colorado with Estelle, Dempsey displays a string of fish which seem not to have soiled his saddle oxfords, argyle hose, or his checked plus fours.

Culver

Jack Dempsey training at Stillman's on Sixth Avenue, for decades the most famous gym in the world of boxing.

Handlers rush to the aid of Jack Sharkey following his knockout by Jack Dempsey, the deposed champion, in the seventh round of a fight held in Yankee Stadium on July 21, 1927.

Wide World

After Gene Tunney defeated Jack Dempsey on September 23, 1926, Dempsey attempted to regain his title one year later in a fight at Chicago's Soldier Field. Above, Dempsey lands the blow that sent Tunney to the canvas for the famous "long count" in the seventh round.   *United Press International*

A publicity shot for the movie *The Prize Fighter and the Lady*. Left to right: Joe Rivers, Spike Robinson, Bull Montana, M. Lubisch, James J. Jeffries, Max Baer, Jack Dempsey, Primo Canera, Jess Willard, director W. S. Van Dyke, Strangler Lewis, Billy Papke, Jackie Fields, Frank Moran, and Dan Tobey.

James J. Corbett was heavyweight champion, 1892–1897. He and Jack Dempsey posed for this picture in Milwaukee in 1929, when Gentleman Jim was sixty-three years old. *United Press International*

Jack Dempsey, who remained a public idol throughout his active life, was constantly photographed at public functions. Here in 1937 he and the famous Irish tenor John McCormack and an actress, Jerry Lawlor, are watching Ellsworth Vines and Fred Perry in a tennis match at Miami Beach.

United Press International

If he was not at the Argonne Forest, Jack Dempsey was at Okinawa. Here Commander Dempsey of the United States Coast Guard is going ashore in April, 1945, a few hours after the initial attack in the Ryukyus.

United Press International

This picture of the former heavyweight champion and his daughters, Barbara and Joan, was made in Chicago in July of 1947. *United Press International*

Both pictures above were made in Jack Dempsey's restaurant, popular with
New Yorkers and tourists for a quarter of a century. Top, he poses in 1972
before a mural depicting his knockout of Jess Willard. Below, he sits alone
on the evening that the restaurant's doors were closed for the last time in
1974. *Wide World*

A scene from *Requiem for a Heavyweight* in which Jack Dempsey made a cameo appearance with Jackie Gleason at the bar in Dempsey's.

somehow convinced themselves that Carpentier had a chance. Frank Parker Stockbridge, a columnist and artist for the New York *Times*, told his readers that the shape of the skull was the most important factor. Carpentier's dolichocephalism (long-headedness), Stockbridge maintained, was a distinct advantage over the brachycephalic (round-headed) Dempsey. Similarly, William Judson Kilby of the New York *Evening World* suggested, "There is every indication, such as the width between the ears and the look of sincerity, that Carpentier is an unusually brave man." Not to be outdone, a New York *World* reporter wrote that Carpentier would undoubtedly win because the Frenchman's muscles were long, not spherical like Dempsey's. As ingenious as these theories were, the most telling comment was voiced by the dapper ex-champion James J. Corbett. Gentleman Jim confidently picked Carpentier to win. It was the kiss of death. In his long and illustrious career as a pugilistic soothsayer, Corbett had never predicted a winner.[42]

Explanations of the phenomenal interest were as many and as complicated as the predictions of the outcome. But through the most reasoned explanations ran a common thread: the bout symbolized the triumph of man over systems and machines. In an age where man seemed to be guided by amoral forces beyond his control, the Dempsey-Carpentier fight represented man as master of his fate. "In days when we think in terms of politics and theologies and economic systems," wrote psychologist P. W. Wilson, "Dempsey and Carpentier declare unto us that it is, ultimately, the man who counts. His food, his muscles, his habits, his frame of mind, his morale, matter infinitely to the whole world."[43] Perhaps Wilson was right, that the bout was a glorification of man, a mass to the human spirit, the final cry of "I am" in the face of the machine. But regardless of the answer, the fact remained: millions of people from all over the world who previously had expressed no interest in boxing were now very interested in the outcome of one particular fight.

By the day of the fight, July 2, the world had turned its attention to a tiny boxing ring in Jersey City, New Jersey. In Paris, Frenchmen gathered around newspaper buildings in the hope of being among the first in their country to learn the outcome of the contest. Once the news reached Paris, six army airplanes stood alert to transmit the

119

verdict to the city by flashing red lights if Carpentier was the winner or white lights for Dempsey. In America the schemes of criminals and reformers alike were thwarted. Several counterfeit ticket rings were discovered before they could unload the forgeries, and the International Reform Bureau failed in its last attempt to have the fight canceled.[44] But such activities went unnoticed in the general excitement about the bout. It was the outcome—and only the outcome—that held any interest.

When the sun rose on July 2, it was greeted by thousands of people who had waited all night in the muddy fields surrounding the arena in the hope of buying a ticket. What tickets that were available were quickly sold, and at nine o'clock the gates were opened. From then until the time of the main event, a steady stream of men and a "noticeable sprinkling of women" filed into the saucer-shaped arena. The process was unusually orderly, and reporters commented upon the surprising absence of crooks and bootleggers. Ushers worked effectively. Even though the crowd was the largest ever to witness a sporting event in America, there were few incidents. "An hour before the 'Battle of the Ages,'" wrote Fred Hawthorne for the New York *Tribune*, "there did not seem to be a round dozen vacant seats in the immense arena." It was reported the next day that over 90,000 persons crammed into the arena, although the official figure was 80,183. Yet the difference between the reported and the actual numbers was hardly significant, for almost every inch of space was occupied. The filled stadium was best described by Arthur Brisbane, who said the ring looked like a small, square lump of sugar at the bottom of a bowl covered with 10,000 black flies.[45]

The attendance insured financial success; the fight grossed $1,789,238, well over twice as much as any previous fight. But of more importance to Rickard, the match was an unqualified social success. Perhaps never before in history had so many famous Americans been gathered together in a single place. Irvin S. Cobb, feature writer for the New York *Times*, noted, "The arts, sciences, drama, politics, commerce and bootlegging industry, have all sent their pink . . . to grace the great occasion. The names at ringside would sound like the reading of the first hundred pages of 'Who's Ballyhoo in America.'" For many newspapers, the only adequate manner in

120

which to deal with the number of "names" was to list them alphabetically. The lists contained hundreds of names of persons who traveled to Jersey City in limousines, private railway cars, yachts, and chartered tugboats. Three of Theodore Roosevelt's children were there—Kermit, Theodore, Jr., and Alice Roosevelt Longworth. Joining them at the ringside seats were a dozen Philadelphia Biddles, several Rhinelanders, William H. Vanderbilt, George H. Gould, Percy Rockefeller, Jr., Henry Ford, Harry Payne Whitney, George J. Gould, Joseph W. Harriman, Sailing Baruch, Vincent Astor, George F. Baker, Jr., and other leading American blue bloods. The Spanish ambassador was there, as were Prince Antoine Bibesco, the Rumanian Minister, Herbert Asquith's son-in-law, the Netherlands' chargé d'affaires, a counselor from the Russian Embassy, the Earl of Drendonald, the ambassador from Peru, several members of Parliament, and too many counts, countesses, sirs, and ladies to mention. Al Jolson led the show business contingent which included Sam H. Harris, George M. Cohan, David Belasco, Owen Moore, and Colonel Jacob Ruppert. Rickard was numb with pleasure. "Look at all them fine people," he kept muttering. "I never seed so many millionaires. Can you imagine all them fine people coming here to patronize Tex Rickard?" His day was complete when he was allowed to escort John D. Rockefeller, Jr., to a better seat. Rickard's biographer, Charles Samuels, claimed, "It was the greatest day in Tex's life."[46]

Rickard feared only two things. First, he was afraid that it might rain and ruin the event. His fears were not unjustified. It was a hazy day, the type that might hold rain in store. Around one o'clock, when the first preliminaries were being staged, it did start to sprinkle, but no sonner had the rain begun than a breeze from the west blew the rain clouds away. Thereafter, the sun emerged bright and strong. The sun turned the haze into steam until the arena resembled a gigantic outdoor Turkish bath. Indeed, men began to disrobe to such an alarming extent that Fred Hawthorne wondered if a fat man seated near to him "would eventually be reduced to athletic underwear." Only the "hard-boiled" women resisted the temptation to remove clothes. They did not even take off their hats.[47]

The second thing that Rickard feared was that Dempsey might ruin the day by killing Carpentier. As much as Rickard knew about

121

promoting fights, he understood very little about the fights themselves. Before the Dempsey-Willard bout, Rickard cautioned Willard
not to kill Dempsey. After Dempsey defeated the gigantic Willard so
easily, Rickard became convinced that not only was the champion
unbeatable, but only an act of God could save Dempsey's opponents
from being beaten to death. With this fear in mind he approached
Dempsey shortly before the fight. "Listen, Jack," Rickard said. "This
Carpentier is a nice feller, but he can't fight. I could lick him myself.
So I want you to be careful and not kill him." Dempsey just looked at
him. "I meant that, Jack," Rickard continued. "If you kill him all
this will be ruined. Boxing will be dead." Again Dempsey refused to
commit himself, forcing Rickard to leave with a sick feeling in his
stomach. "Imagine that," Dempsey recalled over one half century
later. "That damn fool must have thought we were going to fight a
duel with guns or something."[48]

As Rickard left the dressing room, Dempsey was talking with
Gene Fowler, and Kearns was nervously kneading the champion's
shoulders. Outside, the preliminaries were well under way. It was a
good card. Irish Johnny Curlin won a popular decision over Mickey
Delmont in the first preliminary. In another preliminary Dempsey's
sparring partner, Babe Herman, hammered a New Orleans fighter,
Joe Matranga, all over the ring. More fights followed, and between
bouts Tom Mix performed tricks with a Mexican hat. Finally came
the semifinal bout, the last match before the main event. In this contest, Gene Tunney, who was later to defeat Dempsey, soundly defeated Soldier Jones; in the seventh round referee Danny Sullivan
stopped the fight to save Jones from losing too much blood. All the
preliminaries were good action-filled fights, but the spectators had
not come to Jersey City to see preliminaries. During the matches,
commented Jack Lawrence, "the crowd was phlegmatic and disin-
terested to the point of being bored. It seemed to view the appetizers
to the main course as necessary annoyances."[49]

Just about 3 o'clock, Carpentier, escorted by two policemen,
walked down the alleyway and climbed into the ring. His blond hair
brushed back off his forehead, Carpentier, remarked Lawrence,
looked "like anything but a professional prizefighter." Sophie Treadwell, who was commissioned by the New York *Tribune* to write a

feminine report of the bout, claimed Carpentier's clothes "spelled unconscious distinction." Resplendent in a dove-gray bathrobe, decorated with black cuffs and edges, the challenger was close shaven, unusually pale, and wore "a strange, strained and crooked smile." In fact, wrote Treadwell, "he looked exactly like a clever, elusive, but guilty young gentleman who knew at last that the jig was up and was going along to headquarters to face the music."[50]

Carpentier's entrance into the ring was greeted with wild applause, especially from the hundreds of reporters and thousands of women present. The foot-stamping and cheering, however, almost ended the day's activity on a tragic note. Quite simply, the arena was never meant to hold 80,000 people. Rickard's original plan was for the arena to seat 50,000, but as interest in the fight mounted the stadium was expanded to hold 70,000 spectators. This expansion was done cleverly but dangerously by loading the additional sections atop the original framework by extending projecting ribs far beyond the ground support. Thus when the spectators began to cheer, the upper sections of the arena swayed frightfully. People seated in the $5.50 and $10.00 seats cried out for everyone to sit down, but their voices were drowned out by the applause and the brass band playing the Marseillaise. [51]

Minutes after Carpentier climbed through the ropes, Dempsey entered the ring. He was perhaps twenty-five pounds heavier than the challenger but the difference seemed somehow greater. Treadwell was one of the many reporters who noted the difference. Dempsey, she said, "led and towered." He wore a red sweater, and a cap was jauntily tilted on the back of his head. Stitched to the belt section of his long white trunks was the American flag. Around his waist were red, white, and blue strips of ribbon. Reporters were surprised to hear more cheers for Dempsey than for Carpentier, but the champion enjoyed the greeting. He smiled through a heavy stubble of beard that "gave a tramplike and frightening look to his threatening and heavy face." His step was swinging and carefree. At ringside the wife of a sportswriter gripped Sophie Treadwell's arm and said, "It's all over."[52]

The bout was delayed several minutes when a number of airplanes appeared over the arena. This was no small matter. Rickard had prohibited aerial photographs to be taken during the bout, and Mayor Hague had warned fliers to keep away. Both men feared that a plane might attempt to fly too close to the arena and crash into the stands. Less than one year before, navy lieutenant James Murry Grier, a distinguished member of the Lafayette Escadrille, had ventured too close to the Forest Hills Tennis Club during the finals of the United States championships and crashed barely two hundred yards from center court. But regardless of the prohibition, the airplanes circled over the arena, dipping low enough that the photographers inside could be seen grinding out their film. Carpentier gazed aloft, "apparently oblivious to his mundane surroundings." Fred Hawthorne guessed that the airplanes reminded Carpentier of the battlefields of France. "To Dempsey," he added, "it was just an aeroplane."[53]

After the planes had vanished, the fighters were given their instructions by referee Harry Ertle. After months of preparation and millions of words of publicity, the fight was about to start. At ringside Major Andrew White and J. O. Smith had started their radio broadcast, the first broadcast of a championship boxing match.[54] All the ex-champions, near champions, and current champions at the fight had been introduced and escorted out of the ring. Tex Rickard, dressed in a blue suit and wearing a Panama hat, had received his ovation. At 3:16 the bell rang.

The two men's styles were as different as their temperaments. Carpentier was more the classic fighter with his left extended from his body, his right held in reserve, and his knees bent ready to spring into action. He fought along straight lines, attacking and retreating in the manner of a fencer. His head was held immobile as he watched the movements of his opponent with an almost detached interest. He displayed little emotion. By contrast, Dempsey was a study in motion and emotions. He moved from side to side, bobbing his head and rolling and dipping his shoulders as he shifted his weight to impart the maximum power with each punch. Usually his bobbing head was buried deep in his shoulders, protecting a chin that needed little protection. But when the champion's face was exposed to his opponent it was filled with expression. One reporter at ringside said Dempsey's look was "a sardonic grin which was half sneer." Certainly it was the expression of a man who got a grim enjoyment from his work.[55]

During the first round the action was relatively calm; Carpentier displayed his plan early. He would watch the champion, and then suddenly leap and try to hit Dempsey with a right, hoping thereby to end the fight with one punch. At times his strategy was partially successful. He hit Dempsey with several hard rights, but they had absolutely no effect on the champion. Carpentier's punches, said W. O. McGeehan, were shells "bursting against an impenetrable armor plate."[56] Dempsey, on the other hand, seemed content to play a waiting game; he appeared in no hurry to end the fight. When he was rushed by Carpentier, Dempsey directed his attack to the Frenchman's body, landing hard punches, but not the kind that end fights. The few blows that were aimed at Carpentier's head, however, were devastating. One brought blood from the challenger's nose; another opened a cut over Carpentier's right eye.

In the second round Dempsey increased his attack, crowding Carpentier and throwing more punches. But Carpentier easily avoided Dempsey's charges, making, as W. J. Macbeth claimed, "a veritable monkey of the champion."[57] Toward the middle of the round, Carpentier went on the offensive. He hit Dempsey with a solid right, a left, and two more rights. Less hurt than surprised, Dempsey went on the defensive, but still Carpentier attacked. Then with dramatic suddenness, the Frenchman landed his best blow of the fight, a straight overhand right to Dempsey's jaw. The punch, however, hurt Carpentier more than Dempsey, for the challenger broke his thumb in two places and sprained his wrist. Angered by the punch, Dempsey fought back with added vigor. By the end of the round, the champion opened another cut below the left eye of Carpentier.

The more romantic sportswriters at ringside believed that in the second round Carpentier was on the verge of knocking out Dempsey. Heywood Broun claimed that Carpentier was "within a punch of the championship." He maintained that it was fate—the tragic muse—that made Carpentier miss the left uppercut after he landed his big right. In the actions of fate, Broun glimpsed a cosmic idea: "The tragedy of life is not that man loses but that he almost wins." Other writers agreed with Broun's essential point: Carpentier had victory within his grasp in the second round. It was a warming thought, that had fate smiled for a second longer on Carpentier, then the champion, would have been a Frenchman. But like so many pleasant thoughts it was entirely void of truth. At least one unromantic curmudgeon at ringside, H. L. Mencken, realized that "Dempsey was never in any more danger of being knocked out than I was, sitting there in the stands with a pretty gal just behind me and five or six just in front." In brief, Mencken continued, the story that Carpentier almost won or ever had the slightest chance of winning was "apocryphal, bogus, hollow and null, imbecile, devoid of substance." Mencken spoke the truth, even though he knew that "from remote missionaries on the Upper Amazon to lonely Socialists in the catacombs of Leavenworth, and from the Hon. Warren Gamaliel Harding on his alabaster throne to the meanest Slovak in the bowels of the earth," he would be universally disbelieved and ignored.[58] But the fact remains, Carpentier's fabled second round was the product of one gigantic wish shared by most of the sportswriters in Jersey City.

Carpentier supporters found nothing to cheer about in the next two rounds. Dempsey was relentless. Francis Hackett, feature writer for the *New Republic,* summed it up best: Dempsey was not "cruel or humiliating. Dempsey [was] not brutal. He [was] simply superior."[59] In the third round the champion hammered Carpentier with lefts and rights to the body. The fourth round saw Dempsey shift his attack to the challenger's head. A right to the jaw floored Carpentier. He lay still, but at the count of nine he literally sprang to his feet. Dempsey moved in, landed several hard body blows, doubled up Carpentier with a right to the heart, and then knocked down the challenger again with a right to the jaw. Carpentier did not move until Ertle reached the count of eight; then he struggled briefly to regain his feet. But the effort was in vain. At the count of ten he was still stretched out on the canvas. At 3:27 the Battle of the Century ended. The fight that was so assiduously promoted and that attracted the interest of much of the world was not a very good fight.

Regardless of the fight's quality, the press announced the outcome in regal terms. The conclusion of a major war or the election of a new president would hardly have received more attention from the nation's press. Even a newspaper as traditionally conservative in its treatment of sports as the New York *Times* announced the result of the bout in three streamer headlines running all the way across its front page. Evidently, the newspaper that prides itself on printing all the news that's fit to print felt that information about the fight was, indeed, all the news that *was* fit to print. Most of the first thirteen pages were devoted to coverage of the bout. An exception was a one-column article on the front page entitled "Harding Ends War." The war, of course, was the Great War, the conflict that Dempsey had sidestepped. Less than one hour after Dempsey faced Carpentier in front of over 80,000 spectators, Harding affixed his signature to a treaty that officially ended World War I. Scarcely thirty people witnessed Harding's historic signing. But in the carnival mood that prevailed on July 3, no one seemed interested in the war issue any more. Dempsey had won. The American champion, albeit one with notable defects, had triumphed over the European champion. The American public, as reflected in the press, seemed satisfied.[60]

In the wake of the Carpentier fray, Dempsey was once again placed in a pantheon reserved only for unblemished idols. An editorialist for the *Japan Times* wrote that Dempsey's name was far better known than Lloyd George's and that thousands of boys would "rather be Dempsey . . . than be President of the United States or the greatest force in the world of finance, art or letters." Other newspapers and magazines echoed the opinion of the distant editorialist. Superior in action, modest in victory, Dempsey's name took on an almost mythical stature. Dan Daniel, one of the many young sportswriters in the press box, remembered the looks in the spectators' eyes as Dempsey helped the battered and bleeding Carpentier to the Frenchman's corner at the end of the bout: "'My God,' their [the spectators'] eyes said. 'This is not a man, not a boxer. He's a god. He's immortal.'"[61]

Perhaps of even more interest than the praise for Dempsey was what the fight's result represented for American society. On one level, many ministers and moralists in America believed along with Dr. John Roach Straton that the bout was clear proof that "we have relapsed into paganism." From his pulpit at Calvary Baptist Church in New York City, Straton condemned every aspect of the fight. As he told his congregation, he went to the fight so he would have a firsthand knowledge of corruption. And what he saw shocked every bone of his frame. The fight, Straton preached, was a glorification of rampant "materialism, militarism, lawlessness, and immorality in American society." For Straton, however, the most disgraceful aspect of the contest was the large number of women and "little girls" who were exposed to the "half naked" men.[62]

A cross section of ministers surveyed agreed that the fight was a "collective sin" shared by all those who enjoyed the event. The *Christian Century*, an "undenominational" newspaper, believed that boxing was "an outlaw in the civilized world." Another religious newspaper, the *Universal Leader*, expected that "It will take years to bring back our youth to sober sanity from these months of beastly intoxication incited by our newspapers." Finally, the Catholic journal of Dubuque, the *Daily American Tribune*, breathed a sigh of relief and said, "Thanks be to God, the 'great' day of shame, national shame, is over!" Similar opinions were also expressed in most of the churches in New York City on the day after the fight.[63]

But to others, the affair represented less a shift toward barbarism than an indication of the weakening of the power of the pulpit. According to an editorialist for the New Haven *Journal-Courier*, the masses were no longer content to follow blindly the moral precepts of the "intemperate and insolent, overbearing and dictatorial." The American people, the editorialist concluded, would no longer follow religious crusaders such as those who pushed through the Eighteenth Amendment. An editorialist for the New York *Times* also maintained that the bout was a positive sign: Dempsey symbolized the physical superiority that conquered Indians, frontiers, and Germans.[64]

If the fight highlighted a conflict in the moral predilections of society, it was also employed to demonstrate a growing rift between "highbrows" and "lowbrows." The rich or well-educated, from Heywood Broun in America to George Bernard Shaw in Europe, mourned Carpentier's defeat. Similarly, from the readiness of the public to forget the war issue, one suspects that Dempsey had a large following among the literarily inarticulate. By 1921 many people were beginning to question American involvement in the Great War. Wilsonian idealism had been crushed by the League debates, Red Scare, and race riots of 1919. Nowhere was this mood of disillusionment better summed up than in an editorial in the St. Louis *Post-Dispatch*:

The highbrows have had their day. They have wrangled over world peace and protection against future war for nearly three years, and they have accomplished neither. They have left no brain cell unagitated to resume the turning of the economic wheels, but in vain. Now, let us see what the lowbrows have done. In gate receipts alone they have shaken into circulation $1,600,000 from the pockets of people who have been holding back on the monopoly game. Of this, $400,000 is going into the Federal Treasury, where it will pay for a coat of paint and possibly a big gun or two on one of our sorely needed battleships. . . . A Dempsey-Carpentier fight in every state . . . would put old doldrums on the blink.[65]

Thus, in America, the Dempsey-Carpentier bout became more than an athletic contest between two men. Through the workings of the press, it was transformed into a platform for debating the grave moral, social, and political issues of the day, issues that were central to the 1920s.

Even the French, who crowded in the streets of Paris only to see white lights in the planes that announced the result of the fight, found some good portents in the bout. The newspaper *La Victoire* consoled its readers with the fact that Dempsey was a compatriot of the two million "mighty lads" from the United States who dealt a "mighty blow and thrust [to] the *Boche.*"[66] As in the United States, nobody harped on Dempsey's war record; the villain of the fight no longer seemed so evil. Indeed, during Dempsey's career he would again be cast as a scoundrel, but his character would never again be painted in such dark hues, and never again would he face an opponent who appeared to be so pure.

CHAPTER VII

A Question
of
Morals

A FTER several weeks, Dempsey's name left the front page; the
editorialists grew tired of reviewing his draft record and listing
Carpentier's admirable qualities. So completely was the Frenchman defeated that many Americans felt a little silly for ever thinking the smaller fighter had a chance to uncrown the champion. But
the hoopla and the ballyhoo had served its purpose: boxing had become an American obsession. Tex Rickard had taken a dream and
parlayed it into a million-dollar gate. He had transformed prizefight
promotion into an art form, replete with characters, plot, and dramatic tension. The Dempsey-Carpentier bout was his modern masterpiece; it was his twentieth-century drama where virtue goes unrewarded and the cruel amoral forces of nature triumph. Rickard
realized that he had discovered the magic formula, but, like the wise
conservationist, he did not want to squander the ingredients.

With this in mind, he suggested that Dempsey take a vacation
from the ring.[1] His reasoning was sound: let Dempsey rest for a
period and give another contender a chance to acquire a reputation.
Dempsey and Kearns readily agreed to the suggestion. From 1916 to
1921 Dempsey had fought sixty fights and numerous exhibitions. He
was ready for a vacation; but nobody guessed at the time that Dempsey's vacation would last a full two years. The length of his inactivity was due, however, more to the internal conflicts in boxing and
the tragedies in Rickard's personal life than to the champion's need
for a rest.

Dempsey's major vacation of the two-year period was his trip to

Europe in the spring of 1922. By this date, of course, Europe was in an abyss of political and economic decay. The western European countries suffered from inflation, and many commentators predicted that Europe would never regain its prewar status. Indeed, in 1922 the German Oswald Spengler published the second volume of his *Decline of the West*. This apocalyptic tome gave for many the proof that the "West-European-American" culture was about to tread the path of the late Roman Empire. The German motif of decay that surfaces in works as different as Thomas Mann's *Buddenbrooks* and *The Magic Mountain* and the movie *The Cabinet of Dr. Caligari* found a receptive audience in other western European countries. Marcel Proust died, in 1922, leaving a work, *Remembrance of Things Past*, that caused Edmund Wilson to call Proust the historian "of the Heartbreak House of capitalist culture." In the same year, across the channel in England, James Joyce's *Ulysses* was published, and it was soon regarded as an indictment of a western culture in decay.[2]

Dempsey had not read *Buddenbrooks* or even heard of Proust, but during his trip he witnessed different aspects of the decay. However, when the champion boarded the Cunard steamer *Aquitania* on April 11, 1922, the malaise of European civilization was far from his mind. His immediate concern was getting out of New York's harbor. A bevy of stage beauties, including Florence Walton, and scores of other women crowded the ship's main deck in an attempt to give Dempsey an "osculatory" goodby. The New York *Times* reported that hundreds of women roamed the deck crying, "Oh, where is he? Where is Jack Dempsey?" And one man was pushed down a companionway when he was mistaken for the champion. Finally, Dempsey was locked in his cabin on B deck, and the ship was cleared of stray women, reporters, and photographers.[3]

Although Dempsey expressed fear of becoming seasick, the voyage was a pleasant one. With an entourage that included Kearns; Teddy Hayes, his trainer; Joe Benjamin, his sparring partner; Tom O'Rourke, a representative of the New York Boxing Commission; Val O'Farrell, a private detective; and Damon Runyon, who acted as the official historian of the trip, Dempsey soon found himself the center of attention. Even the Dolly Sisters, a popular singing act, and D. W. Griffith failed to attract as much publicity as the champion. Dempsey whiled away his time boxing with the children and giving conditioning advice to the men. According to Runyon, the champion was popular with every one of the 1,480 passengers aboard the *Aquitania*. [4]

After more than one week at sea, the *Aquitania* moored at the harbor in Southhampton. Lord Melford, a leading patron of boxing in England, remembered the arrival of Dempsey, dressed in a blue serge suit and a light-grey plaid overcoat, long after the event took place. He recalled later the gleam of Dempsey's teeth and "what at first sight seemed a rather cruel, menacing expression." Lord Melford was not the only boxing enthusiast who made the trip to Southhampton to greet the champion. Kid Lewis, the English lightweight champion, was there, as was a host of other English fighters. Promoters, reporters, photographers, and hundreds of the merely curious joined the pugilists in cheering the champion and welcoming him to England. The London correspondent for the New York *Tribune* said the advance publicity that Dempsey received from the London press would have done justice to a visit by Charlie Chaplin or Woodrow Wilson. By the time Dempsey reached Waterloo Station in London the crowd had swelled to thousands. Through it all, the champion maintained an admirable equanimity, occasionally doffing his lemon-colored cap or waving to the well-wishers. [5]

Once settled into his comfortable rooms at the Savoy Hotel, Dempsey began his flirtation with the English people. He visited Epsom Downs, remarking that "over home we race on tracks that are, just how should I call it—well, just soil, without covering." He stood on his toes to catch a glimpse of the king and queen, and in the big City and Monarch race he bet—and lost—a small sum of money on King George's entry. At the dinner given in his honor by such English sportsmen as Major J. Arnold Wilson and Douglas Stuart, Dempsey was on his best behavior, smiling, well mannered, and considerate. On meeting the champion, Lord Melford found him to be a "master of himself, easy, natural and unaffected, and free from any pose." In all ways, the press and society of London were captivated by the "schoolboy-like" champion. [6]

As Dempsey's visit to England drew to a close, the flirtation between the champion and the English people turned into a mild love affair. On the eve of Dempsey's departure from London, Lord Northcliffe, the wealthy owner of the *Times, Daily Mail,* and other news-papers, invited the champion to a dinner at his London town house. Northcliffe, described by Dempsey as a "brainy man," was over-whelmed by the champion's charm. Called upon to make an after-dinner speech, Dempsey said he felt like the untalented Irishman who was invited to a fancy dinner to entertain the guests: "I can't sing, I can't dance, and I can't tell a story, but I will tell you what I'll do. I'll fight anybody in the house." The following day the *Times* printed an article, undoubtedly written by Northcliffe, about the champion. The writer expected Dempsey to be a loud mouth, "loud in voice, loud in dress, and loud in manner." But, he admitted, "I was wrong in every way." Instead of a swaggering bully, the writer met a man who was "quiet spoken, almost excessively modest," "re-fined" in his speech, and with "perfect" manners. By the end of his visit to England, Dempsey ironically found himself in the position of an Irish-American who was more popular in England than in the United States. Of all the countries he visited, the champion always retained a special affection for England.[7]

From London, Dempsey traveled to Paris, and his thoughts turned to more ethereal subjects. When asked if he was anxious to visit Montmartre, the center of Parisian nightlife, Dempsey replied that he was far more interested in seeing the serious and eternal side of Paris. Overcome by the attitude of a dutiful sightseer, determined to absorb culture no matter how unenjoyable, the champion told re-porters, "I want to see everything one should see." And see he did. He took early morning strolls along the Seine, walked the length of the Champs Elysées, visited the Arc de Triomphe, inspected the weapons at the Hôtel des Invalides, stood respectfully in front of the Tomb of Napoleon, and viewed the art works at the Louvre and the Pantheon. At the Louvre his pugilistic instincts were aroused by the Farnese *Hercules.* "I'm glad they don't grow them like that today," he told reporters.[8]

But for all his noble intentions, he did not ignore the gayer as-pects of the city. On one afternoon, accompanied by Irving Berlin and Berry Wall, the American Beau Brummell, he picked four win-ners in six races at Longchamps. During the nights he made the rounds of the city's cafés, seldom ever stopping in any one longer than fifteen or twenty minutes. He was roundly applauded at the Casino de Paris, where American singer Pearl White was performing; at Zelli's Café the orchestra struck up "The Stars and Stripes Forever" when he entered; he visited the Folies Bergère as a guest of Irving Berlin; and one night he even refereed a French middleweight championship bout between Billy Balzac and Maurice Prunier.[9] Whether it was the influence of the artistic aura of Balzac's name or the pronunciation of Prunier's name that influenced Dempsey most in his choice of the winner is not known.

As with his visit to England, Dempsey was the center of attention wherever he went in Paris. Men stopped him on the streets to discuss the Carpentier fight or to shake his hand, and women were drawn to him like moths to a flame. During an interview with *Excelsior*, the popular French newspaper, Dempsey reportedly said, "I'd [like to] take back une jolie petite Parisienne to marry," one who could "keep house à la Française, who could cook, wee, à la Française, and bring up des jolis bébés ` la Française." although it is doubtful that Dempsey ever mouthed those words, the effect was nevertheless real. Thousands of French women volunteered their services. In fact, when Dempsey left Paris en route to Berlin several days later, one French midinette labeled Dempsey the "champion flirt" for his unwillingness to make good his offer.[10]

In France and England, Dempsey was received as a symbol of America. The power and surge of the United States, which had insured an allied victory only three years before, was given symbolic form by Dempsey's visit. Less than six months before, the *Neue Zürcher Zeitung*, a liberal Swiss daily, had remarked that America, the "democratic giant," was "dramatically incorporated in Dempsey's powerful, brutal, natural strength, born of the American West." About the same time, a French newspaper, *La Victoire*, had editorialized to the French nation to "remember that Dempsey is the compatriot of 2,000,000 mighty lads who came from the other side of the Atlantic to deal a mighty blow and thrust the *Boche* beyond our boundaries."[11] Thus something of the reception Dempsey received in England and France was tinged by gratitude to an entire nation.

The champion's reception in Berlin is more difficult to explain. Greeted at the Berlin train station by a "riotously welcoming

Teutonic crowd" of seven or eight thousand, Dempsey was treated to a "stupendous, unprecedented and spontaneous popular demonstration" of German hysteria. No sooner was he off the train than the large crowd swallowed him, grabbing for his hat and tearing at his coat and shirt. For more than half an hour the German police issued orders in "typical Prussian" tones, but with no result. Finally, the noted six-day bicycle racer Walter Rutt was able to smuggle Dempsey into the basement of the train station and from there to engineer the champion's escape. Such a reception was unexpected in a country that did not participate in the sport of boxing before the fall of the Kaiser.[12]

Dempsey was shocked by the decadence of postwar Germany. He told reporters that he liked the people, but added, "as for the vice there, I wouldn't have believed there was anything like it in the world." One evening Kearns and he visited a cabaret that featured women boxing. What Dempsey believed would be a form of comical entertainment turned out to be a bloody and brutal affair, one in which jaws were broken and eyes were cut. Kearns enjoyed the action; during one of the fights he even entered the corner of one of the boxers to give her instructions. But Dempsey, who maintained "diplomatic neutrality" during all the bouts, was frankly disgusted by the entire affair. By the time he left the morally and economically diseased city, his only comment was, "I've seen all I want to see of that burg."[13]

By the end of the first week in May, Dempsey and Kearns were ready to return to the United States. Throughout the trip Kearns had harbored plans for staging a championship fight in Europe, but he sadly came to recognize the dismal economic conditions of the different countries. In addition, there were simply no good heavyweights in Europe. Therefore, on May 13 Dempsey and his entourage left Southhampton for the voyage back to the United States. A week later they were greeted by a large crowd at the New York harbor. "Sporting a monocle," which Kearns correctly noted made him "look like an ass," Dempsey told reporters that he had enjoyed Europe but was "glad to be home." As for boxing, he hoped that Rickard would soon promote another bout, for Dempsey expressed his willingness to fight any contender.[14]

135

But no match was made. Dempsey extended his vacation. In July he enjoyed a week's vacation at a resort village near Saranac Lake, New York. Part of September he spent hunting in the woods of northern Maine. When he grew tired of Maine, his hunting party ventured farther north. Near Havelock, a village in New Brunswick, Canada, Dempsey was nearly gored by a bull moose which he later killed. During these and other trips the press was quick to comment upon Dempsey's many manly virtues. His love of the outdoors was noted, as was his fondness for good healthy exercise. When in Canada he met a fifteen-year-old boy who was smoking a cigarette, the champion "reprimanded the lad in a fatherly way and pointed out the evils of cigarette smoking before maturity." During these vacations the public was not reminded of Dempsey's war record or the other less attractive aspects of his personality. The Dempsey the public met was the champion who entertained the Boy Scouts at the New York Hippodrome or the boxer who had "gone clean loco about dogs."[15] But while Dempsey's image was being polished, events in the boxing world were tarnishing the sport.

The major reason that Dempsey enjoyed such an extended vacation was that Tex Rickard was embroiled in an ugly personal scandal. At the start of 1922 Rickard had been sanguine about the future. In addition to promoting the first million-dollar gate, he had been able to reshape the finances of Madison Square Garden and turn the structure into a profitable proposition. The Garden controlled boxing in New York City, especially after the elegant International Boxing Club on Lexington Avenue had gone bankrupt. Furthermore, the Garden featured wrestling matches, basketball games, six-day bicycle races, and Sunday night dances. Thus sitting in his office in the Garden Tower, Rickard had every reason to be optimistic. However, by the end of January, 1922, the Garden's finances no longer seemed important to Rickard.[16]

On Saturday, January 21, three girls checked into New York City's Bellevue Hospital with torn clothing and a bizarre tale. According to the three young girls—Alice Ruck, age fifteen; Elvira Renzi, age twelve; and Anna Hess, age eleven—they had been lured into a taxi by a strange man, sexually assaulted, and, when they resisted, were forced to inhale iodine. When they awoke they found themselves along the banks of the Hudson River. Upon examination no traces of iodine were found on any of the girls. However, a physician for the Society for the Prevention of Cruelty to Children said that Ruck had been assaulted. After intensive verbal examination the girls admitted that the entire story was just that—a story. Afraid to return home late in the evening, the girls had concocted the tale to avoid parental discipline.[17]

But the girls had another story that had far more wide-reaching repercussions. They told a sordid tale of sexual intimacies they had had with a prominent New York City man. The man they named was George L. "Tex" Rickard. According to the girls, they had met Rickard at the Madison Square Garden swimming pool, where he was friendly with them and often presented them with gifts of money. In time Rickard invited them up to the Garden Tower, gave them wine, fondled their breasts, and took other sexual liberties with them. Their story was replete with descriptions of Rickard's Tower bedroom and other apartments where the promoter had taken them. Assistant District Attorney Ferdinand Pecora issued a warrant for Rickard's arrest, and the next day, Rickard, denying the story, turned himself in.[18]

In the days and weeks that followed, the case expanded and assumed the aura of a class B mystery movie. First, other girls were found to support the story of the original cast of juveniles. Mary Horbetch, age eleven, from the Lower East Side, told authorities that although she had never done anything improper with Rickard she knew of the activities of the other girls. More serious, Sarah Schoenfeld, age eleven, added that she both knew of the activities of the other girls and had engaged in sexual intercourse with Rickard herself. At the Grand Jury hearing before Magistrate George W. Simpson, Ruck and Schoenfeld retold their stories. They told of their trips to the Garden Tower and to two apartments that Rickard had access to on West Forty-seventh Street. They described furnishings and named dates. Under cross-examination their stories remained essentially unshaken. Indeed, when the Grand Jury testimony was completed, Magistrate Simpson admitted that the statements by the girls "bore the imprint of truth."[19]

But before the Grand Jury could return an indictment, intrigue

137

entered the case. The cloak and dagger activity took several forms. Nellie Gasko, yet another girl who had admitted her involvement with Rickard, was kidnapped by Nathan Pond, a former fighter and friend of Rickard, and spirited away to his farm in Wappingers Falls, New York. Pond claimed his actions stemmed from concern "for her health"; the police, after they arrested Pond, called the act "bribing and deceiving a witness in a pending criminal action." Next, an employee of Madison Square Garden vanished. Walter Field, the lessee of the apartments named by the girls as the scene of some of the sexual crimes, left New York City under suspicious circumstances. Later, when asked where Field was, Rickard said he probably went to his mother's house in New Jersey. But as to why Field left New York Rickard expressed neither knowledge nor interest. Finally, the janitor of the apartment building containing the two apartments was drawn into the act. Herman Verch, as he was later to testify, had been told by Rickard, "Some persons are going to get after me—a frame-up. If you know anything, keep quiet."[20] Verch had seen Rickard at the apartment buildings. He did not keep quiet.

Intrigue, however, was not limited to the friends of Rickard. One night Rickard received a telephoe call requesting him to go to a bar in the Hell's Kitchen district, one of the toughest sections of New York City. Accompanied by a detective from the Val O'Farrell Private Detective Agency, Rickard went. There he met two men who worked for the Society for the Prevention of Cruelty to Children. According to later reports, the men wanted $50,000 to forget the entire affair. They warned Rickard that if he did not pay the money he would certainly go to jail. Rickard refused to pay the blackmail money, telling the two men that he felt confident that he would be cleared of the charges in court. The two men, William Kelleher and D. J. Supple, were later dismissed from the Society for trying to blackmail Rickard.[21]

If Rickard wished for his day in court, he was not long denied. On February 16 the Grand Jury indicted him on two counts of both assault and abduction. Several days later two more counts of abduction were added. Less than one month later the trial began. In a tense courtroom from which all women were barred, Sarah Schoenfeld took the witness stand. "Grinning broadly," the "obviously imma-

138

ture" girl told her story once again. Again the courtroom heard about the nights in the Garden's tower, the same tower which Stanford White had used during his celebrated affair with Evelyn Nesbit. Once again the crowded courtroom was informed about the doings at the two West Forty-seventh Street apartments. As Rickard's ears reddened, Sarah, who spoke with a lisp because she was missing her four front teeth, looked the picture of innocence and told her sordid tale. The prosecuting attorney, Pecora, even produced a letter written on Madison Square Garden stationery, sent by Rickard to Sarah's mother. The letter informed Mrs. Schoenfeld that Rickard would write the governor of Wisconsin in an attempt to get her son out of jail.[22]

The next day Rickard's attorney, Max D. Steuer, tried and failed to shake Sarah on the witness stand. Similarly, Steuer was unable to dent the story told by Nellie Gasko. By the third day Steuer changed the thrust of Rickard's defense. Instead of trying to disprove the girls' stories, he attacked the girls' characters. He showed that Sarah was having sexual intercourse with a young boy about her own age. He proved that Nellie was a veritable dictionary of criminal offenses; under pressure from Steuer, Nellie admitted to practicing forgery, burglary, robbery, truancy, and making untrue statements under oath. Before the all-male audience, Steuer was relentless in his assassination of the characters of the two girls.[23]

After the prosecution rested, Steuer used the same technique in reverse. Through a series of character references, the lawyer attempted to build Rickard into a citizen above reproach. Charles E. Herron, the owner of several Alaskan newspapers and canning plants, attested to Rickard's financial integrity. An official of the National City Bank in New York, Eugene F. Ailes, confirmed that in Nome, "Mr. Rickard's name was good for whatever he wanted." Major Anthony J. Drexel Biddle, the rich Philadelphia sportsman, testified that Rickard was a man of moral and civic virtue. As proof of this, Biddle noted that Rickard had "purified" boxing. However, the most memorable character reference was supplied by Kermit Roosevelt, the son of the former president and long-time friend of Rickard's. Asked by Pecora if the running of a gambling house was not proof of Rickard's bad character, Kermit replied with a candor which would have pleased his father: "A man who runs a gambling house isn't necessarily a bad character, any more than a man who runs a church is necessarily a good character." Roosevelt's statement drew heated criticism. On Sunday the Reverend Dr. Christian F. Reisner condemned the comment before his Methodist congregation. And the same day, an editorialist for the New York *Times* wrote that all gamblers "who really deserve the name—the professionals, that is, who as a business exploit the common human tendency to risk money on opinion or luck—are and should be objects of condemnation by economists and moralists alike."[24]

In addition to his stable of character references, Steuer established iron-clad alibis for Rickard. The single most important date on which Gasko and Schoenfeld said that they had been with Rickard was November 12, 1921. Steuer proved that on that day Rickard had been at the Polo Grounds watching the Dartmouth-Pennsylvania football game with his press agent, Ike Dorgan, his matchmaker, Francis Flournoy, and another Garden associate. His alibi for the night was equally sound. Although Gasko had earlier demonstrated that she did not know whether September preceded or followed August, and although Rickard did not remember who won the football game or even what color uniforms either of the teams wore, the alibi went unchallenged. Several days later, after only slightly more than one hour and thirty minutes of deliberation, Rickard was found "not guilty" by the all-male jury. As the decision was read, Rickard "gripped the rail and almost fell to his knees in his emotion." The courtroom then erupted into a frenzy of cheering, handclapping, and handshaking.[25]

The day after Rickard was arrested, New York State Boxing Commissioner William Muldoon told the press, "Boxing as an institution is not directly concerned with the situation." Muldoon was wrong. He was as mistaken as the movie studio owner who said that the film-making industry was not affected by the Fatty Arbuckle case. Just as the reputation of boxing was affected by Dempsey's draft trial, so too the sport felt the shock of the Rickard scandal. For although Rickard was cleared, many people still doubted him. Many years after the event, one person who knew Rickard remarked, "I knew the man and I did not like him. . . . He was a no good sonofabitch." When

140

pressed for a reason, he answered that he had seen Rickard enter hotels with young girls.[26] Rumors of this nature continued to float down from the Garden Tower, and they made it difficult for Rickard to promote another major heavyweight championship fight in 1922 and early 1923.

Promotion of a title fight was further complicated by the complexion of the heavyweight division. The list of good heavyweights was a trifle thin in 1922. In fact, the only heavyweight worthy of consideration was Harry Wills. Ably managed by Paddy Mullins, Wills had achieved his number one ranking by virtue of a three-round knockout victory over Fred Fulton in July of 1920. In 1921 Wills had been active. Among other boxers, he defeated Bill Tate three times, twice by knockout, and battered to the canvas both Jeff Clark and Gunboat Smith, two ring veterans who had long since passed their prime. His size was as impressive as his record; at six feet, four inches, and 220 pounds, he was a well-proportioned athlete who could box as well as punch. To the casual observer, a bout between Wills and Dempsey appeared to have all the elements of a classic match.[27]

However, Wills's fate was hampered by two shadows. First, he was black, and, although in the 1920s blacks were permitted to fight for the title in lower divisions, they were not allowed to compete for the heavyweight crown. This situation was an heirloom of Wills's second shadow: Jack Johnson. Everytime a Wills-Dempsey bout was proposed, the image of the gold-toothed, smiling former champion surfaced in the minds of race-conscious promoters. All black heavyweights between 1908 and the mid-1930s were handicapped by the stigma of Jack Johnson. It became so difficult for a black to get a match with a good white fighter that the leading black boxers were forced to fight each other numerous times. For example, Sam Langford, who after Johnson was perhaps the best black heavyweight during the first quarter of the twentieth century, fought Sam McVey fifteen times, Joe Jeannette fourteen times, Jim Barry twelve times, Jeff Clark eleven times, and Harry Wills twenty-three times.[28] Similarly, Wills had an extended series of bouts with Jeannette, McVey, Clark, John Lestor Johnson, Jack Thompson, and Bill Tate.

By the 1920s it became increasingly difficult to ignore black heavyweights. To be sure, the three best blacks of the Johnson era—Langford, McVey, and Jeanette—were too old for serious consideration, but Wills could not be circumvented without notice. The new organization of the sport made Wills's plight more visible. In February of 1922 Nat Fleischer, a boxing reporter, started publication of the *Ring*. In the foreward to the first issue he wrote, "*The Ring* will stand by the public, by the boxers, by those who give honestly their share to the great and glorious game." In the months that followed, the *Ring* established itself as the leading boxing periodical, replacing the *Police Gazette*. Fleischer made a serious effort to accumulate accurate records, publish lists of leading contenders, and insure that the sport imbibed liberally the virtues of honesty and integrity that he preached. "Nat Fleischer and *The Ring* made the sport respectable," his son-in-law, Nat Loubet, claimed. "Before Nat any manager could say his boy was 48 and 0 with 42 knockouts. Nat checked the records; he made damn sure the manager was on the up and up."[29]

No sooner had Fleischer established his magazine than he started a crusade to eliminate the color line in the heavyweight division. Acting as editor, business manager, circulation manager, and general handyman of the *Ring*, Fleischer risked financial suicide by pleading Wills's case in the third issue he published. Speaking for the magazine, Francis Albertine wrote that "it seems only just that prejudices be eliminated in every clean sport, and that if boxing is to hold its place in the field of athletic activities, discrimination must not be countenanced." Albertine continued by asserting that Wills, unlike Johnson, "is a clean athlete, a splendid sportsman, a boxer of high ideals who has proved himself a credit to the game and to his race." Several months later George B. Underwood, another writer for the *Ring*, resumed the argument: "It would not be stretching the truth to say that Wills is running Booker T. Washington a good second in the Africo-American [sic] Stakes."[30] Again, the editorial staff of the *Ring* demanded that Wills be given the opportunity to battle for the title. As Fleischer published more articles in favor of a Dempsey-Wills bout, public pressure began to mount in favor of the match.

This pressure was given direction by Wills's manager, Paddy Mullins. The crafty manager realized that after the Fulton bout only Wills blocked Dempsey's complete domination of the heavyweight division. He believed that given enough time and pressure from the public, Dempsey's pride would force the champion into a contest with Wills. Furthermore, Mullins recognized that his fighter was past his prime. In 1922 Wills was thirty-three years old, an advanced age for a boxer. With these two factors weighing heavily on his mind, Mullins decided on his course of action: he would apply pressure to Dempsey's pride, twitting the champion about this inactivity whenever possible, and allow Wills to fight only inept newcomers to boxing or well-tamed veterans. Of course, Mullins' strategy did not go unobserved. Grantland Rice commented that three of Wills's 1922 fights did not prove the contender's ability, for "Kid Norfolk was too small and too scared, and the two Jacksons, Tush and Tat, were too clumsy, too light and too scared."[31] But Mullins' program was at least a partial success; Wills, fed a diet of well-chewed meat, remained the leading contender, and the public began to clamor for a Wills-Dempsey bout.

For his part, Dempsey was perfectly willing to fight Wills. True, after Dempsey won the championship in 1919, he was quick to draw the color line, saying that under no circumstances would he pay any attention to a "negro challenger." But Dempsey's attitude was not inflexible; he had fought blacks before and he was willing to do so again. After he returned from Europe, for instance, he told reporters that he would not draw the color line. If anything, Dempsey was irritated by the controversy. As a fighter, he was fully confident that he could defeat any man in the world. Any suspicions that Dempsey was afraid to fight Wills are nonsense. Years later, Dempsey said that he had wanted to fight Wills, but "Doc and Tex didn't think it would draw."[32]

Whether Rickard and Kearns were convinced that the fight would not draw a large gate is uncertain; but there can be no doubt that after the fiasco of the Johnson-Jeffries bout, a match that Rickard promoted, the Madison Square Garden czar opposed interracial heavyweight title fights on principle. Rickard believed that to promote an interracial title bout was to tamper with the delicate balance of race relations in the United States. He certainly did not want to see a reenactment of the race rioting of 1910. Furthermore, he contended that the "political forces"—he always used the term rather nebulously—of America were against the bout. On the state level, he felt that the match would aid the antiboxing forces that were attempting to repeal the Walker Boxing Law in Albany. Rickard also once told Nat Fleischer that "powerful forces" in Washington told him not to promote the fight.[33]

Rickard's method of satisfying the public that favored the bout was to promise to make the match but never to produce it. He hoped that his policy of active inaction would eventually outlive the public's interest in the fight. So he announced on June 22, 1922, that he would promote the fight, without saying when or where it would be staged. Rickard did not take one step to promote the fight, but when pressure arose again, he signed the two fighters to a contract that stated no terms, time, or site. As one sportwriter noted, the contract was only "indication of good faith." And where there was little "good faith" such a document was worthless. A New York *Times* editorial appaluded Rickard's signing of the bout but questioned "When?"[34] This question—along with queries about where and under what contions—Rickard was unwilling to answer. Undoubtedly he would have continued his active inaction had not events given him an out.

Rickard could thank William Muldoon, chairman of the New York State Athletic Commission. Fearing commercialism in the sport, Muldoon made an unexpected announcement in early September. Because "money-mad people in boxing have simply gone crazy," Muldoon took it upon himself to name the conditions under which a heavyweight title fight could be staged in New York. First, he said, at least forty thousand tickets had to be offered to the public at the price of two dollars or under. In addition, the top ringside seat could not be priced over fifteen dollars. Under these conditions, and only under these conditions, Muldoon added, would he sanction a Dempsey-Wills or a Dempsey-Willard bout. Rickard's reaction to Muldoon's conditions was uncharacteristically brief: "impossible."[35]

Caught in the middle of the controversy, Dempsey could only wait. He must have agreed with Don Marquis, then writing for the New York *Tribune*, that when the talking ended and the fighting commenced it would probably be 1982.[36] Certainly that date was

144

agreeable to Rickard vis-à-vis a Dempsey-Wills fight. What was not so sure was the position that Muldoon would take. Would he force Dempsey to fight Wills or would he ignore the issue? Indeed, what, if any, power did Muldoon actually possess? During the last third of 1922 these and other questions were discussed and debated, but not answered. Although the question of racism was not new to boxing, there was no precedent for the handling of the issue of commercialism. In early 1923, however, Muldoon found a solution for both problems.

CHAPTER VIII

Shelby
Under
Attack

O LYMPIA, the rambling, barrackslike wooden structure overlooking Long Island Sound and located in the rustic village
of Purchase, New York, was the home of the Muldoon
Hygienic Institute, the 1920s equivalent to today's jet-set health spa
where the rich go to shed pounds and firm up their bodies. The owner
of the institute, William Muldoon, was recognized at the turn of the
century as the world's strongest and most perfectly developed human.
In 1923, at the age of seventy-eight, he was still a marvelous physical
specimen; indeed, his physical measurements were almost identical
to what they had been a quarter of a century earlier when he was the
heavyweight wrestling champion of the world. He was a man who
inspired awe and trust. His taut, chestnut-brown face was perfectly
complemented by his short gray hair, well-trimmed gray mustache,
square jaw, and the cleft chin that jutted out to a position parallel
with his well-formed nose. Except for his twisted, cauliflowered ears,
he was a remarkably handsome man. In fact, in physical appearance,
moral tenacity, and sheer forthrightness, he resembled Sir Arthur
Conan Doyle.[1] Undoubtedly, Muldoon's respectability as much as
his athletic background influenced Governor Nathan L. Miller's decision to make him chairman of the New York State Athletic Commission in June, 1921. As Nat Fleischer, editor of the *Ring* reported
in early 1922, Muldoon was the ideal commissioner.[2]

On February 4, 1923, Muldoon summoned New York City sports
reporters to an impromptu press conference at his Olympia estate.
His subject for the day's lecture was most serious: heavyweight cham-

pionship bouts. As the reporters scribbled notes, Muldoon said he would not sanction any heavyweight title matches in the state of New York. His primary concern was the erosion of the moral integrity of boxing, which he believed to be caused by cancerous commercialism. How, he asked, could Americans tolerate a heavyweight champion making more in ten minutes than the president of the United States makes in four years? Furthermore, he lambasted the press for its excessive coverage of the heavyweight division. In short, his reason for barring heavyweight title fights in the state of New York was the same as the explanation he offered several days earlier when he refused to sanction a Dempsey-Wills or a Dempsey-Willard fight in his jurisdiction: "It is the commercialized condition produced by money-mad promoters and managers which is responsible for the commission's opposition."[3]

Muldoon's position is probably unique in sports history. In essence, the legal representative of boxing was decrying the expenditure of too much money and an excess of publicity given to his sport. His actual motives for banning heavyweight title fights, however, were not as pure as his public statements. In a classic example of cutting off one's nose to spite one's face, Muldoon chose to prohibit a championship fight because he did not want Dempsey to battle Harry Wills, the black New Orleans heavyweight who was the current number one contender. To be sure, Muldoon never said as much; his racism, although bone deep, was not the ugly, public brand. And his friend and biographer, Edward Van Every, claimed that "orders from a very high place" forced him to prohibit the contest. However, Muldoon's constant references to commercialism and his continued claims that all talk of discrimination and racism was "laughable" were just a well disguised front for his deeper feelings. Even Nat Fleischer, who firmly defended Muldoon in the face of heavy criticism, was "opposed to his continued ban against Harry Wills . . . for no other reason than [that] he is a negro."[4]

Had Tex Rickard demanded the match, however, Muldoon would certainly have relented. But Rickard was in no position to push. His personal problems of 1922 had shaken him to such an extent that his close friend Rex Beach believed he would never be able to recover. The sense of humiliation hung over him like a dark cloud, but even if he had been as exuberant as he was in 1921, it is doubtful whether he would have tried seriously to match Dempsey and Wills. As Nat Fleischer wrote, Dempsey and Wills "never fought because Tex Rickard refused to promote it."[5]

As a result of these problems, Dempsey and Kearns found themselves shut out of the major boxing state. They were not in an enviable position. If 1922 had been a year of relaxation and fun, it had also been expensive. Dempsey, in addition, had not engaged in serious training for over a year and a half, and for a boxer such a layoff can mean professional suicide. Boxing is a sport of motion and reactions, where a contest might well be decided by a split-second turn of the head or an equally quick shrug of the shoulder. Each move depends, contrary to popular mythology, not as much on instinct as on training. It is no wonder that by the early months of 1923 Kearns was looking frantically about for a possible match. He was in a mood to listen to any offer, no matter how bizarre.

The offer Kearns received was certainly odd. In early April, 1923, Kearns was notified that a group of wealthy bankers, oilmen, and cattlemen from Montana wished to stage a heavyweight championship fight between Dempsey and Tommy Gibbons in Shelby. Kearns had never heard of Shelby and, if pressed, would not have been able to put it in the right section of the United States, let alone in the correct state. Kearns's ignorance might justifiably be excused, for Shelby, Montana, was not important enough to have found its way into the 1900 and 1910 census reports. Although it had grown to a town with a population of 537 by the time of the 1920 census survey, it was still not the sort of place to attract Kearns's attention.[6]

But the leading citizens of Shelby formed an ambitious and optimistic group. In 1923 they believed that Shelby was destined to become one of the great cities of the Northwest. People had not always thought as much of Shelby, however. Located in northcentral Montana, in Toole County, Shelby in 1923 looked like the kind of cattle town that western movie producers are always trying to construct out of papier-maché. In the nineteenth century the region of sage and parched grasses was the heart of the Blackfoot country, and these Indians usually wintered around the site on which Shelby was later built. In 1891, when the builders of the Great Northern Rail-

148

road were forging across the prairies toward Marias Pass, a group of railroad men threw off a boxcar at the cross-trails in the coulee and named it Shelby Junction, after Peter P. Shelby, the general manager of the Great Northern in Montana. Unimpressed, Shelby is said to have remarked: "That mudhole, God-forsaken place . . . will never amount to a damn!" [7]

For a generation Shelby's assessment of the town held remarkably true. As a distributing point along the Great Northern, Shelby provided a needed, if undramatic, function. Chuck wagons drove in from the south, from the settlements along the Marias River, and men from the Sweetgrass Hills region to the north came into Shelby for supplies. And occasionally a cowboy or a sheepherder would wander into one of several honky-tonks in Shelby to relax after months on the range. But generally the town slept in peaceful anonymity. Between 1891 and 1921 the only moment of excitement in Shelby was when several of the "town playboys" held up an opera troupe that was passing through the town on the Great Northern. A *Police Gazette* report noted that the good-natured bandits shot out the engine headlight, the car windows, and the red signal light. The episode concluded when the conductor was forced at gunpoint to execute a clog dance. [8]

In 1921 the town awoke. After making some preliminary surveys, geologist Gordon Campbell started to drill in the Shelby area for oil. On March 22, 1922, his hopes were confirmed. Before long the oil-rich Kevin-Sunburst field stretched north as far as the Canadian border, and for most of the 1920s it ranked first among all Montana fields. From 1922 until 1929, the Shelby area seemed to hold an unlimited supply of crude oil. In 1923 the Kevin-Sunburst field yielded 441,531 barrels, a figure that rose to 6,457,217 in 1926. What is more, over the next three years production rose an incredible 1,362.5 percent. [9] As the oil came flowing from the derricks, wildcatters became rich, land values in the area skyrocketed, and Toole County entered a period of optimism and prosperity.

Peter P. Shelby's "mudhole" was rich. If Shelby's population was less than a thousand in 1923, the leading citizens of the town expected a rapid increase. Between oil speculators and real estate men buying land to sell to oil speculators, the price of land climbed be-

149

yond even the most sanguine expectations. If there was any obstacle to the rise, it was that Shelby was still generally unheard of. According to popular legend, a group of civic-minded men met one January night in 1923 to decide how to solve their problem. Sam Sampson, a storekeeper and landowner, suggested that a world's heavyweight championship bout would certainly capture the attention of the rest of America. As the men drank, the idea became more and more appealing. By the early morning hours it seemed positively brilliant. They were, after all, ambitious and optimistic men.[10]

Two Montana citizens were especially enthusiastic about the idea. James A. Johnson, the mayor and president of the First State Bank of Shelby, was the leading promoter in the town. A large, hearty man with sleepy eyes and a bushy walrus mustache, Johnson rode the range for thirty-five years before settling down in Shelby. He was a gambler: more than once he risked a five-figure sum on the turn of a card. Although he had become wealthy, drawing a hefty income from ranching, real estate, and oil, he had never lost his love of gambling. His entire life was an open challenge to the assumption that age breeds conservatism. At the age of fifty-eight in 1923 he looked upon the idea of staging a heavyweight championship fight as an exciting bet.[11]

The other motivating force in the initial dealings was Loy J. Molumby, a popular Great Falls attorney who had been a flyer in World War I and was now state commander of the American Legion. Somewhat younger than Johnson, Molumby had a comical appearance. A thick nose and lips combined with floppy ears and shock of coal black hair with a single white streak in the center gave him a slightly lopsided mien. But his appearance was deceptive. As events were to show, Molumby possessed the uncomical ability to convince other people to spend their money on risky ventures. Furthermore, his gift of fast talking was essential in arranging the bout.[12]

Johnson, Molumby, and a group of other Montana businessmen initiated their plans by contacting Mike Collins, a Minneapolis promoter whom they mistakenly believed to be the manager of the St. Paul heavyweight Tommy Gibbons. Wrong about Collins' connections with Gibbons, the informal committee was nevertheless astute enough to know that Gibbons was a highly rated boxer. In addition,

150

Shelby was connected with St. Paul by the tracks of the Great Northern. Thus the bout did generate enough promise to draw Collins from Minneapolis—at the expense of the Shelby group—to Montana to listen to the plans. Collins was startled by the piddling size of the town and its complete lack of facilities, but when the Shelby men drew $26,000 from their collective pockets and promised to raise that figure to $100,000 at the signing of the bout, Collins began to believe that their plan was worthy of serious consideration. He left Shelby promising to relay their plan to Dempsey and Gibbons.[13]

By April, Molumby decided that Collins was not moving fast enough. If anything was to be arranged, he reasoned, the Montana group had better do it themselves. Climbing into his single-engine airplane, Molumby began his crusade to sign Dempsey to fight in Shelby with all the religious conviction of a medieval Christian going to visit the bones of St. James. It was not an easy task. One night he had to force land in Buffalo, Wyoming, because a heavy snowstorm made the crossing of the Big Horn Mountains a dangerous gamble. In addition, Doc Kearns proved difficult to find. Through the first two weeks in April neither Molumby nor Eddie Kane, Gibbons' actual manager, was able to locate Dempsey's elusive manager. To complicate matters even further, Molumby became aware of disgruntled voices back at home. The Custer County Post of the American Legion issued a declaration, with the solemnity of the Pope issuing a bull, announcing that they would have nothing to do with the bout; that is, if Kearns was ever reached and if the bout was ever made. Their only reason was that Dempsey was a "great slacker." Similarly, an editorialist for the Helena *Independent* suggested that Molumby forget his plans before he was "snubbed, for the pugilist and his manager are looking for the almighty dollar always. Former service men count nothing with them." By the end of April the same editorialist repeated his suggestion that Molumby "quit flying around the county and come home."[14]

But spring is the season of hope. Molumby hoped that Collins' public statement that Dempsey must either accept the Shelby offer or else "crawl in his shell" would elicit a reaction from Kearns. Eventually Kearns did respond, although he initially seized the proposal

151

only as a weapon to use in his constant financial battles with Rickard. But the idea that he could control matters began to have a growing appeal for Kearns. As with the Dempsey-Miske bout of 1920, Kearns found the thought of working without the help of Rickard particularly satisfying. Finally, in the first week of May, Kearns traveled to Chicago to enter into negotiations. Molumby, who in the past weeks had slept little, changed his clothes seldom, and bathed even less frequently, had achieved his goal.[15]

They met in Chicago, and Kearns, much to his enjoyment, soon discovered that he could manipulate Molumby as easily as a five-dollar wrist watch. The negotiations at the Morrison Hotel, where Kearns and Molumby were staying, must have been amusing, if slightly suspicious, to passing bellhops and assorted guests. Molumby, whose face was showing the effect of several weeks without washing, evidently had never considered how much money the Shelby committee was willing to pay Dempsey for the fight. Given carte blanche to choose his own price, Kearns suggested and Molumby granted the figure of $300,000 plus $10,000 for training expenses, which was the same amount he received for the Carpentier fight. For a town without a boxing ring, promoter, or large city within five hundred miles, Kearns's price was more than he hoped to gain. Eddy Kane, Gibbons' manager, who had to be dealt with through an intermediary because for several years he and Kearns had refused to be in the same room with each other, was promised 50 percent of the gate from $300,000 to $600,000 and 25 percent on everything after that. After five days of negotiations, the contract was signed on May 5, 1923.[16]

The contract that Kearns signed showed all the machinations of his suspicious and cynical mind. Not only did he demand $300,000, but he required that it be paid in three installments. The first installment of $100,000 was paid when the contract was signed. The second installment of $100,000 was to be paid on June 15, and the final $100,000 had to be handed over to Kearns on July 2, forty-eight hours before the bout was scheduled. If at any time the Shelby group failed to make a payment, the bout was to be canceled and no money would be returned. With the first certified check for $100,000 in his hands, Kearns had more reason than anyone else to be optimistic about the contract.[17]

152

If, as John Lardner has suggested, Molumby tried to learn the boxing business in a few weeks and flunked the course, his return to Montana was accompanied by victorious celebrations. "Packing ten days' accumulation of Michigan Avenue grit and grime," the Great Falls *Tribune* noted, Molumby told a gathering of joyous Montanans that he expected the fight to earn from $1,000,000 to $1,400,000. He felt confident that besides making money, the bout would put Shelby on the map. As he picked and loosened dirt from his face, he told of his experiences in Chicago and then retired to his home, for "he had not washed or bathed for two weeks."[18]

Not everyone shared Molumby's optimism. A Billings *Gazette* editorial observed that the bout would cost Montana a great deal of money. Tex Rickard also suspected the fight would not be staged on firm financial ground. True, Rickard had promoted major bouts in such towns as Toledo, Reno, and Goldfield, Nevada, but, as he told reporters, those matches had not guaranteed the champion $300,000. If, Rickard continued, Shelby could draw enough people to make the fight a financial success—a not very likely possibility—there would be no way for the cowtown authorities to control, feed, or house the people. On this sour note, Rickard wished Shelby all the luck in the world.[19]

By the middle of May, Dempsey was training in Montana. His arrival in Great Falls, where he had chosen to set up his training quarters, drew the largest crowd ever at the Great Northern terminal. Laughter and cheers greeted the champion as he paraded through the city's business district, and the crowd was overjoyed when Dempsey jumped off his car's running board, marched with the band, and even tried his hand at beating the big drum. The town's display of emotion was so overwhelmingly in favor of the champion that a self-righteous editorialist for the Helena *Independent* saw fit to review Dempsey's past and caution the Great Falls populace about being overenthusiastic.[20]

The editorial fell on the deaf ears; Great Falls continued its love affair with Dempsey. And the champion returned the affection. His every public action was tempered with kindness and simple humanity. He attended the Montana Hereford Breeders' Association show, praised the stock, and ended the night by purchasing the two prize bulls. At his training camp he refereed on his knees a bout between two kids, occasionally sinking to the canvas himself when one of the pipecleaner-armed children accidentally hit him with a pillow-sized glove. Another night he raised three hundred dollars for the St. Thomas orphanage by boxing an exhibition bout with Billy Wells, the welterweight champion of England. The town's attitude toward Dempsey was aptly summarized by Bob Dorman, who wrote a personal interest story on the champion. The card-playing, animal-loving boxer was pictured as an "overgrown boy," more at home climbing a tree or executing a practical joke than battering another man's face.[21]

Of course, much of Dempsey's good humor can be attributed to the benevolent attitudes of those who wrote about him. Yet Dempsey did enjoy the training period. He felt at home among the cotton-woods and cold, clear streams. His training was frequently interrupted for fishing trips to the Missouri River or for walks into the hills around his Cascade County training site. When he celebrated his twenty-eighth birthday on June 24, he was joined by his father, two brothers (Johnny and Bernie), a cousin, and a host of friends and hangers-on. His camp was given a final rustic touch by scores of barnyard animals that wandered around the grounds during the training.[22]

The upcoming bout, however, was never far from the front of Dempsey's mind. Grantland Rice remembered that the champion gave himself daily facials with bear grease to toughen his face to the "general texture of a boar's hide." Dempsey understood that two years of easy living had to be tortured out of his body before he climbed into the ring with Gibbons. Those who had to pay for Dempsey's return to physical greatness were his sparring partners. In the ring, whether with a sparring partner or a leading contender, he showed no mercy. In Freudian terms he was the embodiment of the unleashed, primitive id. Most boxers, when they were training, would let up when they hurt a sparring partner, reasoning that nothing would be gained by flooring an inferior fighter. But, as Paul Gallico has commented, Dempsey "treated each and every one of them as his personal enemy as soon as he entered the ring. He seemed to have a constant and bottomless well of cold fury somewhere close to his throat."[23]

Today we see only the stained glass image of Dempsey, the genial, smiling former champion, quick with a slap on the back and an offer of a drink. The cruel, merciless Dempsey is buried deep, or, possibly, has been driven out of his body. But the Dempsey of 1923 wore his violence as proudly as his crown. Gallico recorded a wrestling match between Dempsey and Joe Benjamin, a lightweight fighter who was kept at the Great Falls camp as a stooge and a jester, that ended with the champion bringing his knee up into Benjamin's groin. This variety of playfulness was common. In amiable roughness, Dempsey once hit Gus Wilson, a friend and occasionally his trainer, a "playful tap" on the side which caused Wilson to be hospitalized and have his kidney removed. Such a man was not easy to spar with.[24]

Getting ready for Gibbons, Dempsey hit his sparring partners with a fragilely controlled savagery; he split open their skin, broke their noses, bruised their lips, and damaged their ribs. When one was knocked down, he waited for him to rise and then knocked him down again. Occasionally, some aspiring heavyweight with more ambition than intelligence would challenge Dempsey to box several rounds. One such fighter, Ben Wray, stood seven feet two inches and weighed over 250 pounds. A crowd of fifteen hundred persons watched Dempsey shatter Wray's jaw in less than half a minute. Fortunately, Wray did not have to fight the champion again, but Jack Burke, Frank Powers, Marty Farrell, George Godfrey, and other sparring partners had to fight Dempsey day after day.[25]

As Dempsey honed himself to do violence, Shelby prepared for its day of glory. Shelby had all the personality of a boom town. Its rutted, dirty Main Street—not a road in Shelby or a highway leading into the city was paved—was lined with billiard halls, drugstores, and an assortment of other stores that usually began their names with "Oil City." Although most of Shelby's bars had been forced by the prohibition laws at least to remove their signs, Aunt Kate's Cathouse still proudly and publicly advertised its business. When there was no rain the narrow streets bustled with competition between Model-T Fords and horses, but when the streets were wet the horses were left without rivals. It was a town, then, that in many ways recalled the late nineteenth-century towns of Deadwood, Dodge City, and

155

Cheyenne, a town where horses still fed in troughs along the streets and men occasionally wore guns.[26]

The excitement generated by the upcoming fight did not change Shelby so much as it accelerated the community's tendency toward sordid activity and lawlessness. As early as the end of May, the Helena *Independent* noted that "cafés, cabarets and dance halls with names rivaling those of San Francisco and New York are springing up like mushrooms." The observation makes a fine distinction: the Shelby establishments rivaled their counterparts only in colorful names, not in the quality of their offerings. But one could dance at such dancehalls as the King Tut or the Green Lite, if one could find a woman in a town whose population counted only one female for every twenty males. And a visitor could discover some sort of rudimentary entertainment at such cabarets as the Days of '49, the Black Cat, the Blue Goose, the Cave, or the Day by Day in Every Way, the Red Onion, the Pup, the Turf, and Jack and Jill might even be visited by an adventurous person who was looking for something different in the line of cuisine. This atmosphere was extended to twenty-four hours per day when Mayor Jim Johnson eliminated the traditional ten o'clock curfew. After the symbolic burial of the keys to the dancehalls under the site for the forthcoming fight, the sheiklike orchestra at the King Tut could compete all night and day with the country band at the Mustang.[27]

With daily reports of liquor-guzzling and gambling streaming out of Shelby, it was not long before John Law intervened. Before the end of the first week in June, the Montana attorney general, Wellington D. Rankin, cautioned the town either to "clean up" and restore "law and order" or to suffer the consequences of a canceled fight. "Shelby," said Rankin, "shall not be the rendezvous of thugs, yeggs, plug-uglies, pickpockets, gamblers, rum-runners, or any other class of anarchists who make a living by defying the law and the constitution." However, after Rankin visited Shelby, he reported to Montana that perhaps the descriptions of lawlessness and debauchery in Shelby had been exaggerated. This general conclusion was substantiated by several Great Falls reporters who ventured into Shelby in search of "wild and woolly and wicked" activities. They tried the Black Cat and then visited the Days of '49, but in both places the most wicked thing to be found was the horrible bray of the local jazz bands.[28]

Nightlife, however, was not Shelby's only area of expansion. In order to stage the bout and accommodate the expected sudden increase in the town's population, the leading citizens of Shelby began a program of frenzied building. John Humphrey, a Montana building contractor, was hired to construct an arena to house the event. He responded by employing over two hundred carpenters who built a solid, wood hexagonal arena which could seat 40,268. In addition, the Great Northern Railroad laid over thirty-five miles of side tracks to meet the needs of the forthcoming fight. The visiting spectators would eat and sleep in the railroad cars that carried them to the fight.[29]

Because the railroad was the only sure way into and out of Shelby, railway facilities gained an increased importance. Special Pullman trains were commissioned to carry people from Philadelphia, New York, Boston, Chicago, San Francisco, and other major cities to Shelby. The Metropolitan Special out of New York, for example, promised an eight-day excursion that included sightseeing, fight tickets, sleeping accommodations, and meals for only $150.[30] The promoters of the affair counted on these special trains to carry enough spectators to Shelby to make the bout a financial successs. And the plan was not an altogether bad one. But it did leave them particularly susceptible to train schedules and, more important, vulnerable to doubt. Any doubt that the bout would occur would have a devastating effect on the gate.

This doubt arose when the second payment was due, and the Shelby boom almost became an onomatopoeia. As the day for the second payment of $100,000 drew nearer, the Shelby group confidently told the press that the money was already in the bank. Mayor Johnson, who had become the leader of the group, treated the financial matters as if they were the least of his worries, so when Kearns was called to a hurried meeting about heretofore unmentioned problems he assumed a shocked, even hurt, attitude. As the promoters told Kearns on the afternoon of June 15, they were unable to pay him the entire $100,000. When pressed by Kearns for a more specific figure, Johnson revealed that there was only $1,600 available. If

157

Kearns's earlier surprise and shock were faked, there was nothing counterfeit about his reaction to this revelation. He told the press that if the money was not in his hands in twenty-four hours he would entertain offers for a new site for the fight.[31]

Kearns's willingness to bolt Montana and his near eagerness to move the bout to another city was as unnerving as the promoters' lack of funds. Conferences were called, and a new cast of characters entered the limelight. Molumby, who was under attack from the national American Legion organization for his participation in the affair, dropped entirely out of the picture; as a boxing promoter he was now a recognized and an experienced failure. Mayor Johnson also dropped from public view, though he continued to be the single most powerful force behind the scenes. The new group of promoters, representing the business elite from the Great Falls area, was headed by George Stanton, the thin, gray-haired president of the Stanton Bank and Trust Company. He was joined by Dan Tracy, mining operator and hotel owner; Shirley Ford, vice-president of the Great Falls National Bank; Russell and Arthur Strain, department store owners; and Senator J. W. Speer, lawyer and former judge. It was this group, which comprised the financial and moral leadership of Great Falls, that met on the evening of June 15, to decide how the reputation of Montana could best be saved.[32]

The new committee tried to convince Kearns to take the remainder due to himself and Dempsey from the gate, but the wily manager refused to modify the contract. It was a matter of principle, he said; whenever money owed him was at stake, Kearns was one of the most principled men who ever lived. When the committee raised their offer to 50,000 sheep in lieu of the money, Kearns continued to stand on the "principle of the thing"; furthermore, as he later reported, "what the hell would I do with 50,000 sheep in a New York apartment?" He gave the full story to the reporters who gathered in the lobby of the Great Falls hotel where he was staying: "Dempsey wants to fight and we are ready to go, but I want these promoters to live up to their contract. They have got until 12 o'clock tonight [June 16] to make good." Otherwise, Kearns revealed he would accept a generous offer to transfer the bout to Cleveland.[33]

The crisis was averted on June 16. The full $100,000, was paid to

Kearns, who then admitted that he had always had the most implicit trust in the integrity of the honorable men with whom he was dealing. Fortunately, Kearns did not know how close the committee had been to allowing him to shift his show to Cleveland. The $100,000 was raised only through the personal force of Mayor Jim Johnson. Johnson leased his own cattle and oil land, borrowed from close friends, and "begged" the rest from Stanton. Although Stanton eventually succumbed to Johnson's pressure, he insisted on a complete reorganization of the promotional committee. As a result, Dan Tracy, the bull-necked, balding owner of the Park Hotel in Great Falls, was given full authority over all future negotiations with Kearns. Known for his conservative business habits, Stanton correctly guessed that Tracy would take a more serious look at the financial underpinnings of the match.[34]

Stanton's committee may well have won the battle and lost the war. The fragile public confidence that lay beneath the eggshell promotional techniques used by Johnson and his cohorts had been shattered by Shelby's failure to raise the second $100,000. At the Higgins Cigar Store in Shelby, the official site for buying tickets, requests for tickets began to dwindle. An editorialist for the Helena *Independent*, who had been against the bout from the first, rhetorically asked what happened to Shelby's fabled, oil-rich millionaires. He added that it was a shame that Great Falls citizens had also "lost their heads over a prizefighter." But of even more concern was the reaction of the large urban centers. The New York *Times*, which had earlier commended Shelby's promotional efforts, now remarked that "the promotion of a big bout is nowadays a business for experts."[35] The adverse publicity threatened ticket sales and train charters.

Installed into his new post, Dan Tracy began the herculean task of extricating the bout from the financial quagmire and placing it on solid, black-ink ground. He checked the books— or what passed for the books—oversaw ticket sales, and tried to grasp the subtle intricacies of the concession business. But he always returned to the crucial question raised by the New York *Tribune* when he took over his new duties: where will the third $100,000 payment come from? It was not an easily answered question, but after wrestling with it for eleven sleepless nights, Tracy emerged with an answer: simply put, there was no possible way that Shelby, Great Falls, or Montana citizens could raise the money short of a large tax on cowboy boots. Once Tracy realized that making the third $100,000 payment was beyond hope and that he could not guarantee that any investor would be repaid, he submitted his resignation and returned to the hotel business.[36]

In the midst of the dismal financial revelations, Shelby lost something of its carefree spirit and became more like a town occupied by foreign troops. Grantland Rice, who traveled to Shelby to cover the fight for the New York *Tribune,* commented that although Kearns had not yet seized the oil wells or the post office, Shelby must certainly know how Germans in the Ruhr Valley felt. Assuming the role of a Shelbyite, he declared, "Germany's lucky compared with us," and he enunciated the motto of "peace at any price." The New York *Times's* correspondent in Shelby, Elmer Davis, sounded a similar note. Noting that both in Shelby and in Germany the people who signed the contracts were soon replaced, Davis wrote that "Shelby and Great Falls are full of ex-managers, ex-treasurers, and ex-attachés of the fight, just as Berlin is full of ex-excellencies." Finally, the continual rainfall and the muddy streets and fields led another sports writer, who had been a war correspondent in France, to remark that "next to the late war this prize fight [is] the muddiest and muddiedest affair [I] have ever seen."[37]

If Shelby was an occupied town, then the general of the army of occupation was Kearns. To say that he became one of the most hated men in Montana as the fight neared would be an understatement. To the small-town westerners, who already distrusted anything that smacked of an eastern city, Kearns symbolized the big city slicker. In an attempt to live up to his title of the "Beau Brummel of Main Street," Kearns roamed the streets of Shelby and Great Falls in a pleated Norfolk jacket, neatly fitted riding breeches, and stylish leather riding boots. His slick, urbane image was accentuated by his pugnacious attitude toward money. He became the Shylock who demanded his pound of flesh in three installments. He was doggedly determined to have the $300,000 in cash before Dempsey took one step into the ring with Gibbons. Far from sympathizing with Shelby's plight, Kearns repeatedly announced his readiness to move the fight elsewhere. After Tracy's resignation, for example, Kearns told reporters that a St. Paul promoter, with the symbolical name of Jack Reddy, was willing to pay him $200,000 to stage the fight in Gibbons' home town. By the end of June the reporters for the New York *Times* and New York *Tribune* noted that the financial problem and Kearns's inflexibility guaranteed that the bout would be "a bust."[38]

Just as the match seemed on the verge of complete collapse, Shelbyites and Montanans mustered new optimism. George H. Stanton again was the man to make the announcement. After a night of conferences and negotiations, he told reporters that "the $100,000 due Jack Dempsey next Monday has been raised, and will be in cash in the banks here [Great Falls] not later than tomorrow night." The plan to raise the money, as Stanton disclosed, involved a pledge from twenty prominent Montanans to contribute $5,000 each. It was not an investment for financial gain; it was an investment for the honor of Montana. "We felt," Stanton said on behalf of the group, "that Montana owed it to the world to stage this fight. . . . It would have been a disgrace to have the fight called off." Furthermore, Stanton named Major J. E. Lane of Lewistown, Montana, as the trustee for the entire twenty. Lane had already invested heavily in the arena, and he had been injured in an airplane crash during a promotional tour with Loy Molumby and one of Jim Johnson's sons. Therefore, to enter once again into promotion of the bout was, as Elmer Davis observed, "an act of commendable heroism which few men would have attempted."[39]

Kearns accepted Stanton's announcement with a face "wreathed in smiles." After Kearns turned down a ranch said to be worth $150,000 in lieu of the last payment, Montana's attorney general, W. D. Rankin, criticized the manager's ruthless commercialism, and suggested that Kearns should give Montana a "sporting chance" and forget about the final $100,000. But Kearns proved to be no sport. He wanted his money, all $100,000, paid on July 2. As a New York *Times* editorialist commented, to forget the last payment "might be generous—it even might be noble—but it would not be business, which is what pugilism has come to be."[40] The nation's leading newspaper was correct; boxing had become a business, subject to agreements, provisions, attachments, contracts, and injunctions. And the leading manager-cum-businessman was Doc Kearns.

On the morning of July 2, Kearns, full of the spirit of free enterprise, went to Stanton's bank to collect the final payment. He was met by Stanton who informed him that many of the Montanans who had pledged $5,000 had not lived up to their commitments; and the money that was received had been sent back to the proper owners. In short, there was no $100,000. Another series of conferences and more confusion followed. There was talk of moving the fight either to July 20 or 25. The New York *Tribune* greeted eastern readers with a headline announcing, "Fight Is Called Off." Throughout the day of July 2, hundreds of people milled around Stanton's bank waiting for some word about the status of the fight. But no messages leaked out of the closed doors; no announcements were made.[41]

Inside the bank, Kearns conferred, uninterrupted, with Lane, Stanton, Molumby, and Judge Roy E. Ayres, who had become involved in the promotion after Tracy's resignation. They talked, adjourned to eat, regrouped, talked some more, and then went home without a decision. About 11:00 P.M. Kearns and several other men met again at the bank. Shortly before midnight, Lane was awakened and brought to the conference room. At 2:43 A.M., the announcement was made. The bout would be staged as planned. Kearns, Lane added, had agreed to take over the promotion of the fight, and the gate receipts with it. Kearns and Dempsey were to get the first $100,000 of the revenue taken in, and the original promoters were to pay the expenses, including the purses of the preliminary fighters, Dempsey's training expenses, and the salary of the referee.[42]

Only on the day before the fight was there any guarantee that there would be a fight at all. Thus the eastern crowd was all but eliminated. Of course, the reporters from the East were there, and Grantland Rice informed his eastern readers about his trip west in a parody of "The Road to Mandalay":

Where the mist is on the wheatfields and the
sun is droppin' low:
Where the Rockies rise in splendor is the
route that I must go:
Where the caravan is windin' through the
sultry sweep of June,
And I only hope that Dempsey doesn't end
the show too soon.[43]

162

But except for the reporters, few eastern accents were heard in Shelby in the days before the bout. Even the Pacific Northwest failed to supply the crowd that the promoters had anticipated. At the end of June, Stanton had assumed that "the northwest will put the fight over. The Dakotas, Wyoming, Idaho, Washington, Oregon and western Canada will send at least 15,000 people to Shelby."[44] Yet if the Northwest sent 15,000 people to Shelby, very few of them had purchased tickets by the eve of the fight.

The men—and a very few women—who wandered about the muddy streets of Shelby on the eve of the bout resembled a frontier fight crowd. The arrival of Battling Nelson, the unabashedly unhygienic, former lightweight champion who caused such a stir in Toledo, was prepared for with an extra barrel of lemonade in case the Battler got the swimming urge again. From Palm Beach, the Baker party found its way to Shelby. Mrs. Raymond T. Baker, formerly Mrs. Alfred G. Vanderbilt, was joined by several other New York and Boston worthies who had been vacationing in Palm Beach. The other end of the social spectrum was admirably represented by One-Eyed Connolly, whose sole occupation seemed to involve crashing the gates of parties and prize fights. These people were joined by a liberal sampling of oil millionaires, cowboys, Blackfoot Indians, shepherds, sports writers, and sleepless local citizens.[45]

The local citizens were not the only people who went without sleep on the night before the fight. Although most of the publicity Shelby attracted was undesirable, it is a fact that the town had become the focal point of the nation. The scenario was to be repeated in other small towns in the 1920s. Dayton, Tennessee, for instance, was to have its flirtation with immortality in the summer of 1925. But Shelby was the first of the instant fame towns of the twenties, and nobody there wanted to miss any of the action. The girlie tent shows, the best of which featured a blonde named Patsy Salmon in such short dramas as *Which One Shall I Marry?*, *The Tie That Binds*, and *The Sweetest Girl in Dixie*, played to full houses. And Aunt Kate's Cathouse did not lack customers. But mostly the people just wandered around the small town, breathed in the prefight atmosphere, and waited for the sun to rise and chase away the chilly night.[46]

The streets were crowded early on the day of the fight. Some

163

people had tried to sleep for several hours in their automobiles, but even in the twenties cars were not built to provide sleeping quarters for five or more persons. Visitors who slept for a few hours in hotels were, in many cases, packed ten to fifteen persons per room. Grantland Rice estimated that each person received a space just large enough for a cot. It was not surprising, then, that the cloudless sky and early morning heat made the day impossible for late sleepers.[47]

By late morning the crowd began to move toward the arena on the outskirts of town. Two bands, the Montana State Elks band and the Scottish Highlanders of Calgary, led the way with an appropriate selection of marching tunes. However, only a few of the estimated 10,000 people in the crowd produced one of the poorly printed tickets (a Chicago printer had spelled the name of the county O'Toole rather than Toole) and entered the stadium. The rest milled around the entrance gates, complaining about the high price of the tickets and generally just waiting to see what would happen. Eventually, about 2:50, the cut-rate prices were announced, and the remainder of the crowd filtered into the arena with tickets costing only about 20 percent of their original value. One-Eyed Connolly lived up to his promise to crash the gate, and when a spontaneous rush was made from the cheap seats to the expensive seats, One-Eyed led the charge.[48]

The inside of the arena presented a picture which would strike fear into the heart of any promoter. "Picture a feast fit for the gods," a reporter for the Great Falls *Tribune* wrote, "a banquet table groaning with epicurean delights, set for hundreds. Then visualize a few dozen guests strolling in, and one has something of the Dempsey-Gibbons fight atmosphere." The expensive seats were filled with somewhere between 10,000 to 25,000 spectators, but the rest of the 40,000-seat arena was empty. The stadium looked like a large white saucer with a spoonful of peas in the center. For the promoters, the empty seats marked the difference between a financial success and a bust. The total gate for the fight was only slightly over $200,000.[49]

By one o'clock, when the first preliminary was scheduled to begin, the sun made the pine arena a hot and uncomfortable place. Sitting at ringside, Grantland Rice was unable to touch the steel frame of his typewriter. The oldest and most illustrious member of the press corps, Otto Floto of Denver, who had covered every heavyweight championship bout in the last forty years, told Rice that the only fight that he could remember that was held on a hotter day was the championship fight between John L. Sullivan and Jake Kilrain in July, 1889. The heat forced men to remove their coats and collars and to mop their faces with gaudy colored handkerchiefs. Only James K. Keeley, a Pullman Company official who was dressed in a white linen suit and wore an African pith helmet, seemed prepared for the heat.[50]

The early bouts generated little interest, but many spectators paid more respectful attention when Sergeant Jim McMahon entered the ring at one o'clock. The American military hero who had gone overseas in 1914 with the Canadian forces and who had been blinded during the war was led into the ring where he sang several stirring ballads. Rice and other reporters were reminded of Dempsey's war record, an issue that was not quite dead. Indeed the New York *Tribune* had noted that same day that neither state nor national honor meant anything to Dempsey: "He is no more willing to fight for the honor of an individual state in 1923 than he was to fight for the honor of his nation in 1917."[51] But this issue lost substance in Shelby when it was remembered that Gibbons also stayed in America during the war years.

At 3:36 Dempsey slipped between the ropes and entered the ring. His entourage was large: in addition to such usual cornermen as Kearns, Bernard Dempsey, and Jack Burke, it contained two heavily armed bodyguards, "Senator" Wild Bill Lyons, and Mike Trent. As his cornermen rubbed his shoulders and legs and used an umbrella to shield the champion from the sun, Lyons and Trent suspiciously watched the crowd. Although Dempsey had disagreed with Kearns's policy of holding out for the full $300,000, the crowd tended to identify the champion with crass commercialism. Dempsey's reception reflected this animosity; the applause he received was mixed with boos and was far short of an ovation. But he was brown as a nut and ready to fight.[52]

Five minutes after Dempsey entered the ring, a chorus of cheers greeted Gibbons. The city of Shelby had openly adopted the St. Paul fighter who kept his wife and kids at his training camp and was willing to fight Dempsey knowing full well that he would not receive a nickel for his efforts. It was a case of a gambling town falling in love with a gambling fighter; or, perhaps, it was the psychic affinity that links losers. Gibbons was small for a heavyweight; indeed, boxing authority Nat Fleischer refused to recognize Gibbons as a heavyweight but ranked him as the eighth-best light heavyweight of all time. Although he never won a title, he boxed such champions as George Chip, Battling Levinsky, Harry Greb, Georges Carpentier, and Gene Tunney. Furthermore, it was not until his last fight in 1925 against Tunney that he was knocked out. Altogether, his boxing skill, ring savvy, and record earned him induction into the Boxing Hall of Fame in 1964, three years after he died and five years after his brother was given the same honor.[53] However, when Gibbons entered the Shelby ring in 1923 he had just passed his peak, and he knew that the Dempsey fight would be his only chance to win the title.

It was unusual for the champion to climb into the ring before the challenger, but a far more bizarre circumstance faced the two fighters. There was no referee in sight. James Daugherty, Dempsey's old friend whom Kearns had named as the referee in the contract signed in Chicago, had been guaranteed $5,000, been paid nothing, and so refused to enter the ring until he received the money. Unlike Gibbons, Daugherty was not willing to work for free, and he knew Kearns too well to expect to be paid after the bout. So while the fighters waited under ring umbrellas, Daugherty was on strike in the locker room area. Finally, about four o'clock, Daugherty ended his holdout, climbed into the ring, and started the fight. It was official: after more than two months of uncertainty, a heavyweight championship fight was underway in Shelby.[54]

The actual bout was a classic matchup that fell far short of being a classic fight. It featured boxer versus puncher, but something in the chemistry of the matchup was amiss. Dempsey started the bout as usual by pounding away at his opponent's body. He crowded Gibbons, forcing him into the ropes, and scoring with short lefts and rights to the stomach and kidney region. Gibbons responded by back peddling and clinching. Without doing anything spectacular, Dempsey fought three solid rounds and then shifted his attack from the body to the head. To do this, Dempsey had to stop crowding Gib-

166

bons; he needed leverage and distance to obtain knockout power. However, when Gibbons had the room and the time to maneuver, he was easily able to outbox Dempsey and to avoid being hit. In the fourth, fifth, and sixth rounds Dempsey received a boxing lesson. Nine minutes of frustration were enough to convince Dempsey to go back to his crowding, pushing style. He returned to the heart and rib punches and was successful. Round after round, Dempsey flailed away. Gibbons was never again in control. For the remainder of the fight it was "Dempsey tearing in, his lip often curled back over his white teeth as a wolf sometimes looks, driving desperately to bring his man down." But at the end of the fight Gibbons was still on his feet. Certainly, Dempsey was the clear victor, but the gold of Toledo and Jersey City was tarnished.[55]

When the bout ended and the decision was announced, bottles and seat cushions were thrown into the ring; it was not a protest against the decision as much as it was a comment on the entire affair. Kearns, of course, recognized the signs of discontent—a bottle barely missed his head—and along with Lyons and Trent quickly ushered the champion out of the arena. By private car he was taken to the Shelby railroad station, and from there he was shipped to Great Falls. The next day, accompanied by his father, Trent, and several other friends he left Great Falls en route to Salt Lake City. Both his eyes were discolored and there was a small cut above his left eyebrow, but he joked with the large crowd that showed up at the train station to wish him well. Behind lay the twenty-one-room mansion that had served as his home for the past several months. The same day a $1,750 suit for damages to the house was filed in circuit court. As a local reporter commented, with the exit of Dempsey, "Great Falls started the march back to normalcy."[56]

Kearns's exit lacked the tranquility of Dempsey's departure. Carrying the gate from the fight—estimates range from $30,000 to $80,000—in two large canvas sacks, Kearns slipped out of Shelby under the cover of night. He had been scheduled to meet Johnson and the other promoters at one of the local saloons, but at the last moment he decided that there was nothing to talk about. For $500 an engineer hooked a caboose to his engine and took Kearns to Great Falls. He spent that night in the cellar of a Great Falls barbershop.

The next day he left Montana. From the first he had looked upon the bout only as a business venture, but there were many Montanans who believed that Kearns's sense of business was a trifle too highly developed.[57]

Montanans were not the only Americans who doubted the propriety of Kearns's business ethic. In the 1920s sports became a big business, and no sport more so than boxing. The days when men fought for a ten-dollar side bet and a round of beers ended about the same time that the Great War concluded. In the twenties boxing was commercialized; it became a "'big business,' an industry controlled by big businessmen, run on business principles, financed by banks and licensed and supervised by state laws and officials, just as banking and insurance." The transition from amateurism to commercialism in sports that took place during the decade brought with it a host of questions. Many Americans believed it was immoral to pay an athlete more money than the president earned. Others found the notion that a man could become rich by playing games a disquieting thought. Even supporters of the sport questioned the propriety of the situation. Nat Fleischer, editor of the *Ring*, believed that Kearns and Dempsey were killing the goose that laid the golden egg: "The bloomer at Shelby was the butcher ripping open the goose." Another advocate of the sport noted that in the "old days" fighters engaged one another for the love of the sport or the desire for fame. But those days had vanished: "The modern fighter of any distinction fights for the clang of the cash register, and the clang of the cash register never echoed more loudly than in the recent contest between Jack Dempsey and Tom Gibbons."[58]

It was in Shelby that the new status of boxing was most painfully felt. Early reports claiming that the businessmen of Shelby, Great Falls, and other Montana towns had lost only about $80,000 in the fight were overly optimistic. It was later revealed that Jim Johnson, the mayor of Shelby who paid much of the first two payments out of his own pocket, personally lost at least $140,000. In addition, the lumber used in the construction of the stadium was never fully paid for, nor did the concessionaires make a profit.[59] Except for a few hotel and restaurant owners, not a man in Montana made a cent from the fight.

But the most unfortunate fact was that hundreds of people who had absolutely nothing to do with the promotion of the bout lost money. On July 9, 1923, less than one week after the bout, the Stanton Trust and Savings Bank of Great Falls closed its doors. The bank's failure was blamed on the general postwar economic conditions; but Montanans realized that $73,000 of the second $100,000 payment had come from Stanton's bank. The run was on. On the next day, the First State Bank of Shelby, whose president was Mayor James A. Johnson, was forced to close its doors. This time it was publicly admitted that the money spent on the promotion of the fight had left the bank short of funds. The following afternoon, the First State Bank of Joplin, Montana, an affiliate of Stanton's bank, was forced to suspend operations. The closing was "generally accredited" to the championship bout. On August 16 the First National Bank of Shelby was closed by its board of directors. In his later years, Kearns was fond of leaning back in his well-stuffed chair in his Madison Square Garden office and telling how Dempsey and he—with the emphasis on the *he*—broke four Montana banks.[60]

Shelby recovered. Fresh strikes in the Kevin-Sunburst oil field restored the town's shaken economy and rebuilt the personal fortunes of such men as Johnson. A native of Montana, Tony Dalich, was proud to write in 1965 that "today the [banking] institutions and economy of Shelby are notably solid." But Shelby did not forget. The fight put Shelby on the map, and even today its claim to notoriety is that it staged a heavyweight championship fight between Jack Dempsey and Tommy Gibbons on July 4, 1923. As Mayor Johnson was leaving the arena on that hot July day, a reporter asked him for a comment, and he replied, "Well, we saw a fight, didn't we?"[61]

CHAPTER IX

The Greatest Fight
Since the
Silurian Age

E IGHT days after Jack Dempsey defeated Tommy Gibbons, Jess
Willard attempted a comeback. Although he was nearly
forty-two years old, Willard was still a commanding figure at
the box office. On July 12, 1923, when he fought Luis Firpo at
Boyle's Thirty Acres in Jersey City, close to 100,000 people attended
the match. Before the fight the tunnels under the Hudson River were
crowded with traffic, and every ferry boat to Jersey City was brimming with passengers. An additional 5,000 fans milled around the
New York Times Building on Times Square awaiting news of the
event. At the scene of the bout, it appeared to one reporter that "Every high-pitch man, soft-drink vendor and peanut man east of the
Mississippi . . . had been conscripted to service." [1] It was the greatest
crowd ever to witness a sporting event in America up to that time.
Sitting at ringside were Flo Ziegfeld, Mrs. W. K. Vanderbilt, James
M. Cox, Charles Ried, James Hill, A. J. Drexel Biddle, Jr., and Sr.,
Walter Phelps, and many other noted figures. In fact, the list of important persons present at the fight filled an entire column—from
top to bottom—in the New York *Times*. Everyone had assembled on
the hot night to watch the aged Willard box the virtually unknown
Argentine fighter. Surveying the crowd, columnist Boyden Sparkes
of the New York *Tribune* commented that only a duel between
George Washington and Simon Bolívar would have attracted as
much attention. [2]

For seven rounds Willard avoided Firpo's wild rushes and parried
the Latin American's telegraphed punches. Firpo's complete lack of

skill and anything resembling finesse was apparent to everyone who watched the bout. But Firpo was equipped with strength and limitless courage, two factors that became evident as the fight progressed and Willard tired. In the eighth round Firpo once again rushed wildly at Willard, but this time he landed a solid right cross on the former champion's jaw. The crowd, which had been overwhelmingly for the North American, was shocked and quiet as the referee counted over Willard. At the count of six, Willard struggled to get up, but his right leg was twitching with temporary paralysis. Slumping back down onto the canvas, he was counted out. Then the cheering started again, this time for Firpo. Sparkes believed there was a noble element in the renewed excitement: "When [the Latin Americans] read [about the applause] in the morning's issue of 'La Nacion' perhaps they will be less resentful of the Monroe Doctrine, of marines in Nicaragua, of the Panama Canal, of the Mexican War and Yankee—as they interpret it—imperialism." Then, he concluded, Latins will begin to buy "American automobiles, American drugs, American hardware, [and] American clothing."[3]

If Sparkes misjudged the economic consequences of the fight, he was nevertheless correct in his belief that the outcome would not be ignored. Two men at ringside at once understood what the fight portended in terms of dollars and cents. Doc Kearns remarked to Tex Rickard that Firpo would make a splendid opponent for Dempsey. He suggested Labor Day as a possible date for the fight, and Rickard agreed. Firpo's victory came as a windfall to Rickard and Kearns. If the Latin was an unknown quantity, at least he had never been beaten by Dempsey. If Firpo was not a good fighter, he was exciting and wild and promotionally attractive. Before Rickard left Boyle's Thirty Acres, he was determined to promote a Dempsey-Firpo contest.

Not everyone at ringside, however, was so sanguine about the possibilities of a Dempsey-Firpo contest. After watching Firpo rush about the ring like a bull out of control, many spectators concurred with the New York *Times:* "In his victory Firpo showed little which would justify matching him against Dempsey, not at least, until he has further seasoning and plenty of it." Until then, a fit Dempsey "would slaughter Firpo." Jimmy DeForest, Dempsey's former trainer who had been hired to train Firpo, agreed. If Firpo attempted to fight Dempsey in less than four months, DeForest told reporters, he would be "entering a slaughter house." Perhaps the most cogent assessment of Firpo's ability appeared in the editorial column of the New York *Tribune*'s sports section. The writer noted Firpo's remarkable strength and "untamed and untaught right hand," but concluded that an "uncultivated right hand is a meager weapon with which to attack Jack Dempsey."[4]

Firpo's lack of seasoning did not influence Rickard, who remained deaf to all criticism of the Argentine. As Rickard demonstrated in the Dempsey-Carpentier bout, he intuitively understood the dynamics of promotion. When he watched Firpo, Rickard was more impressed by the crowd's reaction to the Latin than by Firpo's fighting ability. More than anything else, Firpo inspired passion. Ruggedly handsome, his hair swept back off his forehead in a smooth, greasy pompadour, and with great, soulful eyes, Firpo had the appearance of a matinee idol. In Latin America, and especially Argentina, he had become a national hero even before the Willard fight. One sportsman who had spent a year in Latin America during Firpo's rise to prominence reported that Latin entrepreneurs were producing Firpo Film Remover toothpaste, Firpo cigars, Firpo Form Fitting Shoes, Firpo Fedoras, Firpo Fuzz Eradicator razors, Firpo Soap, Firpo Form Fitting evening suits, Firpo Finger Rings, and Firpo Fantasy perfume. Streets were being renamed Firpo Avenue, and babies were being christened Firpo or Firpoa, depending upon their sex. When this charisma was coupled with the cheering Rickard heard after the Firpo-Willard fight, the promoter was convinced that a Dempsey-Firpo match would be a powerful drawing card.[5]

After the fiasco in Shelby, both Dempsey and Kearns were willing, even eager, to have Rickard promote future championship fights. For if Kearns regarded the Shelby promotion as a precious memory, Dempsey, whose personality was always the more placid of the two, remembered his fight with Gibbons as a nightmare. Of course, Kearns was not about to accept the first set of terms Rickard offered. The two men agreed that Dempsey should fight Firpo, but they differed on the matter of money. Rickard believed that $300,000 and a share of the motion picture rights, the same deal as the Carpentier fight, was a fair set of terms for Dempsey and Kearns. It was Kearns's conviction that he and Dempsey should receive more money. Promoter and manager conferred on July 14, but after an hour and a half they could only agree that Dempsey and Firpo would, indeed, be a great match. More conferences in Rickard's Madison Square Garden office followed. Eventually, the two men discovered a price that they could both agree upon. Dempsey and Kearns would receive 37.5 percent of the gate, which, as it turned out, meant that the two earned over $500,000. Firpo agreed to accept 12.5 percent of the gate. At a press conference, Rickard announced that the bout would be held on September 14 at the Polo Grounds.[6]

Once again there was outrage over the price Kearns demanded and received. It was reasoned that after the Shelby fight promoters and boxers would return to the saner, i.e., lower, financial ground of the pre-Dempsey era. After noting that professional boxing had lost "all sense of proportion," an editorialist for the San Francisco Chronicle continued, "Fortunately, the Shelby affair has given the public a jolt. There may be a chance now that prize fighting will get back on a more sensible plane." But he was mistaken; few people could understand that professional boxing was not going to return to its pre-World War I economic or social status. Throughout Dempsey's career moralists would continue to protest the boxer's salary and the propriety of prize fighting, but to no effect. As writers proclaimed from their columns in the New York Times, boxing had become a "key industry" and prize fighters had become "capitalists."[7]

Financial criticism, pro or con, did not concern Rickard as he prepared for the bout. Of more immediate concern was Firpo. His boxing ability was, of course, very limited, and he never made an effort to improve his technique. A friend of Firpo, John V. Grombach, noted that the Latin took a fatalistic view of his career: "He refused to train because he sincerely believed that his success lay in his natural and unorthodox style, and that his unusual strength and phenomenal right hand would carry him farther than any attention to technique or training." So tenaciously did he resist learning that he seldom bothered to train seriously or to observe even the rudimentary rules of prefight tradition. His diet, although immense, was not proper. Grantland Rice remembered that Firpo had a habit of eating gargantuan breakfasts and then lying on a couch "like a python who'd just swallowed a calf."[8] Furthermore, Firpo eschewed both roadwork and serious sparring.

As deplorable as Firpo's training habits were, however, Rickard was concerned most by the Argentine's near-religious parsimony. To say that Firpo was frugal or even stingy understated the case. He was cheap on a heroic scale. One reason he never developed good boxing and training habits was that he was too cheap to employ a manager. No one could convince him that a manager was worth one-third of his ring earnings. William A. Brady, the theatrical producer who also had advised James J. Corbett, Bob Fitzsimmons, and James J. Jeffries on important financial and career matters, offered his services to Firpo, but the boxer replied through an interpreter, "Fitzsimmons is dead. Jeffries has no money. Corbett is all through." Jimmy De-Forest, the experienced trainer who had guided Firpo's American career, was fired when he asked for a raise. Instead of trainers and managers, Firpo hired "business representatives" and "private secretaries," paying an average of twenty-five dollars per week to each. His "business representatives" doubled as chauffeurs or chefs, and his "secretaries" assumed the roles of trainers, sparring partners, bedmakers, or interpreters.[9]

Like all bona fide misers, Firpo's stinginess extended to the trivial. He wore fifteen-dollar suits, kept his celluloid collars until they turned a rich yellow, never tipped, accepted all invitations for free meals, and willingly signed pictures or boxing gloves for show windows in return for free clothes, shoes, and hats. He paid a second for the Willard fight a niggardly ten dollars, and his sparring partners were paid ten to fifteen dollars below the per diem standard. What was more, Firpo continually fleeced the spectators who ventured to the Atlantic City Race Track to watch him prepare for his fight with Dempsey. More than once Rickard had to go to Atlantic City to tell Firpo not to overcharge the patrons.[10]

The aspect of Firpo's parsimony that worried Rickard most was the Latin's willingness to do anything for money. In boxing circles it is generally agreed that Firpo was, as John Lardner said, "the most spectacular lone-wolf financial genius the sport has ever known." For example, his first fight in the United States was against Sailor Tom

Maxted on March 20, 1922. Although Maxted was an unimpressive club fighter, Firpo arranged for the bout to be filmed. Firpo knocked out Maxted in the seventh round, and several months later he returned with the film to South America. In the next year the film was shown in Montevideo, Santiago, Buenos Aires, and, according to Lardner, "virtually every town and city between the Guianas and Tierra del Fuego." Because Maxted was billed by Firpo as one of the leading North American heavyweights, the Argentine boxer increased both his reputation and his pocketbook.[11]

The same ingenuity that engineered the Maxted film coup also discovered a way to make money while training. Firpo's plan was simple: instead of hiring sparring partners, he would tour the country and fight second-rate fighters. This program for training frightened Rickard, who worried that Firpo might look bad or get hit by a lucky punch and ruin the million-dollar gate he had planned for September 14. Given the state of Firpo's boxing ability, Rickard's fears were not unfounded. Firpo's activity likewise upset many followers of boxing. Nat Fleischer, editor of the *Ring,* could not "understand why promoters . . . are willing to pit Firpo against boxers who are so far outclassed that they invite a fatality which may kill the sport. . . . The sport cannot permit Firpo to continue to meet set-ups for the sake of gathering in good American gold." After the signing of the Dempsey-Firpo bout, Rickard's and Fleischer's worst fears almost materialized. Against Homer Smith in Omaha and Joe Downey in Indianapolis, Firpo appeared slow and sluggish, failing to knock out either opponent. After the latter bout, Downey collapsed and was rushed to the hospital. Fortunately, it was nothing serious and he was released the next day.[12]

Finally, much to Rickard's comfort, Firpo ended his road trip and settled down to training for his fight with Dempsey. Less than three weeks before he was to fight Dempsey, Firpo began to train at the same Atlantic City site that Dempsey had used to prepare for his match with Carpentier. Visitors to Firpo's camp found only the pleasant temperatures and a gentle ocean breeze to enjoy; Firpo was uncommunicative to the point of being rude. Elmer Davis, reported in the New York *Times* that Firpo ignored the North Americans who desired only to wish the boxer good luck.[13] Hampered by various lawsuits, unshaven, and essentially bad-tempered, Firpo's attitude made his camp an unpleasant place to visit.

No more striking contrast could have been found than the atmosphere of Dempsey's training camp at Sulphur Springs, New York, close to Saratoga Springs. Looking as "cool as an ocean breeze," Dempsey left New York City in early August accompanied by Kearns and his Greek trainer, Jerry Luvadis. When the trio arrived at Thomas C. Luther's Sulphur Springs Hotel, they were greeted by a large and friendly crowd. They set about at once to establish a typical Dempsey and Kearns camp. The young Paul Gallico, who was assigned to write color pieces about the camp for the New York *Daily News*, remembered "the grand, exciting, bawdy atmosphere" of Uncle Crying Tom Luther's Hotel. Years later in his masterpiece on sports in the 1920s, Gallico said the camp was "gay, low, vulgar, Rabelaisian, and rather marvelous." There were the sparring partners with "bent noses and twisted ears," state troopers in gray and purple uniforms, "doubtful blonds who wandered in and out of the lay-out of wooden hotel and lake-front bungalows, and blonds about whom there was no doubt at all." There was Kearns, "smart, breezy, wise-cracking, scented"; Dempsey, "slim, dark-haired, still crinkled nose . . . dressed in trousers and an old gray sweater, playing checkers on the porch of his bungalow with a sparring partner"; and Uncle Tom, "always crying and complaining over the Gargantuan pranks of the sports-writers." Walking about the camp was an assortment of visiting managers, broken-down pugilists, gamblers, and men such as One-Eyed Connolly who had no fixed occupation. Sports writers drifted about asking questions and inventing stories. One writer called the twenties the golden age of sports writers. At one time or another all of the great ones surfaced at Dempsey's camp: Damon Runyon, Grantland Rice, Bill Corum, Westbrook Pegler, Ring Lardner, W. O. McGeehan, Heywood Broun, Jim Dawson, Hype Igoe, and a host of others. Added to this selection of individuals were thousands of people who came simply to watch the champion train, from Harry F. Sinclair, Consuelo Vanderbilt, and Mrs. Albert Fall, to shoe salesmen and factory workers.[14] At the time, nobody realized that Dempsey's picturesque late-summer camp was the swan song of old-style training camps.

Few of the thousands who traveled to Sulphur Springs failed to find something of interest. As always, Dempsey trained hard and Kearns employed excellent sparring partners. George Godfrey, a leading black heavyweight, was paid $1,500 per week to spar with the champion. He was joined by other fighters of note, such as Jack Thompson, Jules Rioux, Jack Burke, Jack McAuliffe, the Jamaica Kid, Jack Bernstein, and Billy DeFoe. Dempsey sparred with every class of fighter from lightweights like Bernstein to heavyweights like McAuliffe, whom Firpo had fought earlier in the year. And if the champion was kind to the lighter fighters—he was not always—he was brutal to the bigger men. In one sparring contest, Dempsey battered McAuliffe's right eye shut and tore the Detroit fighter's left ear. Another day he beat Jules Rioux, a large Canadian heavyweight, senseless.[15]

Toward the end of August it began to rain more, and the cool showers canceled several days of training. One rainy afternoon in early September when Kearns was in New York City obtaining state licenses for himself and his fighter, Dempsey was sitting on the porch of his cottage. Paul Gallico approached Dempsey and asked if the champion would mind sparring several rounds with him. "What's the matter, son?" Dempsey inquired in his high-pitched voice. "Don't your editor like you no more?" Gallico explained that he believed a sports writer should understand what it was like to be knocked down and dazed in order to write first-class articles in boxing. Gallico's only fear was that he might not be able to take a hard punch in the stomach region. Therefore, he requested Dempsey to restrict his blows to the head. "I think I understand, son," Dempsey said after some reflection. "You must want a good punch in the nose." "Exactly," Gallico agreed. With the rules established, Dempsey said he would fight Gallico the following Sunday.[16]

Before the Dempsey-Gallico fight took place, Kearns returned to Sulphur Springs from New York City. He knew nothing of the participatory journalism, so when he heard that Dempsey was scheduled to box a reporter he immediately became suspicious. What if Gallico was not a reporter, Kearns asked himself. Possibly Gallico, who was six feet three inches tall and weighed about 190 pounds, was a "ringer" from Firpo's camp, sent to Sulphur Springs to "butt, cut, or otherwise injure" Dempsey before the fight. Kearns's suspicious nature found no anodyne during a conversation with Hype Igoe and Damon Runyon, two reporters assigned to Dempsey's camp. Both writers agreed that Gallico had the rugged look of a ringer, and they cautioned Kearns to be careful with the champion. Although Kearns was unable to convince Dempsey to cancel the bout, the manager did arouse suspicions in the champion's own mind.[17]

On Sunday, September 9, less than one week before he was scheduled to fight Firpo, Dempsey gave Gallico a chance to "get a feel" for boxing. It was a splendid sunny day, and about three thousand spectators were scattered around the outdoor ring. While Dempsey fought his other sparring partners, as a preliminary for his contest with Gallico, the sports editor for the *Daily News*, Gallico's boss, explained to Kearns exactly what he and Gallico wanted: "Tell him [Dempsey] to hit us as hard as he can because we want to know just how a knockout feels." Afterwards, added Grantland Rice, Gallico would "report his impressions for the paper, provided, of course, his head was still hanging on by a thread. In case he was killed Mr. Gallico was to write nothing but to communicate if possible through Conan Doyle from the spirit world." As the time for his fight grew near, Gallico began to have second thoughts. When Hype Igoe asked him about the fight, Gallico, in an attempt to soothe his own anxieties, remarked, "we're just going to fool around. Dempsey's going to take it easy." "Son," Igoe said with a look of pity, "don't you know that man *can't* take it easy."[18]

After Dempsey knocked out Farmer Lodge, one of his best sparring partners, Kearns called Gallico into the ring. Dempsey was in near perfect condition, hard and tan and not at all friendly looking. Gallico, dressed in swimming trunks and a Columbia crew shirt—he had captained the eight-oared shell team for that Ivy League institution the year before—later remembered that he was not angry at Dempsey but the champion seemed irritated with his presence. But Gallico had little time for thought. The bell sounded and Gallico assumed "Pose A" from the *Boxer's Manual*. He timidly stuck out his left hand, which Dempsey ran into. Next, he tried a few tentative jabs with surprising success. Just when he was beginning to enjoy the sport everything went black. When he opened his eyes, he was sit-

178

ting on the canvas with his legs collapsed under him. He was "grinning idiotically." As he later remembered, "I held onto the floor with both hands, because the ring and the audience outside were making a complete clockwise revolution, came to a stop, and then went back again counter-clockwise." He struggled to his feet and Dempsey, who by this time realized he was not a ringer, pulled him close and said, "Hang on and wrestle around until your head clears, son." As Dempsey spoke, he hit Gallico a half-dozen affectionate taps on the back back of the neck. But even these blows, which Dempsey executed out of habit, proved too strong for Gallico. Once again he dropped to the canvas. This time he did not get up, and Kearns, who was no longer suspicious and was enjoying himself immensely, counted ten over Gallico's prostrate body. One reporter for the Washington *Post* called the fight "the big laugh of the day." But Gallico, who suffered a cut lip, bloody nose, and headache, had a different impression of the one-and-one-half minute fight. Gallico's only consolation was that he received a by-line for his courage against the champion.[19]

Several days later Dempsey ended his training. For the first time in his life he had been unhampered by criticism. He tried hard to be a popular champion. At the camp, reported Elmer Davis, Dempsey was "rather boyish and good-natured" as he greeted people, signed autographs, and talked with reporters. During one day he fought two exhibition fights for charity, the first in Schenectady against Floyd Johnson and the second in Saratoga against Charles Schwartz. If his draft record was not forgotten, it was at least not used against him. A new attitude toward Dempsey was given voice in an editorial in the New York *Times*. When Dempsey "was younger and less sensible," the editorialist commented, "he made a very serious mistake which turned public opinion strongly against him. It was not the sort of mistake that can be undone, but by modesty and good behavior he has done what he could to live it down."[20] Thus, as Dempsey broke camp, he found himself in a very comfortable position.

Dempsey was not the only person connected with the fight who was happy. Ticket sales for the event guaranteed that Rickard would also be pleased. Although the New York State Boxing Commission set limits on the price of tickets—the most expensive was only $27.50—by September 8 it was clear that Rickard would achieve another million-dollar gate. Four days later, on the eve of the fight, advance ticket sales surpassed the $1,000,000 mark, and aides at Madison Square Garden expected that figure to rise as high as $1,300,000. But the interest in the bout was even greater than the prefight gate indicated. Ticket speculators, such as Mike Jacobs, found it easy to sell ringside seats for $200. Even criminals attempted to capitalize upon the interest in the bout. In New York City six men were arrested for trying to sell over $100,000 worth of bogus tickets, and the same day another forgery attempt was uncovered in Boston. The reason for the interest was clear: Dempsey and Firpo, wrote Grantland Rice, "between them carry a greater amount of raw mule power in their fists than any other contending heavyweights of the decade."[21]

The interest in the bout was not restricted to the United States. Latin Americans viewed the fight in terms of a battle between cultures—Latin vs. Nordic. As one American editorialist commented, Firpo was "not merely the idol of the Argentine people but of all the Southern continent"; he was, a Peruvian said, "the glory of the Latin American race." To the North American press, there was something sinister about the big, hairy Latin, almost as if an air of some prehistoric creature surrounded him. At different times, New York *Tribune* writers compared Firpo to a "caveman" and labeled him an "efficient and zealous... disbeliever in Nordic supremacy." The same newspaper, however, found cause for hope even if the representative of the Nordic culture should fall before the primordial Latin: though "Nordic supremacy may be at present in eclipse," some other "Nord" would surely surface to vanquish the Latin threat.[22]

Thus as September 14, the day of the fight, grew nearer, Firpo found himself praised and feted by Latin Americans as if he were the most important Latin dignitary. On the day before the fight, over two thousand Latins, including eighteen consuls from different Latin American republics, crowded the streets around the Union Benefica Española, a leading club for Spanish-speaking people, to greet Firpo. Fireworks colored the evening and friendly embraces were exchanged. In Buenos Aires, European affairs and the news of Premier Mussolini's entanglement in Corfu were of "secondary consideration." All eyes were focused on the news of the upcoming bout. As

180

one news correspondent stationed in the Argentine capital reported, "The habitual activities and normal pre-occupations of the public have been set aside and are dominated by a visible anxiety over to-morrow's fistic combat."[23]

Excitement intensified with the arrival of Dempsey and Firpo in New York City. Newspapers across the country devoted entire pages to the bout, speculating, predicting, and giving opinions of every sort. Facts about the boxers' weights, reaches, records, and fighting styles were consumed with breakfast and lunch by millions of people who a month before did not know the difference between a haymaker and a hayloft. Professor R. M. Elliott, of the department of psychology at the University of Minnesota, attributed the interest to the "herd instinct" of mankind, that drive which "sends people to see thrills they wouldn't try themselves."[24]

Vicarious thrills, the essence of Professor Elliott's theory, undoubtedly contributed to the public's fascination with the two fighters. However, the interest had deeper, more profound roots. More than a result of the need for nerve excitement, the bout was a symptom of a larger and far more serious disease. Because of increased technology, many Americans believed that man's fate was being taken out of his own hands. Man was a cog in a machine, impotent of action, subject to forces beyond his control. Through the gray technological fog, however, Dempsey and Firpo were glimpses of sunlight. "These men are deciding their own fates," wrote Bruce Bliven in the *New Republic*. "They wade unmindful through seas of agony to the preconceived goal." Boyden Sparkes agreed. In an age dominated by half-truths and propaganda, Dempsey and Firpo represented truth and information.[25]

Such philosophical queries, however, were far from Dempsey's and Firpo's minds on the day before the fight. Dempsey's thoughts centered, as they always did before a fight, on "getting in there." Firpo was also anxious to enter the ring, but he was equally intrigued by the economic aspects of the fight. More particularly, he was concerned about the amount of money he would have to pay to the federal government in taxes. He hated taxes of all kinds. Even during the 1920s, when tax burdens were excessively light, Firpo struggled under his airy load, said John Lardner, "like Atlas beneath the tall

181

pillars that hold heaven and earth asunder." On the eve of the bout, W. O. McGeehan visited the hotel room where Firpo was staying. He found the challenger "sitting at a table stark-naked, with a pencil in a huge fist." Firpo explained in Spanish that he was calculating how much income tax he would have to pay to the United States government for his fight with Dempsey.[26]

Firpo almost avoided the tax burden altogether, for on the day of the fight the bout was nearly canceled. The problem arose during Firpo's physical. Earlier in the week, Firpo had injured his left arm during a training session, and when Dr. William A. Walker gave him his prefight examination, the arm was still tender. Under Firpo's smile there were lines of pain, and though he insisted that the arm was fine, Walker, Muldoon, and Rickard were seriously concerned. Nat Fleischer, who was one of the three boxing writers privy to the meeting, later reported that Firpo slammed his left fist into the training table to prove the strength of his arm. Finally, after consideration of the financial implication of a canceled bout, Firpo was deemed fit to fight by Walker and Muldoon.[27]

On the day of the fight, King Alfonso's fear of revolution in his Spanish homeland, Mussolini's consent to withdraw his troops from Corfu, the Yokohama earthquake that killed over 500 people, and even a man found garrotted among the weeds and sunflowers in Long Island failed to rival the top story of the day: 85,000 people were expected to witness the Dempsey-Firpo bout. After over a month of escalating newspaper coverage, the second "Battle of the Century" since 1920 was about to begin. Very few people actually believed that Firpo had a chance to dethrone Dempsey, and the betting on the fight continued to be light. But there was always the chance that Firpo might land one big punch. Most of the experts agreed with the "comment" section of the New York *Times* sports page: "Firpo may prove easy for Dempsey, but nevertheless, he is a dangerous opponent even for the champion."[28]

Dempsey and Firpo were scheduled to begin their bout at 9:30 at night, but long before then the crowds of people were gathering in front of the Polo Grounds' ticket offices. Hundreds camped beside the arena for as long as forty-eight hours to guarantee themselves a general admission ticket. When the tickets were put on sale at 4:30

on the day of the fight, they were all sold within an hour and a half. Indeed, by 6:00 it was difficult to move anywhere within several blocks of the Polo Grounds. The large doorways were jammed with people. It was possible around some gates to lift one's feet off the ground with no fear of falling. When the tickets were counted, 88,228 people were said to be present, and it was estimated that another 35,000 were turned away from the gates. Even with the low price for tickets, the official gate exceeded $1,127,800.[29]

Rickard, who watched as ushers escorted the spectators to their seats with surprising efficiency, was pleased by the mass of people who attended the fight. But he was overjoyed by the quality of those present. The leaders of American industry and society were gathered in the first twenty rows around the ring. Archie and Kermit Roosevelt sat close to those faithful fans, A. J. Drexel Biddle, Sr., and Jr. Elihu Root was within shouting distance of W. K. Vanderbilt, George Gould, Forbes Morgan, L. H. Rothschild, William A. Brady, and Henry Payne Whitney. The rich and influential, and the sons and daughters of the rich and influential, were seated next to the most illustrious show business entertainers and athletes in America. Florenz Ziegfeld, John Ringling, James J. Corbett, Mickey Walker, John J. McGraw, and Jess Willard were ushered to their seats without notice. Some excitement was caused when Babe Ruth took his seat during the second preliminary, but that thrill vanished when the rumor began circulating that the Prince of Wales, who had been visiting Canada, was present at ringside. The Prince was not there, but, as far as East Coast society was concerned, everybody who was anybody was present. As one reporter noted, "The roll call of ringside ticket-holders, in addition to reading like an abridged edition of the Social Register, contained the names of well-known persons in every walk of life."[30]

For the many wealthy women present, furs were the uniform. Autumn was in the air. The temperature was in the mid-fifties, and flocks of wild geese were spotted flying south over the Polo Grounds. The crisp fall air was complemented by a cool, northwestern breeze and a cloudless sky. Reporter Dan Daniel later remembered that it was a perfect night for a fight: "it was cool and you could cut the tension with a knife." And as the preliminary bouts were fought, the

183

air got cooler and the tension mounted. By 9:30, when a ringside band commenced playing a Latin tune, the 88,000 spectators and 250 reporters who "made use of every available inch of seating space" were ready for the main event.[31]

Firpo was first into the ring. Wearing a long, black and gold checkered bathrobe, he also wore, remarked Jack Lawrence, "the saddest expression we have ever seen on his face." Within seconds, Dempsey climbed into the ring, walked directly over to Firpo's corner, shook hands with the challenger, and waved confidently to the crowd that cheered his appearance. Instead of his usual, good-luck maroon sweater, he had a long-necked white cardigan draped over his shoulders. Such a tempting of fate, perhaps, indicated an overabundance of confidence. Certainly Rickard said nothing to undermine Dempsey's belief in himself. Shortly before the champion left his dressing room, Rickard had said, "We got another million-dollar gate. If you put this poor dub away with one punch all those people out there won't get their money's worth. . . . I hate to think of all those nice millionaires going out of here sore at both of us." Dempsey, who was never very eloquent or good-natured before a fight, had replied, "Go to hell."[32] But Dempsey's confidence was nevertheless clearly visible as announcer Joe Humphreys introduced the two fighters.

At the bell the two fighters spun 180 degrees around on their toes and faced each other. In five minutes the fight would be over, but for pure intensity of motion and fighting it would never be equaled. Dempsey rushed across the ring to meet Firpo and threw a wild right hand. For one of the few times in his ring career, Firpo executed a classic move: he side-stepped Dempsey's right and countered with a perfectly-timed short left uppercut. Less than ten seconds after the opening bell, Dempsey's knees hit the canvas. The impact of the exchange upon the spectators was immediate. "The entire crowd," wrote Paul Gallico, "got to its feet and remained standing for the balance of the fight, yelling, screaming, climbing up on the benches, falling down, clawing at each other, roaring forth a wild, tumultuous cataract of sound in the greatest sustained mass audience hysteria ever witnessed in any modern arena." Within this cataclysm was complete confusion. Benches, set up on the Polo Grounds' infield especially for the fight, toppled over, scattering spectators on the grass; tempers flared as men pounded upon the backs of those in front of them; Babe Ruth took a swing at welterweight champion Mickey Walker after the boxer had pushed him off a bench; and in the more stable, if cheaper, seats one man died of heart failure.[33]

Within the ring the action was also confused. Firpo's uppercut had served only to intensify Dempsey's attack. Dempsey's primary trait as a fighter was the ability to fight with reckless abandon when he was hurt. In fact, he was often at his best when he was injured. After being knocked down, he sprang to his feet before the referee began to count and wrestled Firpo into a clinch. Holding Firpo with one hand and punching with the other, Dempsey began to attack the Latin's body. Seconds later, at about the half-minute mark of the first round, Dempsey landed a right hook to Firpo's chin. Down went the challenger. At the count of nine, Firpo regained a standing position, but the posture was temporary; for after another flurry of blows the challenger again fell to the canvas. For the second time, Firpo arose. The two fighters exchanged right hands and then, as if by mutual consent, fell into another clinch.[34]

Referee Johnny Gallagher, who was having trouble following the action, demanded the fighters break the clinch. Firpo, who obviously had not been tutored on what to expect from Dempsey, dropped his hands and took a step backward in response to Gallagher's orders. It was a costly mistake. As Firpo stepped back Dempsey stepped forward and delivered a hard uppercut to the Latin's chin. Firpo dropped to the canvas as if he was unconscious. After the fight, Dempsey would be soundly criticized for this and other conventionally "foul" tactics. Grantland Rice and Allan Davis both noted Dempsey's "deceit and treachery" in the ring. Although the critics were technically correct, they failed to understand Dempsey as a fighter. Under the rules of boxing, Dempsey was a fouler, "rough, anxious to hurt, and careless with his punches." But, as Paul Gallico has cogently observed, "psychically Dempsey actually never was a foul battler, because in his simple way he recognized no deadlines on the body of his opponent and certainly asked for none to be enforced upon his."[35] Once the bell rang to begin a fight, Dempsey fought, refusing to acknowledge that the verb *fight* might be modified by adverbs such as *fair* or *foul*.

Fight stood alone; either it was or it was not; either one did or one did not. And if it was and one did, then it was best to protect oneself at all times and not look toward such niceties as *break clean* and *beltline* for comfort.

After Dempsey had knocked down Firpo for the third time, he stood close to his fallen foe and waited for the Argentine to rise. As soon as Firpo's hands left the canvas, Dempsey was on the attack. Seconds after Firpo arose Dempsey scored another knockdown with a right uppercut to the heart. While on the canvas Firpo tried to crawl out of Dempsey's reach, but when he regained his feet the champion had circled behind him. Before Firpo even saw Dempsey, the champion knocked him down with a right uppercut. This time, Firpo got up swinging and hit Dempsey with a right hand that traveled about four feet. Dempsey fell to his knees but was up before Firpo could take one step backward. The two fighters exchanged right hands and Firpo went down again, got up, and was knocked down once more. Confidently, Dempsey stepped over Firpo and stood in the near corner, fully expecting the challenger to stay down for the count. In less than two minutes, Dempsey had been knocked down once to his knees and once to his hands; Firpo had been floored seven times. "I just relaxed," Dempsey later recalled. "I didn't think the man would get up again."[36]

But Firpo did get up, and what happened in the next fifteen seconds was destined to become one of the most famous exchanges in the history of boxing. After Firpo arose Dempsey landed a very solid right to the challenger's ribs. Firpo ignored the punch and threw a right of his own, which he launched from over his head. Dempsey staggered backward toward the ropes, where Firpo trapped him. Using his fist like a gloved club, Firpo hit Dempsey with four more right hands. Dempsey, clearly shaken, was trapped with his back on the middle rope and his heels on the canvas. With Firpo's next punch, a right hand which was as much a push as a blow, the middle rope and the upper rope separated and the physics of the situation forced Dempsey out of the ring. Had the ring been more tightly strung, Dempsey undoubtedly would not have fallen out of the ring.

Yet fall he did. One second, champion, challenger, and referee were grouped together along the ropes. "A second later," wrote reporter Frank G. Manke, "only two figures were visible. The king of kings . . . suddenly disappeared as though a trap door had opened and swallowed him." Dempsey fell straight back onto the typewriters of the New York *Tribune* reporters. In the process, he cut his lower back. But his only thoughts were on getting back into the ring. Jack Lawrence, whose typewriter cushioned Dempsey's fall, reported the champion said, "you big ——————, get me back in there; get me back in there, I'll fix him." In a rage, Dempsey twisted and reached for the lower rope, accidentlly hitting judge Kid McPartland in the eye as he struggled. Finally, with the aid of Lawrence and Perry Grogan, a Western Union Morse operator, Dempsey was pushed back into the ring. Defending their actions, Lawrence and Grogan claimed they were pushing Dempsey off of themselves and not trying to help the champion back into the ring.[37] Regardless of the intention, when the referee's count reached nine Dempsey, whose feet never left the ring's apron, had appeared in the ring as quickly as he had vanished.

Back in the ring, Dempsey had a glazed look in his eyes, a blank, expressionless stare with which Gallico probably sympathized. Dempsey tried to force Firpo into a clinch, but the challenger responded with more wild punches, few of which landed solidly. Ducking and bobbing out of habit, Dempsey escaped further punishment. He even recovered enough to throw several punches of his own. At the bell, both fighters were throwing haymakers; defense had been silently declared anathema. When Firpo heard the bell he made his second misjudgment of the fight: he dropped his hands and turned toward his corner. Dempsey, either too excited to hear the bell or too dazed to understand what it signified, continued to fight, hitting the defenseless Firpo with three lazy left hooks, which he threw in the manner of a friendly tap on the back.

The din and confusion of the spectators were matched in Dempsey's corner. Kearns met Dempsey at the center of the ring and led his fighter back to his corner. To clear the champion's thoughts, Kearns emptied a bucket of cold water over Dempsey's head. However, Kearns had forgotten where he had put the smelling salts, and he kept yelling instructions to Jerry Luvadis. Communication was impossible; Ludvadis kept trying to tell Kearns that the smelling salts were in the manager's pocket, and Kearns made equally futile attempts to tell Luvadis to get the smelling salts. Finally, Luvadis reached for Kearns's pocket and the manager punched him. Dempsey's only question was what round it was.[38]

The second round began as the first round ended—heavy punching and no defense. Dempsey landed a right, clinched, and then hit Firpo as the referee called for them to break. During the next clinch Dempsey literally threw Firpo to the canvas with a move not unlike the cross-buttock of the bare-fisted days. Firpo rose swinging and walked into a Dempsey left. As Firpo was falling to the canvas—for the ninth time—Dempsey delivered another right hook. Stretched out on the canvas, arms and legs spread as if he was trying to cover as much space as possible, Firpo did not move until the count of six. Then he rolled over onto his stomach and again spread his arms and legs. At the count of ten he was in the process of doing a fair imitation of a push-up. But the fight was over. Dempsey rushed over to Firpo and picked up the 220 pound Argentine as if he weighed no more than a bale of hay. Firpo was bleeding from the nose, mouth, and ears. His eyes had lost their focus. Bruce Bliven, in his article on the fight for the *New Republic,* wrote, "We may have come in a good mood for blood; but if so, we have had our fill of it."[39]

No fight in the history of boxing ever generated as much disgust and praise, controversy and reform. Sports writers found inspiration in the poetry of the blood and motion. The first round, claimed James Crusinberry of the Chicago *Tribune,* was "the greatest round of battling since the Silurian Age." The stone-age metaphor was used by other writers. Bruce Bliven imagined he saw in the bout acts similar to those committed by "our Cro-Magnon ancestors." Superlatives governed the reporters' accounts. The "most sensational," said Grantland Rice; "no parallel," echoed Jack Lawrence; "the greatest," agreed Jim Dawson. Nat Fleischer, editor of the *Ring,* observed that for thrills no fight in modern times could match the contest; furthermore, "It was one of the greatest dramas ever staged. [Neither] Shakespeare nor Shaw could have constructed a greater drama." Comments along this vein were seemingly endless. Suffice it to say that if one liked to see fighting—not to be confused with boxing—at its best, "It was one sweet quarrel."[40]

Another class of people was pleased with the outcome of the fight for quite different reasons. After all, it was a contest between a person from the United States and a man from a Latin American country. There was, then, a matter of prestige, of national honor, to be determined. Or, at least, this was how many perceived the fight. Bruce Bliven gave a perfectly blunt reason for going to the fight: "We are here to see the Nordic race defend itself against the Latin." Viewed from this perspective, the match was a resounding victory for the United States. One editorialist for the Brooklyn *Eagle* noted the "international significance" of the fight: "One shudders to think of what might have happened to the Monroe Doctrine if Firpo had won. To-day it is safe to say that South America has more respect for us than ever before. If Europe would only send over a first class challenger, Mr. Dempsey might do something to restore American prestige abroad."[41]

For others, however, the bout represented a cancerous growth on the American social body. The fight was, commented a New Haven *Journal-Courier* editorialist, "a study of national degeneracy." The *Christian Science Monitor,* a newspaper that seldom acknowledged the existence of prizefighting, agreed that the bout was a sordid and disgraceful affair. The "Yankee doughboys" who braved the horrors of war to make America and the world a safer place "must wonder at the national temperament that leaves them to shift as best they may for a livelihood, while giving $500,000 and unbounded adulation to a pugilist who carefully avoided the trenches." The post–World War I tendency to seek thrills and to titillate the nerves was a clear indication that American civilization was on the decline. The roar that filled the Polo Grounds, reasoned those who maintained this Spenglerian philosophy, was no different from the noise that echoed through the Coliseum when the Romans fed Christians to the lions or the sound that drifted across the dark jungle when primeval, weak-brained men fought one another with sticks and rocks.[42]

The fear raised by the Dempsey-Firpo fight was very real. On the Sunday after the bout, sermons were given in which the topic was the fight. In New York City, the Reverend Doctor Christian F. Reisner, pastor of the Chelsey Methodist Church, told his congregation that America was becoming a land of hypocrisy: "We are talking about peace and yet developing a lust for blood." Reisner found himself supported by ministers of different denominations. Doctor S. Edward Young of the Bedford Presbyterian Church in New York City agreed that hypocrisy and Romanism threatened America. The thought that the money spent on the fight would have furnished a copy of the Holy Scriptures to every person in the world infuriated Young. Indeed, most reform organizations from the Methodist Board of Ministers to the Board of Temperance condemned the brutality and avarice that they believed were the outgrowth of professional boxing.[43]

Unfortunately for the reformers, most of their criticism of boxing fell upon deaf ears. A New York *Times* editorialist spoke for many citizens when he declared his weariness with discussions about boxing leading to the "Decline and Fall" of American civilization. One minister even felt compelled to defend the sport. The Reverend Frederick E. Hopkins, pastor of the First Presbyterian Church of Michigan City, Illinois, said the Dempsey-Firpo fight, far from being evil or decadent, gave a "healthy holy thrill" to millions of people. Bill Muldoon, he continued, had certainly contributed as much to American society as the president of Harvard.[44] Thus by 1923 religious and moral reformers found their ranks growing thin. To be sure, some believed that boxing indicated the decline of a civilization, but a far greater number saw no reason to link boxing with some vague apocalyptic message.

Paradoxically, the bout aroused the most concern in the least likely place. Within the boxing community, people were appalled by Dempsey's unethical and, at times, illegal method of fighting. Nat Fleischer, for one, admitted that he was "mighty happy" to see the heavyweight crown resting upon an American head, but "disregarding personal feeling" he believed that "Firpo should today be wearing the crown." Dan Daniel agreed wholeheartedly. Years later he remarked that "Firpo was cheated; by all rights he should have been the champion."[45] Both men emphasized Dempsey's cavalier attitude toward the rules and regulations of the boxing code. The outcome of the controversy over the fight resulted in the rewording and future enforcement of two rules.

Most commentators on boxing maintain that the neutral corner

190

rule was an outgrowth of the Dempsey-Firpo fight. They believe that before the fight it was unethical, but not illegal, for a boxer to stand over a fallen opponent, hoping to hit the unfortunate foe as soon as his hands and knees left the canvas. However, this notion was erroneous. Even before the Dempsey-Firpo bout such a tactic was illegal. The rule was quite clear on the neutral corner point: "When a contestant is down, his opponent shall retire to the farthest corner and remain there until the count is completed. Should he fail to do so, the referee and timekeeper may cease counting until he has so retired." Thus referee Gallagher was at fault when he permitted Dempsey to stand over Firpo. After the fight, the rule was reworded so that the decision was taken out of the referee's hands. The "may" in the rule became a "must"; no count would be permitted to start until the neutral corner rule was observed.[46] Four years later to the month, this addition to the boxing code would come back to haunt Dempsey in a case of poetic justice in its truest sense.

The second rule that was altered concerned a boxer knocked out of the ring. Again, Fleischer led the crusade to clarify the rules, for he felt that the assistance Dempsey received when the champion was battered out of the ring should have led to a disqualification and a new heavyweight champion. The ambiguous wording of the rule was the crucial point in the controversy. It said that if a fighter did not return to the ring "immediately," the referee "may count him out as if he were down." Conceivably under this rule, a fighter who was knocked out of the ring might be given a minute or more to reenter the fighting arena. In addition, the rule said nothing about aid in returning to the ring. To clarify the matter, the rule was reworded to say that any boxer who was knocked out of the ring was required to return within ten seconds "under his own power."[47]

Regardless of the controversy, Dempsey was still the champion. If anything, the controversy added to his attractiveness as a boxer, for it kept his name in front of the public. But after two fights in less than three months, Dempsey wanted a rest. In terms of boxing he was no longer a young man, and the Firpo fight was an indication that he was no longer invincible. The January, 1924, issue of the *Ring* printed a cartoon of Dempsey that aptly commented upon his career. Drawn by Robert Ripley and entitled "He stands Supreme," its message was clear. A boxer labeled "Dempsey" stands on top of a mountain, labeled "the peak," with one foot on the downhill side.[48] As unsubtle as the cartoon was, it was nevertheless prophetic. In Dempsey's next fight he would be defeated. But the fight would not take place for another three years.

CHAPTER X

The Nose
Makes
the Man

BETWEEN Dempsey's dramatic defeat of Firpo and the rainy night in Philadelphia when he was outboxed by Gene Tunney, there stretched three eventful years. Although he did not defend his title, he was seldom far from the minds of the millions of Americans who so keenly followed his career. His name continued to dominate the sports pages of American newspapers, occasionally creeping onto the front page and editorial pages as well. His face, similarly, could not be forgotten. From the heights of the silver screen, vaudeville stage, and Broadway stage, Dempsey's face and movements were studied by millions of people who, if not captivated by his acting talent, were awed by his magnetic presence. From their darkened seats in filled theaters they watched as Dempsey changed. The rough mannerisms of hungry western youth gave way to a rude but sincere sophistication of the earnest, nouveau riche man of leisure. The rugged features—facial scars and broken nose—were transformed, smoothed, and straightened. The loud clothes, which had been cultivated through too close an imitation of his manager, were subdued. In short, between 1923 and 1926 Dempsey changed both inwardly and outwardly. If the savage in him was not tamed completely, it learned to pass invisibly before the public.

In the three years following the Firpo fight, Dempsey's public image was carefully cultivated, both by himself and the manipulators of the media. Rarely would the question of Dempsey's war record be raised. Rather the champion would always appear before the public as a kind, gentle, and considerate man. This is not to say that the popular image of Dempsey varied greatly from the actual personality of the fighter. After four years of unpopularity that he believed was wholly undeserved, the champion hungered for the admiration of the public. Unlike Kearns, who was cold and scornful of the public, Dempsey was sensitive about his image. He wanted to be liked, even loved in the same manner as the public took Babe Ruth and Little Billy Johnston to their hearts.[1] Therefore, during his hiatus from the ring, Dempsey courted the public; his accessibility and willingness to chat with anybody or to sign autographs was uncommon even for the 1920s when popular heroes were often before the public.

But Dempsey needed periodic rests. Immediately after the Firpo bout, he became tired of New York City and the controversy over his methods of battling the Argentine, so he went on a hunting trip with three of his closest friends, Teddy Hayes, Jerry Luvadis, and Mike Burke. Dempsey longed for the "open life," as he told reporters. Certainly he found what he was looking for in the rugged mountains of northern New Mexico, where he and his colleagues plowed through deep snow in search of bears, deer, and mountain lions. The hunt lasted about a week, and Dempsey reportedly killed a seven-prong, three-hundred-pound buck, the largest deer killed in the Elks Mountain region that year. But by early December, Dempsey was prepared to leave the "open life" for the more confined life of "the city."[2]

The city, for Dempsey, was New York City. It was there that Kearns was eagerly trying to capitalize on his fighter's title. After boxing several exhibition bouts in Chicago and St. Louis and visiting his family and friends in Salt Lake City, Dempsey joined Kearns in New York City. But there was little time for a joyful reunion. Dempsey was upset over the death of his friend and rival Billy Miske, who died on January 1, 1924. With characteristic exaggeration, Kearns called Miske "one of the greatest boxers of his weight in the history of the ring."[3] Dempsey, however, could not be reached for a comment, for on January 2 he was on a train bound for Jacksonville to start a tour of a southern vaudeville circuit.

For most of January, Dempsey traveled the South on the Pantages Circuit, a small but respectable show that served as a training ground for new acts. Although the pay was not very good, the circuit was

excellent for breaking in an act in front of small, but usually enthusiastic and uncritical, audiences in towns the major circuits
bypassed. It served Dempsey well. Never particularly comfortable on
the stage or in front of the movie camera, he needed uncritical audiences to bolster his confidence. This short tour allowed him time to
learn his lines for future engagements on the more prestigious circuits. It even drew a short but kind comment from Nellie Revell, a
feature columnist for *Variety*. [4]

When not stumbling through his lines and stiffly moving across
the vaudeville stage, Dempsey was served up to his ample admirers in
a more familiar form. Before packed houses, he fought exhibition
bouts in the major cities in the South. He knocked out Dutch Seifert
in Memphis and two days later fought two rounds each with Martin
Burke, Tommy Martin, and Dan O'Dowel in New Orleans. [5] Other
exhibitions were staged in Pensacola, Raleigh, and Charlotte. The
contests were exceeded in popularity only by Dempsey himself.
Wherever he went he was cheered. On the street people would reach
out to touch him or even his clothes, as though contact granted some
mystic association with his power.

On his return to New York City, after finishing his vaudeville
and exhibition engagements, Dempsey received an invitation to visit
the White House. Filled with irony, the short stay in Washington
exemplified how far Dempsey and boxing had moved toward social
acceptance since the end of the Great War. The vilified draft dodger
of 1920 was photographed standing silently before the tomb of
Woodrow Wilson where he had just placed a wreath. Later in the
day, the champion boxer was greeted at the White House by an unusually talkative Calvin Coolidge. The president introduced Dempsey to his aides as "one who has been before the public longer than I
have," and when told that the champion could knock out an opponent with a two-inch punch replied, "Well, that is two inches more
of a punch than I would like to get from you." [6] The meeting marked
the coming of age of professional boxing. No longer was prizefighting
an unacceptable barroom sport, a contest between rough, brutal men
for the enjoyment of rough, sadistic men. If the national symbol of
the chilly Yankee ethic invited a boxer to the national home, then,
indeed, the sport and the man had arrived.

Noting Dempsey's return to New York City, a Washington *Post* sports writer commented upon the champion's inability to sit still. What the reporters assumed was restlessness was actually a symptom of hemorrhoids, from which Dempsey had suffered for years. Late in the afternoon of February 27, the champion underwent surgery, and Dr. Robert E. Brennan, who performed the operation at the Polyclinic Hospital in New York City, described Dempsey's problem as an uncomplicated case of fistula, but as the champion's stay in the hospital lengthened, the sports-obsessed public began to speculate, and rumors spread quickly, due in part, perhaps, to the rumors of Babe Ruth's ill health. In Hot Springs, Arkansas, the Babe was suffering from a serious attack of influenza that fans feared might lead to pneumonia. So newspaper readers were ripe for rumors that the boxing champion suffered from a hernia which would end his career. Finally the secrecy was ended, and it was disclosed that Dempsey had been operated upon for hemorrhoids as well as fistula.[7] With the rumors quieted, Dempsey finally was allowed by reporters to rest in the hospital.

For Dempsey, as for other fighters, New York City's night life had always been a temptation. From the pugilistic dives on Eighth Avenue to the best clubs in the city, boxers, and especially champions, have always been welcome. Dempsey continued to be well known at the El Morocco, Delmonico's, the Cotton Club, "Legs" Diamond's Hotsy Totsy Club, "21," and the other neon landmarks of the 1920s.[8] Rich food, easily accessible liquor, and even more easily acquired women were constant enticements for the champion. In addition, the training quarters of New York City were not conducive to good health. Stillman's, the premiere gym in the city, was a dirty, grimy, poorly ventilated, ill-smelling breeding ground for future champions. For a fighter on the make Stillman's smoke-filled world was bearable, but for a champion it was different. Although Dempsey trained in Stillman's whenever he was in New York City during the next three years, his conditioning was never very strenuous or regular. Eighth Avenue was a difficult street to enter after long hours on Broadway.

Temptation and poor training areas also strained the pocketbook. In New York City the champion was expected to buy drinks, overtip, and give expensive parties. Kearns, a master of spending his and other people's money, had educated Dempsey to do the same. But money so easily spent was difficult to make in New York City. Outside the ring Dempsey had few marketable talents; he passed his days talking with sports writers and footing bills. Challengers were discussed. The abilities of Gibbons, Wills, Firpo, and other leading heavyweights were compared. New challengers such as Prince Mohammed Ali Ibrahim of Egypt, whose trainer Blink McCloskey said had a punch called a "pyramid punch" that "lands with the force of a falling pyramid and knocks a rival stiffer than a sphinx," were noted.[9] But the drain on Dempsey's financial and physical resources continued. A splendid place to visit, New York City was certainly no place for the heavyweight champion of the world to live.

Dempsey favored living on the West Coast. Two years earlier, he had purchased a large ranch-style house in Los Angeles, where, along with Kearns, he also had bought a $350,000 apartment complex. As Dempsey had learned in 1920, the West Coast was a land of abundant financial opportunities. Every day new celluloid idols were being manufactured in Hollywood, and the avenues open to heroes from other exciting fields were unlimited. Of all athletes during the decade, Dempsey was the most feted and pursued. And this popularity was easily converted into cash. In early April, Carl Laemmle of the Universal Picture Corporation signed Dempsey to a movie contract. Laemmle's plan was for Dempsey to star in ten films and to train at Universal City. For his work Dempsey was guaranteed $1,000,000, a princely sum even in Hollywood. As Allen T. Treadway, a Republican congressman from Massachusetts, remarked only partly in jest, perhaps the Federal Trade Commission should inquire into the agreement, for considering Dempsey's thespian abilities the public was bound to be overcharged at the box office.[10]

Moving to Los Angeles with his mother, sister, and several brothers, Dempsey was immediately accepted into the Hollywood community. Boxing attracted the stars of the motion picture world like no other sport; the pace and drama of the ring, the sudden shifts of fate that spelled the difference between winning and losing, were intuitively understood. Douglas Fairbanks, the trim, athletic idol of millions of moviegoers, confessed that his true passion was boxing, and during periodic breaks from acting he was known to spar with Bull Montana and other ex-boxers. Other actors who supported the sport in Hollywood included Charlie Chaplin, Peggy Joyce, Harold Lloyd, and Carter De Haven. They were, as one article noted in typical Hollywoodese, "wild about boxing." Even during Dempsey's trial for draft dodging, the show business trade journal *Variety* had constantly stood on the side of Dempsey and boxing, steadfastly refusing to believe that either the sport or the man might be impure.[11]

Into this world of glamour and surface appearances Dempsey moved with graceful ease. Universal wanted a hero, a woman-saving, child-loving, scoundrel-hating idol. Dempsey accepted his role. He lived the role, at least publicly, on and off stage. Discarding his fighting trademark, his punch-flattened nose, Dempsey had his nose recast along more Grecian lines. Proud of the miracle of surgery, Dempsey told reporters that besides making him look better it aided his breathing. But more than that, the remodeled nose helped to create a new image of Jack Dempsey. The hungry, hard, mean, poorly educated Dempsey was removed by the surgeon's knife and skillful hands, and replaced by a controlled, gentlemanly, kind and considerate champion. The old Dempsey evaded the draft and threw punches aimed at the groin; the new Dempsey bought new homes for his mother and established bank accounts for orphans.[12]

The different forms of the media also helped to establish the new Jack Dempsey. Universal cast him in movies that catered to the public's immense capacity for hero worship. W. O. McGeehan, the New York *Tribune* sports journalist, was surprised at the change in Dempsey wrought by the motion picture industry. "Our foremost demonstrator of modified murder," wrote McGeehan, has been "transformed by the art of the make-up man into a somewhat sheepish and harmless-looking young man who makes moon faces at the heroines and pats the hand of a tubercular stage mother with the fist that fractured the jaw of Mr. Jess Willard." Not only was Dempsey's nose reformed, beetle-brows plucked, and rebellious hair smoothed, but his entire appearance seemed to McGeehan to have been "softened." Added to this was the high moral tone of the picture being reviewed. "There is nothing in them [Dempsey's movies] to bring the blush of shame to the most sensitive cheek," rhapsodized McGeehan. "Of course there is a hint of what they call 'sex' in these films. But it is handled with a delicacy that would even get by the judge who maintained that all literature should be denatured to suit a seminary girl of the mid-Victorian period." Instead of making love with the "brazenness of a Valentino," Dempsey "merely looks at the 'goil.' He does not manhandle her. There are no shameless petting parties in this clean and wholesome Dempsey film." [13]

What McGeehan wrote about *Jack O'Day*, one of the *Fight and Win* serials, was true of all the pictures in which Dempsey performed between 1924 and 1926. The roles changed and he was called upon to play a lovable Mexican bandit, a cake-eater, and a rube for the "fillum," but the wholesome, all-American symbol Dempsey came to personify and the elevated moral tone of the pictures remained constant. In the films Dempsey starred in there were no "brilliant men, beautiful jazz babies, champagne baths, midnight revels, petting parties in the purple dawn, all ending in one terrific smashing climax that makes you gasp"; there were no "neckers, petters, white kisses, red kisses, pleasure-mad daughters, sensation-craving mothers"; and there was nothing that was sinful, immoral, or ribald. There was instead a simple hero who, much in the tradition of Tarzan, Leatherstocking, D'Artagnan, or the Scarlet Pimpernel, righted all wrongs, safeguarded virtue, and generally made certain that the white forces of good knocked out the darker shades of evil. He was a hero, in short, who echoed the calls for duty and morality sounded in the nineteenth century, trumpeted into the blood of youths who were raised long before the Great War shattered the optimistic belief in the perfectability of mankind. The Dempsey of the silver screen almost fit the hero of Douglas Dwikin's *The Lobstick Trail*, a popular novel of the 1920s: "His blood was clean, his body knit of fiber woven in God's out-of-doors, his mind fashioned under a clear sky in a land of wide horizons." [14]

The new image of Jack Dempsey, so assiduously manufactured in Hollywood, was given further treatment on painters' canvases. On display at the Kansas City Art Institute was a portrait in oil of Dempsey by the Seattle artist Alonzo Victor Lewis. In the impressionistic portrait, Dempsey is pictured as a serious, noble youth with pensive eyes and a sober mouth; arms crossed, tilted hat, heavy jacket, his understanding—even wisdom—seems boundless. As a subject, commented a viewer of the portrait, Dempsey possessed "native grace, physical beauty and a prowess which has fired the imagination of the world." [15]

Dempsey was also a subject of one of the leading artists of the 1920s. George Bellows, the famous exponent of the Ashcan School, had always been intrigued by the ring, by the dramatic clash of motion, color, and bodies when two fighters battled each other. His boxing paintings, among them *The White Hope, Counted Out, Introducing Georges Carpentier, Between Rounds, Stage at Sharkey's, Knockout, Ringside Seats,* and *Introducing John L. Sullivan,* had won him considerable fame by the mid-1920s. Therefore it came as no surprise for Bellows when he was commissioned by the New York *Evening Journal* to cover the Dempsey-Firpo fight. Out of the experience was produced *Dempsey-Firpo,* Bellows' best-known boxing painting. Hung among the nudes and nobles on the walls of New York's Metropolitan Museum of Art, the painting shows Dempsey being knocked out of the ring by a Firpo left. The punch that accomplished the task was an overhead right, but artistic license considered, the painting is an impressive testimony to Dempsey's status as a hero. As Dempsey falls, hands reach to push him upright, mouths drop open in horror, and faces contort with agony. There is no pleasure in the faces, no desire to see a new champion crowned. There is only fear that Dempsey, the hero and the champion, is finished. The impact of the painting was quickly understood by Heywood Broun: "Bellows painted well and for all time. By and by everything the sports writers ever said of Dempsey will be forgotten. He will belong, then, to the ages and the art critics." [16]

But Dempsey, in Hollywood in 1924, was not overly concerned about the future ages, and he was even less interested in art critics. He was, to be sure, aware of the changes in his image. The cheers that greeted him when he appeared at fights or other public occasions and the complete absence of criticism over his inaction during the Great War did not pass unobserved. Even when a Massachusetts branch of the American Legion issued a resolution calling for people to boycott Dempsey films, it was done to force Dempsey to fight in the ring and was not a criticism of his war record. This elevation to a national pedestal had, in turn, a calming effect on the champion. Instead of becoming bloated with ego, Dempsey became kinder and more considerate of others' feelings. He willingly signed autographs, chatted with sports writers, boxed exhibitions, and smiled gently at the countless numbers of people who tore at his clothes or tried to feel his muscles. Surprisingly, nothing went to his head—not success, money, or the change in his social position. He was one of the few celebrities, Paul Gallico observed, who remained "unspoiled, natural and himself."[17] If anything, his disposition vis-à-vis the world at large improved.

Life in California relaxed Dempsey; his thoughts and actions separated him farther and farther from boxing. Entrenched in Hollywood, concerned with his movie career and with having a good time, he announced in July that he would not defend his title in 1924. This announcement was made certain several weeks later when he was injured in an automobile accident near San Juan Capistrano. Although his injuries were not serious—a dislocated right elbow, strained ligaments in his neck, abrasions on his right knee, and a small cut on his scalp—they were extensive enough to curtail any more ring activity for several months.[18] Dempsey, however, was not concerned; he had discovered that his popularity could be converted into money without the risk either of title or body.

Movies, of course, provided most of the money Dempsey earned between 1924 and 1926, but they were not the only source of revenue. In early October the champion, assisted by Kearns, returned to the vaudeville stage. Joining the Loew Circuit, one of the largest in the East, Dempsey and Kearns spent a week each in Buffalo, Newark, Brooklyn, Boston, and New York City. It was Dempsey's first time on an eastern circuit, and he was paid $5,000 per week, the largest sum ever paid to an entertainer on the Loew Circuit. But Dempsey proved to be a sound investment. Everywhere he played, the house was packed and the previous records broken. At Loew's State Theater on Broadway, for example, the performances headlined by Dempsey grossed over $41,000 and more than seventy-six thousand people saw him on stage during his week's engagement. The previous record for a week's gross was $28,000. Even election day failed to lessen the flow of traffic to Loew's State, but, to be fair, as poor as Dempsey's act was, it still provided more excitement and interest than Coolidge's victory over John W. Davis.[19]

The $25,000 that Dempsey was paid by the Loew Circuit represented a fraction of his income for 1924. In that year he paid $90,831.31 in income taxes alone, which represented the tax on an income of about $275,000. What was more, Kearns paid $71,657.96 into the federal coffers, the taxable figure on an income of approximately $225,000. Kearns's income can be viewed as an extension of Dempsey's earnings, for until early 1925 Dempsey paid his manager about 50 percent of his income. Dempsey's income, then, for 1924 was close to $500,000. In an age when a man could buy a large house, own an automobile, raise a family, and live comfortably on $300 to $350 a month, Dempsey's income was embarrassingly high. Without climbing into the ring he earned more than any other professional athlete during that year. The highest paid baseball player, Babe Ruth, was paid $52,000 by the New York Yankees in 1924, and the second highest paid Yankee, Home Run Baker, was content with making $16,000 for the year. Although no gauge can indicate exactly what Dempsey's income would be worth today, it would be safe, even conservative, to say that $500,000 in 1924 would be equal to $10,000,000 in 1978.[20] By the end of the year, therefore, Dempsey was not even considering reentering the ring in the near future.

Boxing, in fact, was the farthest thing from Dempsey's mind. Lavishly paid, loved by his public, and welcome at the mansions of the most beautiful people in Hollywood, the champion's most serious concern centered on a matter of the heart. Kearns, whose attitude toward women might be best described as misogynistic, had always encouraged Dempsey to follow his example in handling females: never become involved in any relationship that extended beyond one night. And, from 1917 to 1923 when Dempsey was never far from Kearns's watchful eyes, the manager made sure that his fighter steered clear from any tender entanglements. But throughout 1924 Dempsey and Kearns were seldom together. Kearns preferred the fast pace of New York City and Dempsey was equally content in Hollywood. Free from Kearns, Dempsey began to cultivate his romantic tendencies. And Dempsey was a romantic when it came to women. He had a true Irishman's respect for females, a reverence that extended from the near worship of his mother to the most profound deference toward the women he met in Hollywood. Unlike Kearns, Dempsey never enjoyed the life of one night stands. He was never a "woman chaser" or a "swinger," said his friend Nat Loubet. Rather he preferred to settle down with one woman; he was a "family man."[21]

Rumors that the champion was indeed about to "settle down" became common gossip in Hollywood as early as August, 1924. Earlier that summer, Dempsey met Ida Estelle Taylor Pencock who was working in *The Alaskan,* a feature film for Paramount. In true Hollywood fashion it was love at first sight; the hobo turned pugilist turned actor fell madly in love with the glamorous starlet.[22] A five-foot-four-inch brunette, Estelle was beautiful by the standards of her day. She had dreamy, bedroom eyes and a sensual, fleshy body. In dress and actions she was a flapper. Her hats covered her eyebrows, and she was extremely opinionated. As a success symbol, she represented everything Dempsey longed for or ever hoped to obtain.

As far as her career was concerned, Estelle was an ambitious, second-rate actress. Although she was under a personal contract with Cecil B. De Mille in 1924, when she met Dempsey her career was on the downswing. She was originally discovered by William Fox, who saw her play a small role in George V. Hobart's play *Come-on Charley.* After a successful screen test, Fox cast her as the leading lady in *Broadway Saint* (1919), *While New York Sleeps* (1920), *A Fool There Was* (1922), and several other productions. But the temperamental brunette from Wilmington, Delaware, failed to excite the public. In addition, her reputation in Hollywood had been dragged through a series of gutters. Her name was prominent in George Walsh's divorce scandal, and before she quit Paramount in the middle of 1924 it had been rumored that Walter Wanger, the head of production for the company, was about to fire her.[23] In short, Dempsey's "success symbol" was a well-used piece of merchandise.

When rumors began to circulate in Hollywood that Dempsey and Estelle were engaged, both parties were anxious to quell the reports. Several reasons were involved. For his part, Dempsey did not want Kearns to know that he was serious about a woman. Similarly, Estelle was willing to forego the publicity of her engagement to the world's heavyweight boxing champion to keep her husband, Malcolm Pen-cock of Philadelphia, in the dark. However, the rumors were difficult to suppress, especially after the two took the same train east in September, 1924. Contacted in Atlantic City, Dempsey said it had been a coincidence that he and Estelle had departed at the same time, and, he added, his only interest in traveling east was to see the Firpo-Wills bout. Estelle, coincidentally contacted at the same hotel in Atlantic City, said that Jack was just a good friend.[24]

After Estelle's divorce from Pencock for "cruel and barbarous treatment" in early January, 1925, the rumors of 1924 were confirmed. Their engagement was announced on January 16, and Dempsey said, they planned to marry in either May or June. On second thought, they decided not to wait. After a day at a Tijuana race track, Estelle and Dempsey were married at the First Presbyterian Church in San Diego by Reverend Wallace M. Hamilton on the night of February 7. It was a small, informal wedding, witnessed by only Helen Taylor, Eddy Conners, Celia Dempsey, and Joe Benjamin. After the wedding, Estelle confessed herself to be "too happy to talk" and Dempsey spoke about plans for a honeymoon in Europe. But both expressed a weariness of publicity and the wish to be left alone.[25] Newspaper reporters, engrossed with the ordeal of Floyd Collins in Mammoth Cave, granted the newlyweds their wish.

The tragedy of the marriage, remembered Paul Gallico, was that Dempsey loved Estelle "terribly... too terribly." But husband and wife had no common interests upon which to base a marriage. Estelle was a frustrated actress trapped in a career that was going nowhere. Looking for reasons for the failure of her career, she blamed Dempsey. An actress needs social contacts to succeed in Hollywood, she reasoned, and being married to a pug hurt her socially. Coupled with her belief that Dempsey was bad for her career was Estelle's loathing for everything about the world of boxing. She hated fights, fight talk, and fighters; she was digusted by her husband's career and friends. As for Dempsey, the actor's makeup was a thin disguise. Scrape off the pancake makeup and look past the remodeled nose and the fighter was all too evident. At his home in Los Angeles, Dempsey entertained a steady stream of ex-fighters. His house was their base, and the broken-nose pugs came and went as they pleased, often spending all night in the house reminiscing about the time Joe Gans fought forty-two rounds with Battling Nelson under the Nevada sun and other such stories. In this company Dempsey felt relaxed; there was no need to worry about subject-verb agreement or which fork to use in front of these men. But the conflict with Estelle unavoidably emerged from their divergent interests. "Had he met and married Estelle in his last phase, after he had quit the ring, when his restless, rising gorge was crushed deeper and deeper within him through experience, through living, and, above all, through disuse," judged Gallico, "this love-match might have lasted. But in those days he was still too close to the disgusting things that every prizefighter needs in his trade."[26] From the first, then, love and hopeless incompatibility earmarked their marriage.

Not that Dempsey did not try to change, for he did. He bought a spacious house in Beverly Hills which Estelle had wanted. Architecturally, the house could be described as a cross between a Renaissance palace and a quaint English country home with a bit of Versailles added to keep things honest. It was pure 1920s Hollywood and not nearly as attractive as Dempsey's ranch-style mansion on Western Avenue in Los Angeles. Estelle was also given carte blanche in the interior decorations department. Jim Tully, a boxer turned writer, described the result as "middle-class elegance in many colors." Bric-a-brac, lace, and silk dominated the inside of their love nest. The boudoir was draped in silk and satin, and on the bed—Jack Dempsey's bed—were stuffed taffeta and lace pillows and large painted dolls with bisque heads and nothing but voluminuous satin skirts for bodies.[27] One can only imagine Dempsey's justified sense of self-sacrifice when he crawled into bed at night and snuggled next to a bisque-headed baby doll.

On their European honeymoon, delayed because of business engagements in Los Angeles, Dempsey also acquiesced to his wife's whims. They sailed from New York City on May 6 aboard the *Berengaria*, the old White Star liner *Superator* which had been rechristened when it had been purchased by Cunard. Like the *Aquitania* aboard which Dempsey sailed to Europe in 1922, the *Berengaria* was a fine old vessel, the kind which made the North Atlantic crossing an engagement with the utmost luxury. Fully booked, the ship could accommodate nearly fifty-five hundred people. She had a pillar-free vista the entire length of her enormous first-class lounge, a swimming pool that gave the appearance of being set in a mosaic temple supported by Doric columns, a large searchlight to comfort iceberg-conscious passengers, and hot and cold running water. The voyage was peaceful, the waters unusually calm, but Estelle spent most of her time in her cabin suffering from seasickness. When not attending to his wife, Dempsey mingled with the other passengers, signing autographs, and once even staging an exhibition bout with the butcher's mate.[28]

He and Estelle had come to Europe, Dempsey told reporters, just to "loaf around," but their hectic pace allowed little time for loafing. There were dinners given in his honor in London, chats with old friends and ex-fighters, and luncheons given in his honor in Paris. He spent two weeks in Berlin boxing exhibition bouts at the Lund Park for $15,000 each week, and he earned another $10,000 in Vienna for an exhibition bout. In London, Paris, Berlin, Cologne, and Vienna he was followed by crowds of people, and his every action was applauded. His appearance at the Gaumont Palace in Paris, for example, was greeted by the biggest round of applause since Marshall Joffre appeared there to witness a film commemorating the first Battle of the Marne.[29] In Europe, as in America, Dempsey's popularity was on the rise.

There were only two problems: taxes and Estelle. Calling himself "a victim of the Dawes Plan," Dempsey was forced to pay a $6,000 tax on the $28,000 he made boxing exhibition bouts in Berlin. His money was further drained by Estelle's spending. In Paris she bought the latest fashions, more dolls were purchased in Germany, and England was searched for antiques. At one point Dempsey remarked to reporters, only half in jest, that his exhibition work in Germany was made necessary by Estelle's spending.[30] Few things, it turned out, made Estelle more happy than spending money.

However, one of those few things was indulged in by Estelle in Europe. She loved dogs, big ones and small ones, but especially expensive ones. Dempsey also enjoyed dogs, though he tended to favor fighting canines like pit bulls. In Germany, Dempsey bought a large blue boarhound named Castor for Estelle. According to Gene

206

Fowler, perhaps Dempsey's closest friend, Castor "weighed almost three hundred pounds, ate four times a day . . . looked like the Abominable Snowman . . . and [lacked all] the social graces." Estelle fell immediately and madly in love with the beast, though, it seemed, he did not return the emotions. The uneven romance lasted for some months and left its trail of broken furniture, destroyed rooms, lawsuits, and costly bills across western Europe and the United States.[31]

After Dempsey purchased Castor from Joe Edwards, a former lightweight champion of England, the original owner initiated a lawsuit to reacquire the pet. After months of litigation and expensive legal bills, the Berlin courts found in favor of Dempsey, but the lawsuit was only the beginning of the troubles that followed Castor. Estelle insisted that Castor accompany Dempsey and her on their many sightseeing tours, but no automobile could be located that was big enough to hold the newlyweds, chauffeur, and dog. Therefore, two chauffeurs had to be hired for each trip, one for the Dempseys and the other for Castor. Unfortunately, Castor did not like to travel alone, and he harbored a grave mistrust of chauffeurs, growling at them and finally biting one who tried to pet him during a visit to Sans Souci. The episode cost Dempsey several hundred marks.[32]

Estelle, who believed Castor was being systematically provoked by the European chauffeurs, convinced Dempsey to employ a full-time escort for Castor. Lee Moore, a former lightweight boxer and close friend of Dempsey, was hired as the dogsitter. His tenure lasted about one week. One morning when Moore was about to take Castor for a walk, Estelle called her dog. The problem was that Moore was at the top of the grand staircase at the Hotel Adler in Berlin and the dog's leash was securely looped around his wrist. Estelle's unprompted call set Castor charging down the steps while Moore performed a series of "involuntary head stands, high dives, and pratfalls." After Moore's broken arm was set and his assortment of contusions treated, he resigned from the job. To add insult to injury, Estelle made Dempsey convince Moore to apologize to Castor for calling the untrained hound a "son of a bitch."[33]

Similar problems followed Castor's tour of Europe and visit to the United States. He ruined an Aubusson rug in Paris, exhibited a true German dislike for Frenchmen, and resisted all efforts toward house training. On the trip back to the United States he became seasick, and Estelle, who thoroughly sympathized with him, spent a large part of the trip cradling him in the ship's kennel. In Chicago, Castor was caught in the revolving doors at the Morrison Hotel. Once freed, he proceeded to do $500 worth of damage to the lobby of the hotel. In California he developed the habit of fighting other dogs, once even killing a game airedale. Finally for a price Dempsey convinced Moore to adopt Castor, but not before the dog cost the champion over $10,000 in fines, court costs, and damages.[34]

Problems with Castor, of course, dominated Dempsey's tour of Europe, but the champion nevertheless found time to honor certain commitments, the most important of which was a promise to box a charity exhibition in Brighton on July 4. The English, said a writer for the *Times,* were "grateful" to Dempsey for delaying his return trip to box for the Royal Sussex Hospital benefit. It was a friendly affair. Dempsey was kind, holding back on his punches and smiling. He "was not quite the Dempsey of our nightmares," wrote the *Times* reporter. In all, he sparred thirteen rounds against four British boxers, the most memorable of whom was "Fainting Phil" Scott, who so disliked being hit that he once won nine consecutive fights by falling to the canvas and claiming foul at the first suggestion of a low blow. Several days later, Dempsey, wife, and dog left from Cherbourg aboard the White Star liner *Homeric* for their return voyage to America.[35]

During the trip Dempsey had catered to Estelle's every desire. But their marriage continued down its ill-fated path. Estelle's career showed no signs of improving, and she continued to blame her husband. Even the movie they made together, *Manhattan Madness,* failed to lift her spirits. Advised by Estelle, Dempsey had invested heavily in the film, but it was released the same year as such films as *The Phantom of the Opera* and *The Gold Rush* and failed to attract much public attention. Obsessed by her failure, Estelle began to listen to friends who disliked Dempsey. Lupe Velez told Estelle that being married to a prizefighter would ruin her career. Estelle listened and agreed. The rift widened.[36]

Estelle's fears about her own career and jealousy over her husband's success affected Dempsey. He attempted to cultivate more friendships within show business circles and, one by one, he began to prune his own garden of boxing friends. Estelle's antagonism to members of the pugilistic world increased until it became an obsession. She complained about the ex-pugs who littered her home; she grew to hate broken noses and the slurred speech patterns of fighters who had fought too often. Gradually, she came to recognize one person as the symbol of everything that to her was slimy and corrupt about her husband's trade. She grew to hate Doc Kearns.

For his part, Kearns violently disliked Estelle from the moment he learned that Dempsey had married her. Suspicion was his most prominent characteristic, so he viewed the marriage in terms of a power play: Estelle, he believed, was trying to muscle in on his action. When Dempsey telephoned Kearns to announce his marriage, the champion was greeted by icy silence and then the equally cold click of the telephone receiver. This reception was followed several weeks later by an ugly confrontation at the Montmartre, a Hollywood café. In tones that resounded throughout the café, Kearns criticized Dempsey and threatened to uncover some shady and publicly unknown aspect of Estelle's career. Tempers erupted on both sides, and, for all intents and purposes, the partnership was ended with Kearns's drunken attack on the champion and his wife.[37]

In the months that followed both Dempsey and Kearns denied that they had parted company. Certainly, they told reporters, each had developed interests that excluded the other. Kearns had extended his managerial services to the welterweight champion of the world, Mickey Walker, and he even attempted to sign Gloria Swanson to a personal contract. In addition, at various times he announced that he would become a movie producer. As for Dempsey, a demanding wife and a movie career occupied most of his time. But the public statements provided for the press by Dempsey and Kearns failed to prevent their split from becoming general knowledge. As Jim Tully wrote in mid-1925, "A woman had come between two men whose friendship was the greatest in the annals of the prize-ring. The mighty Dempsey cannot serve two masters. He has chosen the lovelier but not more sagacious one of the two."[38]

Tully's estimation of the situation, however, was only partially true. To be sure, Estelle provided the catalyst for the Dempsey-

Kearns fission. But before Estelle entered the champion's life there had been signs of a crack in the men's relationship. Money had been a constant problem. Kearns freely spent his earnings, and, whenever possible, he just as freely spent a portion of Dempsey's money. To insure that he would receive his fair share of the gate from his bout with Firpo, Dempsey had personally collected his money from Rickard on the morning following the fight. This enraged Kearns, as did Dempsey's growing tendency for looking toward Rickard for sound financial advice.[39] Mature enough to recognize Kearns's faults, Dempsey was concerned about his own future. He did not want to retire broke; he wanted to avoid the gutter-to-millionaire-to-gutter syndrome. He knew fighters who perpetually jerked their heads to one side because economic necessity forced them to fight for too many years, and he saw the ex-champions who in their declining years earned a living by shining shoes or selling hand-painted ties. Dempsey did not want to be one of those pathetic tie vendors who blinked his eyes every other second because of some pressure on his brain.

Dempsey's marriage further aggravated the situation. He used it as a pretext for altering the fifty-fifty agreement that he and Kearns had always worked under. Fifty percent, he told Jim Tully, was too much for Kearns to demand from a married man. The champion told reporters that Kearns would accept 35 percent or nothing at all. He managed himself before he met Kearns and he was confident he could do so again. Kearns, in turn, insisted that he would continue to receive 50 percent of everything the champion earned.[40] There was no room for reconciliation or compromise. Both men wholeheartedly believed their demands were just. Although it would not be officially confirmed until 1926, the partnership had ended.

They went their separate ways. Kearns successfully guided Walker's fortunes. Although Walker lost the welterweight crown to Pete Latzo in early 1926, he recovered his old form and won the middleweight title from Tiger Flowers later in the year. A spender like Kearns, Walker was a perfect fighter for the spendthrift manager. Dempsey stayed in Hollywood and made pictures, or, occasionally, fought exhibition bouts. For each exhibition Dempsey was guaranteed at least $5,000, and although he never fought a good boxer, the contests were usually very successful. In one match in Mexico City a crowd of well over 20,000 people had to be controlled by the army or it would have smothered Dempsey with affection. He was called the most popular foreigner ever to visit Mexico. On the way to Havana for another exhibition, the champion was paid $10,000 per day for two days' public relations work with a Miami real estate firm.[41] He had become a very popular champion.

But something was missing. After reminiscing with Jim Tully about his early days in the ring, Dempsey said, "I had something then I haven't got now—I don't know what it is—I just know I haven't got it, that's all." He missed the ring. After almost three years of pugilistic inactivity he was ready to return. He did not have to return to fighting for financial reasons; though he made far less money in 1925 than he did in 1924, he was still a wealthy man. His motives were internal, not external. Perhaps he questioned his own mortality after the death of several friends during his inactive years. Billy Miske's death had upset Dempsey, and the champion was further saddened when Bill Brennan was shot down by thugs at the Tia Juana Club on Broadway. Then came the death of another friend, Rudolph Valentino, after the "Pink Powder Puffs" affair. Only a month before, Estelle had signed a contract with Feature Productions to play the leading lady in Valentino's next film.[42] Perhaps Dempsey simply missed practicing his trade.

CHAPTER XI

And Ghastly Thro' the Drizzling Rain

NEVER in the history of the modern heavyweight division has a champion gone as long without defending his title as Dempsey did. From September 1923 until September 1926 Dempsey neither defended his crown nor engaged in any sort of match more serious than an exhibition. He lived the life of a celebrity without an occupation. Trips to Europe, movie contracts, and vaudeville tours became the by-products of a trade he no longer practiced. During his three years of inactivity, Dempsey's trips to the gyms of the east and west coasts became less frequent, and although he never looked out of shape, he was never wholly in shape either. Sportswriters realized that the champion's years of inactivity would not serve him well when he decided to fight again. His "youth has slipped away from him," commented George B. Underwood. "Changed habits and environment have softened his hickory fiber. . . . Dempsey has passed his peak."[1]

Various reasons can be offered for Dempsey's not fighting between 1923 and 1926. One moralistic cartoon in the *Ring* suggested the champion was the victim of the "the soft life, idleness, the movies, [and] success."[2] To be sure, success—and especially the rewards of success—did cause Dempsey to become complacent about his boxing career. Similarly, his marriage to Estelle and estrangement from Kearns interrupted his ring activity. His wife hated boxing and Kearns hated his wife. The situation made it difficult for Dempsey to resume his career under the same manager. Yet as valid as these reasons were, the major reasons for the champion's inactivity stemmed from the nature of the heavyweights. Two of the better fighters in the division, Gibbons and Firpo, had already been defeated by Dempsey, and most of the others were either too inexperienced, too old, or too unimpressive for serious consideration. For example, Tex Rickard's ranking of the heavyweight division in 1925 listed Jack Renault as the fourth-best fighter. A former sparring partner for the champion and only a cut above a club fighter, Renault could never have been matched against Dempsey for the title. The sixth-ranked boxer, George Godfrey, had served as Firpo's sparring partner before the latter's fight with Dempsey. The remainder of the list was equally unimpressive: Young Bob Fitzsimmons' major qualification was that he was the son of a former champion; Emilio "King" Solomon, who billed himself as the heavyweight champion of Central America, was untested in the United States; Harry Persson, from Jarva, Sweden, was better known for his tattoos than for his fighting ability; Bud Gorman was a capable but undramatic tradesman; and Jack Sharkey and Paulino Uzcudun were still several years away from being boxers of championship caliber.[3] In fact, the only two heavyweights worthy of consideration between 1923 and 1926 were Harry Wills and Gene Tunney.

Wills, of course, labored under a stigma of a different kind. He was the black man in a white man's division. Throughout Dempsey's reign as champion, Wills was always the number-one contender. In 1922 Dempsey and Wills had signed a contract to fight, but the match was never promoted. Early in 1923 William Muldoon, chairman of the New York State Athletic Commission, said that until Dempsey fought Wills the champion would be barred from boxing in New York, but a few months later the Dempsey-Firpo bout was staged at the Polo Grounds. On May 1, 1924, Rickard announced that he would promote the match, then two months later he said Dempsey would not fight in 1924. Following the well-established pattern, in 1925 Rickard, Kearns, Dempsey, and the New York State Athletic Commission continually assured the public that a Dempsey-Wills bout would be held, but again no match was forthcoming.[4] By 1926 it was painfully obvious to everyone connected with the pseudopromotion that the fight would never be held.

Yet if the men on the inside realized this, the public and the sportswriters who constantly called for the contest did not. Indeed, equipped with a good record for the years between 1923 and 1926 and a resourceful manager, Wills became the cause célèbre of boxing in the 1920s. In 1924 Wills defeated Bartley Madden, a "leading contender" in the heavyweight division, and won an easy if unimpressive newspaper decision over Luis Firpo. He continued his string of victories in 1925 by knocking out Charley Weinert and Floyd Johnson, two tradesmen who had spent more time on the floor than on their feet during the mid-1920s. Given these wins to work with, Wills's manager, Paddy Mullins, kept pressuring Kearns and Rickard for a chance at the title.[5]

Journalists were swift to shoulder Wills's cause. In the name of "fair play" they demanded that Dempsey defend his crown against Wills. "It is evident," said an editorialist for *Opportunity*, a leading black journal in the 1920s, "that beneath the racial sentiments upon which prejudice rests there is a sense of fair play among the rabble." This "sense of fair play," he continued, will make "white America" ashamed of "honors gained through a limited competition" and will prevent Dempsey from hiding behind "the hobglobin of race feeling or race riots." In complete agreement was an editorialist for the New York *Sun and Globe* who maintained that the "race question has ceased to influence ring followers." Nat Fleischer, editor of the *Ring*, similarly supported Wills's case. Dismissing side issues of patriotism and race pride, Fleischer said "the matter is one purely of fair play." Either Dempsey showed his sportsmanship and fought Wills or he went contrary to the sporting tradition of fair play. For Fleischer, Spike Webb, America's Olympic boxing coach, and hundreds of other journalists, it was a very simple issue.[6]

Unfortunately for the well-intentioned journalists, the issue was not at all simple. Nor was the problem Dempsey's fault. Essentially, the problem was a political football thrown around by Rickard, the New York State Athletic Commission, and a group of politicians in Albany. Rickard opposed interracial heavyweight championship fights on principle, but by 1926 he would probably have promoted a Dempsey-Wills bout for the sake of expediency. The commission, being composed of political appointees, was subject to the will of Albany; and the will of Albany was sensitive to the political vibrations of a Dempsey-Wills fight. At one moment, wishing to please black voters in New York, political leaders in Albany and the commission would insist that Rickard promote the bout. Then, after Rickard had made plans for the fight, state authorities would countermand their orders because they feared the bout might be followed by race riots more extensive than those in 1910. As Charles Samuels, Rickard's biographer, wrote, "The politicians, being politicians, played both ends against the middle—and Tex Rickard was the middle."[7]

The other major contender for Dempsey's crown in 1926 was Gene Tunney, a superb defensive boxer who lacked a hard punch and a killer instinct, and was, therefore, not very popular with the public. Actually, Tunney's lack of a punch was largely a myth originated in sportswriters' columns early in his career. Tunney was afraid to hit an opponent with a hard punch for fear of breaking his brittle hands. Relying instead on his ability to outbox or to cut an adversary with his punches to win bouts, he was labeled as a "light puncher." But by 1926 Tunney had overcome his hand problems. A winter working as a lumberjack in Canada and a series of hand exercises had toughened his tender fists, and after 1923 he was seldom troubled with sore hands. Nevertheless, the myth remained; until the end of his career, Tunney never overcame the stigma of being the heavyweight who could not punch.[8]

As for the other labels—"defensive fighter" and "lack of the killer instinct"—Tunney never denied their truth. He modeled his fighting style after Mike Gibbons, a crafty middle and light heavyweight who popularized defensive boxing. Like Gibbons, Tunney's objective was always to win a fight without, if possible, ever being hit. He did not care in the least whether he won by a knockout or not. As he later admitted, "I found no joy in knocking people unconscious or battering their faces. The lust for battle and massacre was missing."[9] In an age when the most popular fighters were of the hit and be hit variety, Tunney was an artistic boxer, a master of the hit without being hit. So it was not surprising that Tunney was not a very popular fighter.

Popularity, however, had nothing to do with Tunney's worthiness as a contender. His record in the mid-1920s was the best in the heavyweight division. In 1922 he won the American light heavyweight title from Battling Levinsky. In the next three years he defeated many of the best fighters of his day. After an initial loss to Harry Greb, he thrice defeated the Pittsburgh boxer, considered by boxing experts to be one of the best of all time. In addition, Tunney defeated Jack Burke, Charlie Weinert, Tommy Loughran, Jack Renault, Jimmy Delaney, Georges Carpentier, Bartley Madden, Johnny Risko, and Tommy Gibbons. Against Gibbons, Tunney accomplished something that even Dempsey failed to do; he knocked out the crafty St. Paul boxer.[10] By 1926, then, Tunney's record placed him beside Wills as one of the only two logical opponents for Dempsey.

An elimination bout between Wills and Tunney would have been the logical way to decide which of the two should meet Dempsey. Indeed, Tunney suggested such a match. But Paddy Mullins would have nothing to do with an elimination bout. He was confident that the New York State Athletic Commission would force Dempsey to fight his boxer. Mullins believed that the pressure of thousands of votes in Harlem would influence enough politicians to force a Dempsey-Wills showdown. To fight Tunney, Mullins maintained, would needlessly risk Wills's chances for a championship fight. In short, Mullins wanted a political, not a pugilistic, decision.[11]

In 1926 Mullins won his political showdown with Dempsey, but he lost his chance for a Dempsey-Wills bout. The process by which Dempsey was matched against Tunney rather than Wills was one of the most confusing in the history of boxing. Simplified, it went like this: In New York boxing was a politicized business. Controlled by the governor's office, boxing provided a variety of patronage jobs, positions that ranged upward from examiners, clerks, and deputies to licensing officials and commissioners. The top jobs, of course, were the three commissioners' posts. At one time during his term as governor, Alfred E. Smith had fifty applications on his desk for two commissioners' jobs. In part, the political aspects of boxing in New York helped to insure that the Walker Boxing Law would never be repealed. Even Governor Nathan L. Miller, who publicly expressed his disdain for boxing, was quick to hand out the lucrative patronage jobs connected with the sport.[12]

By late summer, 1926, when the Dempsey-Wills-Tunney controversy reached its climax, the three-man New York State Athletic Commission was composed of William J. Muldoon, a Republican who had been appointed by Miller, and two loyal Democrats who had been appointed by Smith—James A. Farley and George E. Brower. Within the politically divided commission, and possibly overriding purely political loyalties, was a monstrous clash of ambitions and egos. In 1922 Muldoon had been elected commission chairman, but in 1924 Brower and Farley elected Brower commission chairman over Muldoon's protest. "The courteous thing," said the sulking former chairman, "would have been to elect me." Then in 1925, when Brower was in the hospital having his throat X-rayed, Farley and Muldoon elected Farley chairman. "The position must rotate," a vindictive Muldoon told reporters. "It rotated from me."[13] On such petty practices as back-stabbing and symbolic revenge, the commission functioned.

The same practices characterized their attitude on the Dempsey-Wills-Tunney controversy. In 1922 and early 1923, Muldoon, at least publicly, had favored Wills as an opponent for Dempsey. However, after Jimmy Walker was elected mayor of New York, Muldoon switched his position; it has been suggested that Muldoon's about-face was motivated by his personal hatred of Walker, who was an ardent advocate of a Dempsey-Wills bout. Muldoon's position on Wills was nevertheless the minority one, for both Farley and Brower favored a Dempsey-Wills match. Thus in early June, 1926, Dempsey was given an ultimatum by the commission: he must either defend his title against Wills or be prohibited from boxing in New York. When the champion failed to reply to the commission's demand, he was duly declared ineligible to box in New York. Only Muldoon, of the three commissioners, stood on Dempsey's side in the controversy.[14]

No sooner had the commission voiced its decision, however, than it reversed it. For some unknown reason, Brower suddenly saw his duty to his state and city in a new light. This new-found sense of duty, he said, caused him to change his vote in favor of a Dempsey-Tunney bout. On July 27 Brower and a very happy Muldoon voted formally in favor of a Dempsey-Tunney fight and recommended that the champion be granted a license to box in New York. This time

217

Farley filed the minority report. Farley, more than the other two commissioners, knew his politics; he foresaw the votes that the Democratic party would lose in Harlem if he reversed his stand. The future New York Democratic boss and later postmaster general, therefore, remained firm in his support of Wills.[15]

All would have appeared, then, to be set for a heavyweight championship fight in New York, but the New York State Athletic Commission did not have the final say in such matters. Working both jointly with and independently of the commission was the license committee, and before Dempsey could fight in New York he had to be granted a license. John Lardner said the relationship between the commission and the license committee "bordered closely on chaos," and he was undoubtedly correct. Like the commission, the license committee was composed of three members. One member was a close friend of Governor Smith's and stood in favor of a Dempsey-Tunney match. The position of the other two members, D. Walker Wear, a Binghamton Democrat, and Colonel (later General) John J. Phelan, a National Guard leader and importer of ladies' undergarments, was unknown at the time of the commission's decision to sanction a Dempsey-Tunney match. Phelan, the chairman of the license committee, thoroughly enjoyed his moment in the public limelight, for, as Lardner judged, he suffered from three faults: a weakness of syntax (he once declared, "There's no man alive who can accuse me of being honest!"), job enthusiasm that once caused him to break his own glasses while demonstrating a rabbit punch, and a fondness for positions of power.[16]

Forced by circumstances into the public spotlight, Phelan showed a real reluctance to vacate it. First, he postponed the case while he led his Sixty-ninth Regiment of the National Guard through maneuvers at Peekskill. Next, on August 10, Phelan and Wear met at the Flatiron Building in New York City to discuss the case. After two hours, while a crowd of five thousand people waited below, Phelan announced that the committee had granted Tunney a license but had decided to spend more time examining Dempsey's qualifications. During the next week the New York State Athletic Commission and the state attorney general, Albert Ottinger, recommended that Dempsey be issued a license, but Phelan continued his independent evaluation of the case. Finally, on August 16, Phelan announced his final decision: in behalf of himself and Wear, he said that until Dempsey fought Wills there would be no Dempsey-Tunney fight in New York. Although Attorney General Ottinger recommended a court case to test the license committee decision, it was clear that any championship bout involving Dempsey and Tunney for 1926 would have to be staged outside of the state of New York.[17]

Rickard, who was not about to initiate legal action, responded quickly. On August 18, he announced that the title bout would be held in Philadelphia at the new Sesquicentennial stadium. Both Governor Gifford Pinchot and Mayor Richard Kendrick welcomed the match. "New York's loss," commented a New York *Times* editorialist who disagreed with the decision of the license committee, will be "the gain of Philadelphia." Similarly, Tunney's gain proved to be Wills's loss. After six years of chasing the title, Wills and Mullins had reached the end of their quest. Later in the year Wills would fight a younger and hungrier fighter, Jack Sharkey. For twelve rounds Sharkey would batter the black fighter; then in the thirteenth round Wills would be disqualified for repeated fouling.[18]

Once the controversy was settled, the public became interested in Tunney's personality. Most boxing fans were acquainted with Tunney's record. His victories over Erminio Spalla, Carpentier, Italian Jack Herman, Johnny Risko, Bartley Madden, and Gibbons had been well publicized, and even people who did not follow the sport very closely were aware of his fights with Harry Greb. However, Tunney's personality remained largely an enigma. Other than his service record, Tunney's personal life—his likes and dislikes—had remained a mystery; not a guarded mystery, simply a mystery no one had been interested in enough to explain.

Actually, few boxers have been as attractive on a surface examination as Tunney. Horatio Alger could not have invented a better prototype for the mythic American hero. Born into a poor but honest family in the Greenwich Village section of New York in 1898, Tunney had attended St. Veronica's parochial school and LaSalle Academy. After completing his education he got a job as a stenographer for the Ocean Steamship Company, at a weekly wage of twelve dollars. At night he studied law at New York University. Although he boxed in preliminary contests, he gave little thought to fighting as a profession. Essentially, boxing was only a form of conditioning for the handsome Irishman.[19]

In 1918 he enlisted in the Marine Corps. For Tunney, war provided an unequaled opportunity for romantic heroism. As he explained in his autobiography—one of the few boxing autobiographies actually written by a pugilist—"I was reading 'The Three Musketeers' at the time, and like countless other lads, was intoxicated by the dashing doings of D'Artagnan. . . . I lived D'Artagnan adventures in imagination, with visions of flashing swords. I dreamed of myself as a soldier of the king, or of the U. S. A." A member of the Thirteenth Marines, Tunney went to France, but his unit never saw any action.[20] Still the romantic naïveté that characterized Tunney's enlistment was and remained the essential ingredient in his personality. He was a dreamer. He dreamed of being D'Artagnan and saving his country; he dreamed of smashing the death blow to the evil Hun; but most of all, he dreamed of moving up the social ladder, becoming wealthy, achieving a sophisticated level of education, marrying a socially prominent woman, and entering into the exclusive ranks of the American aristocracy. Tunney, then, was a dreamer, but like a hero from one of Alger's novels, his ambitious dreams came true.

It was while he was in the Marines, sailing past castles on the Rhine River, that Tunney devised a plan for the realization of his dream. At the time Tunney was boxing exhibitions for the AEF, of which he was the light heavyweight champion. As the castles passed his view, he discussed the upcoming Dempsey-Willard fight with a Corporal James McReynolds, who before the war had been a sportswriter in Joplin, Missouri. "He'll murder Willard," McReynolds said of Dempsey. "He's a big Jack Dillon." The conversation made Tunney think: Dillon, a murderous puncher, had been beaten by the sharp defensive boxer Mike Gibbons. Possibly, Tunney told McReynolds, the same would happen to Dempsey. The former reporter agreed, "Yes, when Dempsey is beaten, a fast boxer with a good defense will do it." At that moment, while he was little more than a glorified amateur, Tunney decided that someday he would defeat Jack Dempsey.[21]

During the years after his decision to channel all his efforts into preparing himself for a match with Dempsey, Tunney single-mindedly pursued his goal. "Perhaps it was not an obsession," wrote Mel Heimer, "but it was awfully close." After Tunney fought Soldier Jones on the same card that featured the Dempsey-Carpentier bout, the ring novice, still dressed in his bathrobe, crouched next to the ring and studied the champion's moves. At other times, he studied the films of Dempsey's other defenses. And he learned. Gibbons and Bill Brennan showed Tunney that a clever boxer could avoid Dempsey's wild rushes. Carpentier and Firpo demonstrated that the champion could be hit by a straight right hand. Every move and fault Dempsey had in the ring was filed away in Tunney's brain for future use. Even away from the ring, Dempsey was never far from Tunney's mind. Playing golf with the Scottish professional Tommy Armour a year or two before 1926, Tunney would hit his drives and then run after the ball, shadowboxing, hooking, jabbing, and muttering "Dempsey, Dempsey."[22] The champion and the championship gave Tunney's life a purpose.

Outside the ring, Tunney also fit into the typical Horatio Alger mold. A writer for the New York *World* remarked that Tunney looked "more the matinee or screen idol than a relentless foe with padded mitts." Tunney, he continued, "looks and acts clean. His private life has been above reproach. . . . Socially, [he] is a charming, cultured gentleman, as much at home in the smartest of smart drawing-rooms as he is . . . in the company of big men." To the press as a whole, no single person in sports better exemplified the virtue of the American character than Tunney. Enraptured by his ample qualifications, the New York *Times* editorialist noted that Tunney had a "flawless record." Before Tunney fought for himself, he battled for his country. Furthermore, "of unblemished character, representing the highest ideals in American manhood, an example for the younger generation, modest, retiring, unassuming, well read and educated—he combines every desirable characteristic."[23] More than anything else, Tunney resembled one of those romantic Horatio Alger characters that he so loved to read about.

But Tunney also had a tragic flaw—tragic, that is, at least in the eyes of the public. An ambitious, self-assured, self-educated man, he was, alas, something of a prig. After reading Shakespeare's A Win-

221

ter's Tale shortly after he landed in France in 1918, Tunney began to view himself as a literary critic. He read, he said, to relax, and, it would seem, he relaxed most when there was a reporter nearby, for the closer the journalist the weightier the volume by Tunney's side. Brian Bell, a feature sportswriter, first drew attention to Tunney's reading habits when he found the challenger reading Samuel Butler's *The Way of All Flesh*. Tunney explained to Bell that the bulky novel about three generations of English curates provided a rest from his hours of training. Soon every visitor to Tunney's camp discovered a different volume in Tunney's hands. Shakespeare, Somerset Maugham, and George Bernard Shaw were but a few of his favorite writers. Not every visitor, however, was impressed by the breadth of Tunney's knowledge. Ring Lardner, accompanied by Grantland Rice and the female members of their families, visited Tunney's Stroudsburg, Pennsylvania, training quarters, where, according to Lardner, Tunney was never without a thin volume. At the dinner table and even during chats, Tunney would lay the book face down at his side. Lardner wisely decided not to ask the name of the volume, but one of the ladies in the group succumbed to the temptation. "Oh, it's just a copy of *The Rubaiyat* that I always carry with me," Tunney informed the lady.[24]

If Tunney's display of books did not alienate enough of the reporters and public, his conversational technique took care of the rest. Evidently, Tunney's reading of the classics led him to believe that real people actually spoke in blank verse. Tunney's affected, convoluted speech patterns were as foreign to most Americans as an untranslated poem by Baudelaire. Upset with a group of sportswriters for a particularly cutting story, Tunney lectured the group: "Your conduct... was most unbecoming, when I acted the man, for you to construe, as you did, my actions to your ends. That's the sort of ungentlemanly thing that makes it so difficult for you chaps to get what you want." Trevor Wignall, an English friend of Tunney's, admitted that the boxer "affected a superiority" and "used long words when shorter, more easily understood words would have served a clearer purpose."[25] But it was all part of the dream; the Tunney of Tunney's dream spoke as if he had just stepped out of the pages of a romantic novel.

Also part of the dream and another reason Tunney was disliked was his circle of friends. The challenger avoided members of his profession like the plague. Instead he tried as much as possible to associate with the wealthy and the artistic. Industrialists, the social elite, writers, aristocrats, bankers, and professors were among Tunney's favorite people. After he won the title he lectured on Shakespeare before Professor Wendell Phelps's class at Yale, corresponded with George Bernard Shaw, took walking trips in Europe with Thornton Wilder, married a socially prominent woman, and regarded the public with a lofty indifference.[26] Even before he won the title his tendency to reach upwards was present. It was also obvious.

In short, what the public learned about Tunney's character in the weeks before the fight was not always to its liking. Watching the challenger train at the Glenbrook Country Club on the edge of Stroudsburg, many viewers saw something fully as alien as Carpentier. Here, certainly, was a boxer who was very different from Dempsey. Dempsey trained at race tracks, on battleships, or in ballparks—but never at a country club. Dempsey's championship years had been scarred by his war record and his smaller moral improprieties, but he was always accessible to and open with the public and reporters. On the surface Tunney appeared to be a more perfect hero than Dempsey, but after scratching the surface people were not so sure.

At Dempsey's training camp in Atlantic City the friendly, carefree atmosphere of his earlier camps was totally absent. Gone, also, were the colorful characters and scenes. Instead, visitors to the dog track where Dempsey trained found a grim camp, guarded like an army arsenal. Night and day, Dempsey himself was guarded by an expensive team of private detectives headed by his friend Mike Trent. Surrounded by his sparring partners and a group of close friends, Dempsey was unusually reserved and nervous, withdrawn and paranoid.[27]

The champion's changed attitude was not without cause. In the eyes of his former manager, Doc Kearns, Dempsey was a marked man. A resourceful ally, Kearns was just as crafty an enemy, and from the time he split with Dempsey, he was the champion's foremost adversary. Kearns maintained that Dempsey was his property, that at least one-third of everything Dempsey made was rightfully his, and that to split things otherwise was the grossest display of ingratitude on the part of the champion. To exact revenge, he decided to harass Dempsey. In August, before Dempsey went to Atlantic City, Kearns's legal agents seized Dempsey's Rolls Royce from Estelle, an action that enraged her even more than Dempsey.[28] Dempsey regained the car by proving that it belonged to Estelle, but the legal hassle—the heart of Kearns's vengeful program—was nonetheless real and annoying.

Kearns's attack on Dempsey's patience and nerves increased as the days before the fight decreased. Kearns filed a suit which demanded that Dempsey pay him $333,333.33, the amount of money, the manager said, which would have been his share of a Dempsey-Wills and a Dempsey-Tunney fight. Another suit tied up $150,000 in the champion's New York bank account. Two days before the championship fight, Kearns filed still another suit. This one was for $250,000 and represented what Kearns believed was his deserved portion of Dempsey's "entertainment" earnings. If these actions were not enough, Kearns teamed up with B. C. Clements, a Chicago promoter who held an unconsummated Dempsey-Wills contract, to file a "taxpayer's suit" which, if successful, would prevent Dempsey and Tunney from collecting any fight earnings until it was proved that the bout had been honest.[29] All totaled, Kearns sued Dempsey for over $700,000. None of the vicious suits were successful in the courts.

The rocky state of his marriage with Estelle added strain, and in the weeks before the fight Dempsey's health began to break down. Suffering from dermatitis, brought on by stress, Dempsey's skin cracked and peeled, and each day he drank olive oil to calm his troubled digestive tract. He even had trouble sweating, a certain sign that there was something wrong. Dan Daniel, who visited Dempsey's camp as a reporter, remembered that he and his fellow sportswriters noticed that the champion looked sick but they convinced themselves that it was nothing serious.[30]

Dempsey's treatment of his sparring partners was further evidence that something was amiss. As always, he tried to hurt his sparring partners, but his timing was off. Bill Tate, Mike Burke, Jimmy Roberts, Johnny Saxon, Joe Karp, and others escaped from their matches with the champion unbruised. Tommy Loughran, the future light heavyweight champion, was hired to imitate Tunney's style. Loughran did his job too well. He stabbed and jabbed Dempsey as he pleased, shifting easily from his right to his left and avoiding the champion's wild rushes with frightening ease. Day after day, as thousands of spectators watched in grim silence, Loughran made Dempsey look like a novice. Less than one week before the championship fight, the small boxer even bloodied the champion's nose. Paul Gallico, who witnessed these contests, recorded his and the other sportswriters' feelings: Loughran "wrote Dempsey's finish in letters large enough for all of us to see, except that we, too, were blinded by our own ballyhoo and the great Dempsey legend that we had helped to create." They kidded themselves that Dempsey was just taking it easy on Loughran because the light heavyweight was of championship caliber. "That was a laugh: Dempsey, who never went easy on anybody, would have broken Loughran in two if he could have caught him." The whole scene was, for Gallico, added proof of "the strange grip" that Dempsey had upon the imagination of his age.[31]

Nearly everyone who followed boxing was influenced by the Dempsey legend. His years away from the ring seemed miraculously to have increased the proportion of his image. In the days before the fight, former champions and sportswriters confidently predicted that Dempsey would easily knock out Tunney. One was Gentleman Jim Corbett, the old heavyweight who had popularized scientific boxing. Corbett had advised his friends at the Friars Club to bet on Dempsey regardless of the prohibitive odds. Corbett, however, was notorious for his unblemished reputation as a false prophet. Mindful of this fact, and not wishing to allow Corbett to destroy such a fine record, Gene Fowler, who as Corbett's ghost writer submitted daily articles to the Hearst Universal Service, reversed Corbett's prediction. Across America, newspaper readers were informed by Corbett-Fowler on the day before the fight that Tunney would win a decision after ten rounds of left jabs and superb footwork. Fowler, of course, did not believe a word that he put in Corbett's mouth; he only wanted to insure that Gentleman Jim would once again be wrong. Corbett never read the articles printed under his name, so the day after the fight he believed that the telegrams and telephone calls of congratulations were the work of sarcastic sportsmen. When Corbett did learn the truth, he puffed up with pride and told any sportswriter who would listen about the process behind his logic. "By the time he got back to New York," wrote Fowler, "Gentleman Jim believed that he really *had* chosen Tunney to win."[32]

Sportswriters who actually gave Tunney a chance were laughed at. W. O. McGeehan was ridiculed when he picked Tunney; friends of McGeehan suspected that his choice was influenced more by a dyspeptic nature than sound knowledge. Similarly, the opinion of Bernard Gimbel, an amateur boxer and member of the famous mercantile family, was dismissed as idle speculation. With the exception of these two men, public opinion was solidly, if sometimes mournfully, behind Dempsey. The student of Shakespeare was given little chance of dethroning the product of the hobo jungle.[33]

Nevertheless, interest in the fight was high. It was the first heavyweight championship in three years; that fact alone guaranteed interest. Beyond this was the interest generated by the symbolic nature of the contest. Dempsey and Tunney represented two different visions of America. Dempsey was a fighter; he disliked the term boxer. From the rural West, his virtues and strengths were those of a frontiersman—individualism, straightforwardness, and, above all, brute strength and determination. Outside the ring, he was not concerned with rules and laws. Tunney was from the urban East, and his virtues were similar to those of the businessmen he so admired. He was organized; he planned, studied, analyzed, rehearsed, pondered, and practiced. His style was synthetic, the result of careful planning and practicing.[34] A "boxer" whose method resembled a well-oiled machine, intricate and subtle, Tunney was unemotional inside the ring. For him, boxing was a vehicle for success—a means to an end, and not the end itself. In short, boxing was a business for Tunney. Fighting was a way of life for Dempsey. Such a symbolic contrast heightened interest in a fight not between two men, but between two visions of America, two ways of life.

On the day of the fight, September 23, both men traveled to Philadelphia. Tunney used the trip to gain a psychological edge over Dempsey, for he covered the eighty-mile journey between Stroudsburg and Philadelphia in a plane piloted by stunt flier Casey

Jones. In an age when only brave men and fools traveled by air, Tunney's act was a public warning: neither the air nor Dempsey frightened him. In fact, if anyone was frightened by the stunt, it was Rickard, not Tunney. "Goddam that son of a bitch!" Rickard said when he learned of Tunney's exploit. "What's he trying to do to me?" "To you?" replied the cynical W. O. McGeehan. The trip did affect Tunney's stomach, however. At the mid-afternoon weigh-in, Tunney appeared pale and airsick, and after Frank Weiner, chairman of the Pennsylvania boxing commission, weighed the challenger, he told a friend that Tunney looked "scared" and was "as white as a sheet." Unaffected, Tunney went to the apartment of a friend to sleep and, later, to eat a steak.[35]

Dempsey's trip from Atlantic City to Philadelphia was by more conventional means—a train. By the time the train reached Broad Street Station in the City of Brotherly Love, the champion knew that something was wrong. He felt queasy; his legs were rubbery. Eventually, he began to vomit. For the next several hours, he continued to retch, and his condition was complicated by a rash. With each passing minute more of his strength passed out of his body. If by fight time Dempsey's adrenalin gave him enough power to compete, he still was in no condition to win. Mentally and physically, at bell time Dempsey was a defeated man.[36]

What he suffered from has never been discovered. Obviously, it was some sort of poisoning, probably ptomaine. Several months after the fight, Dempsey's condition became a subject of heated debate. Police Captain Charles J. Mabbutt of Atlantic City, who had been assigned to Dempsey's camp, told a reporter for the Baltimore *News* on December 1, 1926, that the champion had been poisoned. According to Mabbutt, "a poisonous substance was introduced into the cream used by our party" for breakfast on the day of the fight. Everyone connected with the camp denied Mabbutt's poisoned cream story. Sergeant Mike Trent, Dempsey's bodyguard, said Mabbutt never ate with the champion, not on the day of the fight or any other day. Dempsey admitted to being ill but discounted deliberate poisoning. However, the possibility of deliberate poisoning did not fade away. As recently as 1977, Trent's actions on the day of the fight have been questioned. Jerry Luvadis, Dempsey's trainer, supposedly told Gene Normile that Dempsey became sick only after Trent gave the champion some olive oil. Furthermore, Trent was conspicuously absent from Dempsey's corner during the fight. The day after the fight, Normile fired Trent, explaining to Dempsey that the bodyguard was involved with gamblers. All talk of deliberate poisoning, though, lacks a shred of proof. As far as Dempsey was concerned, his illness was accidental, a trick of fate, and, besides, he says, "Tunney would have won anyway."[37]

Only a handful of people on the night of September 23 knew of Dempsey's condition. What interested the mass of people who came to Philadelphia for the fight was the event itself. Actually, it was more than an event; it was a *happening* in the fullest sense of the word. Under overcast skies, as the temperature dropped to the lower 40s, people from every walk of life filed into the Sesquicentennial stadium. The next day, the newspapers reported that 135,000 people paid to attend. Officially, the figure has been revised downward, to 120,757. The fight grossed $1,895,733. For the time, both figures were records for all sporting events, not just for boxing. Millions more people listened to the fight on the radio. Everyone, it seemed, was interested. The New York *Times* reported that in Jacksonville, Illinois, an interpreter, standing beside an Associated Press telegraph operator, passed round by round details about the fight via sign language to a group of deaf-mutes from the Illinois School for the Deaf waiting in the street below. After the fight, a writer for *Labor*, a railway union newspaper, estimated that 114,900,000 Americans out of a total population of 115,000,000 were for Tunney.[38] The pro-Tunney guess was undoubtedly wrong, but the claim that 115,000,000 Americans were interested in the outcome was not far from the truth.

H. L. Mencken had described the crowd at the Dempsey-Carpentier fight as "well-dressed, good-humored and almost distinguished." The gathering at the Dempsey-Tunney affair was that and more so. Earlier in the month, the New York *Times* predicted that more than 2,000 millionaires would attend the fight. Although nobody counted, the estimate must have been accurate. Led by Secretary of the Treasury Andrew Mellon, the ringside sections were filled by such multimillionaires as Charles M. Schwab, Percy Rockefeller, Vincent Astor, William Randolph Hearst, Joseph Pulitzer, Anthony J. Drexel Biddle, Jr., W. Averill Harriman, Harry Payne Whitney, and Kermit and Archie Roosevelt. Athletes and those who owned the athletes were present: Gertrude Ederle, Babe Ruth, Tim Mara, John McGraw, Jacob Ruppert, and Wilbert Robinson. Ambassadors, diplomats, governors, mayors, cabinet secretaries, assistant secretaries, undersecretaries, and other high government officials filled an entire column in the *Times*. If Mayor James J. Walker was the most flamboyant of the group, he was far from the most prestigious. On this night wealth, sports, and politics mixed with show business and crooks. The Hollywood contingent included William Fox, Charlie Chaplin, Norma Talmadge, Tom Mix, and Billy Hart. William A. Brady and Florenz Ziegfeld represented Broadway. Gamblers, the most notorious of the 1920s, were everywhere. Arnold Rothstein, the man behind the 1919 World Series fix, was joined by Abe Attell and Philadelphia's own Boo Boo Hoff. Significantly, the "smart money" was on Tunney. Finally, every major sportswriter of the twenties was there—Grantland Rice, Dan Parker, Paul Gallico, Ring Lardner, Ed Sullivan, Westbrook Pegler, Damon Runyon, Red Smith, Jim Dawson, W. O. McGeehan, Hype Igoe, and the rest. It was estimated that over two million words were sent over the hundred telegraph lines installed for the fight. Looking over the crowd, Rickard remarked, "I ain't never seed anything like it."[39]

The crowd was large but surprisingly orderly. An army of ushers and 4,000 Philadelphia policemen kept order, preventing the gates from being crashed and refusing to accept counterfeit tickets. Through most of the preliminaries, the crowd was quiet, erupting only when Tommy Loughran, a local favorite, won a six round decision over Jimmy Delaney. For the most part, the fans simply waited for the championship fight and for the dark clouds over the stadium to break. They did not have long to wait for either event.[40]

Tunney was first in the ring. Handsome, dressed in a scarlet-trimmed blue robe with the Marine Corps emblem on the back, Tunney received an uproarious cheer. A few minutes later, Dempsey climbed through the ropes. Philadelphia rules required a fighter to be clean-shaven, so the champion was without his usual two-day growth. Otherwise, he looked fit, at least to the spectators who were

229

sitting some distance from the ring. When Dempsey was introduced boos rocked the amphitheater. It was a pro-Tunney crowd. Perhaps, as Nat Fleischer guessed, Dempsey's long delay in defending his title was viewed cynically by the audience. For three years, Fleischer wrote, "Dempsey has used the heavyweight title as a medium for almost everything but defense." Perhaps, too, the crowd, like most crowds, was just cheering for the underdog. After all, a recent popularity contest to determine America's favorite athlete placed Dempsey third behind Babe Ruth and Helen Wills.[41]

The two fighters met in the center of the ring. "Hello, Champion," the smiling Tunney said. "Hello, Gene," Dempsey replied. As they parted Tunney said, "May the better man win." Somewhat startled at such a thought, Dempsey only muttered, "Yeh, yeh." Swiftly, as if in an attempt to beat the rain, referee Tommy Reilly gave the fighters their instructions. Dempsey was warned against rabbit-punching and low blows, but he did not appear to be listening. Back in their respective corners, both men had their hands wrapped. At shortly before 10:00 the bell rang, and almost immediately luminous streaks of rain filled the bright ring.[42]

The first round started as everyone expected it would, with Dempsey rushing Tunney, throwing left hooks. Tunney, who, after all, enjoyed Shakespeare more than fighting, was content to parry Dempsey's blows and back pedal. Sensing that his opponent was afraid to throw punches, Dempsey began to pressure Tunney even more. For Tunney it was a dream come true. Overconfident, Dempsey was doing just as Tunney planned; the champion, who fought by instinct and not by plan, was falling into Tunney's trap. Suddenly, as Dempsey launched another left, Tunney stepped in toward the champion and snapped off a straight right hand. It was a move that Tunney had practiced since he saw Carpentier hit Dempsey with an identical punch in 1921. But like Carpentier's blow, Tunney's punch landed high, on the cheek instead of the jaw. "Perhaps if the punch had landed on Jack's jaw," Tunney wrote years later, "I might have knocked him out." Even high, though, the punch hurt. Dempsey staggered back, sagging a little, and then clinched, trying to gain time for his head to clear. Few in the crowd realized what had happened. Everyone knew that Tunney had won the round, and most cheered accordingly. But nobody knew how much the punch had taken out of the champion. Sitting in his corner between rounds, breathing smelling salts, Dempsey later said he thought, "I'm an old man."[43]

Tunney knew the effect of the punch: Dempsey, he said, "never got over the punch . . . that blow won the fight." What followed was confirmation of Tunney's belief. A pattern was set: Dempsey would rush the challenger, throwing wild rights and lefts; Tunney would elude or block the punches and counter with left jabs and an occasional straight right. If it were not a heavyweight championship fight and a major upset, the fight would have been boring. Dempsey seldom landed a solid punch, and Tunney was too cautious to try to knock out the champion. The crowd sensed Tunney's timidity. Tunney's plan was to win by taking the fewest possible chances. He outboxed Dempsey, but after the first round, he did not try to knock out his opponent. Even when Dempsey was bleeding and groggy, Tunney showed no taste for blood.[44]

Only in the sixth round did Dempsey land a good punch, a left to the adam's apple which was serious enough that for days after the fight Tunney was hoarse and coughed blood. Otherwise, the fight was marked by a grim monotony. Dempsey was cut over the right eye in the fourth round. By the eighth round his left eye was closed. At the bell for round ten, the last round, both the champion's cheeks were bruised, his jaw was swollen, and he was bleeding from the mouth. The rain, which fell heavily throughout the fight, mixed with his blood and gave the champion's face a ghastly appearance. For the first time in his life, he drew pity from a fight crowd. Mixed with the sympathy, however, was respect. On the wet canvas, Dempsey could not get enough traction to land a knockout blow, and a knockout was his only chance for victory. Nevertheless, he did not quit. The tenth round serves as an example. After touching gloves, "Dempsey, with the urge of the old Dempsey still upon him, even if the effectiveness was gone, went on the offensive. He rushed blindly, although eagerly, it seemed, only to miss."[45] When the bell ended Dempsey's futile efforts, there was no question about who had won the fight. Dempsey did not win one round.

He had lost, but in losing he achieved a dignity that was to become legendary. After the decision was announced, Dempsey, sick and unable to see, grabbed Philadelphia Jack O'Brien, a former light heavyweight boxer who acted as a second for the champion, and said almost incoherently through thick bruised lips, "Take me to him. Take me to him." Ushered across the ring by O'Brien and Normile, Dempsey hugged Tunney. "All right, Gene," he said slowly. "All right, good luck." There was nothing else to say. Turning, leaning heavily on O'Brien, Normile, and Luvadis, Dempsey was helped out of the ring. Then it started—the cheering, not for the new champion but for the old champion, for Dempsey. It grew louder and louder, "deafening," as Dan Daniel described it. And Dempsey heard it, until his dressing room door closed out the noise. Then, through swollen, bloody eyes, he cried.[46]

Nobody knew exactly what to say. Bill Tate, who had been with Dempsey since 1918, looked glumly at the floor. Normile and Luvadis followed Tate's example. As Dempsey lay on the rubbing table a doctor stitched his cut eye. Finally, Normile said something, but Dempsey did not answer. Even when he was shaken slightly, he refused to say anything. "Let him alone. He's tired," the doctor said. He issued only one statement to the press. It was simple, sincere, and offered no excuses: "I have no alibis to offer. I lost to a good man, an American—a man who speaks the English language. I have no alibis."[47] It seemed that the important thing was not losing the title but to whom one lost it.

As Dempsey was dressing, his wife learned about the outcome of the match. She was in Fort Wayne, Indiana, aboard the Pennsylvania Limited bound for Philadelphia. She did not like boxing, and Dempsey did not believe a wife should see her husband fight; therefore, she did not attend the championship contest. That night, when Estelle reached Dempsey by telephone, she asked, "What happened, Ginsberg?" Dempsey's answer was as good an explanation for why a fighter loses as has ever been advanced. "Honey," he said, "I just forgot to duck." For Dempsey, the mysteries of fighting were that simple. Fights were won by hitting and ducking, not by studying and planning. And when one lost, it was best to accept the pain, offer no excuses, congratulate the winner, and go on from there. Something in the uncomplex way Dempsey viewed the situation appealed to people. Even the anti-Dempsey writer for *Labor* had to admit that the former champion was splendid in defeat.[48] After the public learned how Dempsey accepted defeat, his public image was forever altered. People realized that the dethroned lion was not so bad after all.

Dempsey, however, was about the only person who did not offer excuses for his loss. Why Dempsey lost became the subject of controversy and wild speculation. Every theory started at the same point: Dempsey at his best would have soundly defeated Tunney. The question was why Dempsey was not up to par. The most commonly offered excuse was that Dempsey had stayed away from boxing for too long. The New York *Times* expressed this opinion. Dan Daniel was also inclined toward this view in the *Ring*. From there, theories became more strained. Many people believed the poisoned cream theory was the best explanation. Nat Fleischer maintained that a poison of a different kind spelled the champion's end: "Dempsey was poisoned by worry." As Dempsey explained to Fleischer, he was worried about his condition and Kearns's continual harassing attacks. In the end, he became "a victim of his own forebodings." Still another theory asserted that Dempsey's muscle failed in its battle with Tunney's brain. As the Philadelphia *Inquirer* explained, Tunney's superb use of human psychology was the primary difference in the fight. Finally, there was the theory that bypassed logic and searched the soul of human emotion and devilment. Ring Lardner championed this cause. The fight, Lardner wrote to F. Scott Fitzgerald, was a "frame-up." Lardner, who bet fifty dollars on Dempsey, informed his friend, "The thing was a very well done fake. . . . The championship wasn't worth a dime to Jack; there was nobody else for him to fight and he had made all there was to be made (by him) out of vaudeville and pictures."[49] Fortunately, almost nobody believed Lardner.

For those who believed in fate, there was even an easier explanation: 1926 was a bad year for champions. Within two weeks, three of the great athletes of the 1920s were defeated. Big Bill Tilden was dethroned by René Lacoste, Bobby Jones was defeated by George Von Elm, and Dempsey lost to Tunney. Furthermore, four other boxing champions besides Dempsey lost their crowns between January and October, 1926. Harry Greb, Mickey Walker, Rocky Kansas, and Paul Berlenbach lost their titles.[50] Every explanation of why Dempsey lost the title was offered except one: Tunney was a better fighter.

The fight was interesting from a social perspective. All levels of American society seemed to have accepted prizefighting. Although Dempsey received $717,000 for the fight—by far his largest purse until that time—commercialism was not an issue. If press reaction is indicative of the American temper, then Americans had finally accepted the commercialistic nature of professional boxing. The moral position of the sport and the harmlessness of attending a prize fight was a second social issue settled by the match. No longer were women criticized for watching two men box, and the voices of reformers and religious leaders against boxing were surprisingly quiet during the entire affair. Certainly, opponents were not totally mute. The Reverend Dr. Clarence Edward Macartney of the Arch Street Presbyterian Church in Philadelphia criticized the government officials who attended the "recrudescence of paganism" in his city. How, Macartney asked, could America maintain its elevated moral position in the world when "Cabinet [members], Governors . . . and men high in politics and business of the country sit by the ringside and join the multitude as they acclaim a new champion?"[51] Such voices, however, were futile cries in the night that, for the most part, fell upon deaf ears. By 1926 Americans realized that professional boxing was here to stay. Many people may have secretly resented the fact, and still more may have been openly envious of a fighter's wage, but no one felt compelled any longer to try to reverse the irreversible.

The entrenched position of professional boxing was the result of two men—Tex Rickard and Jack Dempsey. The former was a genius of promotion; the latter was the greatest single drawing card who ever lived. The name—Dempsey—was a magnet that attracted money. Before the twenties there was never a million dollar gate, and after the twenties there were only four between 1930 and 1960. But during the twenties there were five million-dollar gates. Dempsey participated in all five of them. But after the rainy night in Philadelphia, Rickard had lost his champion, his drawing card. Saddened by the beating Dempsey took, Rickard told reporters that there would be no rematch: "I wouldn't want to put him through it again." In a private meeting with Rickard several days after the fight, Dempsey expressed similar sentiments. "I've had it," he told the promoter. By early December, however, both men had had more time to think, and each had changed his mind.[52]

CHAPTER XII

I'm Fighting
for the
Glory

WHEN a legend is debunked, questions are bound to arise. Shock and disbelief underlined the public's reaction to Dempsey's loss. Had the Lone Ranger been unmasked and exposed as a woman, the surprise could not have been greater. For seven years—longer than any modern heavyweight to that time—Dempsey had been the heavyweight champion of the world. His image had ruled the public imagination of what a fighter should be like; Dempsey, the hungry kid from the West who fought all-out, all the time, ignoring defense while continually advancing and punching, was for millions of Americans simply and totally "the fighter." Americans, Dan Daniel said, loved a puncher, and above all else, Dempsey was a puncher.[1] Yet suddenly, and, to many, inexplicably, Dempsey was no longer the champion. Instead the heavyweight division was ruled by a cold, aloof intellectual boxer, who, unlike every heavyweight champion before him, did not win the title by a knockout but by a decision. The consensus among Americans was that something was wrong with the fight game.

After his initial shock at Dempsey's defeat, Rickard began to tap this public sentiment. Dempsey's loss, Rickard soon realized, made the former champion an even more lucrative commodity: one loss might be rationalized as a fluke or a fix, but two losses would be a sure indication that Dempsey was human after all. Furthermore, Rickard saw that the loss increased Dempsey's popularity. Less than one month after their fight, both Dempsey and Tunney attended a contest between Jim Maloney and Arthur de Kuh. When introduced,

Dempsey was greeted by uproarious cheering; the noise lasted several minutes, and he was showered with paper thrown by spectators in the second balcony. For Tunney there were scattered cheers mingled with boos. Similar outbursts greeted Dempsey in the various cities he visited after he lost the title. And when he became ill in February, 1927, his recovery was followed by millions of Americans.[2] Indeed, losing the title may have tarnished his reputation, but he was still the most popular fighter in the world. Rickard, who noted the public's interest in Dempsey, knew that cheers could be converted into dollars if the former champion would attempt a comeback.

Dempsey balked. For personal as well as professional reasons, he did not want to fight again. His marriage was faltering; an attempted comeback would only further complicate it. Estelle's hatred of boxing increased at the same rate as her career declined, and by early 1927 there were doubts that she had any career left. Added to his marital problems, Dempsey suffered doubts about his own ability as a fighter. At the age of thirty-one, he realized that he was past his prime, and he honestly doubted that he could ever defeat Tunney. "I was beat like no man should be beat," he said years later. "I just didn't think I had enough left in my legs to catch a *real* boxer anymore. And I had doubts about what I could do if I did catch him [Tunney]."[3] Therefore, when Rickard approached him about returning to boxing, Dempsey refused to leave the comfort of retirement. Could he beat Tunney? Retired he would never know. Only a fight would answer the question, and he feared the answer more than the fight.

Although he kept repeating that he would not come out of retirement, Dempsey found it difficult to cut his ties with boxing. As if by habit, he continued to train after returning to Los Angeles. In an effort to keep his weight down, he did his road work and engaged in light gym workouts. By the spring his exercising took a more serious course. Isolated from curious reporters, Dempsey started to train in earnest in the mountains near Ojai, California. He chopped trees, punched the heavy bag, and even sparred on occasion. Next he moved to the Ventura Mountains, where his old trainer, Gus Wilson, added more organization to his schedule. For almost three months he trained outdoors, letting the sun and time heal his injured body and ego. By April, Dempsey was ready to leave retirement to

237

those persons over sixty-five. He was once again ready to fight whomever and whenever Rickard chose.[4]

One person Rickard did not choose was Tunney. Publicly, Rickard announced that Dempsey would have to earn a rematch with Tunney. As he told the press, he hoped to match the winner of the Paulino Uzcudun-Knute Hansen fight with either Jack Sharkey or Jim Maloney, with the victor in that match to meet Dempsey.[5] Such an elimination tournament would mean large gates for Rickard's Madison Square Garden. Although a Paulino-Hansen match held little intrinsic interest, the idea that the winner might possibly be Dempsey's next opponent added color to an otherwise drab affair. Similarly, an elimination tournament had another advantage that, if he realized it, Rickard did not care to make public. There was a very good chance that Dempsey would lose a rematch with Tunney; therefore an elimination tournament would allow Rickard to promote at least two more fights that involved Dempsey. With the former champion on a card a million-dollar gate was almost certain. Without Dempsey such a gate was much less sure.

In Rickard's makeshift elimination tournament, Paulino defeated Hansen in a fight staged in Madison Square Garden. On April Fool's Day, Paulino won another crucial bout, this time against the Australian heavyweight Tom Heeney. Suddenly, the thick-set, beetle-browed Basque, whose left arm was frozen in a permanent forty-five degree angle as a result of a poorly set broken arm, became the leading contender to face Dempsey. Paulino was a curious man; a product of an elaborate press campaign, he always looked far more ferocious than he actually was. A report from Cuba said that he had once killed three wild boars single-handedly, shooting one, clubbing another, and finishing the last with his bare fists. Furthermore, his crouching style of fighting and sledgehammer left hooks appealed to the boxing public. As far as Rickard was concerned, a Paulino-Dempsey fight appeared to be an ideal match.[6]

However, Paulino was soon to leave the picture—not the heavyweight picture, to be sure, for Paulino's career lasted until 1935 when Joe Louis altered the bone structure on the left side of the Basque's face. But for some inexplicable reason known only to Rickard, Paulino was dropped from the elimination tournament. Instead, Rickard decided to pit Dempsey against the winner of the Sharkey-Maloney fight. On May 20, 1927, the two Bostonians were matched in Yankee Stadium, and the winner was scheduled to meet Dempsey. Before the bout started, the ring announcer, gravel-voiced Joe Humphreys, informed the crowd that Charles Lindbergh, in the *Spirit of St. Louis,* was three hundred miles at sea and on course, and he asked the spectators to observe a moment of prayerful silence for the daring pilot. With Humphrey's impassioned speech concluded, the spotlight fell upon Sharkey and Maloney. It was, at least pugilistically, Sharkey's night; the seven-to-five underdog knocked down his neighborhood rival three times before stopping Maloney in fifty-two seconds of the fifth round. After the fight, Sharkey told reporters that he wanted to fight Tunney, "but if I have to, I'm ready to battle Dempsey."[7] Unfortunately for Sharkey, he would have to fight Dempsey.

On June 10, Rickard announced that he would match Dempsey and Sharkey in Yankee Stadium on September 21. Two weeks later, Dempsey traveled to New York to sign a contract for the fight. After signing into the Hotel Belmont, he met in private with Rickard. Following that conference, the former champion "tirelessly" answered questions posed by the press. With his wife at his side, he told reporters that he was not coming back for financial reasons. "I'm fighting for the glory," he sheepishly said. Then he added, as if to justify his first remarks, "I'm fighting because I want to fight. It's my business. I'm not dead by a jugful." Finally, he hit upon the real reason for his comeback: "I want to be convinced I'm wrong [for coming back] and that my ring days are positively over. Maybe Sharkey can convince me," he said with a shrug.[8] Beneath Dempsey's quiet good humor was a note of desperation: at the age of thirty-one he feared that his career was close to its end.

The next day he met Rickard and Sharkey formally to sign the articles for the fight. The ritual was scheduled for Rickard's Madison Square Garden office, but a mass of reporters, photographers, and hangers-on forced Rickard to move the ceremonies to the Garden's boxing ring. It was an appropriate site. Dempsey kept everyone waiting. When he arrived, the mood of the gathering changed. The usually jaunty Sharkey, who had been joking with reporters only minutes before, became oddly quiet, and the press corps fell into an argument over the color of Dempsey's shirt; it was "smoke-blue," decided Jim Dawson of the New York *Times*. Dempsey was also rather solemn. After asking Sharkey about his wife, who was sick in a Boston hospital, Dempsey eyed the former sailor straight on, giving him "the fiercest conceivable glare from beneath a penthouse of frowning and beetle brows." The contract was then signed, which guaranteed Dempsey 27.5 percent of the gate. As the two fighters left Madison Square Garden, they were cheered by a crowd of young boys who waited outside. It was now official. Dempsey had ended his short retirement.[9]

Dempsey's return to the ring was applauded by nearly everyone who followed boxing. The extraordinary appeal that boxing exerted on millions of men and women was the result of Dempsey's personality. Hype Igoe, said in the New York *World*, that "the affable, likable, magnetic Dempsey" was the center of attention at the Garden signing; everyone present followed his every move as if they were watching the actions of a famous Greek god. Although most sportswriters believed that Sharkey would defeat his aging opponent, nobody expected the Boston fighter to replace Dempsey. Watching Dempsey sign to fight Sharkey, journalist Walter Trumbull reported the thoughts of many of the followers of the great fighter. After writing that Dempsey's body "would bring joy to the soul of a sculptor" and that the fighter's toes were as ideal as those of a Greek statue, Trumbull wrote, "Jack isn't the lean, swift, vicious youngster of Toledo, but he looks bigger, stronger, and still the fighting man."[10] On that point everyone agreed: Dempsey was still a "fighting man." Opinions differed on whether Dempsey's will to fight could be translated into action once he was in the ring.

After signing to meet Sharkey, Dempsey retired to Uncle Tom Luther's White Sulphur Springs Hotel to prepare himself to do battle. It was a more relaxed camp than Dempsey's Atlantic City quarters a year before. For the most part, Kearns had given up suing Dempsey, and the former champion appeared to Jimmy DeForest, his old trainer, to be cheerful, clear-minded, and mentally alert. Unlike those in Atlantic City, Dempsey's workouts were spirited and organized. Part of the change was the result of the addition of Leo P.

Flynn as Dempsey's new manager and trainer. Flynn, a silver-haired old-timer who had managed Bill Brennan, David Shade, Bud Gorman, and Jack Renault, was Rickard's idea. The promoter maintained that Dempsey needed a real fight manager to replace Kearns, and Flynn suited both promoter and fighter. Under Flynn's guidance, Dempsey began to develop a strategy to defeat Sharkey. With Flynn doing the thinking, the fighter showed remarkable improvement over the previous year. By the end of June a team of eight physicians—"medicos" as they were called by sportswriters— declared that Dempsey was in splendid condition. One doctor told reporters that he was particularly impressed by the "absence of that strained brain which he exhibited before the Tunney fight."[11] Taken together, the presence of Flynn and the absence of a "strained brain" meant that Dempsey was more relaxed than he had been for years.

Perhaps Dempsey was too relaxed. When trouble came, he was taken by surprise, and for that reason it hurt all the more. On July 2, less than three weeks before he was scheduled to fight Sharkey, Dempsey rose as usual at about 7:00 to do his roadwork. After running, he ate breakfast and rested, again as usual. Just before noon, as he was relaxing on the front porch of his cottage, Dempsey received a telephone call from Schenectady, New York, a mere twenty miles from where he was training. He was informed that his older brother, Johnny, and his sister-in-law, Edna, were dead. For years Johnny had been a drug addict, and during the previous year Edna had left him. Johnny had traveled to Schenectady with hopes of reconciliation. When Edna refused, Johnny had shot her and then had fired a bullet through his own head. Dempsey was requested to travel to Schenectady to identify the bodies.[12]

"It's terrible, a terrible thing," Dempsey told reporters after making the identifications. "He was sick . . . subject to moods. He must have been in one of those moods when he did it; must have been out of his mind." As he spoke, Dempsey's eyes filled with tears. Tragedy was not new to him; less than ten years before a younger brother had been stabbed to death while selling newspapers in Salt Lake City. But this tragedy was greater, for Dempsey felt partially responsible. He had introduced Johnny to Wally Ried, with whom the older brother had developed a dependency on heroin. Over the years that fol-

241

lowed, Dempsey had supported his brother and paid all Johnny's medical bills. Yet Johnny resented his more famous brother; he was jealous of Dempsey's success and suspicious that he was popular only because he was the brother of the heavyweight champion. Over the years, the resentment had grown and festered and been distorted by drug abuse until Johnny was indeed "out of his mind."[13]

After Dempsey gave instructions to send the bodies to Los Angeles, he returned to camp, his eyes still bloodshot from crying. Rumors circulated that the Sharkey fight would have to be postponed, if not canceled. Flynn was frankly confused about what to do: if he tried to make Dempsey train too soon after the tragedy, he might "ruin" his fighter, but the result might be the same if Dempsey quit training and brooded over his loss. "Such a thing is a terrific blow at any time," Flynn told reporters. "To a man training for one of the most important fights of his life it is a crushing load to have to carry." For once, the manager understated the case; to continue training after such an event was a herculean task. But the next day Dempsey was awake at 7:00 to continue his schedule.[14]

A new mood, however, engulfed the camp. Flynn gave orders that all of Dempsey's workouts would be held in secret, and his command was strictly followed. Thousands of would-be spectators and hundreds of reporters were turned away from the camp by four state troopers with Colt .45s at their sides and several of Tom Luther's husky employees. More dedicated than ever, Dempsey's physical condition rapidly improved. Even though a heat wave settled over most of the East in the week before the fight, Dempsey's pace did not slacken; he continued to cut and batter Martin Burke, Johnny Saxon, Allentown Joe Gans, and his other sparring partners.[15] When he ended his training, Dempsey was as fit as a fighter of thirty-two could hope to be. Certainly, he was in much better condition than when he had fought Tunney ten months before.

If Dempsey hoped to defeat Sharkey, his condition would indeed have to be excellent, for the Bostonian was a very good heavyweight at the peak of his career. Sharkey, whose real name was Joseph Paul Zakauskas, bore a striking resemblance to the Dempsey of 1918–1921. Six feet tall, he had a perfectly proportioned 196-pound body and the ability to box as well as punch. To complement his physical attributes, Sharkey added valuable mental qualities. Above all, he was supremely confident. Sharkey believed—and eagerly informed anyone who would listen—that he was the best fighter in the world. As Sharkey told Grantland Rice shortly before his fight with Dempsey, Rickard had offered him a title contest with Tunney, but he wanted to fight Dempsey first: "I know I can lick Dempsey, and by beating him I figure it will be better buildup for Tunney." And Sharkey had reason to be confident, if not conceited, which he was. In the two previous years, he had defeated such leading heavyweights as Jack Renault, Jim Maloney, King Solomon, Bud Gorman, Johnny Risko, George Godfrey, Harry Wills, and Mike McTigue. Roundly prophesied as a future heavyweight champion—which he became in 1932—ring authorities agreed that in all probability Sharkey, who was only twenty-eight, would defeat Dempsey. Even more telling, professional gamblers made Sharkey anywhere from a two-to-one to a seven-to-five favorite.[16]

Interest in the nontitle fight mounted in the days before July 21, and the tickets for the match were sold quickly. In fact, the tickets were sold so fast that their black market price skyrocketed. The New York State Athletic Commission set the top ticket price at $27.50, but on the black market speculators demanded and obtained up to $200. The fault, Boxing Commissioner George F. Brower told a *Times* reporter, was the commission's: "If the price is fixed below that which the public is willing to pay speculation is bound to result." The problem was aggravated, however, by the number of good tickets available, for many companies and individuals used political pull to buy large sections of ringside seats. Hayden, Stone and Company, for instance, purchased 500 tickets to dole out to business associates, and Franklin Delano Roosevelt bought a half-dozen tickets. The commissioners themselves received, according to Rickard, 594 free tickets worth $18,316, though James A. Farley maintained that the tickets were not free.[17] Thus, to get a ringside ticket on the day or two before the fight, one simply but regrettably had to pay the speculators' price, and since many persons wanted tickets, the cost rose like the stock market.

The speculators, Mike Jacobs and his associates, had their day—or, more properly, days—but the soft summer night of July 21,

1927, was all Dempsey's. It was Dempsey whom the majority of 72,283 persons had come to see. Officially, the gate was $1,083,529 and Dempsey earned $317,000, though unofficially the gate was considerably higher, and it was rumored that Rickard paid the former champion $352,000. In addition, it was the sort of crowd that Rickard liked. Damon Runyon wrote that as he made his way down an aisle, he "fell under the hurrying hoofs of fourteen kings of the world of finance, twenty-nine merchant princes, six bootleggers and five ticket speculators, all owners of estates on Long Island and of Rolls-Royce cars." So impressive was the gathering that few people doubted Runyon. Commander Richard E. Byrd and Clarence D. Chamberlin "didn't get a tumble" when they walked to their ringside seats. There were simply too many celebrities to lavish much attention on any one; as the *Times* reporter observed, to the fight crowd, Byrd and Chamberlin "were just two more celebrities." The next day the list of notables who attended the match ran several columns in the *Times*. Tunney was there, of course, to watch his opponent emerge. But the future president of the United States, Franklin D. Roosevelt, was also there, as was Sam Harris, David Belasco, Irving Berlin, Colonel Jacob Ruppert, the faithful Major Anthony Drexel Biddle, "Big Bill" Edwards, Flo Ziegfeld, Tom Mix, the Maharajah of Rutlam (a ranking Indian potentate), John Ringling, and hundreds of other actors, industrialists, socialites, bankers, soldiers, politicians, and journalists. They had come to be seen, but also to see. Like the unknown people in the least expensive seats, they had come to see Dempsey's comeback.[18]

When Dempsey entered the ring the crowd displayed its new-found affection for the former champion with a barrage of hand-clapping, foot-stamping, and whistling. It had been rumored that Dempsey had been killed in an automobile crash, so just his appearance in the ring came as a relief for many spectators. Stripped of his robe, he looked good. No longer was his body sinewy and lean as it had been when he defeated Willard, but there was still very little fat, and if his muscles looked a trifle thick, they held the promise of power unmatched. Furthermore, according to astrologist Gradney Gray, Dempsey's astral number was in harmony with the astral number of the date of the fight. Dempsey's number *eight*, commented

244

Gray, was a "steady, hammering, boring-in, never-let-up number."[19] To possess the body and the number must have been a comfort to the fighter.

Any feeling of comfort, however, vanished for Dempsey into the pleasant summer evening when the fight started.[20] Before the fight, Sharkey told reporters, "I am going in there to knock out Jack Dempsey." And that was his actual intention. Sharkey was an excellent boxer, undoubtedly good enough to outbox Dempsey as Tunney had done, but unlike Tunney, Sharkey fought emotionally; he was excited by a large cheering crowd and determined to win with a knockout. Thus from the opening bell, Sharkey forced the fight. Dempsey, whose best defense was his offense, waited, half-crouched, for the attack. In the first round, Sharkey hit Dempsey with long left and right leads. Toward the end of the round, Sharkey landed a solid left hook which split open Dempsey's lower lip and sent a stream of blood flowing down the center of his chin. Sharkey connected with another left to the jaw at the bell, and Dempsey was clearly wobbly as he walked back to his corner.

Dempsey looked better the next round. After missing several wild swings, the former champion landed his first solid punches, a stiff left and right to the jaw. Forcing Sharkey to the ropes, Dempsey landed two more solid uppercuts. But something happened that surprised nearly everyone. Nothing happened. Dempsey's punches had no visible effect on Sharkey; indeed, the Bostonian actually seemed to rally under the attack. In this round and the next, whenever Dempsey attacked, Sharkey simply redoubled his own defense. Later, Dempsey told reporters, "He couldn't miss me with his left. He moved like a good middleweight. I thought he was going to knock me out." At the close of the third round, as the crowd cheered wildly for Dempsey, Sharkey turned to the spectators at ringside and yelled, "Here's your cheese champion." Years later, comfortably behind his bar, Sharkey remembered, "I thought I had him. In the third, fourth, fifth—I knew it was just a matter of time before I knocked him out."[21]

The fourth, like the first three, was another good round for Sharkey. In the third Sharkey had opened a cut over Dempsey's left eye, and in the fourth the cut was further torn open. Half blinded by the blood, Dempsey was hit again and again. Although he landed several telling blows to the body, the big punches—those to the face—were scored by Sharkey. To James P. Dawson, the leading *Times* reporter at the fight, Dempsey looked "slow and awkward, cumbersome, stiff and [he] has not a remnant of his former fighting speed and agility left." Dempsey, he concluded, was a mere "shell" of his former self.[22] By the round's end, he was bleeding from cuts around both eyes, and his nose and mouth were smeared with blood.

The fifth was even. Although Dempsey did not land any hard punches to Sharkey's head, the former champion stayed close and punched away at the Bostonian's stomach and kidneys. Between rounds Leo Flynn told Dempsey to concentrate on Sharkey's body: "Keep boring in. Keep pounding 'em home until he folds up." In the sixth round Dempsey followed Flynn's instructions perfectly. Blindly, savagely, Dempsey bore into Sharkey's body. Even when Sharkey landed a hard punch—and he landed many—Dempsey refused to alter his style. At the bell to end the sixth round, Dempsey was still throwing punches. In fact, he continued even after the bell, hitting Sharkey twice in the face. When Sharkey retaliated he was roundly booed.[23]

In the seventh round, Dempsey continued to throw punches at Sharkey's belt line, with some landing above and some below. After one exchange, early in the round, Sharkey complained to referee Jack O'Sullivan. "Watch your punches, Jack," O'Sullivan warned, and then realizing that both fighters were named Jack, he added, "I mean you, Dempsey!" Unimpressed by O'Sullivan's caution, Dempsey threw several more punches into the same area. The first, a right hand, connected with Sharkey's left thigh. Where the next punches landed depended upon where one sat. Dawson maintained that those people sitting on the third base and left field sides of Yankee Stadium had the best view. Sitting on that side himself, Dawson saw Dempsey hit Sharkey with four straight rights to the region below the belt. Grantland Rice, W. O. McGeehan, Bill Corum, Damon Runyon, and Benny Leonard also said they saw the low blows. However, Jim Corbett, Paul Gallico, Tommy Loughran, Westbrook Pegler, Ed Sullivan, and Gene Tunney maintained that there were no foul punches thrown by Dempsey. The film of the fight is of no help in determining where the punches landed. Based on the angle of the camera, it *appears* that the punches were headed toward the foul area, but it is impossible to see exactly where the blows actually landed.[24]

There was no doubt, however, about what happened next. Sharkey grabbed his groin and started to launch a verbal protest against Dempsey's punches. As his eyes turned toward the direction of O'Sullivan and his mouth opened, Dempsey hit Sharkey with a perfectly timed left hook that traveled only about twelve inches. But every ounce of Dempsey's shifting weight was behind the punch. Justifying the punch later, Dempsey said, "What was I going to do— write him a letter?" At the instant the punch landed it was clear that the fight was over; Sharkey dropped as if he had had a heart attack. His hands were still clutching his groin when his face hit the canvas. On the floor, he groveled in the resin dust trying to hold his groin and his head at the same time.[25]

The focus of everyone present then shifted to O'Sullivan. He could do one of two things: award Sharkey the fight on a foul or begin to count. He hesitated, unable to decide which course to take. Next, he bent over the prostrate Sharkey and shouted, "You better get up, Jack, because I'm starting to count." Turning to timekeeper Kid McPartland to pick up the count, he began to do just that. Sharkey could not get up, however. His face was contorted with pain, and his clear blue eyes had turned wild. He was a portrait of misery. At the count of ten, Dempsey rushed across the ring, grabbed Sharkey around the midsection, and half-carried, half-dragged the ex-sailor to a corner. Even as Dempsey carried him, Sharkey continued to hold his head and his groin. Although Dempsey was bleeding from his nose, mouth, and a dozen other cuts on his face, it was obvious that Sharkey was in worse condition.[26]

In the dressing room, Sharkey was examined by the State Athletic Commission physician, Dr. William H. Walker. The doctor could find "no surface indication of a foul," but he refused to rule out the possibility. In many such cases, he said, the result of a low blow may not be seen for hours or even days. Johnny Buckley, Sharkey's manager, continued to protest, but Sharkey accepted the official decision as philosophically as possible. "Ah, shut up," he told Buckley, "it's all in the game." After adding that he had not been impressed with Dempsey's punch, Sharkey headed for the shower. He had won three other fights on fouls; now that his luck had run out he did not complain.[27]

The crowd at the fight was generally happy with the outcome, but, of course, there was considerable debate over Dempsey's method. The victory, according to the *Times,* was a decision for age and experience; America, he added, will welcome back its hero. Robert Edgren agreed; Dempsey's "superior courage" was an inspiration to every spectator at Yankee Stadium. Even crusty Westbrook Pegler had to admit that Dempsey was a fighter's fighter, though he added that Sharkey was a "trifle yellow." As for reversing the decision, James Farley put to rest any hope that the boxing commission would change O'Sullivan's verdict. The commission had never reversed a decision of its officials, and, according to Farley, probably never would.[28] Dempsey had won, regardless of the ethics of his method. There would be a second Dempsey-Tunney bout.

One indication of the popularity of the decision was the reception Dempsey received in the various cities he visited in the days after the fight. In his wife's hometown of Wilmington, Delaware, an immense crowd gave him a rousing welcome. An even greater welcome was extended to Dempsey in New Orleans. Three times in a single day, Dempsey was mobbed by enthusiastic supporters. Chants of "give Gentleman Gene what you gave Sharkey" were heard from the train station to the French Quarter. One man, intent on shaking the hand that knocked out Sharkey, thrust his own hand through a window of the automobile in which Dempsey was riding. Though his hand was painfully cut, he insisted upon congratulating the former champion. Whatever secret ingredient comprised popularity and attracted boundless adulation, commented an editorialist for the New Orleans *Times-Picayune,* Dempsey certainly possessed the magic "it."[29]

And no man was more pleased with Dempsey's victory than Tex Rickard. Watching from ringside, Rickard clearly understood that the seventh round guaranteed his—and Dempsey's—fifth million-dollar gate, perhaps even a two- or three-million-dollar gate. His only concern was the proper place to stage the Dempsey-Tunney rematch. For several reasons, he objected to holding the contest in New York. The Athletic Commission's insistance on a $27.50 top ticket was one problem. Another was that there was no stadium large enough to hold the crowd that Rickard envisioned.[30] In addition, there were objections of a more personal nature. Both Tunney and Rickard remembered the troubles that the commissioners had given them in 1926, and they now saw their chance to exact revenge by taking a great title fight out of New York. For Tunney, a New York boy deprived by the commission of winning the crown before a hometown audience, the revenge was particularly sweet.

After considering a number of possible sites, Rickard chose Chicago. It was a city that was desperately hungry for the big fight. Earlier in the year, Mayor William "Big Bill" Thompson had organized a three-hundred man committee of the city's leading businessmen and executives to "do things for Chicago." Thompson's first order to George Getz, the wealthy coal dealer who headed the committee, was to secure the Dempsey-Tunney rematch for Chicago. Getz did everything in his power to satisfy the mayor. As an inducement for Rickard, Getz promised to allow forty-dollar tickets to be sold. What was more, Soldiers' Field in Grant Park was larger by far than any stadium in New York. Getz's argument convinced Rickard, and so with Getz as the promoter of record—Illinois law prohibited an out-of-state person to fill that spot—Rickard set up a ticket office in Chicago's Palmer House.[31]

Not all went according to plan, however. Mostly, it was a conflict in names: Dempsey and Soldiers' Field struck a disharmonious note in the minds of many observers. It seemed somehow a defilement of America's shining effort in the Great War to allow Dempsey to earn hundreds of thousands of dollars in an arena that was dedicated to the men who participated and died in the war. When Soldiers' Field was mentioned as a possible site, four of Chicago's aldermen objected. Speaking for the group, Alderman John W. Chapman criticized Dempsey's war record and said it would be a "travesty" to permit the former champion to do battle in Soldiers' Field. Former congressman Frederick Landis, brother of baseball czar Kenesaw "Mountain" Landis, agreed with Chapman. Addressing the Chicago chapter of the American Legion, he pleaded that Chicago's war monument be kept pure. Spreading his arms open wide, he ended his speech by imploring his fellow Legionnaires to "Stop it! Stop it!"[32]

As rousing as Landis' speech was, it did not help; the fight was set for Soldiers' Field.

That boxing was legal in Illinois at all was an indication that the values that Landis represented were in decline. Rural Illinois, the region that had once elected Landis, had always opposed the legalization of boxing, just as adamantly as it had sponsored the prohibition of alcohol. To the rural mind, boxing represented a curious jumble of interests that included crude commercialism, cheap sensationalism, unearned money, immigrants, gamblers, and criminals. In 1919, when there was a movement to legalize the sport in Illinois, proponents of a boxing bill made every concession to the rural regions by placing boxing on a local option basis, promising to pay commissioners from the receipts of matches, banning Sunday fights, making the use of liquor illegal (the Eighteenth Amendment had not yet been ratified), prohibiting gambling on bouts, and penalizing fixed fights. Although the powerful support of Cook County pushed the bill through the house, it was defeated in the senate. Two years later a bolder bill that eliminated the rural concessions met with the same fate; it passed the house over rural opposition but was stymied in the senate. Again in 1923 a boxing bill was introduced, and again the rural representatives in the senate had the final say. Finally in 1925 the persistence of the cities was rewarded in a bill that guaranteed that boxing contests would only be held in cities that approved of the sport in a referendum. Only a year before Dempsey lost the title, then, did Illinois obey the voices of the cities.[33]

Perhaps Rickard best expressed the general public's attitude concerning Dempsey's draft record: "That war-record business is old stuff. The war is a long way behind us." What concerned Rickard was arranging the bout. Since Chicago enjoyed a reputation as a wide-open town, the promoter saw few problems in his way. Promising Chicagoans that the bout would be "better than a national Republican convention for Chicago," Rickard made plans to hold the contest on September 15. However, at Dempsey's request the date was moved back one week. By the beginning of August everything was set—date, time, ticket prices, and location. Even before the first ticket was sold, tension and excitement began to mount.[34]

Chicago was a good choice. Tickets sold fast. In one day,

$200,000 worth of tickets were sold. By early September, Rickard announced that a three-million-dollar gate might be achieved, and though that sanguine estimate was not reached, $2,250,000 was collected by September 19. In Chicago, the mood was jubilant, even ribald. Although several hotel owners complained about the influx of visitors, most Chicago businessmen accepted the additional burden—and income—without protest. As the September days grew shorter, the fight triumphed over other national issues for the public's attention. Even the debate over the execution of Sacco and Vanzetti on August 23 took second place to the fight as the big day approached. "A changing world," wrote an editor for the *Literary Digest*, "has taken pugilism to its bosom. . . . The democracy of fandom has embraced it as a release . . . for pent-up emotions of the cave-man type. The once gentle sex has exalted it to an idolatrous rite." The fight, he concluded, "promises abundant food for the social philosopher as well as the sportsman, and [it] may be expected to launch formidable reverberation alike in the printing-presses and pulpits of this lively old planet." The New York *Times* added the future social historian to the list of people who would be interested in the contest, for the fight "will reveal to the historian how much the twentieth-century American was willing to pay for thrills."[35]

If the fight was the stage where the public focused its attention, Dempsey was in the spotlight. Certainly, Tunney was not ignored; his reception in Chicago, according to the New York *Times,* rivaled for warmth and color the greeting Lindbergh received in New York. Applauded by tens of thousands of spectators, Tunney told the gathering, "The talk seems to be about some fight that is to be held, about which I know nothing. I am here to train for a boxing contest, not a fight. I don't like fighting. Never did. But I'm free to admit that I like boxing." Fortunately, the crowd that laughed and applauded loudly did not realize that Tunney was serious. Yet for all the newspaper coverage extended to Tunney, Dempsey was the real center of interest. Marie Hannon, his secretary, and Leonard Sachs, his troubleshooting lawyer, reported that Dempsey received about five thousand letters a day from "just plain fans," an additional one thousand involving business propositions, and several hundred telegrams. Shortly after his arrival in Chicago, an event which was observed with wild

251

celebration, Dempsey was made an honorary member of the Chicago Police Department. A few days later, he was made a full Indian chief of the Blackfoot tribe and given an eagle-claw necklace, said to be 1,200 years old, for a good luck charm.[36] Indeed, everywhere Dempsey went and everything he did was closely followed and duly reported in magazines and newspapers across the country.

Dempsey's training sessions were particularly well scrutinized. On one day, Governor Len Small of Illinois and Will Rogers visited his camp at the Lincoln Fields racetrack, and his sparring sessions were broadcast by station WLS in Chicago. Often he was watched by crowds of as many as eight thousand people. Sports writers and lay spectators alike watched for signs of the former champion's fitness: note was taken of the easy manner in which Dempsey handled Big Boy Peterson, Whitey Allen, Allentown Joe Gans, Joe Williams, and his other sparring partners, and similar interest was displayed when crafty Dave Shade gave the former champion trouble. Finally, in an effort to secure some privacy for Dempsey, Flynn switched to secret nighttime training sessions. The switch was denied by everyone at the camp, but Dave Shade's black eye and the bruised sparring partners confirmed the reports.[37]

The mood of the camp was unlike any other in which Dempsey trained. If the tension of his 1926 Atlantic City camp was absent, so also was the hearty fun of the Great Falls and Saratoga Springs quarters. Paul Gallico recalled the quiet dullness of the weeks before the second Dempsey-Tunney contest. Dempsey kept pretty much to himself, living alone and exercising with a grim determination. No longer an "ignorant, hungry, inarticulate, half-savage fighter," wrote Gallico, Dempsey had grown into a man who was sensitive to his surroundings. He read what was written about him, and when it was bad, which it often was, he worried. Then there was Estelle, in the background tottering on the verge of a nervous breakdown. Her career was in its final stages, and her marriage was beginning to break up. On occasion she would show up to watch Dempsey train, but more often she would remain in bed under medication for her nervous condition. The combination of worries—Tunney, press, and Estelle—made Dempsey more than a little edgy, and at times he was positively testy.[38]

252

Perhaps the worries explain Dempsey's open letter to Tunney which was published in the Chicago *Herald-Examiner* on Monday, September 19, three days before the fight. In the letter, which Dempsey later claimed as his own, the former champion accused Tunney of conspiring with Max "Boo Boo" Hoff and Abe Attell to fix the first Dempsey-Tunney fight. According to the letter, Hoff, whom Westbrook Pegler called "a sinister citizen of Philadelphia," had attempted to fix the fight by "getting to" the referee and one of the judges. "I was to lose the decision," Dempsey said, "and if I hit you [Tunney] at any point lower than the top of your head and dropped you, that somebody would yell 'foul!' in your behalf." Although the plans fell through, Dempsey still maintained that Tunney had a good bit of explaining to do, especially over his exact relationship to Hoff and Attell.[39]

The letter aroused a lot of controversy. Tunney, who first said that he would not "dignify the charges with a denial," later called the letter "trash" and "a cheap appeal for public sympathy." Billy Gibson, Tunney's manager, similarly believed that the letter was simply a ploy to endear Dempsey to the public. Yet the matter could not be passed over so easily. Rumor of an attempted fix is a contagious thing; once started it is difficult to contain. If Hoff, a relatively minor underworld figure on the national scene, could fix a fight in Philadelphia, what could a Capone do in Chicago? Soon it was everywhere said that the second Dempsey-Tunney fight would certainly be rigged. Reports that Capone had bet $45,000 on Dempsey did nothing to soothe the public mind on the matter. In the days before the rematch, the Cook County Board of Commissioners did everything within its power to dispel the rumors, and both Dempsey and Tunney denied that there would be any hanky-panky in the upcoming title contest. "There will be no feigning on my part," said Tunney. Although Dempsey used different words, he too said that the fight would be fair. About the only man who was not concerned about a fix was Tex Rickard. For him the rumors were simply a part of the grand equation: rumors generated interest and interest equaled money. It was little wonder that some sportswriters had trouble keeping a straight face when Rickard, suddenly turned holy, said, "This stuff makes me sick!"[40]

The rumors did heighten public interest in the bout. By September 22, the day of the fight, interest reached a fever pitch. It was a cool, crisp day; the smell of autumn was in the air. From every major eastern and midwestern city—from New York, Newark, Rochester, Cleveland, Columbus, Cincinnati, Detroit, Boston, Toledo, Louisville, Philadelphia, and many more cities—special trains detailed to carry spectators to the fight rolled into Chicago. All the $30 and $40 seats were sold, and it was estimated that over $10 million had been bet on the fight. Several counterfeit ticket rings had been crushed, as had been religious opposition to the contest. Both fighters expressed confidence. After going for a long walk, Tunney retired to the library of Fred Ludlin, perhaps to finish *Of Human Bondage,* the book he had been reading during the preceding weeks. Asked for a prediction, he replied, "My first defense of the title finds me quite confident that I will be victorious." After a morning run, Dempsey told reporters, "I'll knock that big bookworm out inside of eight rounds." A cartoon on the front page of the Chicago *Tribune* best expressed the mood of the country: pictured was a content-looking, middle-aged man inspecting his easy chair, radio, slippers, ottoman, and framed pictures of Dempsey and Tunney. "There!" the caption read. "I guess ever' thing's all ready." Everything was ready. Professor Henry J. Cox of the Chicago Weather Bureau gave the final bit of information. He predicted that there would be no rain, and that by fight time, 10:00, the temperature would drop into the lower fifties. He was right, but few spectators needed a sweater to keep warm.[41]

Not everybody in the world was concerned over the outcome of the contest, but the interest generated by the fight would, as gamblers say, do for openers. In London, Englishmen crowded around telegraph stations on Fleet Street and waited in the early morning hours for round-by-round reports of the fight. Across the channel in Paris, American Legionnaires and Frenchmen sat in all-night cafés that issued reports on the progress of the match. France's former and future enemy, Germany, was similarly captivated with the fight; one Berlin critic was particularly impressed by Tunney's "metaphysical studies." In Buenos Aires, the world champion chess match, which was being held there, was momentarily forgotten as

Latins searched for a place to hear reports of the title contest. The same was true in Rio de Janeiro, where men crowded into Carioca Square to read bulletins about the fight, and in San Juan, where the reception was amazingly clear, and in Lima, Peru, where the corridors of *El Commercio* were jammed by interested Peruvians. It was the same story on board the *Berengaria,* sailing in the mid-Atlantic, and in the clubs and hotels of Shanghai. Thousands of people in Cape Town and Guayaquil also waited eagerly for news of the fight. Indeed, if, as a writer in the Vatican newspaper *Osservatore Romano* claimed, boxing represented "the resurrection of paganism" and "the return to barbarianism," then the Dempsey-Tunney rematch exposed millions of pagans and barbarians throughout the world.[42]

The interest displayed the world over was, of course, multiplied many fold in the United States. The night show of the American Dahlia Society was canceled to allow flower-lovers to listen to the fight. At the New Jersey State Prison in Trenton, the match was listened to by all the inmates except the four who were on death row and barred from radio privileges. At Sing Sing, even the prisoners on death row were allowed to listen. In New York and Chicago and other cities, theaters and movie houses played to below normal crowds. The entire affair was carried to its logical conclusion at the 71st Regimental Armory in New York City, where two boxers, one dressed in black trunks to represent Dempsey and the other clothed in white trunks to portray Tunney, reenacted the fight blow-by-blow as reports came over the telegraph wires.[43]

Chicago was a madhouse of pushing, crowding people. The sidewalks of the Loop and Michigan Boulevard were jammed by ticket holders and other people interested in the fight. The closer one got to Grant Park, the home of Soldiers' Field, the worse the congestion became. Inside the stadium, enclosed by Doric columns and bathed with the pale white of powerful searchlights, over 100,000 spectators—reports vary between 105,000 and 150,000—were ushered to their seats, the location of which had been the most closely guarded secret about the affair. They came clothed in furs and overcoats, expecting cold weather, but they were greeted by a light rain—which soon stopped—when the first preliminary began. They paid a total of $2,658,660, by far the largest amount ever paid to see an athletic contest up to that time and perhaps the largest ever paid to see any event. Even when Big Boy Peterson fought Johnny Grosso in the first preliminary, there was high drama in the air. At ringside, Graham McNamee, the radio announcer, surveyed the humanity surrounding him and began his broadcast by saying, "All is darkness in the muttering mass of crowd beyond the light. It's like the Roman Colosseum."[44]

Beside and around McNamee was the cream of American society, politics, business, industry, arts, athletics, show business, and life. From Hollywood came Gloria Swanson, Joseph Schenck, Norma Talmadge, Jackie Coogan, William Fox, and M. P. Bernstein, vice-president of the Metro-Goldwyn company. From Washington Assistant Secretary of War Hanford MacNider traveled to the fight with a bevy of lesser officials. Former governor James Cox of Ohio was at ringside, as was Governor Len Small of Illinois and eight other governors. Charles M. Schwab, head of Bethlehem Steel, sat close to Gerald Swope, president of the General Electric company, and Roy Howard of the Scripps-Howard newspapers. Phil Wrigley, John McGraw, and Colonel Jacob Ruppert represented the world of baseball, just as Jack Johnson and Jack Sharkey represented heavyweight champions of the past and the future. Sprinkled among the men and women who earned their fame were the sons and daughters of famous families—the Astors, Vanderbilts, Talbotts, Whitneys, Harrimans, Carters, and Biddles. From across the ocean came the foreign royalty—Princess Xenia of Greece, the Marquis of Blandford, the Marquis of Douglas and Clydesdale, Viscount Castlereagh, Lady Ravensdale, and lesser nobility. They and many others—famous, not-so-famous, and unknown—had come to see and be seen. They had also traveled to Chicago to watch, depending upon whom one asked, Dempsey fight or Tunney box. Grantland Rice, who was one of the hundreds of representatives from the working press at ringside, later wrote, "Never again will I witness the mass of seething humanity that jammed Soldiers' Field."[45]

Dempsey was the first to enter the ring. He was wearing black trunks and had a white robe draped over his shoulders. Around him were his seconds—Flynn, Luvadis, Fred Tapscot, Gus Wilson, and Bill Duffy. "Men and women," wrote James P. Dawson, "arose as if pulled erect by some giant magnet" when Dempsey was seen in the ring. As he danced around the ring, shook hands with notables, and waved greetings to friends he recognized at ringside, the crowd cheered wildly. It was obvious that Dempsey was the favorite of the vast majority of people at the fight. A New York *Times* editorial, written a month before the contest, predicted as much. "Youth, good looks, some acquaintance with books, and a commendable war record" meant nothing when matched against Dempsey's popularity. Indeed, the debonair, "scientific" Tunney was "suspiciously regarded as a superior fellow." At ringside, Paul Gallico noticed the same thing. Tunney was the villain; he was pictured as a "priggish, snobbish, bookish fellow, too proud to associate with common prizefighters," and comparatively few people at Soldiers' Field rooted for the champion.[46]

After Tunney climbed into the ring all the floodlights were directed at the twenty-foot square in the middle of the football field. In relation to its surroundings, the ring appeared small, but it was adorned for the regal show that was to follow. The ring posts were gilded and in the corners gold-painted containers swung on hinges. Everything was just as Rickard had planned. Turning to Hype Igoe, who sat beside Rickard at ringside, the promoter said, "Kid, if the earth came up and the sky came down and wiped out my first ten rows it would be the end of everything. Because I've got in those ten rows all the world's wealth, all the world's big men, all the world's brains and production talent. Just in them ten rows, kid. And you and me never seed nothing like it."[47] As the gloves were tied on to the fighters' hands with blue ribbon, Igoe was forced to admit that he had never "seed nothing like it."

Dempsey opened the first round as he had begun almost every fight in which he had engaged: he charged savagely at Tunney. Although he did not hit Tunney, Dempsey looked better than he had a year earlier in Philadelphia. He was tan, and his body was firm; his balance and timing looked excellent. Furthermore, his defense was better. Tunney, with his white Irish body, had difficulty landing right-hand punches. Soon a pattern developed: Dempsey circled Tunney, "like a wild beast stalking its prey," said Dawson. The pace was perfect for Tunney, who boxed with professional ease, occasionally jabbing or hooking but always moving to his left and thus away from Dempsey's left hook. In short, though Dempsey looked better than he had in Philadelphia, Tunney still controlled the fight, dictating its pace and winning the early rounds. [48]

As the fight progressed, Dempsey became more careless, both of himself and where he punched. His face contorted with rage, he became absolutely vicious. In the second and third rounds he repeatedly hit Tunney low with long-range leads and short punches during the clinches. Although Dempsey was warned to watch his punches by referee Dave Barry, a gray-haired veteran of the ring, the former champion continued to attack as persistently, tirelessly, and ruthlessly as before. When Tunney opened a cut over Dempsey's right eye in the fourth round, it only increased the anger that was visible on the ex-champion's face. Throughout the fifth and sixth rounds, Dempsey, oblivious of the price, forced the action. At times he landed solid punches both to the head and to the body, but he did not connect with enough blows to affect Tunney. And for every punch Dempsey landed, Tunney landed five or six. By the end of the sixth round, Dempsey was beginning to look like a defeated fighter. His right eye was cut, his left eye was swollen badly, and his left ear was bleeding profusely. Perhaps Dempsey won one or two rounds of the first six; regardless of the number, it seemed certain that Dempsey had to knock out Tunney if he wished to avoid losing another ten-round decision.

The seventh round began and for about fifty seconds looked like all the rest. Then it happened. Dempsey launched a long right which landed high and followed with his best punch to that point, a left hook to Tunney's chin. Tunney appeared annoyed that he would allow himself to be hit with a left hook, the very blow he had trained himself to avoid. Years later he wrote, "For a boxer of any skill to be hit with a left swing in a commonplace maneuver of sparring is sheer disgrace." His only excuse was that an eye injury suffered during his training had left him with a blind spot. [49] But Tunney had little time to worry about the "how" during the seventh round. After landing the left, Dempsey drove Tunney into the ropes with another straight right. As Tunney careened off the ropes, Dempsey stepped forward and landed a perfectly timed left hook to the champion's jaw. Everything about the punch was right: both Dempsey and Tunney were moving forward when the blow connected. Perhaps Tunney was unconscious a moment after the second left landed, for he fell back into the ropes and his hands dropped carelessly to his side. He started to fall, or, rather collapse to the canvas. But before he did, Dempsey vented his year of frustration, his rounds of impotence. As Tunney slid to the canvas, Dempsey hit the champion with a left-right, left-right combination, his body rotating with the punches, a metronome of destructive power. For a moment it was again 1919.

When Tunney fell to the canvas, Dempsey reacted as he always had: he remained as close to the fallen champion as possible. Standing in a corner, just a few feet from Tunney, Dempsey waited for the champion either to get up or be counted out. Neither happened. Instead referee Barry yelled at Dempsey to go to the farthest neutral corner, as the rules required. "I'll stay here," Dempsey told Barry, as if that was concession enough to the new laws of the ring. Later, Dempsey told Dan Daniel, "I couldn't move. I just couldn't. I wanted him to get up. I wanted to kill the sonofabitch."[50] Barry, however, refused to allow Dempsey to remain near Tunney. So, grabbing Dempsey by the arm, the referee half-shoved, half-escorted him to the farthest neutral corner.

While Barry and Dempsey debated their differing interpretations of ring behavior, Tunney was sitting on the canvas. As Tunney fell, he instinctively reached for the lower rope, but he was visibly shaken. After the fight, Tunney admitted that he remembered nothing of Barry's argument with Dempsey. By the time Barry returned from escorting Dempsey, four seconds had lapsed; in fact, the timekeeper, Paul Beeler, was calling out "five" in order to give Barry a count to pick up. But instead of starting his count at six, Barry shouted "One!" At the count of three—or seven seconds after the knockdown—Tunney lifted his head and looked at Barry. In turn, Barry moved closer to Tunney so that the champion could hear the count above the din of the crowd. At the count of four, Tunney probably could have got up. But that would not have been the intelligent thing to do; the wise boxer takes a count of nine before he rises. If nothing else, Tunney was an intelligent boxer. He waited until Barry shouted "nine" before he regained his feet.

The "long count" was over, but the controversy over the "long count" lingers on. If Barry had started his count with five, could Tunney have got up? If Tunney had beat the count, would he have been alert enough to avoid another barrage of punches? Nobody can definitively answer either question. Tunney believed he knew the answer to the first: "Could I . . . have got up? I'm quite sure I could have." As for the second question, even Tunney was unsure of the answer.[51] As in a good horserace, everyone had an opinion about the "long count," but nobody really knows what would have happened "if . . . ."

What did happen was that Tunney got up thinking. Although he had never been knocked down in his boxing career, he was not without a contingency plan—or, more precisely, plans—to cover the event. Like a military strategist, Tunney had a plan to cover any possible event. Before he got up to face Dempsey, Tunney considered three possible courses of action. First, he could hold and clinch, hoping to get extra time to recover his scrambled senses. But he decided against this course because Dempsey "hit too hard and fast with short punches for it to be at all safe." Besides, in a clinch Tunney would have been susceptible to Dempsey's rabbit punches, an illegal blow to the area where the base of the skull meets the cervical vertebra, known to doctors as the medulla oblongata. Punches of this variety dull the reflexes of a fighter and cause numbness. Tunney's next alternative was to surprise Dempsey by attacking. He expected Dempsey to attack with little thought of defense; if, Tunney thought, he could land a solid surprise blow to Dempsey's jaw, it might thwart the former champion's attack. But in seventeen rounds, when Tunney had possessed all his wits, he had been unable to land a solid blow to Dempsey's jaw. Dempsey, as Tunney knew, fought instinctively with his head tucked against his chest. Thus he decided against the second course. Tunney's last plan was to retreat. He knew that Dempsey's legs were weaker than they had once been, and he was willing to bet his title that Dempsey would not be able to catch him.[52]

Tunney's retreat was perfect. As Dempsey rushed wildly, throwing looping lefts and rights, Tunney back-pedaled and circled away from Dempsey's left. Several punches Tunney blocked, a few more he ducked. Most of Dempsey's punches fell a foot or more short of their target. After a half minute or so, Tunney even threw a couple punches of his own. Eventually, Dempsey was too tired to chase Tunney; he was not a smart enough boxer to sidestep, change direction, and herd Tunney into a corner. And at the age of thirty-two, he was not young enough for endless pursuit. Instead of chasing Tunney, he stopped and expressed his emotions in the most graphic manner. Paul Gallico remembered the exact moment, and years later it was still hauntingly fresh in his mind: "over [Dempsey's] swarthy, blue-jowled fighter's face there spread a look the memory of which will never leave me as long as I live. First it was the expression of self-realization of one who knows that his race is run, that he is old and that he is finished. And then through it and replacing it there appeared such a glance of bitter, biting contempt for his opponent that for the moment I felt ashamed for the man who was running away."[53]

What Dempsey wanted was for Tunney to fight. As he watched his retreating foe, Dempsey made a pawing motion with his glove, as if to say, "Enough running. Come on and fight." What Dempsey was asking was certainly no less than he would have done if he were in Tunney's place. Dempsey would not have retreated. He would have fought, just as he had fought back after being hurt by Firpo and Sharkey. Perhaps by fighting back Dempsey would have been knocked out, but, as a fighter, he would have taken that chance. Tunney, however, was a different breed entirely. Tunney was a boxer, and as a boxer he retreated and waited for his head to clear. By the end of round seven, his retreat had accomplished its purpose. His wonderfully conditioned body had recuperated, and he was again in control. At the bell, in fact, Tunney was on the offensive. He landed a blow to the heart that Dempsey later called the hardest punch he ever received: "It was not a question in my mind of being knocked out. I thought I was going to die. I could not get my breath."[54] Dempsey went to his corner after the seventh round a defeated man.

In the final three rounds, Tunney was in complete control. Although Dempsey kept moving forward, he was no match for the champion. Midway through the eighth round, a left hook to the jaw knocked Dempsey down. Ironically, this time Barry started the count before Tunney moved to the farthest neutral corner, but the count did not matter. Dempsey was back on his feet, charging Tunney, before Barry's count reached two. Unlike Tunney who waited before getting up—as any intelligent boxer would—Dempsey resented the feel of the canvas against his back. By the start of the tenth round it was clear that Tunney would successfully defend his title. Even so, Dempsey continued to try. He was cut and bruised, and he had no real chance of winning, but he did not quit. When the bell rang at the end of the tenth round, there was no need for a decision. Tunney had won seven or eight of the ten rounds, and he was still champion.

It was, all things considered, a good fight on which to end his career. Dempsey's paycheck, $425,000, was the largest ever received by a challenger. But more important than the money, the drama of the fight meant that Dempsey's last fight would be remembered for a long time. Listening to the fight on the radio had caused ten men to die of heart failure; half of them died in the seventh round. Estelle, who listened to the fight with her nurse in her room at Chicago's Edgewater Beach Hotel, also suffered during the seventh round. Unable to stand the suspense, she ordered the radio to be turned off. Later, she called Barry's actions "unfair." In the days that followed the fight, Dempsey, his handlers, and interested sportswriters protested, and the fight was discussed in the editorial sections of many of the nation's leading newspapers. As John Kieran wrote in his column in the New York *Times,* "There was hardly as much arguing over the result of the late World War as there is over the more recent Tunney-Dempsey quarrel in Chicago. Most of it is quite interesting, but practically all of it is useless."[55]

The only people who wished to forget the fight were the ministers of America. The Reverend Dr. John Roach Straton called the fight "barbarous," and he believed that it was a clear indication that America was "going the same way that Rome went, through her sensualism and blood-lust." The Reverend Dr. Christian F. Reisner said the contest was "shameful." The Reverend Dr. Cortland S. Myers of the First Baptist Church in Los Angeles, agreed that the match was "brutal, low-down, animal." He called upon America to glorify spiritual strength rather than physical power. In a thinly disguised reference to Dempsey, he said, "A man may be a prizefighter and still a coward and run away from the battlefield and the defense of the flag of his country."[56] However, the religious voice went unheard by the majority of Americans.

Perhaps the most important result of the fight was the increased popularity Dempsey enjoyed afterward. Paul Gallico observed that Dempsey emerged from the match as "the greatest and most beloved sports hero the country had ever known." For in losing he became more human. It was almost as if Dempsey had been crossed by fate; he had hit Tunney hard enough to win—hard enough to keep Tunney on the canvas for fourteen seconds—but fate had robbed him of his victory. His hubris—the desire to win completely—had led to his downfall. As Gallico continued, "That made him human and one of us." And through it all, Dempsey did not complain. His response to the loss was admired because it reflected how every person wishes to handle bad luck. Smiling, calm, with a simple unaffected manner, Dempsey gave his version of the outcome: "It was just one of the breaks. Tunney fought a smart fight."[57] With this statement, the legend, which had already been formed, was institutionalized.

Epilogue: Everybody Give the Big Boy a Hand

AT THIRTY-TWO, a time when most men are just becoming accustomed to their jobs, Dempsey's career as a fighter ended. He was somewhat like Tom Buchanan in *The Great Gatsby*, "one of those men who reach such an acute limited excellence at twenty-one that everything afterward savors of anticlimax." Young by all standards except those of athletics, Dempsey wisely left the profession that had given him much, before it started to take things away from him. More than anything else, he feared ending his career with his pockets empty and his head full of bells. When a doctor told him that another match would mean risking permanent eye damage or even blindness, Dempsey nixed a third fight with Tunney. Although he could have earned over a million dollars by fighting Tunney again, in 1927 he just did not need money that badly.[1]

All Dempsey knew was fighting, so retirement created an assortment of problems. What else could he do? Certainly his name was still marketable. In 1928 he starred, along with his wife Estelle, in *The Big Fight*, a melodrama directed by David Belasco. Although people had paid large sums to see Dempsey fight, they were not willing to do the same to watch him act. The play opened in early September at the Chestnut Street Opera House in Philadelphia. Before a packed house, which greeted him with "one of the noisiest and most prolonged and most sincere" ovations ever heard in the local playhouse, Dempsey moved stiffly about the stage and gave his lines in a voice that threatened to turn into a countertenor. Nevertheless, *Variety* confidently predicted that the play would be a huge success.

But after only moderate success in Philadelphia, the play was met with apathy in New York. Before *The Big Fight* moved to Boston, Estelle quit the cast, reportedly to be operated on for an infected tonsil but actually because her voice was weak and wavered during critical emotional scenes. After a poor showing in Boston, the play closed in New Haven. Although the play was a failure, George Jean Nathan applauded Dempsey's lack of effeminacy, remarking that "nobody could accuse the former champion of belonging to the court of Titania."[2]

Next, Dempsey tried something that was more familiar; with Tex Rickard, he promoted boxing matches. Rickard wanted Dempsey to help promote the Young Stribling-Jack Sharkey bout scheduled for February, 1929, in Miami. Perhaps Rickard hoped to convince Dempsey to meet the winner. However, early in January, Rickard began complaining of nausea and stomach pains. He developed peritonitis, and four days after the diagnosis, with Dempsey at his bedside, he died. Saddened by the death of his friend, Dempsey continued to promote the Stribling-Sharkey match, but after that contest he lost interest in arranging fights between other men.[3]

Dempsey now concentrated on his domestic life, for his fragile marriage with Estelle was cracking under the strain of his retirement from the ring. When his name was linked with Agnes O'Loughlin, a dancer with the Whoopee Show on Broadway, Estelle believed the gossip columnists. And although Dempsey had never met the woman, Estelle used the rumors to justify her bitter attitude, a posture that more reflected an insecurity concerning her career than any wrongs committed by her husband. Inevitably, in the summer of 1930, Dempsey filed for a divorce in Reno, and Estelle did not contest the action.[4]

Before the final separation, however, Dempsey, who had lost over three million dollars in the stock market crash, urgently needed additional income. For a time, he considered a ring comeback. Listening to sycophants and to his own ego, in 1931 and 1932 he fought over a hundred exhibition bouts, sometimes fighting four or five easy bouts on the same night. Most he won by a knockout. Finally, he decided to test himself against Kingfish Levinsky, a top-ranked heavyweight. In a four-round bout held in the Chicago stadium,

Levinsky smothered Dempsey's punches, clinched, and countered sharply. After the contest Dempsey no longer deluded himself about regaining the championship. He was no longer a fighter.

He moved into middle age gracefully; and he found other ways to make money. He refereed boxing and wrestling matches and occasionally, as in *The Prizefighter and the Lady* and *Mr. Broadway*, found work in Hollywood. After the bombing of Pearl Harbor, he attempted to enlist in the navy, but was turned down. His subsequent acceptance by the Coast Guard was for Dempsey the opportunity to settle the slacker charges leveled against him in the 1920s. If he was not at the Argonne Forest, he would be at Okinawa.[5]

When the war ended, Dempsey and Jake Amron opened a new restaurant in New York, and for the next quarter of a century countless New Yorkers and tourists were privileged to stop at Dempsey's to eat and to see the aging champion. The years brought more than financial changes. Dempsey married the beautiful Hannah Williams, raised a family, and became the victim of another sensational divorce. His fourth marriage, to Deanna Piattelli in 1959, proved to be a happy one. Over the years he has known presidents, actors, diplomats, and kings; he has made hundreds of friends and treated them with kindness. If the term *living institution* ever applied to an American, it has applied to Jack Dempsey. As Broadway was transformed from small shops and restaurants to porn shops and peep shows, Dempsey's remained a stable landmark, until it was closed in 1974 and replaced by a fast-order eating establishment. The man Dempsey continued to ride his bicycle through Central Park in the early mornings, even though his hips were racked by arthritis. He remained as solid living proof of another age.[6]

Many years after the second Dempsey-Tunney bout, Gene Fowler wrote his reminiscences of the 1920s. He was then an old man, writing about a decade that he helped to immortalize. The account bears the Fowler stamp of brutal honesty; he refused to overromanticize his youthful years. Toward the end of his narrative, however, he characterizes the decade thus: "The Dempsey legend is like the larger saga of the age that sired his fame, the Roaring Twenties. Both the man and the era had gusto and raw color; but they also had less bombastic overtones." [7] Fowler's point was apt; beneath the surface glitter of the 1920s, under the mountains of sensational stories about gangsters, athletes, flappers, and movie stars, there was a stretch of ten years in which real people were born, lived, worked, and died. Fowler saw the Dempsey legend as the perfect twenties metaphor for the two extremes—the world of tinsel and the world of bone.

Of course, other men have been called symbols of the 1920s. Historian Roderick Nash has suggested that Henry Ford was the ideal symbol for the decade, and literary historian John William Ward has offered Charles A. Lindbergh. Other personalities could be said to symbolize the era for equally sound reasons. But Dempsey's very name evokes the age; they are, as Fowler intimated, inseparable. Ford's and Lindbergh's successes could just as well have been experienced in 1913 or 1933 and the result would have been the same; their triumphs would have represented the same principles. But Dempsey's years in the sun could not have been lived ten years before or ten years later. The time and the man were perfectly suited to each other, and although without Dempsey the twenties might have been the same, without the prosperity, inward-directed interests, slackening of moral restraints, and advancements in promotional techniques of that period, the Dempsey mystique would not have developed.

Essentially, Dempsey is a better metaphor for the 1920s than Lindbergh or Ford because he and his image are more complex. In Ford and Lindbergh we see none of the glitter of the tantalizing scene—from Babe Ruth and Big Bill Tilden to Legs Diamond and Al Capone to Charlie Chaplin, Floyd Collins, F. Scott Fitzgerald, Leopold and Loeb, and the host of others. Not every woman was a flapper who danced the Charleston, nor did every man dance like Valentino, and not everyone drank bootleg gin—but flappers, Valentino, and bootleg gin did exist, and they will always be identified with the 1920s. Dempsey is part of this heritage of glitter.

The Dempsey image, however, reflects another side of the decade, the side that did not roar. By temperament, Dempsey was a quiet, conservative man. His modesty and love of family were not a pose. His genuine respect for traditional values was emphasized by the press, so that in life and legend he was able to bridge two worlds; in the ring and on the movie screen, he appeared larger than life. His exploits were followed by Ring Lardner, Rudolph Valentino, Jimmy Walker, Al Capone, and Babe Ruth; he was a hero's hero in an age that glorified flamboyant individualism. Outside of the ring his attitudes were little different from the vast majority of Americans. Although he was accused of being a slacker, Dempsey was extremely patriotric; he prided himself on being an American and often boasted of his pioneer and Indian blood. Most important, he did not think of himself as remarkable. Years later he said, "I was just a big kid that God blessed with a good punch. Besides that I had no other talents."[8] Thus it was possible for an average man to feel that, blessed with a similar "punch," he too could have been a Dempsey.

Dempsey, in addition, was the physical manifestation of yet another universal impulse: the longing of the average man to destroy the giant. In fiction, David, Siegfried, Beowolf, and Roland did this. But Dempsey did it in real life. He butchered Jess Willard, the giant who defeated the great black giant, Jack Johnson. Then, several years later, he got off the canvas to administer the same treatment to the foreign giant, Luis Firpo. Dempsey, wrote Paul Gallico, "crystallized something that all of us at one time or another long for—to be able to 'up' to someone, a giant, a bully, a tough guy, without qualm or tremor, and let him have it." When Grantland Rice summarized Dempsey's career, the reporter entitled his article "Was Jack the Giant Killer?" Rice's answer was a resounding yes.[9]

Here, then, was Dempsey, the hero and legend who belonged to the 1920s—soft-spoken, gentle, a "giant killer" when aroused. He was the average man who was blessed with just a little something extra. In time he became a metaphor for the ambitions of the American male. This metaphorical quality was recognized by Horace Gregory, who exploits the symbolic nature of Dempsey in a book of poems, Chelsea Rooming-House, published in 1930.

In the poem "Dempsey, Dempsey" the former champion assumes a dual role. First, he is the hero—no longer the champion, but still the great fighter. Only his opponent is not simply another boxer but the evil oppressors of the common man. In this role, the narrator of the poem wants Dempsey to do what he cannot do—destroy those men who hold the ultimate power:

The million men and a million boys,
came out of hell and crawling back,

maybe they don't know what they're saying,
maybe they don't dare,
but they know what they mean:
knock down the big boss,
O, my little Dempsey,
my beautiful Dempsey
with that Godinheaven smile
and the quick, god's body leaping,
not afraid, leaping, rising—
hit him again, he cut my pay check, Dempsey.

In the role of the hero, then, Dempsey is the defender of the common man, a modern-day St. George ready to defeat the dragons that prey upon society.

In his second role, Dempsey represents the common man who is subject to the control of others. Dempsey is no longer invincible; instead, he became the "failure king of the U.S.A." Just when the narrator thinks that Dempsey is about to win, he realizes,

Christ's sake Dempsey,
my god they're killing Dempsey,
It's Dempsey down, Dempsey, Dempsey.

And later, with pain in his voice, the poet cries out, "the bastards are killing Dempsey." Thus, when faced by such an opponent as the Great Depression and ruthless employers, even Dempsey is unable to win. Dempsey, the average man with a little something extra, loses his slight edge and melts into the ranks of the impotent laborers.

It is this destruction of Dempsey as hero that the narrator is unable to face. He instinctively realizes that man must have a hero to place upon a pedestal. Without a hero near-empty lives would be completely empty. Thus the narrator admits his weaknesses:

Listen, they made me go to war
and somebody did something wrong to my wife
while I was gone.

But as he quits, he pleads for Dempsey to remain an untarnished hero:

Hit him again Dempsey, don't be a quitter
like I am Dempsey,
O' for Jesus Christ, I'm out.
I can't get up, I'm dead, my legs
are dead, see, I'm no good

269

down for the count.
They got me and I'm out
I've quit, quit again,
Only God save Dempsey, make him get up again . . . [10]

In the final analysis, it is the human quality of Dempsey that makes him such an appropriate symbol for the age. Other heroes of the twenties gained as much notoriety and lived as glamorous lives, but few seemed as close to the common man as the Manassa Mauler. Hence when the golden age of boxing ended—with Tunney retired and Rickard dead before 1930—Dempsey's name lingered in the popular mind, an echo of an era. Even today, a half-century later, Dempsey himself is an institution, and he is still the popular conception of what a fighter should be. Before his restaurant closed, tourists visited it as if on a pilgrimage. And it is still true, as Paul Gallico noted years ago, that when kids scuffle and brawl in the streets, someone will inevitably say, "Aw, who do you think you are—Jack Dempsey?" [11]

270

Postscript: "Here's to Heroes"

IN THE late afternoon on May 31, 1983, Jack Dempsey died in his home. He was eighty-seven, almost eighty-eight years old—and one of the last heroes of the golden age of sports to die. Although there are few people still living who saw him fight, the dramatic moments of his career—the "long count" and the night Firpo knocked him out of the ring—are still hotly debated. Red Smith, now also dead, remembered a breakfast he had had with Dempsey in Chicago during the summer of 1949. Both were in town to watch Ezzard Charles and Jersey Joe Walcott fight for Joe Louis' vacated heavyweight title. A stranger passing their table recognized Dempsey. Such recognition was the unifying theme of his life. The stranger approached: "Jack Dempsey! Oh, boy, Jack do I know you! Do you remember how you gave it to Jess Willard back there in Toledo!" Then, leaning closer, his mouth at Dempsey's ear in a moment of private confidence, the stranger whispered, "I hope you beat the hell out of that guy tomorrow night." Dempsey had lost the title almost twenty-three years before, but he was still the stranger's champion. Old men became young, looking into the eyes of their childhood hero.

The day after he died, journalists, boxers, politicians, and businessmen genuflected in his direction. "Jack Dempsey was a champion who never lost his title in the hearts of the American people," said President Reagan. "In an era that was hungry for heroes, the first one was Jack Dempsey," added Bert Sugar, publisher of *Ring*. Former head of Madison Square Garden's boxing department Harry Markson noted, "Jack Dempsey *was* boxing." He "was magic," said the eighty-one-year-

271

old trainer Ray Archer. Summing up the attitude of boxers themselves, former heavyweight champion Floyd Patterson said, "Jack
Dempsey was something special."

There was, then, a touch of irony at his death. Although his wake
was open to the public, there were few visitors outside his family and
friends. When Babe Ruth died in 1948, thousands of people waited in
long lines for one last glimpse of their idol. But the Babe had died only
thirteen years after his last game. Dempsey's death came almost fifty-
six years after his last fight. He had outlived his idolators. And this
gave the mourning of Jack Dempsey a certain surreal quality.

The Dempsey legend, though, is immortal. It was difficult to separate the man from the image. There was one line that said Dempsey
was a killer in the ring and a pussycat outside. Grantland Rice said
Dempsey was the finest gentleman, in the literal sense of that word,
he had ever met. Ira Berkow, who only spoke with Dempsey one time,
remembered the "electricity and brute power" that the old champion
always carried. Berkow recalled watching Dempsey leave the Joe Fra-
zier-Jimmy Ellis fight after the third round. On the way out, he saw
Lester Bromberg, former boxing writer for the New York *Post* and an
old-time friend of Dempsey's. In a gesture of friendship, Dempsey
reached down, lifted Bromberg's hand, and bit it. "Caveman," Bromberg told Berkow after Dempsey had departed. "He's always been that
way."

Surely Dempsey's brutal sense of practical joking was the legacy of
a rough childhood and a violent career. It is difficult to believe that
the Dempsey who rode the rods, fought desperate men in saloons, and
pounded Willard's face into a bloody mask was a gentleman. As a contender and champion Jack Dempsey was hungry. In the ring he moved
with restless, violent energy. And for most of his career, he was sullen
and brutal outside the ring; the gentleman inside rarely struggled to
get free.

In retirement the gentle, albeit still physical, man did surface in,
and then dominate, Dempsey. He never lingered on his bad breaks.
He made a fortune, invested it intelligently, and then saw it all lost
in the 1929 market. He didn't complain; he found work where he
could. He trained boxers, refereed wrestling matches, sold a variety of
products, and finally settled into the restaurant business. It was a liv-

ing. But after 1929, Dempsey was never really rich again. When he died, his estate was valued at between $100,000 and $250,000. He lived well without a lot of money.

It is perhaps reasonable to speculate that there was an inverse relationship between Dempsey's kindness and his bank account. Red Smith accurately noted that Dempsey "was warm and generous, a free spender when he had it and a soft touch for anyone down on his luck." Friends told him that he was too generous, that more than a few "strangers and friends" took advantage of his kindness. "Yes," he would reply, "I suppose they do." It was the reply of a man not terribly concerned, the reply of a man who knew himself well enough to know that he was not about to change.

At my only meeting with Dempsey, I was the recipient of his legendary kindness. I was a young graduate student, in New York to research an unusual dissertation. It was the day after Christmas, 1973. I remember that my coat was too thin, my hair was too long, and I had not taken enough money. Nat Loubet, then editor of *Ring*, had given me Dempsey's unlisted phone number. When I called, I didn't talk with Dempsey, but his adopted daughter arranged for me to talk with him at his restaurant that night.

I went to the restaurant long before the hour when we were scheduled to meet. Wandering around, I closely examined the hundred or so autographed pictures and assiduously avoided risking any of my limited funds on a drink. The hour arrived, and Dempsey wasn't there. I was, of course, by this time disconsolate, confident that he would not show. Reassurance from a sympathetic bartender could not penetrate my despair. I was about to order my first drink, a small compensation I had decided to allow myself, when Dempsey walked in.

He gracefully smoothed awkward introductions. And he did much more than simply permit me to interview him. He invited me to join him at dinner with some of his family and friends. This was more than I had dared to expect. Although I was honored by the invitation, I accepted with considerable anxiety, since I hadn't enough money to buy a meal in a good New York restaurant. But this was no time to be timid. I knew this was one chance I had to take.

Dempsey was a gentleman and a perfect host, trying to bring out the best in his guest. He was concerned with the feelings and desires of the people at the table—so concerned, in fact, that at times (I don't care to remember how many) I found myself doing the talking and Dempsey doing the listening. That was no way to conduct an interview. There was never any suggestion that I should pay for my meal, a thought that still brings me relief. He was the host, and I the guest. It was a memorable evening with a memorable man.

The evening made me reflect on Dempsey's life after his retirement. How many thousands of people had interrupted his public meals? How many hundreds of interviewers had been graciously received as guests? How many people with good or sad stories had been treated to free meals or given handouts? What sort of man could have endured such violations of his privacy without complaint or any outward expression of ennui? Perhaps Grantland Rice was correct. It took a remarkably gentle man to live Dempsey's postchampionship life as decently as he lived it.

Notes

CHAPTER I

1 Rupert Hart-Davis (ed.), *The Letters of Oscar Wilde* (New York, 1962), 109–11.
2 Works Progress Administration, *Colorado: A Guide to the Highest State* (New York, 1941), 399; Jack Dempsey and Myron M. Stearns, *Round by Round: An Autobiography* (New York, 1940), 4–6.
3 Gene Fowler, *Skyline* (New York, 1961), 311.
4 Interview, Jack Dempsey, December 26, 1973, hereinafter cited as Dempsey, with date; Jack Dempsey, Bob Considine, and Bill Slocum, *Dempsey* (New York, 1960), 14.
5 Dempsey and Stearns, *Round By Round*, 14.
6 Dempsey, Considine, and Slocum, *Dempsey*, 13.
7 Dempsey and Stearns, *Round By Round*, 15; Dempsey, Considine. and Slocum, *Dempsey*, 14, 16–17; Dempsey, December 26, 1973.
8 Dempsey, Considine, and Slocum, *Dempsey*, 14–17; Dempsey, December 26, 1973.
9 *The Modern Gladiator: Being an Account of the Exploits and Experiences of the World's Greatest Fighter* (St. Louis, 1889), v.
10 Dempsey, Considine, and Slocum, *Dempsey*, 18; Nat Fleischer, *Jack Dempsey* (New Rochelle, N.Y., 1972), 16.
11 Dempsey, December 26, 1973; Dempsey and Stearns, *Round By Round*, 17.
12 William S. Greever, *The Bonanza West: The Story of the Western Mining Rushes, 1848–1900* (Norman, 1963), 183–214.
13 *Ibid.*, 189, 194.
14 *Ibid.*, 186–94; Dempsey and Stearns, *Round By Round*, 13–21.
15 Percy Stanley Fritz, *Colorado: The Centennial State* (New York, 1941), 282–97.
16 Works Progress Administration, *Colorado*, 314; Dempsey, December 26, 1973; Dempsey, Considine, and Slocum, *Dempsey*, 21.
17 Dempsey and Stearns, *Round By Round*, 33–39; Fritz, *Colorado*, 339–40.
18 House of Representatives, Committee on Interstate and Foreign Commerce, *Federal Boxing Commission* (Washington, D.C., 1965), 27–28; Dempsey, December 26, 1973.
19 Dempsey, December 26, 1973; Dempsey, Considine, and Slocum, *Dempsey*, 22–24.
20 Dempsey, December 26, 1973; Dempsey and Stearns, *Round By Round*, 40–49.
21 Bob Waters and Stanley Weston, "Dempsey: 50 Years a Champion," *International Boxing* (July, 1969), 16.

22 Dempsey, Considine, and Slocum, *Dempsey,* 31: See Jack London, *The Road* (New York, 1907), 24–52, for a vivid picture of riding the rods.

23 Nels Anderson, *The Hobo: The Sociology of the Homeless Man* (Chicago, 1923), 125–26.

24 *Ibid.,* 144–47.

25 Dempsey, Considine, and Slocum, *Dempsey,* 32–34; Dempsey and Stearns, *Round By Round,* 50–57.

26 Dempsey, December 26, 1973.

27 *Ibid.;* Rex Lardner, *The Legendary Champions* (New York, 1972), 221; Dempsey, Considine, and Slocum, *Dempsey,* 34–36.

28 Dempsey, Considine, and Slocum, *Dempsey,* 34–36; House of Representatives, *Federal Boxing Commission,* 27.

29 Interview, Dan Daniel, December 26, 1973.

30 Dempsey, Considine, and Slocum, *Dempsey,* 36–37; Dale L. Morgan, "Salt Lake City: City of the Saints," in Ray B. West, Jr. (ed.), *Rocky Mountain Cities* (New York, 1949), 197–200.

31 Nat Loubet et al. (eds.), *Ring Record Book* (New York, 1973), 175–76; Dempsey, Considine, and Slocum, *Dempsey,* 38–55; Dempsey and Stearns, *Round By Round,* 61–99; Fleischer, *Jack Dempsey,* 20–34; Nat Fleischer, *Jack Dempsey: Idol of Fistiana* (New York, 1929), 84–92; Jack Dempsey and Barbara Piatelli Dempsey, *Dempsey* (New York, 1977), 23–34.

32 Rex Lardner, *Legendary Champions,* 221–22.

33 Dempsey, Considine, and Slocum, *Dempsey,* 47–48.

34 Loubet et al. (eds.), *Ring Record Book,* 175.

35 Dempsey and Dempsey, *Dempsey,* 35–36; Dempsey, Considine, and Slocum, *Dempsey,* 50–52; Fleischer, *Jack Dempsey: Idol of Fistiana,* 89–90.

36 Fleischer, *Jack Dempsey: Idol of Fistiana,* 92; Dempsey, Considine, and Slocum, *Dempsey,* 53–55; Dempsey and Stearns, *Round By Round,* 97–99.

CHAPTER II

1 Dempsey and Dempsey, *Dempsey,* 39–42; Dempsey, December 26, 1973.

2 Dempsey and Stearns, *Round By Round;* 101.

3 Rex Lardner, *Legendary Champions,* 143: Loubet et al. (eds.), *Ring Record Book,* 10; Nat Fleischer, "Root Passes at 87," *Ring* (August, 1963), 30–31; John Gallagher and Joseph T. Friscia, "Jack Root: Last of the Giants," *Boxing Illustrated and Wrestling News* (September, 1963), 42–45; Allen Ressler, "The One-Eyed Heavyweight Champion," *Boxing Illustrated and Wrestling News* (March, 1959), 30; Johnny Salak, "The Case For and Against Marvin Hart," *ibid.* (July, 1961), 22–23; Charles W. Meadows, "Forgotten Greats of the Past: Marvin Hart," *ibid.* (May, 1968), 51.

4 Alexander Johnston, *Ten and Out: The Complete Story of the Prize Ring in America* (New York, 1947), 174–81.

5 John C. Betts, "Organized Sports in Industrial America" (Ph.D. dissertation, Columbia University, 1951), 602.

6 Loubet, et al., *Ring Record Book,* 173–74; Lardner, *Legendary Champions,* 174–76.

7 Omaha *Morning World-Herald,* December 26, 1908, p. 1. Actually the bout was stopped by the police to prevent further injury to Burns. Omaha *Daily News,* December 27, 1908, pp. 1, 2.

8 Budd Schulberg, *Loser and Still Champion: Muhammad Ali* (Garden City, N.Y.; 1972), 17–18; Finis Farr, *Black Champion: The Life and Times of Jack Johnson* (London, 1964), 62; Omaha *Daily News,* October 17, 1908, Sports Section, 1.

9 Farr, *Black Champion,* 63–114; Al-Tony Gilmore, *Bad Nigger: The National Impact of Jack Johnson* (Port Washington, N.Y.; 1975), 32–54; Randy Roberts, "Heavyweight Champion Jack Johnson: His Omaha Image, a Public Reaction Study," *Nebraska History,* LVII (1976), 231–35.

10 Omaha *Daily News,* July 2, 1910, p. 6.

11 Omaha *Evening World-Herald*, July 2, 1910, p. 1.

12 Farr, *Black Champion*, 80, 82.

13 Omaha *Evening World-Herald*, July 2, 1910, p. 1; Omaha *Daily News*, July 2, 1910, p. 6.

14 Rex Lardner, *Legendary Champions*, 181–82; Gilmore, *Bad Nigger*, 42; Charles Samuels, *The Magnificent Rube* (New York, 1957), 166–72.

15 Farr, *Black Champion*, 112–14; Jack Johnson, *Jack Johnson Is a Dandy: An Autobiography* (New York, 1969), 123–27; Lester Bromberg, *Boxing's Unforgettable Fights* (New York, 1962), 67–71.

16 *New York Times*, p. 1; Omaha *Daily News*, pp. 1–2; Omaha *Evening World-Herald*, p. 1; Omaha *Daily Bee*, p. 1, all on July 5, 1910.

17 Omaha *Evening World-Herald*, July 5, 1910, p. 1; Gilmore, *Bad Nigger*, 72.

18 *New York Times*, July 6, 1910, p. 3.

19 Stuart Mews, "Puritanicalism, Sport, and Race: A Symbolic Crusade of 1911," in G. J. Cuming and Derek Baker (eds.), *Studies in Church History*, VIII (Cambridge, England, 1972), 305–308.

20 *New York Times*, July 6, 1910, p. 1; Omaha *Daily News*, July 6, 1910, p. 1, July 7, 1910, pp. 1–2; Omaha *Daily Bee*, July 7, 1910, p. 1; Omaha *Evening World-Herald*, July 6, 1910, p. 1, July 9, 1910, p. 10; Gilmore, *Bad Nigger*, 79.

21 Mews, "Puritanicalism, Sport and Race," 311; Gilmore, *Bad Nigger*, 81; Omaha *Evening World-Herald*, July 6, 1910, p. 1.

22 *Congressional Record*, 62nd Cong., 2nd Sess., 7908, 7501, 8551, 9304–9309, 9988.

23 William H. Wiggins, Jr., "Jack Johnson as Bad Nigger: The Folklore of His Life," *Black Scholar* (January, 1971), 35–46.

24 Gilmore, *Bad Nigger*, 95–116; Al-Tony Gilmore, "Jack Johnson and White Women: The National Impact," *Journal of Negro History*, LVIII (1973), 18–38; Farr, *Black Champion*, 115–74.

25 Quoted in Gilmore, *Bad Nigger*, 109.

26 *Congressional Record*, 62nd Cong., 3rd Sess., 502–504.

27 *Ibid.*, 2312.

28 Quoted in Gilmore, *Bad Nigger*, 126–27.

29 Interviewing Dan Daniel, Nat Loubet, Nat Fleischer, Jack Dempsey and reading the literature on the subject will not solve the dispute.

30 Dempsey and Dempsey, *Dempsey*, 43–44.

31 *Ibid.*, 41–44; Dempsey, Considine, and Slocum, *Dempsey*, 59–61; Dempsey and Stearns, *Round By Round*, 100–104.

32 Dempsey and Dempsey, *Dempsey*, 42–44; Fleischer, *Jack Dempsey: The Idol of Fistiana*, 95–96.

33 *New York Tribune*, June 26, 1916, p. 14; Fleischer, *Jack Dempsey: The Idol of Fistiana*, 96.

34 Fleischer, *Jack Dempsey: The Idol of Fistiana*, 97.

35 Dempsey, Considine, and Slocum, *Dempsey*, 61–62; Dempsey and Dempsey, *Dempsey*, 45–46.

36 Dempsey and Dempsey, *Dempsey*, 46.

37 Dempsey and Dempsey, *Dempsey*, 46; Dempsey and Stearns, *Round By Round*, 108; New York *Tribune*, July 15, 1916, p. 13; Dempsey, December 26, 1973.

38 Fleischer, *Jack Dempsey: The Idol of Fistiana*, 99; Dempsey and Stearns, *Round by Round*, 106.

CHAPTER III

1 Dempsey, December 26, 1973.

2 Dempsey and Dempsey, *Dempsey* (New York, 1977), 40–49; San Francisco *Chronicle*, June 10, 1920, p. 13.

3 San Francisco *Chronicle*, June 12, 1920, p. 13.

4 Dempsey and Dempsey, *Dempsey*, 52–57; San Francisco *Chronicle*, June 10, 1920, p. 13, June 11, 1920, p. 13, June 12, 1920, p. 13.

5 Loubet et al. (eds.), *Ring Record Book*, 175, 417–18; Dempsey, December 26, 1973; Dempsey, Considine, and Slocum, *Dempsey*, 77–78; Dempsey and Dempsey, *Dempsey*, 54–56.

6 Dempsey and Dempsey, *Dempsey*, 56.

7 San Francisco *Chronicle*, June 10, 1920, p. 13, June 11, 1920, p. 13, June 15, 1920, p. 7.

8 *Ibid.*, March 22, 1917, p. 11.

9 The official record book for boxing is the *Ring Record Book* edited for years by Nat Fleischer and after his death by his son-in-law Nat Loubet. It is an admirable attempt to accumulate boxer's records, but it will not, unfortunately, withstand close scrutiny. I have made a policy of trusting newspaper accounts, and for April and May the San Francisco *Chronicle* does not mention Dempsey's name. Had he fought, the paper would probably have listed the results. Dempsey, December 26, 1973.

10 San Francisco *Chronicle*, June 12, 1920, p. 13; Jack "Doc" Kearns and Oscar Fraley, *The Million Dollar Gate* (New York, 1966), 77–81; Dempsey and Dempsey, *Dempsey*, 60–65.

11 A. J. Liebling, *The Sweet Science* (New York, 1956), 69; Kearns and Fraley, *The Million Dollar Gate*, 21–73; interview, Jerry McKernan, October 28, 1974; Rex Lardner, *The Legendary Champions*, 224.

12 Dempsey, December 26, 1973; Daniel, December 27, 1973; Rex Lardner, *Legendary Champions*, 224.

13 Nat Fleischer, *Jack Dempsey: The Idol of Fistiana* (New York, 1929), 104–105; "Dempsey and the Fat Sailor," *Boxing Illustrated and Wrestling News* (July, 1962), 32–33; San Francisco *Chronicle*, July 26, 1917, p. 6.

14 Kearns and Fraley, *The Million Dollar Gate*, 82–83; San Francisco *Chronicle*, August 2, p. 7, September 8, p. 9, September 19, p. 10, September 20, p. 11, September 25, p. 6, September 26, p. 7, September 27, p. 7, 1917.

15 James Allen, "Gunboat Smith: The Man and the Legend," Pt. I, *Boxing Illustrated and Wrestling News* (April, 1963), 22–27 and 65–66; Pt. II (May, 1963), 38–43 and 67–69; San Francisco *Chronicle*, October 2, 1917, p. 7, October 3, 1917, p. 11.

16 Dempsey and Dempsey, *Dempsey*, 52–53; San Francisco *Chronicle*, October 16, 1917, p. 10, November 2, 1917, p. 10.

17 San Francisco *Chronicle*, November 3, 1917, p. 9, November 4, 1917, p. 7; Fleischer, *Jack Dempsey: The Idol of Fistiana*, 113–14; Dempsey, December 26, 1973.

18 Kearns and Fraley, *The Million Dollar Gate*, 86–89; Dempsey and Dempsey, *Dempsey*, 72–76; San Francisco *Chronicle*, January 26, p. 10, February 5, p. 10, 1918, February 15, p. 10, 1918; New York *Tribune*, February 5, p. 12, February 15, p. 12; New York *Times*, February 15, 1918, p. 6.

19 New York *Tribune*, February 26, 1918, p. 12; New York *Times*, February 26, 1918, p. 10; San Francisco *Chronicle*, February 26, 1918, p. 10; Dempsey and Dempsey, *Dempsey*, 80–81.

20 San Francisco *Chronicle*, March 18, p. 8, March 26, 1918, p. 9, New York *Tribune*, March 26, 1918, p. 12.

21 New York *Times*, May 4, 1918, p. 12; New York *Tribune*, May 4, 1918, p. 17; San Francisco *Chronicle*, May 4, 1918, p. 8.

22 San Francisco *Chronicle*, May 24, 1918, p. 9; Loubet et al., *Ring Record Book*, 339; *Stars and Stripes*, July 5, 1918, p. 6. New York *Times*, December 19, 1918, p. 12, April 8, 1918, p. 16, April 13, 1918, p. 10, April 24, 1918, p. 14, June 23, 1918, II, p. 5, August 18, 1918, II, p. 2.

23 Major General E. H. Crowder, *The Spirit of Selective Service* (New York, 1920), 155.

24 Marshall Smelser, *The Life That Ruth Built: A Biography* (New York, 1975), 106; Frank Deford, *Big Bill Tilden: The Triumphs and the Tragedy* (New York, 1975), 33.

25 New York *Tribune*, May 24, 1918, p. 15; Thomas Foster, "Why Our Soldiers Learn to Box," *Outing* (May, 1918), 114; Nat Fleischer, "Forward," *Ring* (February 15, 1922), 4.

26 Dempsey, December 26, 1973; San Francisco *Chronicle*, June 15, 1920, p. 7; Fleischer, *Jack Dempsey: The Idol of Fistiana,* 57.

27 Fleischer, *Jack Dempsey: The Idol of Fistiana,* 62; San Francisco *Chronicle*, August 18, 1918, p. 8, June 15, 1920, p. 7. Dempsey's military record receives a fuller treatment in Chapter V, herein.

28 *Stars and Stripes*, May 31, p. 6; July 26, p. 6, December 27, p. 6, 1918.

29 San Francisco *Chronicle*, July 2, p. 6, July 5, p. 12, 1918; New York *Times*, July 5, 1918, p. 13; New York *Tribune*, July 5, 1918, p. 13.

30 Atlanta *Constitution*, July 6, p. 9, July 7, Sec. II, p. 3, 1918.

31 *Ibid.*

32 New York *Times*, February 1, 1917, p. 10; *Stars and Stripes*, July 26, 1918, p. 6; Dempsey and Dempsey, *Dempsey*, 83.

33 New York *Times*, June 2, Pt. II, p. 7, June 18, p. 10, June 23, Pt. II, p. 7, June 27, p. 8, July 2, p. 10, July 4, p. 14, July 21, p. 17, all in 1918.

34 *Ibid.*, July 28, Sec. II, p. 5, 1918; San Francisco *Chronicle*, July 28, p. 2, August 26, p. 10, 1918; New York *Tribune*, July 28, 1918, Pt. II, pp. 1–2.

35 San Francisco *Chronicle*, August 26, p. 10, September 14, p. 10; New York *Times*, September 15, 1918, II, p. 4; Loubet et al., *Ring Record Book,* 175.

36 Robert Coughlan, "Young Jack Dempsey," in *Yesterday in Sport* (New York, 1968), 131; Dempsey and Dempsey, *Dempsey*, 87–88; Fleischer, *Jack Dempsey: The Idol of Fistiana,* 56–57.

37 New York *Tribune*, November 7, p. 13, November 17, Sec. II, p. 1, 1918; San Francisco *Chronicle* November 7, 1918, p. 8; New York *Times*, November 7, p. 12, November 17, p. 21, 1918; New Orleans *States*, November 20, 1918, p. 11.

38 San Francisco *Chronicle*, November 19, p. 8, November 29, p. 11, 1918; New York *Times*, November 17, p. 10, November 29, p. 15, 1918.

39 New Orleans *Times Picayune*, December 17, p. 14, December 15, p. 14, 1918; New Orleans *States*, December 17, 1918, p. 11; New York *Times*, December 17, p. 14, December 31, p. 12, 1918; New York *Tribune*, December 31, 1918, p. 16; San Francisco *Chronicle*, December 31, 1918, p. 12; Loubet et al., *Ring Record Book,* 175.

CHAPTER IV

1 New York *Sun*, July 1, 1919, p. 8.

2 *Ibid.*, June 19, 1919, p. 7; Interview, Dan Daniel, December 26, 1973.

3 John Lardner, *White Hopes and Other Tigers* (Philadelphia, 1951), 53–54.

4 New York *Times*, January 25, 1919, p. 8.

5 Nat Fleischer to Randy Roberts, November 3, 1971.

6 Samuels, *The Magnificent Rube*, 207–208; New York *Times*, February 11, 1919, p. 8.

7 New York *Times*, September 14, 1919, Sec. 9, p. 6.

8 "Tobacco and Pugilism in the Army," *Literary Digest* (August 10, 1918), 32.

9 New York *Times*, January 27, p. 10, February 28, p. 10, February 6, p. 12, March 31, p. 14, 1919.

10 Samuels, *The Magnificent Rube*, 209; New York *Times*, March 2, Sec. 2, p. 2, March 12, p. 12, March 16, p. 17, 1919; Loubet et al. (eds.), *Ring Record Book,* 129.

11 New York *Times*, January 29, 1919, p. 10; James M. Cox, *Journey Through My Years* (New York, 1946), 215–16.

12 John Lardner, *White Hopes and Other Tigers*, 64; New York *Times*, May 6, 1919, p. 17.

13 New York *Times*, May 20, p. 18, May 22, p. 2, 1919.

14 *Journal of the House of Representatives of the Eighty-Third General Assembly of the State of Ohio,* May 26, 1919, p. 1067; New York *Times*, June 20, 1919, p. 14.

15 *Congressional Record,* 66th Cong., 1st Sess., 1898; New York *Times*, June 27, p. 19, June 28, p. 10, 1919.

16 New York *Times*, May 28, 1919, p. 13.
17 *Ibid.*, March 19, pp. 9, 12, June 27, p. 13, 1919; Nat Fleischer, *The Heavyweight Championship: An Informal History of Heavyweight Boxing from 1719 to the Present Day* (New York, 1949), 163.
18 New York *Times*, June 27, p. 13, June 22, p. 21, 1919.
19 New York *Times*, June 22, p. 21, June 24, p. 11, 1919.
20 John Lardner, *White Hopes and Other Tigers*, 58-74.
21 *Washington Post*, July 3, 1919, p. 12; *San Francisco Chronicle*, July 3, 1919, p. 8; *Chicago Daily News*, July 2, 1919, p. 2; New York *Times*, July 4, 1919, p. 6.
22 Daniel, December 26, 1973; John Lardner, *White Hopes and Other Tigers*, 59-60.
23 New York *Times*, June 29, p. 19, July 4, pp. 6, 16, 1919.
24 New York *Sun*, June 19, 1919, p. 7; *Atlanta Constitution*, July 2, 1919, p. 13; New York *Times*, June 5, 1919, p. 7; *Chicago Daily News*, July 2, 1919, p. 2.
25 New York *Tribune*, July 1, 1919, p. 15.
26 *Ibid.*, July 3, 1919, p. 11.
27 New York *Times*, June 29, 1919, p. 19; John Lardner, *White Hopes and Other Tigers*, 68-69.
28 Daniel, December 26, 1973; John Lardner, *White Hopes and Other Tigers*, 60-68.
29 John Lardner, *White Hopes and Other Tigers*, 70; New York *Times*, July 2, 1919, p. 14; St. Louis *Post-Dispatch*, July 6, 1919, p. 1; Lester Bromberg, *Boxing's Unforgettable Fights*, (New York, 1962), 100-101.
30 Dempsey, December 26, 1973.
31 John Lardner, *White Hopes and Other Tigers*, 71; *Dempsey-Willard*, Ring Classics, no. 1. Unless otherwise noted, all descriptions of the fight are based on the film.
32 Kearns, and Fraley, *Million Dollar Gate*, 1-19; St. Louis *Post-Dispatch*, July 5, 1919, p. 3.
33 Interview, Jerry McKernan, October 29, 1974.
34 Fleischer, *Jack Dempsey: The Idol of Fistiana*, 160; Interview, Nat Loubet, December 26, 1973; Daniel, December 26, 1973; John Hollis, "Were Dempsey's Fists Loaded in Toledo?" *Boxing Illustrated and Wrestling News* (May, 1964), 20-24, 66.
35 New York *Times*, July 5, 1919, p. 1; St. Louis *Post-Dispatch*, July 5, 1919, p. 23.
36 New York *Times*, July 6, 1919, Sec. 3, p. 1.
37 San Francisco *Chronicle*, July 6, 1919, p. 8.
38 New York *Times*, July 6, 1919, p. 17; Bogalusa *Enterprise and American*, July 10, 1919, p. 1.
39 St. Louis *Post-Dispatch*, July 6, 1919, p. 1.
40 New Orleans *Times-Picayune*, July 5, 1919, p. 6; New York *Times*, August 12, p. 8, July 13, Sec. 3, p. 2, 1919.
41 "Toledo Clergy on the Prize Fight," *Literary Digest* (August 9, 1919), 31-32.
42 *Atlanta Constitution*, July 11, 1919, p. 10; New York *Tribune*, July 6, 1919, p. 8, Sec. 2, p. 1; San Francisco *Chronicle*, July 7, 1919, p. 18.
43 New York *Tribune*, July 5, 1919, p. 10.
44 Orrin C. Klapp, "Creation of Popular Heroes," *American Journal of Sociology*, LIV (1948), 135.

CHAPTER V

1 Opelousas *St. Landry Clarion*, November 8, 1919, p. 1.
2 Baton Rouge *State Times*, November 8, p. 10, November 10, p. 4, 1919.
3 *Ibid.*, November 6, 1919, p. 8.
4 New Orleans *Times-Democrat*, September 8, 1892, p. 8.
5 Dale Somers, *The Rise of Sports in New Orleans, 1850-1900* (Baton Rouge, 1972), 183; Baton Rouge *State Times*, November 8, 1919, p. 10.
6 New York *Times*, November 9, 1919, Sec. 4, p. 10; Baton Rouge *State Times*, November 9, 1919, p. 4.

7 New York *Times*, November 14, 1919, p. 15.

8 San Francisco *Chronicle*, July 20, 1919, p. 11.

9 Lewis Jacobs, *The Rise of the American Film: A Critical History* (New York, 1968), 159.

10 *Ibid.*, 159-70, 287-301; Kevin Brownlow, *The Parade's Gone By* (New York, 1968), 296-318.

11 David Robinson, *Hollywood in the Twenties* (New York, 1968), 34-35.

12 The actual amount Dempsey received fluctuates according to the source cited. See Kearns and Fraley, *The Million Dollar Gate*, 117-18; Dempsey and Dempsey, *Dempsey*, 124; Dempsey, Considine, and Slocum, *Dempsey*, 109; Fleischer, *Jack Dempsey*, 136.

13 Jacobs, *The Rise of the American Film*, 82, 288, 420.

14 Dempsey, December 26, 1973; John V. Gromback, *The Saga of the Sock: A Complete Story of Boxing* (New York, 1949), 194-236; Donald Barr Chidsey, *John the Great: The Times and Life of a Remarkable American: John L. Sullivan* (Garden City, N.Y., 1942), 173-80; James J. Corbett, *The Roar of the Crowd: The True Tale of the Rise and Fall of a Champion* (New York, 1925), 207; New York *Times*, June 19, 1919, p. 9.

15 Dempsey and Dempsey, *Dempsey*, 124-26.

16 See close-up in Fleischer, *Jack Dempsey: The Idol of Fistiana*, 27.

17 Dempsey and Dempsey, *Dempsey*, 125; Waters and Weston, "Dempsey: 50 Years a Champion," 51.

18 Kearns and Fraley, *The Million Dollar Gate*, 119-20; Dempsey and Dempsey, *Dempsey*, 125.

19 *National Police Gazette*, May 1, 1920, p. 2.

20 Dempsey, Considine, and Slocum, *Dempsey*, 109-112, 196-97.

21 Dempsey, December 26, 1973; quoted in the New York *Times*, January 21, 1920, p. 8.

22 San Francisco *Chronicle*, January 23, 1920, p. 11.

23 *Ibid.*, January 24, 1920, p. 9; Kearns and Fraley, *The Million Dollar Gate*, 122.

24 San Francisco *Chronicle*, January 24, p. 9, January 25, p. 6, 1920.

25 *Ibid.*, January 27, p. 11, January 31, p. 11, 1920.

26 *New York Times*, January 14, p. 4, February 4, p. 20, January 26, p. 8, January 23, p. 14, February 4, p. 20, 1920.

27 New York *Tribune*, January 26, 1920, p. 10.

28 New York *Times*, January 28, 1920, p. 8.

29 *Ibid.*, February 27, p. 12, November 28, p. 6, January 15, p. 18, 1920.

30 Although he makes no reference to Dempsey, Paul Fussell's *The Great War and Modern Memory* (New York, 1975), shows the change in man's concept of heroic action and war.

31 San Francisco *Chronicle*, February 3, p. 12, February 5, p. 9, 1920.

32 *Ibid.*; New York *Times*, February 5, 1920, pp. 1-2.

33 Jack Dempsey, Department of Justice, Mails and Files Division, Record Group: 25-11-51, National Archives; San Francisco *Chronicle*, February 25, pp. 1-2, February 28, pp. 1-2, 1920.

34 Kearns and Fraley, *The Million Dollar Gate*, 120-26. Although Kearns's tale reads more like fiction, circumstantial evidence appears to confirm his story.

35 New York *Times*, April 4, p. 9, May 9, p. 23, May 13, p. 4, 1920.

36 San Francisco *Chronicle*, June 9, 1920, p. 17.

37 *Ibid.*, June 10, 1920, p. 13.

38 *Ibid.*

39 *Ibid.*; New York *Times*, June 11, 1920, p. 17.

40 San Francisco *Chronicle*, June 11, 1920, p. 13.

41 *Ibid.*; New York *Times*, June 11, 1920, p. 7.

42 New York *Times*, June 11, 1920, p. 7; Fleischer, *Jack Dempsey: The Idol of Fistiana*, 62-63.

43 San Francisco *Chronicle*, June 12, 1920, p. 13.

44 *Ibid.*, June 15, 1920, p. 7.

45 *Ibid.*; Fleischer, *Jack Dempsey: The Idol of Fistiana*, 62–63.
46 San Francisco *Chronicle*, June 16, 1920, pp. 1, 5; Dempsey and Dempsey, *Dempsey*, 131.
47 New Orleans *Times-Picayune*, June 17, 1920, p. 8.
48 Atlanta *Constitution*, June 16, 1920, p. 14.
49 Jack Dempsey, Department of Justice, Mails and Files Division, 25–11–51–5; San Francisco *Chronicle*, June 12, 1920, p. 13; Kearns and Fraley, *The Million Dollar Gate*, 120–26.
50 San Francisco *Chronicle*, June 12, 1920, p. 13; Dempsey, December 26, 1973; Daniel, December 26, 1973.
51 New York *Times*, July 28, 1920, p. 14; Fleischer, *Jack Dempsey: The Idol of Fistiana*, 122.
52 New York *Times*, September 3, 1920, p. 20.
53 *Ibid.*, September 1, 1920, p. 10.
54 San Francisco *Chronicle*, February 2, 1920, p. 7; New York *Times*, September 5, 1920, p. 17; Fleischer, *Jack Dempsey: The Idol of Fistiana*, 161–62.
55 New York *Times*, September 5, p. 17, September 6, p. 9, 1920; Fleischer, *Jack Dempsey: The Idol of Fistiana*, 161–62.
56 New York *Tribune*, September 7, 1920, p. 5; New York *Times*, September 7, 1920, pp. 1, 7.
57 New York *Tribune*, September 7, 1920, p. 5.
58 *Ibid.*; Fleischer, *Jack Dempsey: The Idol of Fistiana*, 63–68.
59 Dempsey, December 26, 1973; Loubet et al. (eds), *Ring Record Book*, 440.
60 New York *Times*, September 7, 1920, p. 7; Michael A. Glick, "Boxing's Tender Side," *Boxing Illustrated and Wrestling News* (December, 1958), 35.
61 Loubet et. al., *Ring Record Book*, 81; Daniel, December 26, 1973.
62 Gromback, *The Saga of Sock*, 168; New York *Times*, February 8, p. 20, February 18, p. 19, 1920.
63 Gromback, *The Saga of Sock*, 168–69; Gene Fowler, *Beau James* (New York, 1949), 99–100.
64 New York *Times*, January 15, p. 11, February 8, p. 20, February 18, p. 19, March 8, p. 10, March 25, p. 13, 1920.
65 Fowler, *Beau James*, 98–99; New York *Times*, April 2, p. 18, April 25, p. 19, 1920.
66 Samuels, *The Magnificent Rube*, 222–23; James MacGregor Burns, *Roosevelt: The Lion and the Fox*, I (New York, 1956), 93–94; Richard O'Connor, *The First Hurrah: A Biography of Alfred E. Smith* (New York, 1970), 120–22.
67 New York *Times*, May 9, 1920, p. 17; Fowler, *Beau James*, 100–103; O'Connor, *The First Hurrah*, 119–22.
68 Fowler, *Beau James*, 100–105; O'Connor, *The First Hurrah*, 119–22; New York *Times*, May 25, 1920, p. 13; New York *Tribune*, May 25, 1920, p. 9.
69 New York *Times*, May 25, 1920, p. 13; New York *Tribune*, May 25, 1920, p. 9; Fowler, *Beau James*, 104–105; Samuels, *The Magnificent Rube*, 223–25.
70 Jack Dempsey, Department of Justice, Mails and Files Division, 203014-20.
71 New York *Times*, May 10, 1920, p. 12; New York *Tribune*, April 26, p. 12, May 26, p. 12, 1920.
72 Samuels, *The Magnificent Rube*, 217–22.
73 New York *Times*, August 12, p. 17, November 9, p. 12, 1920.
74 New York *Tribune*, December 10, 1920, p. 17.
75 "This Was Dempsey's Toughest Fight," *Boxing Illustrated and Wrestling News* (July, 1964), 35; Dempsey, Considine, Slocum, *Dempsey*, 113–14.
76 New York *Times*, November 19, 1920, p. 12; New York *Tribune*, December 8, 1920, p. 15.
77 New York *Tribune*, December 15, 1920, p. 1.
78 *Ibid.*
79 *Ibid.*, 15; Fleischer, *Jack Dempsey: The Idol of Fistiana*, 168–76; "This Was Dempsey's Toughest Fight," 39.

80 Dempsey, December 26, 1973; New York *Tribune,* December 15, 1920, p. 15.
81 St. Louis *Post-Dispatch,* December 16, 1920, p. 41.

CHAPTER VI

1 Ring Lardner, "The Battle of the Century," *Some Champions: Sketches and Fiction by Ring Lardner,* ed. Matthew J. Bruccoli and Richard Layman (New York, 1976), 134.
2 Ring Lardner, Jr., *The Lardners: My Family Remembered* (New York, 1976), 148.
3 Ring Lardner, "The Battle of the Century," 135, 136.
4 *Ibid.,* 138, 149.
5 Arnold Bennett, "The Prize Fight," *Living Age* (January 24, 1920), 224–27.
6 Francis Hackett, "The Carpentier Fight: Bennett vs. Shaw," *New Republic* (January 14, 1920), 198–200.
7 Bohum Lynch, *Knuckles and Gloves* (New York, 1923), 170–73; Bennett, "The Prize Fight," 225; quoted in Hackett, "The Carpentier Fight," 199.
8 Bennett, "The Prize Fight," 227.
9 Quoted in Hackett, "The Carpentier Fight," 200; "Georges Carpentier—Gentleman, Athlete, and Connoisseur of the 'Boxe,'" *Literary Digest* (April 17, 1920), 130–33.
10 New York *Times,* December 7, p. 2, December 8, p. 19, December 26, p. 12, 1919.
11 *Ibid.,* September 11, p. 11, September 23, p. 9, 1920; Kearns and Fraley, *The Million Dollar Gate* 138–39; Samuels, *The Magnificent Rube* 230–31; New York *Times,* November 6, 1920, p. 1.
12 Samuels, *The Magnificent Rube,* 229.
13 New York *Times,* November 1, p. 19, November 6, p. 1, 1920; John Lardner, *White Hopes and Other Tigers,* 84.
14 New York *Sun,* July 1, 1919, p. 19.
15 New York *Times,* November 8, 1920, p. 14; quoted in "Boxing Reduced to Sordid Money-Grabbing," *Literary Digest* (February 14, 1920), 124–25.
16 New York *Times,* November 19, 1920, p. 9, January 20, 1921, p. 1; Samuels, *The Magnificent Rube,* 131; Fleischer, *Jack Dempsey: The Idol of Fistiana,* 184–85.
17 Samuels, *The Magnificent Rube,* 1–216; Mel Heimer, *The Long Count* (New York, 1969), 103–12.
18 Samuels, *The Magnificent Rube,* 232–33; Kearns and Fraley, *The Million Dollar Gate,* 145.
19 Samuels, *The Magnificent Rube,* 233.
20 Paul Gallico, *Farewell to Sport* (New York, 1938), 96.
21 *Ibid.,* 97.
22 Quoted in Hackett, "The Carpentier Fight," 199; quoted in John Lardner, *White Hopes and Other Tigers,* 75–76.
23 New York *Times,* May 17, 1921, p. 1; "Carpentier, From Pit-Boy to Esthete of the 'Boxe,'" *Literary Digest* (June 11, 1921), 34; Dempsey and Dempsey, *Dempsey,* 141; Loubet et al. (eds.), *Ring Record Book,* 193; Lardner, *White Hopes and Other Tigers,* 80–81.
24 Quoted in "Carpentier, From Pit-Boy to Esthete of the 'Boxe.'" 36; quoted in "Georges Carpentier—Gentleman, Athlete, and Connoisseur of the 'Boxe,'" 130–34.
25 Quoted in "The War Record of Dempsey," *Literary Digest* (February 4, 1920), 122–24; New York *Times,* January 14, 1920, p. 24.
26 "Georges Carpentier—Gentleman, Athlete, and Connoisseur of the 'Boxe,'" 130–36; "Carpentier: From Pit-Boy to Esthete of the 'Boxe,'" 39; "Georges Carpentier—Gentleman, Athlete, and Connoisseur of the 'Boxe,'" 133.
27 For the views of intellectuals who were interested in boxing, see Bennett, "The Great Prize Fight," 124–27; Hackett, "The Carpentier Fight: Bennett vs. Shaw," *New Republic,* 198–200; Francis Hackett, "Dempsey-Carpentier," *New Republic* (July 13, 1921), 185–87; Heywood Broun, "Mr. Dempsey's Five Foot Shelf," *Bookman* (August, 1921), 521–24;

"Boswell Takes Dr. Samuel Johnson to the Beckett-Carpentier Fight," *Literary Digest*, 127-218; "Shaw Called a 'Colossal Joke' as a Prize-Fight Reporter," 146-48.

28 "Carpentier: A Symbol," *New Republic* (July 20, 1921), 106; New York *Times*, May 18, 1921, p. 14.

29 "Carpentier: A Symbol," 206, 207; Manchester *Guardian*, July 2, 1921, p. 8; London *Times*, July 2, 1921, p. 13.

30 New York *Times*, November 19, p. 9, 1920, February 19, p. 12, March 16, p. 10, March 26, p. 14, March 28, p. 13, March 29, p. 16, April 10, p. 1, April 20, p. 1, April 26, p. 17, 1921; John Lardner, *White Hopes and Other Tigers*, 85.

31 New York *Times*, April 28, p. 10, June 23, p. 13, June 26, p. 2, 1921; John Lardner, *White Hopes and Other Tigers*, 85.

32 New York *Times*, April 1, p. 14, April 21, p. 10, 1921.

33 *Congressional Record*, 67th Congress., 1st Sess, 2297; New York *Times*, June 9, 1921, p. 17.

34 New York *Times*, May 1, 1923, p. 3, May 25, 1925, p. 17, June 11, p. 14, June 18, p. 9, June 29, p. 1, 1921.

35 John Lardner, *White Hopes and Other Tigers*, 85-86; New York *Times*, May 17, p. 1, May 18, p. 14, May 19, p. 12, 1921.

36 John Lardner, *White Hopes and Other Tigers*, 85; New York *Times*, May 26, 1921, p. 15; "Did 'Psychic' Power Aid Brawn When Carpentier Licked Beckett?" *Literary Digest* (January 17, 1920), 121-22.

37 Ring Lardner, "Some Champions," 70; New York *Times*, May 27, 1921, p. 22.

38 New York *Times*, May 7, p. 12, May 23, p. 12, May 29, p. 20, 1921; Dempsey and Dempsey, *Dempsey*, 140; Ring Lardner, "Some Champions," 70.

39 Broun, "Mr. Dempsey's Five Foot Shelf," 522; New York *Times*, May 14, p. 13, May 16, p. 14, 1921.

40 New York *Times*, June 18, 1921, p. 9; Samuels, *The Magnificent Rube*, 237.

41 Quoted in "Fist Civilization vs. Sword Civilization," *Living Age* (September 24, 1921), 773-74; Manchester *Guardian*, July 2, 1921, p. 8; London *Times*, July 2, 1921, p. 13; Japan *Times*, July 2, 1921, p. 2.

42 John Lardner, *White Hopes and Other Tigers*, 76; New York *Times*, June 26, 1921, p. 1; Samuels, *The Magnificent Rube*, 241, 242.

43 P. W. Wilson, "The Big Prize-Fight Psychologically Considered," *Current Opinion* (August, 1921), 175.

44 John Lardner, *White Hopes and Other Tigers*, 87; New York *Times*, July 1, p. 9, July 2, pp. 1, 10, 11, 1921.

45 New York *Times*, July 3, 1921, p. 1; New York *Tribune*, July 3, 1921, p. 4; Loubet et al. (eds.), *Ring Record Book*, 86; Kearns and Fraley, *The Million Dollar Gate*, 147.

46 Loubet et al. (eds.), *Ring Record Book*, 147; New York *Times*, May 23, p. 2, July 3, p. 9, 1921; Samuels, *The Magnificent Rube*, 245-46.

47 Samuels, *The Magnificent Rube*, 246; New York *Tribune*, July 3, 1921, p. 4.

48 Samuels, *The Magnificent Rube*, 247; Dempsey and Dempsey, *Dempsey*, 143; Dempsey, December 27, 1973.

49 New York *Tribune*, July 3, 1921, pp. 1, 6.

50 *Ibid.*, pp. 1, 3.

51 Lester Bromberg, *Boxing's Unforgettable Fights*, 115-16; Samuels, *The Magnificent Rube*, 247-48; New York *Times*, June 9, p. 12, June 23, p. 13, 1921.

52 New York *Tribune*, July 3, 1921, pp. 1, 3.

53 New York *Times*, June 30, 1920, p. 13, July 2, 1921, p. 11; Deford, *Big Bill Tilden*, 38-39; New York *Tribune*, July 3, 1921, p. 4.

54 Loubet et al. (eds.), *Ring Record Book*, 108.

55 New York *Times*, July 3, 1921, p. 1; *Dempsey-Carpentier*, Ring Classics, no. 56. Unless otherwise noted, all description of the fight is based on the film.

56 New York *Tribune,* July 3, 1921, p. 1.
57 *Ibid.,* p. 2.
58 *Ibid.,* p. 1; quoted in "Esthetics of Pugilism," *Literary Digest* (August 27, 1921), 27; H. L. Mencken, *A Mencken Chrestomathy* (New York, 1956), 406.
59 Francis Hackett, "Dempsey-Carpentier," 187.
60 New York *Times,* July 3, 1921, pp. 1–13.
61 Japan *Times,* July 4, 1921, p. 1; Daniel, December 26, 1973.
62 Quoted in " 'Carbuncle' of Boyle's Thirty Acres," *Literary Digest* (July 30, 1921), 31; New York *Times,* July 4, p. 11, July 5, p. 14, 1921.
63 Quoted in " 'Carbuncle' of Boyle's Thirty Acres," 31; New York *Times,* July 4, 1921, p. 11.
64 Quoted in " 'Carbuncle' of Boyle's Thirty Acres," 31–32; New York *Times,* July 5, 1921, p. 14.
65 St. Louis *Post-Dispatch,* July 2, 1921, p. 14.
66 London *Times,* July 4, 1921, p. 14; quoted in "Paris Meditates on Jersey City," *Literary Digest* (August 20, 1921), 19.

CHAPTER VII

1 Dempsey and Dempsey, *Dempsey,* 147.
2 For a short survey of the European intellectual scene in the 1920s, see Raymond J. Sontag, *A Broken World* (New York, 1971), 209–35.
3 *Police Gazette,* May 13, 1922, p. 9; New York *Times,* April 12, 1922, p. 24; New York *Tribune,* April 12, 1922, p. 15.
4 New Orleans *States,* April 12, p. 17, April 17, p. 13, 1922; New York *Times,* April 19, 1922, p. 16.
5 Fred Dartnell ("Lord Melford"), *"Seconds Out!" Chats About Boxers, Their Trainers and Patrons* (London, N.D.), 271–72; New York *Tribune,* April 19, 1922, p. 15; New York *Times,* April 19, 1922, p. 16; New Orleans *States,* April 19, 1922, p. 15.
6 New York *Times,* April 20, p. 14, April 21, p. 5, April 24, p. 11, 1922; New Orleans *States,* April 20, p. 15, April 21, p. 19, 1922; Dartnell, *"Seconds Out!,"* 272; New York *Tribune,* April 21, 1922, p. 13.
7 New Orleans *States,* April 22, 1922, p. 7; New York *Times,* April 23, 1922, p. 15; San Francisco *Chronicle,* April 23, 1922, p. 13; London *Times,* April 22, 1922, p. 6; Dempsey, December 26, 1973.
8 New York *Times,* April 23, p. 25, April 25, p. 18, April 26, p. 16, April 27, p. 14, 1922; New Orleans *States,* April 25, p. 14, April 26, p. 16, 1922.
9 New Orleans *States,* April 24, p. 12, April 25, p. 14, April 26, p. 16, 1922; New York *Times,* April 25, p. 18, April 26, p. 16, 1922; New York *Tribune,* April 23, 1922, p. 19.
10 Quoted in New York *Times,* April 28, p. 13, April 29, p. 11, 1922.
11 Quoted in "Fist Civilization vs. Sword Civilization," 774; quoted in "Paris Meditates on Jersey City," 19.
12 New York *Times,* May 1, 1922, p. 14; New Orleans *States,* May 1, 1922, p. 14.
13 New York *Times,* May 2, p. 16, May 4, p. 17, 1922.
14 New Orleans *States,* May 20, 1922, p. 8; New York *Times,* May 20, 1922, p. 11; Dempsey and Dempsey, *Dempsey,* 148.
15 New York *Times,* July 11, p. 11, September 19, p. 17, September 24, p. 3, September 28, p. 17, 1922; Bill McNulty, "Jack Dempsey's Moose Hunt in Canada," *Ring* (December, 1922), 7; Mark A. Luescher, "Footlights vs. Ringlights, *Ring* (April, 1922), 8; A. D. Phillips, "Pets of Fistic Luminaries," *Ring* (June, 1923), 19.
16 Samuels, *The Magnificent Rube* 252–53.
17 New York *Times,* January 22, 1922, pp. 1, 17.
18 *Ibid.;* Samuels, *The Magnificent Rube,* 252–57.

19 New York *Times,* January 25, p. 10, January 26, p. 3, February 4, p. 6, February 12, p. 9, 1922.
20 New York *Times,* February 8, p. 5, February 9, p. 8, February 10, p. 8, February 11, p. 14, 1922. New York *Tribune,* March 24, 1922, p. 7.
21 Samuels, *The Magnificent Rube,* 255-56; New York *Times,* April 1, 1922, p. 1.
22 New York *Times,* February 17, p. 17. February 24, p. 3, March 22, p. 8, 1922; New York *Tribune,* March 22, 1922, p. 3.
23 New York *Tribune,* March 23, p. 6, March 24, p. 7, 1922; New York *Times,* March 23, p. 6, March 24, p. 6, 1922.
24 New York *Tribune,* March 25, p. 4, March 28, p. 19, 1922; New York *Times,* March 25, p. 4, March 27, pp. 14, 15, March 28, p. 19, 1922.
25 New York *Tribune,* March 23, p. 6, March 25, p. 4, March 29, p. 1, 1922; Samuels, *The Magnificent Rube,* 260-61; New York *Times,* March 29, 1922, pp. 1, 4.
26 New York *Times,* January 22, 1922, p. 17; Name of source withheld.
27 Loubet et al. (eds.), *Ring Record Book,* 459-60.
28 *Ibid.,* 67-68.
29 Nat Fleischer, "Forward," 4; Loubet, December 27, 1973. Also see Nat Fleischer, *50 Years at Ringside* (New York, 1958), 245-51.
30 Francis Albertani, "Harry Wills, Most Logical Opponent for Jack Dempsey," *Ring* (April, 1922), 19; George B. Underwood, "Harry Wills, Giant Negro Gladiator, Credit to the Game," *Ring* (August, 1922), 10.
31 Nat Fleischer, *"Sockers in Sepia":* A Continuation of the Drama of the Negro in Pugilistic Competition, Vol. V of *Black Dynamite* (New York, 1947), 55; New York *Tribune,* September 8, 1922, p. 12.
32 New York *Times,* July 6, p. 17, June 20, p. 16, 1922; Dempsey, December 27, 1973. Also see MacDonald Stringham and Robert J. Thornton, "The Giant Who Might Have Killed Jack," *Boxing Illustrated and Wrestling News* (April, 1964), 44.
33 Fleischer, *"Sockers in Sepia,"* 49; Samuels, *The Magnificent Rube,* 276; Nat Loubet, December 26, 1973.
34 New York *Times,* June 23, p. 14, July 12, p. 7, July 17, p. 10, 1922; New York *Tribune,* July 12, 1922, p. 14.
35 New York *Times,* September 7, 1922, p. 13; New York *Tribune,* September 7, 1922, p. 12.
36 "That Terrible Combat: To a Draw, Between Dempsey and Wills," *Literary Digest* (October 14, 1922), 70.

CHAPTER VIII

1 Edward Van Every, *Muldoon: The Solid Man of Sports* (New York, 1929), ii, 52, 350.
2 Nat Fleischer, "New York State Athletic Commission Standard for Nation," *Ring* (February 13, 1922), 10.
3 New York *Times,* February 3, p. 10, February 5, p. 12, 1923.
4 Every, *Muldoon,* 340; New York *Times,* February 5, p. 12, February 3, p. 10, 1923; Nat Fleischer, "As We See It," *Ring* (May, 1923), 7.
5 Samuels, *The Magnificent Rube,* 262; Nat Fleischer to Randy Roberts, November 3, 1971.
6 Kearns and Fraley, *The Million Dollar Gate,* 163; U.S. Department of Commerce, Bureau of the Census, *Population: Fourteenth Census of the United States,* Vol. I (Washington, D.C., 1921), 250.
7 Byron Crane, *Montana: A State Guide Book* (New York, 1939), 235.
8 *Ibid.*
9 Don Douma, "Second Bonanza: The History of Oil in Montana," *Montana Magazine of History* (Autumn, 1953), 18-30.
10 New York *Times,* May 6, 1923, p. 1; John Lardner, *White Hopes and Other Tigers,* 97-98.

11 Tony Dalich, "Shelby's Fabled Day in the Sun," *Montana Magazine of History* (July, 1965), 3-4.
12 *Ibid.*, 6.
13 *Ibid.*, 4; Lardner, *White Hopes and Other Tigers*, 99.
14 Helena *Independent*, April 14, p. 1, April 12, p. 1, April 7, p. 6, April 16, p. 4, April 30, p. 6, 1923.
15 New York *Times*, April 7, 1923, p. 11; Kearns and Fraley, *The Million Dollar Gate*, 162-65; Lardner, *White Hopes and Other Tigers*, 99-101.
16 Helena *Independent*, May 2, p. 6, May 3, p. 7, May 4, p. 6, May 5, p. 8, May 6, p. 1, 1923; New York *Times*, May 7, 1923, p. 11; Chicago *Daily News*, May 5, 1923, p. 1; Lardner, *White Hopes and Other Tigers*, 100; Kearns and Fraley, *The Million Dollar Gate*, 164-66.
17 Helena *Independent*, May 6, 1923, p. 1.
18 Quoted in Dalich, "Shelby's Fabled Day in the Sun," 5-6.
19 Reprinted in the Helena *Independent*, May 8, 1923, p. 6; New York *Times*, May 7, 1923, pp. 11, 12.
20 Helena *Independent*, May 16, pp. 1-2, May 18, p. 6, 1923.
21 Helena *Independent*, May 18, p. 1, May 24, p. 8, June 1, p. 6, 1923; Dalich, "Shelby's Fabled Day in the Sun," 7.
22 Grantland Rice, *The Tumult and the Shouting: My Life in Sport* (New York, 1954), 124-25; Dalich, "Shelby's Fabled Day in the Sun," 7-8; Lardner, *White Hopes and Other Tigers*, 104.
23 Rice, *The Tumult and the Shouting*, 124; Gallico, *Farewell to Sport*, 19-20.
24 Gallico, *Farewell to Sport*, 18.
25 Helena *Independent*, May 22, 1923, p. 6; New York *Times*, June 14, 1923, p. 15; Dalich, "Shelby's Fabled Day in the Sun," 7-8.
26 Dalich, "Shelby's Fabled Day in the Sun," 5.
27 Helena *Independent*, May 31, p. 6, June 3, p. 8, 1923.
28 *Ibid.*, June 7, 1923, p. 1; New York *Times*, June 7, 1923, p. 15. Helena *Independent*, June 14, pp. 1, 5, June 28, p. 7, 1923.
29 New York *Times*, May 19, 1923, p. 10; Eilleen Humphrey Finley to *Montana Magazine of History* (October, 1965), 8; Helena *Independent*, May 24, 1923, p. 8.
30 New York *Times*, June 21, 1923, p. 16.
31 Helena *Independent*, June 12, p. 1, June 15, pp. 1, 3, June 16, p. 1, 1923; New York *Times*, June 16, 1923, p. 1.
32 Helena *Independent*, June 15, 1923, pp. 1, 3; New York *Times*, June 16, 1923, p. 1; John Lardner, *White Hopes and Other Tigers*, 106.
33 Helena *Independent*, June 16, 1923, p. 7; Kearns and Fraley, *The Million Dollar Gate*, 169-72.
34 Helena *Independent*, June 17, 1923, pp. 1, 7; New York *Times*, June 17, p. 1, June 18, p. 10, June 19, p. 19, 1923.
35 Helena *Independent*, June 16, 1923, pp. 4, 7; New York *Times*, June 18, 1923, p. 11.
36 New York *Tribune*, June 18, 1923, p. 13; Helena *Independent*, June 28, 1923, p. 1.
37 New York *Tribune*, June 29, 1923, pp. 14, 16; New York *Times*, June 29, 1923, p. 13.
38 Helena *Independent*, June 28, 1923, p. 1; New York *Times*, June 29, 1923, p. 13; New York *Tribune*, June 27, 1923, p. 12.
39 Helena *Independent*, June 30, 1923, pp. 1, 8; New York *Times*, June 30, 1923, p. 7.
40 Helena *Independent*, June 29, p. 1, June 30, p. 8, 1923; New York *Times*, June 30, 1923, p. 10.
41 New York *Tribune*, July 3, 1923, p. 1; Helena *Independent*, July 2, p. 1, July 3, p. 1, 1923.
42 Lardner, *White Hopes and Other Tigers*, 110; Dalich, "Shelby's Fabled Day in the Sun," 10-12; Kearns and Fraley, *The Million Dollar Gate*, 172-74.
43 New York *Tribune*, June 26, 1923, p. 12.
44 Helena *Independent*, June 30, 1923, p. 8.

45 *Ibid.*, June 23, 1923, p. 7; New York *Tribune*, July 5, 1923, p. 1; Rex Lardner, *Legendary Champions*, 232.

46 New York *Tribune*, July 5, 1923, pp. 1, 13; John Lardner, *White Hopes and Other Tigers*, 110–11; Dalich, "Shelby's Fabled Day in the Sun," 14.

47 New York *Tribune*, July 5, 1923, pp. 1, 13.

48 *Ibid.*; Lardner, *White Hopes and Other Tigers*, 111–12; Dalich, "Shelby's Fabled Day in the Sun," 21; New York *Times*, July 5, 1923, p. 1, Helena *Independent*, July 5, 1923, p. 1.

49 Quoted in Dalich, "Shelby's Fabled Day in the Sun," 14; Loubet et al. (eds.), *Ring Record Book*, 81.

50 New York *Tribune*, July 5, 1923, p. 13; Helena *Independent*, July 5, 1923, p. 1.

51 New York *Tribune*, July 4, 1923, p. 8.

52 *Ibid.*, July 5, 1923, p. 13; Lardner, *White Hopes and Other Tigers*, 111.

53 Loubet, et al. (eds.), *Ring Record Book*, 10, 420–41; Jersey Jones, "10th Year of Boxing's Hall of Fame," *Ring* (November, 1963), 16–28; "Tommy Gibbons: March 22, 1891–November 19, 1960," *Boxing Illustrated and Wrestling News* (February, 1961), 32–35.

54 New York *Tribune*, July 5, 1923, p. 13.

55 *Ibid.*; Robert Ripley (ed.), *Everlast Boxing Record: 1924* (New York, 1924), 38–42; "Gibbons Only Boxer to Last Fifteen Rounds with Dempsey," *Ring* (January, 1924), 45–47; Fleischer, *Jack Dempsey: The Idol of Fistiana*, 219–23.

56 New York *Tribune*, July 5, 1923, p. 13; Helena *Independent*, July 6, 1923, p. 7.

57 John Lardner, *White Hopes and Other Tigers*, 113–15; Kearns and Fraley, *The Million Dollar Gate*, 175–78.

58 "The 'Big Business' of Prize-Fighting," *Literary Digest* (October 13, 1923), 64; "The Fight Craze," *Literary Digest* (June 28, 1923), 49–55; Fleischer, "As We See It," *Ring* (August, 1923), 9; "From Homer to Hearst," *Outlook* (July 18, 1923), 401.

59 Helena *Independent*, July 5, p. 1, July 8, p. 5, July 12, p. 4, 1923. The July 8 article estimated that the Chamber of Commerce and concessionaires in Shelby lost $300,000.

60 *Ibid.*, July 10, p. 1, July 11, p. 1, July 12, p. 7, 1923; John Lardner, *White Hopes and Other Tigers*, 115–16; Kearns and Fraley, *The Million Dollar Gate*, 177–79; Interview, Dan Daniel, December 27, 1973.

61 Dalich, "Shelby's Fabled Day in the Sun," 23; New York *Tribune*, July 5, 1923, p. 13.

CHAPTER IX

1 New York *Tribune*, July 13, 1923, p. 1.

2 *Ibid.*, pp. 1, 12; New York *Times*, July 13, 1923, pp. 1, 2.

3 New York *Tribune*, July 13, 1923, p. 12.

4 New York *Times*, July 13, 1923, p. 2; New York *Tribune*, July 15, Sec. 3, p. 6, July 16, p. 13, 1923.

5 Vernon Van Ness, "Argentinians Go Wild Over Firpo," *Ring* (June, 1922), 13; Samuels, *The Magnificent Rube*, 264–65.

6 Dempsey, December 26, 1973; Bromberg, *Boxing's Unforgettable Fights*, 141; Kearns and Fraley, *The Million Dollar Gate*, 180–81, New York *Times*, July 15, p. 20, July 26, p. 9, July 29, Sec. 2, p. 1, 1923; New York *Tribune*, July 29, 1923, Sec. 3, p. 1.

7 San Francisco *Chronicle*, July 6, 1923, p. 22; New York *Times*, July 26, p. 12, July 14, p. 10, 1923; New York *Tribune*, July 17, 1923, p. 12.

8 Grombach, *The Saga of Sock*, 72; Rice, *The Tumult and the Shouting*, 120.

9 New York *Times*, September 6, 1923, p. 12; John Lardner, *White Hopes and Other Tigers*, 141; Johnston, *Ten—And Out*, 11.

10 Bromberg, *Boxing's Unforgettable Fights*, 142; Grombach, *The Saga of Sock*, 73–74; W. O. McGeehan, "Battles of the Century," in *Sport U.S.A.: The Best From the Saturday Evening Post*, ed. Harry T. Paxton (New York, 1961), 122; New York *Times*, September 3, 1923, p. 11; John Lardner, *White Hopes and Other Tigers*, 149–50.

11 John Lardner, *White Hopes and Other Tigers*, 138, 143–44.

12 Fleischer, "As We See It," 9; New York *Times*, August 4, p. 10, August 18, p. 6, August 19, p. 22, 1923.

13 New York *Times*, August 23, p. 11; September 12, p. 16, 1923.

14 *Ibid.*, August 5, p. 24, August 27, p. 8, 1923; Gallico, *Farewell To Sport*, 24; Randall Poe, "The Writing of Sports," *Esquire* (October, 1974), 174.

15 Rice, *The Tumult and the Shouting*, 120; New York *Times*, August 15, p. 14, September 8, p. 9, August 23, p. 11, August 31, p. 13, September 1, p. 9, 1923.

16 Paul Gallico, "My Fight with Jack Dempsey," *Reader's Digest* (July, 1954), 11-14; Gallico, *Farewell to Sport*, 290-91; Jerome Holtzman (ed.), *No Cheering in The Press Box* (New York, 1974), 63-64; George Plimpton, *Shadow Box* (New York, 1977), 61-62.

17 Gallico, "My Fight with Dempsey," 12; Kearns and Fraley, *The Million Dollar Gate*, 182-85; Dempsey and Dempsey, *Dempsey*, 157-59.

18 New York *Tribune*, September 10, 1923, p. 12; Gallico, "My Fight with Dempsey," 12.

19 Gallico, *Farewell to Sport*, 291-92; Gallico, "My Fight with Dempsey," 13-14; Washington *Post*, September 10, 1923, p. 10; Holtzman (ed.), *No Cheering in The Press Box*, 64-65.

20 New York *Times*, August 19, p. 24, September 12, p. 16, September 14, p. 18, 1923; New York *Tribune*, August 19, 1923, Sec. III, p. 5; New York *Times*, September 8, p. 9, September 14, p. 18, 1923.

21 New York *Times*, September 8, p. 9, September 12, p. 16, September 13, p. 23, 1923; New York *Tribune*, September 1, 1923, p. 10.

22 New York *Tribune*, September 14, p. 19, September 10, p. 8, July 6, p. 8, July 14, p. 6, 1923.

23 *Ibid.*, September 14, 1923, pp. 2, 14.

24 "The Fight Craze," *Literary Digest* (June 28, 1923), 51.

25 Bruce Bliven, "Arc Lights and Blood: Ringside Notes at the Dempsey-Firpo Fight," *New Republic* (September 26, 1923), 126; New York *Tribune*, September 15, 1923, p. 1.

26 Dempsey, December 26, 1973; John Lardner, *White Hopes and Other Tigers*, 140; McGeehan, "Battles of the Century," 123.

27 New York *Times*, September 14, 1923, p. 14; Fleischer, *50 Years at Ringside*, 122-24.

28 New York *Tribune*, September 14, 1923, pp. 1, 4; New York *Times*, August 20, p. 8, September 9, Sec. 2, p. 1, September 14, p. 14, 1923.

29 New York *Tribune*, September 15, 1923, p. 10; New York *Times*, September 15, 1923, p. 2; Samuels, *The Magnificent Rube*, 266.

30 New York *Times*, September 15, 1923, p. 2; New York *Tribune*, September 15, 1923, p. 10.

31 Daniel, December 26, 1973; New York *Times*, September 15, 1923, p. 2; New York *Tribune*, September 15, 1923, p. 10.

32 New York *Tribune*, September 15, 1923, p. 10; *Jack Dempsey vs. Luis Firpo*, Hauppauge, N.Y.: Ring Classics, no. 16 (hereafter referred to as *Dempsey vs. Firpo*. Unless noted, all fight description is based on the film.); Samuels, *The Magnificent Rube*, 265-66; Dempsey and Dempsey, *Dempsey*, 160.

33 Paul Gallico, "Portrait of a Legend," in *Esquire's Great Men and Moments in Sports* (New York, 1962), 11, 12; Allan Davis, "Lies About the Fight," *Freeman* (October 10, 1923), 114; John D. McCallum, *The World Heavyweight Boxing Championship: A History* (Radnor, Pa., 1974), 97.

34 *Dempsey vs. Firpo.*

35 New York *Tribune*, September 15, 1923, p. 1; Davis, "Lies About the Fight," 114; Gallico, *Farewell to Sport*, 20.

36 Dempsey, December 26, 1973.

37 Frank G. Menke, "Dempsey-Firpo," in *The Fireside Book of Boxing*, ed. W. C. Heinz (New York, 1961), 292; Peter Heller (ed.), *"In This Corner . . . !" Forty World Champions Tell Their Stories* (New York, 1973), 60; Jim Dawson, "Boxing," in *Sports' Golden Age: A Close-Up of the Fabulous Twenties*, ed. Allison Danzig and Peter Brandwein (New York,

1948), 62; Bromberg, *Boxing's Unforgettable Fights*, 145–46; Dawson, "Boxing," 62; Gallico, "Portrait of a Legend," 11; Rice, *The Tumult and the Shouting*, 122–23.

38 Menke, "Dempsey-Firpo," 293; Kearns and Fraley, *The Million Dollar Gate*, 188–89.

39 New York *Tribune*, September 15, 1923, pp. 1, 10, 11, 15; New York *Times*, September 15, 1923, p. 2; Menke, "Dempsey-Firpo," 293; Bliven, "Arc Lights and Blood, Ringside Notes at the Dempsey-Firpo Fight," 126.

40 Heimer, *The Long Count*, 114; Bliven, "Arc Lights and Blood," 126; New York *Tribune*, September 15, pp. 1, 10, 1923; Dawson, "Boxing," 61; Nat Fleischer, "Dempsey-Firpo Bout Most Thrilling of Modern Heavyweight Champion Contests," *Ring* (January, 1923), 42; Fleischer, "As We See It," *Ring* (October, 1923), 29; Gallico, "Portrait of a Legend," 12.

41 Bliven, "Arc Lights and Blood," 115; quoted in "'Big Business' of Prize Fighting," 62.

42 Quoted in "Moralizing on the Million-Dollar Fight," *Literary Digest* (October 6, 1923), 35–36; *Christian Science Monitor*, September 15, 1923, p. 18; Stuart Chase, "The Etiquette of Big Business," *Nation* (October 10, 1923), 383.

43 New York *Times*, September 17, p. 17; Fleischer, "As We See It," *Ring* (October, 1923), 8.

44 New York *Times*, September 17, p. 17, September 18, p. 20, 1923, Fleischer, "As We See It," *Ring* (November, 1923), 1.

45 Nat Fleischer, "As We See It," *Ring* (November, 1923), 9; Daniel, December 26, 1973.

46 See, for example, Bromberg, *Boxing's Unforgettable Fights*, 147; Dawson, "Boxing," 62–63; Fleischer, "As We See It," *Ring* (November, 1923), 9.

47 Fleischer, "As We See It," *Ring* (November, 1923), 9; Bromberg, *Boxing's Unforgettable Fights*, 147.

48 Robert Ripley, "He Stands Supreme," *Ring* (December, 1923), 47.

CHAPTER X

1 Dempsey, December 26, 1973.

2 New York *Times*, November 27, p. 17, November 30, p. 20, December 2, Sec. 2, p. 5, 1923.

3 New York *Times*, November 29, p. 27, December 14, p. 26, 1923; January 2, p. 20, 1924.

4 Joe Lourie, Jr., *Vaudeville: From the Honky-Tonks to the Palace* (New York, 1953), 407; *Variety*, November 12, p. 50, January 10, p. 6, 1924.

5 New Orleans *States*, February 12, 1924, pp. 1–2; New Orleans *Times-Picayune*, February 11, 1924, pp. 11, 15.

6 *Washington Post*, February 23, 1924, pp. 1, 4, New York *Times*, February 23, 1924, p. 1.

7 New York *Times*, February 24, Sec. 2, p. 1, February 28, p. 15, February 29, p. 20, 1924, March 1, p. 10, March 2, p. 23, 1924; Smelser, *The Life That Ruth Built*, 292–93; New York *Tribune*, March 2, 1924, Sec. 3, p. 1.

8 Dempsey and Dempsey, *Dempsey*, 186.

9 Dempsey, December 26, 1973; New York *Times*, March 4, 1924, p. 14.

10 New York *Times*, January 27, 1922, p. 18, January 6, 1923, p. 10, April 1, 1924, p. 15; *Variety*, April 2, April 9, p. 18, 1924; New York *Tribune*, March 25, 1924, p. 16.

11 Al Carson, "Masters of the Seven Arts Keen Students of Boxing," *Ring* (July, 1922), 9; *Police Gazette*, November 18, 1922, p. 11; *Variety*, January 31, 1920, p. 10.

12 New York *Times*, September 1, 1924, p. 10; *Police Gazette*, May 20, p. 19, September 27, p. 9, 1924.

13 New York *Tribune*, June 5, 1924, p. 17; "Dempsey as a Movie Actor," *Literary Digest* (June 21, 1924), 61–63.

14 *Police Gazette*, May 24, p. 4, June 21, p. 1, July 26, p. 13, 1924; quoted in Frederick Lewis Allen, *Only Yesterday: An Informal History of the 1920s* (New York, 1931), 84; quoted in Roderick Nash, *The Nervous Generation: American Thought, 1917–1930* (Chicago, 1970), 142.

15 "Jack Dempsey in Oil," *Literary Digest* (August 18, 1923), 34.

16 Betts, "Organized Sports in Industrial America," 398-99, 655-66; Donald Braider, *George Bellows and the Ashcan School of Painting* (Garden City, N.Y., 1971), 136; quoted in "Dempsey Among the Immortals," *Literary Digest* (October 31, 1925), 50.

17 New York *Times*, August 21, 1924, p. 12; Gallico, *Farewell to Sport*, 27.

18 New York *Times*, July 6, p. 23, July 22, p. 10, August 3, p. 28, 1924; Dempsey and Dempsey, *Dempsey*, 165-66.

19 *Variety*, October 8, p. 5; November 5, pp. 5, 9, November 12, p. 1, 1924; New York *Times*, October 8, p. 13, November 4, p. 27, 1924; Lourie, *Vaudeville*, 121, 126; John E. Dimeglio, *Vaudeville, U.S.A.* (Bowling Green, Ohio, 1973), 129-30.

20 *Variety*, October 29, 1924, p. 3; Robert W. Creamer, *Babe: The Legend Comes to Life* (New York, 1974), 254-55. Based on the conversion of Ruth's income to a 1957 standard.

21 Loubet, December 26, 1973.

22 Dempsey, December 26, 1973.

23 *Variety*, April 16, 1924, p. 26; Dempsey and Dempsey, *Dempsey*, 167-68.

24 Dempsey and Dempsey, *Dempsey*, 168; New York *Times*, September 5, 1924, p. 20.

25 New York *Times*, January 10, p. 15, January 17, p. 7, January 31, p. 10, February 1, p. 1, February 8, p. 1, February 9, p. 6, 1925; San Francisco *Chronicle*, February 8, 1925, p. 1; New York *Herald-Tribune*, February 8, 1925, p. 1.

26 Gallico, *Farewell to Sport*, 26; Dempsey, Considine, and Slocum, *Dempsey*, 155.

27 New York *Times* Collection, National Archives, 306-NT, #13; Dempsey and Dempsey, *Dempsey*, 113; quoted in "Has Dempsey, Like Samson, Been Shorn of His Power?" *Literary Digest* (September 19, 1925), 68; Gallico, *Farewell to Sport*, 26.

28 New York *Times*, May 7, p. 15, May 24, Sec. 10, p. 7, 1925; John Malcolm Brinnin, *The Sway of the Great Saloon: A Social History of the North Atlantic* (New York, 1971), 387, 430; Dempsey and Dempsey, *Dempsey*, 174.

29 New York *Times*, May 13, p. 18, May 19, p. 17, May 20, p. 19, May 24, p. 7, May 27, p. 19, May 31, Sec. 10, p. 6, June 3, p. 19, June 16, p. 19, 1925.

30 *Ibid.*, June 3, p. 19, June 25, p. 16, 1925.

31 Gene Fowler, *Skyline: A Reporter's Reminiscence of the 1920s* (New York, 1961), 264-77; Dempsey and Dempsey, *Dempsey*, 174-76; Dempsey, Considine, and Slocum, *Dempsey*, 156-63.

32 New York *Times*, March 29, 1926, p. 3; Fowler, *Skyline*, 276.

33 Dempsey and Dempsey, *Dempsey*, 175; Dempsey, Considine, and Slocum, *Dempsey*, 157-58; Fowler, *Skyline*, 276.

34 New York *Times*, July 5, 1925, Sec. 2, p. 3; Fowler, *Skyline*, 276-77; Dempsey and Dempsey, *Dempsey*, 175-76; Dempsey, Considine, and Slocum, *Dempsey*, 159-63.

35 London *Times*, July 6, 1925, p. 5; New York *Times*, July 5, Sec. 9, p. 1, July 9, p. 17, 1925; Plimpton, *Shadow Box*, 23.

36 New York *Times*, April 24, p. 14, April 27, p. 10, 1925; *Variety*, July 8, 1925, p. 27; Dempsey and Dempsey, *Dempsey*, 176.

37 Kearns and Fraley, *The Million Dollar Gate*, 199; Dempsey and Dempsey, *Dempsey*, 169-73.

38 New York *Times*, April 10, p. 24, April 11, p. 17, April 15, p. 14, April 18, p. 11, July 18, p. 9, July 21, p. 17, July 30, p. 16, August 12, p. 18, August 15, p. 9, November 5, p. 19, 1925; *Variety*, June 17, 1925, pp. 1, 45; quoted in "Has Dempsey, Like Samson, Been Shorn of his Power?" 68.

39 Dempsey and Dempsey, *Dempsey*, 161-62.

40 "Has Dempsey, Like Samson, Been Shorn of His Power," 68; New York *Times*, April 11, p. 17, July 18, p. 9, 1925.

41 Mickey Walker and Joe Reichler, *Mickey Walker: The Toy Bulldog and His Times* (New York, 1961), 89-147; *Variety*, January 6, 1926, p. 12; New York *Times*, September 8, p. 24, October 28, p. 22, November 2, p. 29, November 6, p. 28, 1925, February 13, p. 20, June 29, p. 24, 1926.

42 Quoted in "Has Dempsey, Like Samson, Been Shorn of his Power?" 70; *Variety*, September 9, 1925, p. 2; *Police Gazette*, July 5, 1924, p. 10; New York *Times*, July 30, p. 19, August 27, pp. 3, 17, 1926.

CHAPTER XI

1 Robert Ripley, *Everlast Boxing Record*, 22.
2 Ed Hughes, "The Jack Dempsey Shadow," *Ring* (November, 1926), 29.
3 "Tex" Rickard, "'Tex' Rickard's Ranking of the World's Boxers on Their Records for the Year 1925," *Ring* (February, 1926), 7; Herbert G. Goldman, "Contenders: Heavyweights," *Ring* (July, 1978), 34-35, 53; "Boxing Thrones That Wobble," *Literary Digest* (February 16, 1924), 68.
4 New York *Times*, August 11, 1926, p. 16.
5 Fleischer, "*Sockers in Sepia*", 46-50, 56-60; "Harry Wills, World's Negro Heavyweight Champion," *Ring* (January, 1924), 19.
6 "Black, White and Yellow," *Opportunity* (January, 1924), 4; Nat Fleischer, "As We See It," *Ring* (August, 1926), 19; Spike Webb, "Harry Wills Has Fine Chance To Beat Dempsey, Heavyweight Champion," *Ring* (April, 1926), 15.
7 Samuels, *The Magnificent Rube*, 276.
8 Gene Tunney, "My Fights with Jack Dempsey," in *The Aspirin Age: 1919-1941*, ed. Isabel Leighton (New York, 1949), 156-57.
9 *Ibid.*, 158.
10 Loubet et al. (eds.), *Ring Record Book*, 176-77.
11 Fleischer, *Sockers in Sepia*, 50; John Lardner, *White Hopes and Other Tigers*, 168.
12 John Lardner, *White Hopes and Other Tigers*, 174.
13 *Ibid.*, 174-75.
14 *Ibid.*, 175; New York *Times*, June 2, p. 19, June 23, p. 21, 1926.
15 New York *Times*, July 28, 1926, p. 1; George Walsh, *Gentleman Jimmy Walker*, (New York, 1974), 92; James A. Farley, *Behind the Ballots: The Personal History of a Politician*, 43-51.
16 John Lardner, *White Hopes and Other Tigers*, 174, 179.
17 New York *Times*, August 11, p. 16, August 13, p. 13, August 15, Sec. 9, p. 1, August 17, p. 16, 1926.
18 *Ibid.*, August 19, p. 1, August 20, p. 16, 1926; *Police Gazette*, September 4, p. 19, October 30, p. 19, 1926; Fleischer, *Sockers in Sepia*, 60.
19 Francis Albertanti, "Tunney Is First New York Born Heavyweight Champion Since Hyer," *Ring* (November, 1926), 6-7.
20 Gene Tunney, *Arms for Living* (New York, 1941), 24; "Lieutenant Tunney, the Pride of the Marines," *Literary Digest*, (October 16, 1926), 44.
21 Tunney, "My Fights with Jack Dempsey," 152-54; Tunney, *Arms for Living*, 95-99.
22 Heimer, *The Long Count*, 9; Tunney, "My Fights with Jack Dempsey," 155-57.
23 Quoted in "Lieutenant Tunney, the Pride of the Marines," 44; New York *Times*, September 27, 1926, p. 18.
24 Tunney, "My Fights with Jack Dempsey," 159-62; Tunney, *Arms for Living*, 200-208, 227-33; Matthew J. Bruccoli and Richard Layman (eds.), *Some Champions: Sketches and Fiction by Ring Lardner* (New York, 1976), 71; Ring Lardner, Jr., *The Lardners*, 148-49.
25 John Lardner, *White Hopes and Other Tigers*, 171; Trevor Wignall, *Ringside* (London, 1941), 103.
26 Allen, *Only Yesterday*, 175.
27 Gallico, *Farewell to Sport*, 25.
28 New York *Times*, August 22, 1926, Sec. 10, p. 1.
29 *Ibid.*, August 17, p. 16, August 26, p. 13, September 17, p. 15, September 21, p. 24, 1926;

John Lardner, *White Hopes and Other Tigers,* 180.

30 Dempsey and Dempsey, *Dempsey,* 198; Daniel, December 26, 1973.

31 New York *Times,* September 12, Sec. 10, p. 1, September 17, p. 15, 1926; Philadelphia *Inquirer,* September 14, 1926, p. 22; Gallico, *Farewell to Sport,* 25.

32 Fowler, *Skyline,* 281-82.

33 Tunney, "My Fights with Jack Dempsey," 158; Tunney, *Arms for Living,* 119-21.

34 Dempsey, December 26, 1973; Tunney, "My Fights with Jack Dempsey," 157-58.

35 Heimer, *The Long Count,* 12-14; New York *Times,* September 24, 1926, p. 1.

36 Dempsey, December 26, 1973; Dempsey and Dempsey, *Dempsey,* 190-91.

37 Heimer, *The Long Count,* 92-94; New York *Times,* December 2, 1926, p. 32; Dempsey and Dempsey, *Dempsey,* 202-203; Dempsey, December 26, 1973.

38 Philadelphia *Inquirer,* September 22, p. 21, September 24, p. 1, 1926; New York *Times,* September 22, p. 21, September 24, p. 1, September 30, p. 18, 1926; Loubet et al., *Ring Record Book,* 86.

39 Mencken, *A Mencken Chrestomathy,* 403; Philadelphia *Inquirer,* September 24, 1926, pp. 1, 2; New York *Times,* September 13, p. 27, September 19, Sec. 11 p. 5, September 24, pp. 1-3, 1926; John Lardner, *White Hopes and Other Tigers,* 170; Heimer, *The Long Count,* 15-17; Walsh, *Gentleman Jimmy Walker,* 92; Rex Lardner, *Legendary Champions,* 263.

40 New York *Times,* September 24, 1926, p. 1.

41 *Ibid.,* Nat Fleischer, "Dempsey-Tunney Fight Would Save World's Heavyweight Title From Strangulation," *Ring* (September, 1926), 4; *National Police Gazette,* June 12, p. 19, June 26, p. 19, July 3, p. 19, July 10, p. 11, September 25, p. 18, 1926.

42 Philadelphia *Inquirer,* September 24, 1926, p. 2; New York *Times,* September 24, 1926, p. 2; Heimer, *The Long Count,* 17-18.

43 Tunney, *Arms For Living,* 124-25; New York *Times,* September 24, 1926, p. 1; Heimer, *The Long Count,* 19.

44 Tunney, *Arms For Living,* 125; *Dempsey-Tunney: Fights 1 and 2,* Universal 8 Films: Classic Fights #8; New York *Times,* September 24, 1926, pp. 1-2; Philadelphia *Inquirer,* September 24, 1926, pp. 1-2; Heimer, *The Long Count,* 19-20.

45 New York *Times,* September 24, 1926, p. 2.

46 Daniel, December 26, 1973; Dempsey, December 26, 1973; New York *Times,* September 24, 1926, p. 2; Philadelphia *Inquirer,* September 24, 1926, p. 25; Heimer, *The Long Count,* 22-23.

47 New York *Times,* September 24, 1926, pp. 1, 5.

48 *Ibid.,* p. 5; Dempsey and Dempsey, *Dempsey,* 202; quoted in New York *Times,* September 30, 1926, p. 18.

49 New York *Times,* September 25, 1926, p. 16; Daniel M. Daniel, "Has Dempsey Gone Back Enough To Lose His World's Heavyweight Title to Tunney?," *Ring* (September, 1926), 5; Nat Fleischer, "Poison of Worry Quenched Spark in Dempsey and Helped Tunney Win Title," *Ring* (December, 1926), 4; Philadelphia *Inquirer,* September 25, 1926, p. 10; Quoted in Ring Lardner, Jr. *The Lardners,* 148.

50 New York *Times,* September 24, pp. 6-7, September 27, p. 24, 1926.

51 Loubet et al. (eds.), *Ring Record Book,* 86.

52 Samuels, *The Magnificent Rube,* 284; Heimer, *The Long Count,* 24; New York *Times,* December 28, 1926, p. 31.

CHAPTER XII

1 Daniel, December 26, 1973.

2 Heimer, *The Long Count,* 60; New York *Times,* March 13, 1927, Sec. 9, p. 7.

3 Dempsey and Dempsey, *Dempsey,* 206-10; Dempsey, December 26, 1973.

4 New York *Times,* January 21, p. 11, June 23, p. 17, April 2, p. 12, 1927.

5 New York *Times*, February 24, 1927, p. 19.

6 *Ibid.*, February 26, p. 9, April 2, p. 12, April 29, p. 17, 1927; Heimer, *The Long Count*, 118–19.

7 New York *Times*, May 21, 1927, p. 13; Heimer, *The Long Count*, 139–40.

8 New York *Times*, June 11, p. 14, June 23, p. 17, 1927.

9 *Ibid.*, June 24, p. 19, June 25, p. 16, 1927; Heimer, *The Long Count*, 155.

10 Quoted in "Million-Dollar Query: Can Dempsey Come Back?" (*Literary Digest*, July 9, 1927), pp. 46, 49.

11 "Million-Dollar Query," 48; New York *Times*, June 24, p. 19, June 25, p. 11, June 26, Sec. 10, p. 8, June 27, p. 15, June 30, p. 23; Heimer, *The Long Count*, 155.

12 New York *Times*, July 3, 1927, Sec. 1 p. 10.

13 *Ibid.* Dempsey, Considine and Slocum, *Dempsey*, 197; Dempsey and Dempsey, *Dempsey*, 212.

14 New York *Times*, July 3, Sec. 9, p. 1, July 4, p. 11, 1927.

15 *Ibid.*, July 5, p. 26, July 17, Sec. 9, p 1, 1927; Heimer, *The Long Count*, 156.

16 Rice, *The Tumult and the Shouting*, 132; Loubet et al. (eds.), *Ring Record Book*, 178; New York *Times*, July 20, p. 18, July 21, p. 15, 1927.

17 *Ibid.*, July 21, 1927, p. 1; Heimer, *The Long Count*, 166; Farley, *Behind the Ballots*, 50–51.

18 Heimer, *The Long Count*, 168–69; New York *Times*, July 22, 1927, pp. 1, 11.

19 *Police Gazette*, August 20, 1927, pp. 6, 19.

20 *Jack Dempsey vs. Jack Sharkey, Ring Classic*: no. 4 (unless noted, all description of the fight is based on the film); New York *Times*, July 21, 1927, p. 15.

21 New York *Times*, July 22, 1927, pp. 10–11; Heimer, *The Long Count*, 170; Interview, Jack Sharkey, June, 1973.

22 New York *Times*, July 22, 1927, p. 10.

23 Heimer, *The Long Count*, 171; New York *Times*, July 22, 1927, p. 10.

24 Heimer, *The Long Count*, 171; New York *Times*, July 22, 1927, p. 1; Chicago *Daily News*, July 21, 1927, p. 1, July 22, 1927, p. 1; San Francisco *Chronicle*, July 22, 1927, p. 1; New Orleans *Times-Picayune*, July 22, 1927, p. 1; New York *Herald Tribune*, July 22, 1927, p. 1; *Police Gazette*, August 6, 1927, p. 19.

25 New York *Times*, July 22, 1927, p. 1; Heimer, *The Long Count*, 172.

26 New York *Times*, July 22, 1927, p. 1; Heimer, *The Long Count*, 172.

27 New York *Times*, July 22, 1927, p. 10.

28 *Ibid.*, July 22, 1927, p. 18; Chicago *Daily News*, July 22, 1927, p. 1; San Francisco *Chronicle*, July 22, 1927, p. 1; Heimer, *The Long Count*, 174.

29 Dempsey and Dempsey, *Dempsey*, 213; New Orleans *Times-Picayune*, July 24, p. 4, July 25, p. 1, 1927; New York *Times*, July 25, 1927, p. 17.

30 Samuels, *The Magnificent Rube*, 289; New York *Times*, July 24, 1927, Sec. 9, p. 1; Heimer, *The Long Count*, 177.

31 Lloyd Wendt and Herman Kogan, *Big Bill of Chicago* (New York, 1953), 277; New York *Times*, July 26, p. 12, July 28, p. 11, July 29, p. 12, August 2, p. 14, 1927; Heimer, *The Long Count*, 177–79.

32 New York *Times*, July 26, 1927, p. 12.

33 Don S. Kirschner, *City and Country: Rural Responses to Urbanization in the 1920's* (Westport, Conn., 1970), 97–110.

34 New York *Times*, July 28, p. 11, July 29, p. 12, August 2, p. 14, 1927; Heimer, *The Long Count*, 180–81.

35 New York *Times*, August 16, p. 23, September 9, p. 21, September 20, p. 23, September 27, p. 11, 1927; *Police Gazette*, September 10, 1927, p. 11; "The Tunney-Dempsey Fight: A World Spectacle," *Literary Digest* (September 17, 1927), 36.

36 New York *Times*, August 22, p. 13, September 5, p. 14; September 3, p. 7, 1927; Heimer, *The Long Count*, 191; *Police Gazette*, October 15, 1927, p. 23.

37 New York *Times*, September 3, p. 7, September 12, p. 18, 1927; Chicago *Tribune*, September 16, 1927, p. 17; New York *Times*, August 27, p. 11, August 31, p. 16, September 5, p. 9, September 12, p. 18, 1927.

38 Gallico, *Farewell To Sport*, 25; Dempsey and Dempsey, *Dempsey*, 205–15; Heimer, *The Long Count*, 183–232.

39 Chicago *Tribune*, September 19, 1927, p. 1; New York *Times*, September 19, 1927, p. 20; Heimer, *The Long Count*, 216–19.

40 New York *Times*, September 19, p. 20, September 20, p. 23, 1927; Heimer, *The Long Count*, 220–32.

41 Chicago *Tribune*, September 21, p. 23, September 22, pp. 1–2, 1927; Heimer, *The Long Count*, 222–32.

42 New York *Times*, September 23, p. 21, September 24, p. 10, July 28, p. 11, 1927.

43 Heimer, *The Long Count*, 234–35.

44 Loubet et al., *Ring Record Book*, 87; quoted in Heimer, *The Long Count*, 238.

45 Chicago *Tribune*, September 23, 1927, p. 5; Rice, *The Tumult and the Shouting*, 152–53.

46 New York *Times*, August 27, p. 12, September 23, 1927, p. 18; Chicago *Tribune*, September 23, 1927, pp. 1–2; Gallico, *Farewell to Sport*, 101.

47 Samuels, *The Magnificent Rube*, 289.

48 *Dempsey and Tunney: Fights 1 and 2*, Famous Fights, no. 8; New York *Times*, September 23, 1927, p. 18.

49 Tunney, "My Fights with Jack Dempsey," 163–64.

50 Heimer, *The Long Count*, 249; Daniel, December 26, 1973.

51 Tunney, "My Fights with Jack Dempsey, 163–64.

52 *Ibid.*, 166–67; Heimer, *The Long Count*, 247–51.

53 Gallico, *Farewell to Sport*, 22.

54 Heimer, *The Long Count*, 253.

55 New York *Times*, September 24, p. 10, September 28, p. 21, 1927; Chicago *Tribune*, September 24, 1927, p. 4.

56 New York *Times*, September 26, 1927, p. 21.

57 Gallico, *Farewell to Sport*, 23.

EPILOGUE

1 F. Scott Fitzgerald, *The Great Gatsby* (New York, 1925), 6; Dempsey, December 26, 1973.

2 New York *Times*, August 12, p. 6, August 31, p. 23, October 22, p. 29, October 23, p. 28, 1928; *Variety*, September 5, pp. 51, 53, September 12, pp. 51–52, September 19, p. 50, September 26, pp. 48, 51, 53, October 17, p. 49, October 24, pp. 50, 52, 1928; George Jean Nathan, "Dempsey as an Actor," *American Mercury* (November, 1928), 377–78.

3 Dempsey and Dempsey, *Dempsey*, 221–26.

4 *Ibid.*, 226–33.

5 Dempsey, December 26, 1973.

6 For a good treatment of Dempsey's later years see, Dempsey and Dempsey, *Dempsey*, 221–309.

7 Fowler, *Skyline*, 312.

8 Dempsey, December 26, 1973.

9 Gallico, *Farewell to Sport*, 15–18; Grantland Rice, "Was Jack the Giant Killer?" *Collier's* (May 28, 1927), 9.

10 Horace Gregory, *Collected Poems* (New York, 1964), 5–6.

11 Gallico, *Farewell to Sport*, 29.

Bibliography

PRIMARY SOURCES

Manuscripts

Jack Dempsey. Antiboxing material. Department of Justice, Mails and Files Division. Record Group: 203014-20. National Archives.

Jack Dempsey. Anti Draft material. Department of Justice, Mails and Files Division. Record Group: 25-11-51. National Archives.

Jack Dempsey. Shelby material. Department of Justice, Mails and Files Division. Record Group: 11-116-1. National Archives.

Jack Dempsey. New York Times Photograph Files. National Archives.

Nat Fleischer to Randy Roberts. Correspondence.

Government Documents

Journal of the House of Representatives of the Eighty Third General Assembly of the State of Ohio. May, 1919, 1067.

U.S. Bureau of the Census. *Fourteenth Census* (1920). *Population: Fourteenth Census of the United States,* Vol. I. Washington, D.C.: Government Printing Office, 1921.

U.S. Congress. *Congressional Record.* 61st Cong., 2nd Sess.; 70th Cong., 1st Sess.

U.S. House of Representatives. Committee on Interstate and Foreign Commerce. *Federal Boxing Commission. Hearings* before the Committee on Interstate and Foreign Commerce, House, on H.R. 8635, H.R. 8676, H.R. 9140, H.R. 9196, H.R. 9426, H.R. 9633, 89th Cong., 1st Sess., 1965.

U.S. Senate. Committee on the Judiciary. *Professional Boxing: Part 1 Jacob "Jake" LaMotta. Hearings* before the subcommittee on Antitrust and Monopoly of the Committee on the Judiciary, Senate, pursuant to S. 238, 86th Cong., 2nd Sess., 1960.

U.S. Senate. Committee on the Judiciary. *Professional Boxing: Part 2 Frank Carbo. Hearings* before the subcommittee on Antitrust and Monopoly of the Committee of the Judiciary, Senate, pursuant to S. 238, 86th Cong., 2nd Sess., 1960.

297

BIBLIOGRAPHY

U.S. Senate. Committee on the Judiciary. *Professional Boxing: Part 3 Legislative. Hearings* before the subcommittee on Antitrust and Monopoly of the Committee on the Judiciary, Senate, on S. 1474, 87th Cong., 1st Sess., 1961.

U.S. Senate. Committee on the Judiciary. *Professional Boxing: Part 4 Liston-Clay Fight. Hearings* before the subcommittee on Antitrust and Monopoly of the Committee on the Judiciary, Senate, on S. 1182, 88th Cong., 2nd Sess., 1964.

U.S. War Department. *Manual of Physical Training.* Washington, D.C.: Government Printing Office, 1914.

Newspapers

Atlanta *Constitution.* 1918–1927.

Baton Rouge *State Times.* 1919–1927.

Bogalusa *Enterprise and American.* 1919.

Chicago *Daily News.* 1918–1927.

Chicago *Tribune.* 1927.

Christian Science Monitor. 1919–1927.

Helena *Independent.* 1923.

Japan *Times.* 1919–1927.

London *Times.* 1919–1927.

Manchester *Guardian.* 1919–1927.

New Orleans *States.* 1918–1927.

New Orleans *Times-Democrat.* 1892.

New Orleans *Times Picayune.* 1916–1927.

New York *Herald-Tribune.* 1925–1930.

New York *Sun.* 1919.

New York *Times.* 1910–1930.

New York *Tribune.* 1916–1924.

Omaha *Daily Bee.* 1908–1915.

Omaha *Daily News.* 1908–1915.

Omaha *Evening World-Herald.* 1908–1915.

Omaha *Morning World Herald.* 1908–1915.

Opelousas *St. Landry Clarion.* 1919.

St. Louis *Post-Dispatch.* 1918–1927.

San Francisco *Chronicle.* 1916–1930.

Stars and Stripes. 1918.

Toledo *Blade.* 1919.

Variety. 1919–1930.

Washington *Post.* 1919–1927.

Articles

"An Odious Comparison." *Freeman*, May 30, 1923.

"Barnum Was Great, But 'Tex' Rickard Gets More Money." *Literary Digest*, June 25, 1921.

Bennett, Arnold. "The Great Prize Fight." *Living Age,* January 24, 1920.

"Benny Leonard Disagrees with Bertrand Russell on Boxing." *Literary Digest,* March 17, 1928.

" 'Big Business' of Prize Fighting." *Literary Digest,* October 13, 1923.

Bliven, Bruce. "Arc Lights and Blood: Ringside Notes at the Dempsey-Firpo Fight." *New Republic,* September 26, 1923.

"Boswell Takes Dr. Samuel Johnson to the Beckett-Carpentier Fight." *Literary Digest,* January 17, 1920.

"Boxing Reduced to Sordid Money-Grabbing." *Literary Digest,* February 14, 1920.

"Boxing Thrones that Wobble." *Literary Digest,* February 16, 1924.

Broun, Heywood. "A Bolt from the Blue." *Nation,* July 31, 1920.

Broun, Heywood. "It Seems to Heywood Broun." *Nation,* August 8, 1928.

Broun, Heywood. "Mr. Dempsey's Five-Foot Shelf." *Bookman,* August, 1921.

" 'Carbuncle' of Boyle's Thirty Acres." *Literary Digest,* July 30, 1921.

"Carpentier: A Symbol." *New Republic,* July 20, 1921.

"Carpentier: From Pit-boy to Esthete of the 'Boxe.' " *Literary Digest,* June 11, 1921.

" 'Champion Fighters' of To-day and Some Days Ago." *Literary Digest,* July 26, 1919.

Chase, Stuart. "The Etiquette of Big Business." *Nation,* October 10, 1923.

"Corbett to Tunney on 'How to Win the Mob.' " *Literary Digest,* January 14, 1928.

Davis, Allan. "Lies About the Fight." *Freeman,* October 10, 1923.

"Dempsey as an Actor." *American Mercury* (November, 1928).

Dempsey, Jack, with Wesley Stout. "Those Were the Days." *Saturday Evening Post,* March 28, 1931.

"Dempsey Among the Immortals." *Literary Digest,* October 31, 1925.

"Dempsey as a Movie Actor." *Literary Digest,* June 21, 1924.

"Did 'Psychic' Power Aid Brown When Carpentier Licked Beckett?" *Literary Digest,* January 17, 1920.

"Esthetics and Pugilism." *Literary Digest,* August 27, 1921.

"Fight Craze." *Literary Digest,* June 28, 1923.

"Fist Civilization vs. Sword Civilization." *Living Age,* September 24, 1921.

Foster, Thomas. "Why Our Soldiers Learn to Box." *Outing,* May, 1918.

"French Scientists on Boxing." *American Review of Reviews,* September 1921.

"From Homer to Hearst." *Outlook,* July 18, 1923.

Gallico, Paul. "My Fight with Jack Dempsey." *Reader's Digest,* July, 1954.

"Georges Carpentier—Gentleman, Athlete, and Connoisseur of the 'Boxe.' " *Literary Digest,* April 17, 1920.

"Georges Carpentier Pens His Opinions of America." *Literary Digest,* March 5, 1921.

Hackett, Francis. "Dempsey-Carpentier." *New Republic,* July 13, 1921.

Hackett, Francis. "The Carpentier Fight: Bennett vs. Shaw." *New Republic,* January 14, 1920.

"Has Dempsey, Like Samson, Been Shorn of His Power?" *Literary Digest,* September 19, 1925.

BIBLIOGRAPHY

"Hit Him in the Slats." *Literary Digest,* June 25, 1921.

"How Painters and Poets Defined the Original Boxing 'Champ.'" *Literary Digest,* November 13, 1926.

Humphries, Rolfe. "The Fight Film." *New Republic,* November 2, 1927.

"Jack Dempsey in Oil." *Literary Digest,* August 18, 1923.

"Lieutenant Tunney: The Pride of the Marines." *Literary Digest,* October 16, 1926.

"Million-Dollar Query: Can Dempsey Come Back?" *Literary Digest,* July 9, 1927.

"Moralizing on the Million-Dollar Fight." *Literary Digest,* October 6, 1923.

Nathan, G. J. "Dempsey as an Actor." *American Mercury,* November, 1928.

"Paris Meditates on Jersey City." *Literary Digest,* August 20, 1921.

"Prize-Fighters in the Opera-House." *Literary Digest,* September 10, 1921.

Pulsifer, Harold Trowbridge. "Diana's Tenants." *Outlook,* November 17, 1920.

Rice, Grantland. "Boxing for a Million Dollars." *American Review of Reviews,* October, 1926.

Rice, Grantland. "The Iron Handshake." *Collier's,* April 13, 1929.

Rice, Grantland. "Was Jack the Giant Killer?" *Collier's,* May 28, 1927.

Rice, Grantland. "You Have to be Hungry." *Collier's,* December 8, 1928.

"Shaw Called a 'Colossal Joke' as a Prize-Fight Reporter." *Literary Digest,* April 17, 1920.

"That Terrible Combat: To a Draw, Between Dempsey and Wills." *Literary Digest,* October 14, 1922.

"Tobacco and Pugilism in the Army." *Literary Digest,* August 10, 1918.

"Toledo Clergy on the Prize-Fight." *Literary Digest,* August 9, 1919.

"Tunney-Dempsey Fight: A World Spectacle." *Literary Digest,* September 17, 1927.

"War-Record of Dempsey." *Literary Digest,* February 14, 1920.

Wilson, P. W. "The Big Prize-Fight Psychologically Considered." *Current Opinion,* August, 1921.

Books

Baker, Newton D. *Frontiers of Freedom.* New York: George D. Doran, 1918.

Bruccoli, Matthew J., and Layman, Richard, eds. *Some Champions: Sketches and Fiction by Ring Lardner.* New York: Charles Scribner's Sons, 1976.

Corbett, James J. *The Roar of the Crowd: The True Tale of the Rise and Fall of a Champion.* New York: G. P. Putnam's Sons, 1925.

Cox, James M. *Journey Through My Years.* New York: Simon and Schuster, 1946.

Crowder, Major General E. H. *The Spirit of Selective Service.* New York: Century, 1920.

Dartnell, Fred (Lord Milford). *"Seconds Out!" Chat About Boxers, Their Trainers and Patrons,* London: T. Werner Lawise.

Farley, James A. *Behind the Ballots: The Personal History of a Politician.* New York: Harcourt, Brace, 1938.

Fleischer, Nat. *50 Years at Ringside.* New York: Fleet Publishing, 1958.

BIBLIOGRAPHY

Fowler, Gene. *Skyline: A Reporter's Reminiscence of the 1920s.* New York: Viking Press, 1961.

Hart-Davis, Rupert, ed. *The Letters of Oscar Wilde.* New York: Harcourt, Brace and World, 1962.

Heller, Peter, ed. *"In This Corner. . . !": Forty World Champions Tell Their Stories.* New York: Simon and Schuster, 1973.

Holtzman, Jerome, ed. *No Cheering in the Press Box.* New York: Holt, Rinehart and Winston, 1974.

Johnson, Jack. *Jack Johnson Is a Dandy: An Autobiography.* New York: Chelsea House, 1969.

London, Jack. *The Road.* New York: Macmillan, 1907.

Mencken, H. L. *A Mencken Chrestomathy.* New York: Alfred A. Knopf, 1956.

Modern Gladiator: Being an Account of the Exploits and Experiences of the World's Greatest Fighter, John Lawrence Sullivan. St. Louis: Athletic Publishing, 1889.

Rice, Grantland. *The Tumult and the Shouting: My Life in Sport.* New York: A. S. Barnes, 1954.

Ripley, Robert, ed. *Everlast Boxing Record: 1924.* New York: Everlast Sport Publishing, 1924.

————, ed. *Everlast Boxing Record: 1925.* New York: Everlast Sport Publishing, 1926.

Stillman, Marshall. *Mass Boxing: Success Through Boxing.* New York: Marshall Stillman Association, 1920.

Tunis, John R. *$ports: Heroics and Hysterics.* New York: John Day, 1928.

Tunney, Gene. *Arms For Living.* New York: Wilfred Funk, 1941.

Interviews

Dan Daniel. December 26, 1973.

Barbara Piattelli Dempsey. December 26, 1973.

Deanna Dempsey. December 26, 1973.

Jack Dempsey. December 26, 1973.

Nat Loubet. December 26, 1973.

Jerry McKernan. October 29, 1974.

Films

Jess Willard vs. Frank Moran. Castle Films, No. 3027.

Jack Dempsey vs. Jess Willard. Ring Classics, No. 1.

Jack Dempsey vs. Bill Brennan. Ring Classics, No. 96.

Jack Dempsey vs. Georges Carpentier. Ring Classics, No. 56.

Jack Dempsey vs. Tommy Gibbens. Ring Classics, No. 28.

Jack Dempsey vs. Luis Firpo. Ring Classics, No. 16.

Jack Dempsey vs. Jack Sharkey. Ring Classics, No. 4.

Dempsey-Tunney Fights 1 and 2. Famous Fights, No. 8.

Jack Dempsey vs. Cowboy Luttrell. Ring Classics, No. 89.

BIBLIOGRAPHY

Boxing Periodicals

Big Book of Boxing. 1974–1978.

Boxing Annual. 1963–1975.

Boxing Illustrated and Wrestling News. 1958–1970.

Boxing and Wrestling. 1961–1965.

Boxing Yearbook. 1964–1975.

Fight Game. 1964.

Inside Boxing. 1963–1964.

International Boxing. 1969–1778.

International Boxing Annual. 1968–1974.

National Police Gazette. 1917–1930.

Official Ringside and Wrestling News. 1964.

Ring. 1922–1978.

World Boxing. 1970–1978.

SECONDARY WORKS

Articles

Betts, John R. "Mind and Body in Early American Thought." *Journal of American History,* LIV (March, 1968).

Betts, John Richard. "Sporting Journalism in Nineteenth-Century America." *American Quarterly,* V (Spring, 1953).

Coughlan, Robert. "Young Jack Dempsey." *Yesterday in Sport.* New York: Time-Life Books, 1968.

Dalich, Tony. "Shelby's Fabled Day in the Sun." *Montana Magazine of History,* July, 1965.

Dempsey, Jack, as told to Bob Considine, and Bill Slocum. "I Had to Fight," *Look,* January 5, 1960.

Dempsey, Jack, as told to Bob Considine and Bill Slocum. "I Was the Right Guy at the Right Time," *Look,* February 2, 1960.

Douma, Don. "Second Bonanza: The History of Oil in Montana." *Montana Magazine of History,* Autumn, 1953.

Gallico, Paul. "Portrait of a Legend." *Esquire's Great Men and Moments in Sports.* Edited by the editors of *Esquire.* New York: Harper and Brothers, 1962.

Gilmore, Al-Tony. "Jack Johnson: A Magnificent Black Anachronism in the Early Twentieth Century." *Journal of Social and Behavioral Sciences* (Winter, 1973).

———. "Jack Johnson and White Women: The National Impact." *Journal of Negro History,* LVIII (January, 1973), 18–38.

Kaplan, Jim, and Dick Weiner. "Jack Johnson: Martyr or Coward?" *Black Sports,* October, 1972, pp. 26–29.

Kearns, Jack "Doc," with Oscar Farley. "He Didn't Know the Gloves Were Loaded." *Sports Illustrated,* January 13, 1964, pp. 48–56.

302

Klapp, Orrin E. "Creation of Popular Heroes." *American Journal of Sociology*, LIV (1948).

―――. "Heroes, Villains, and Fools, as Agents of Social Control." *American Sociological Review*, XIX (1954).

―――. "Hero Worship in America." *American Sociological Review*, XIV (1949).

―――. "The Folk Hero." *Journal of American Folklore*, LXII (1949).

Lewis, William F. "Man to Man: A History of Boxing." *Mankind*, April, 1972.

Meadows, Paul. "Some Notes on the Social Psychology of the Hero." *Southwestern Social Science Quarterly*, XXVI (1945).

Neal, Larry. "Uncle Rufus Raps on the Squared Circle." *Partisan Review*, XXXIX (Winter, 1972).

Paxon, Frederich L. "The Rise of Sport." *Mississippi Valley Historical Review*, IX (September, 1917).

Poe, Randall. "The Writing of Sports." *Esquire*, October, 1974.

Roberts, Randy. "Heavyweight Champion Jack Johnson; His Omaha Image, A Public Reaction Study." *Nebraska History*, LXII (Summer, 1976).

Sipes, Richard G. "War, Sports and Aggression: An Empirical Test of Rival Theories." *American Anthropologist*, LXII (February, 1973).

Strong, Samuel M. "Negro-White Relationships as Reflected in Social Types." *American Journal of Sociology*, LII (1946).

Wiggins, William H., Jr. "Jack Johnson as Bad Nigger: The Folklore of His Life." *Black Scholar*, January, 1971.

Young, A. S. "Doc." "Was Jack Johnson Boxing's Greatest Champion." *Ebony*, January, 1969.

Books

Allen, Frederick Lewis. *Only Yesterday: An Informal History of the 1920's*. New York: Harper and Row, 1931.

Altrocchi, Julia Cooly. *The Spectacular San Franciscans*. New York: E. P. Dutton, 1949.

Anderson, Nels. *The Hobo: The Sociology of the Homeless Man*. Chicago: University of Chicago Press, 1923.

Beisser, Arnold R. *The Madness in Sports: Psychosocial Observations on Sports*. New York: Meredith Publishing, 1967.

Boorstin, Daniel L. *The Image: A Guide to Pseudo-Events in America*. New York: Harper and Row, Publishers, 1964.

Bowen, Ezra, ed. *This Fabulous Century: 1920–1930*, Vol. III. New York: Time-Life Books, 1969.

Braider, Donald. *George Bellows and the Ashcan School of Painting*. Garden City, New York: Doubleday, 1971.

Brinnin, John Malcolm. *The Sway of the Great Saloon: A Social History of the North Atlantic*. New York: Delacorte Press, 1971.

Bromberg, Lester. *Boxing's Unforgettable Fights*. New York: Ronald Press, 1962.

Brownlow, Kevin. *The Parade's Gone By*. New York: Ballantine Books, 1968.

Burns, James MacGregor. *Roosevelt: The Lion and the Fox,* Vol. I. New York: Harcourt, Brace and World, 1956.

Cantor, Norman J., and Michael S. Werthman, eds. *The History of Popular Culture Since 1815.* New York: Macmillan, 1968.

Chidsey, Donald Barr. *John the Great: The Times and Life of a Remarkable American: John L. Sullivan.* Garden City, N.Y.: Doubleday, Doran, 1942.

Cleaver, Eldridge. *Soul on Ice.* New York: Dell Publishing, 1968.

Carter, Paul. *The Twenties in America.* New York: Thomas Y. Crowell, 1968.

Cohane, Tim. *Bypaths of Glory: A Sportswriter Looks Back.* New York: Harper and Row, 1963.

Crane, Byron, ed. *Montana: A State Guide Book.* New York: Viking Press, 1939.

Creamer, Robert W. *Babe: The Legend Comes to Life.* New York: Simon and Schuster, 1974.

Cronan, Edmund David. *Black Moses: The Story of Marcus Garvey and the Universal Negro Improvement Association.* Madison: University of Wisconsin Press, 1955.

Crunden, Robert M. *From Self to Society: 1919–1941.* Englewood Cliffs, N.J.: Prentice-Hall, 1972.

Cuming, G. J. and Derek Baker, eds. *Studies in Church History,* Vol. VIII. Cambridge: Cambridge University Press, 1972.

Danzig, Allison, Peter Brandwein, eds. *Sport's Golden Age: A Close-up of the Fabulous Twenties.* New York: Harper and Brothers, 1948.

Deford, Frank. *Big Bill Tilden: The Triumph and the Tragedy.* New York: Simon and Schuster, 1975.

Dempsey, Jack, as told to Bob Considine and Bill Slocum. *Dempsey.* New York: Simon and Schuster, 1960.

Dempsey, Jack, with Barbara Piattelli Dempsey. *Dempsey.* New York: Harper and Row, 1977.

Dempsey, Jack, with Myron M. Stearns. *Round by Round: An Autobiography.* New York: McGraw-Hill, 1940.

Dibble, R. F. *John L. Sullivan: An Intimate Narrative.* Boston: Little, Brown, 1925.

Dimeglio, John E. *Vaudeville U.S.A.* Bowling Green, Ohio: Bowling Green University Press, 1973.

Dulles, Foster Rhea. *America Learns to Play: A History of Popular Recreation, 1607–1940.* New York: D. Appleton-Century, 1940.

Durant, John. *The Heavyweight Champions.* 4th ed. New York: Hastings House, 1971.

Edmonds, Anthony O. *Joe Louis.* N.d.: William B. Eerdmans, 1973.

Elias, Robert H. *"Entangling Alliances with None": An Essay on the Individual in the American Twenties.* New York: W. W. Norton, 1973.

Every, Edward Van. *Muldoon: The Solid Man of Sport.* New York: Frederick A. Stokes, 1929.

Farr, Finis. *Black Champion: The Life and Times of Jack Johnson.* London: Macmillan, 1964.

Fleischer, Nat, ed. *The 1964 Ring Record Book and Boxing Encyclopedia.* New York: Ring Book Shop, 1964.

Fleischer, Nat, and Sam Andre. *A Pictorial History of Boxing.* New York: Citadel Press, 1959.

Fleischer, Nat. *The Heavyweight Championship: An Informal History of Heavyweight Boxing from 1719 to the Present Day.* New York: G. P. Putnam's Sons, 1949.

————. *Jack Dempsey.* New Rochelle, New York: Arlington House, 1972.

————. *Jack Dempsey: The Idol of Fistiana.* New York: C. J. O'Brien, 1929.

————. *John L. Sullivan: Champion of Champions.* New York: G. P. Putnam's Sons, 1951.

————. *"Sockers in Sepia": A Continuation of the Drama of the Negro in Pugilistic Competition,* Vol. V of *Black Dynamite.* New York: C. J. O'Brien, 1947.

Fowler, Gene. *Beau James.* New York: Viking Press, 1949.

Frank, Stanley, ed. *Sports Extra: Classics of Sports Reporting.* New York: A. S. Barnes, 1944.

Fritz, Percy Stanley. *Colorado: The Centennial State.* New York: Prentice-Hall, 1941.

Fussell, Paul. *The Great War and Modern Memory.* New York: Oxford University Press, 1975.

Gallico, Paul. *Farewell To Sport.* New York: Alfred A. Knopf, 1938.

Gilmore, Al-Tony. *Bad Nigger: The National Impact of Jack Johnson.* Port Washington, N.Y.: Kennikat Press, 1975.

Goldstein, Ruby, as told to Frank Grahm. *Third Man in the Ring.* New York: Funk and Wagnalls, 1959.

Greever, William S. *The Bonanza West: The Story of the Western Mining Rushes, 1848–1900.* Norman: University of Oklahoma Press, 1963.

Gregory, Horace, *Collected Poems.* New York: Holt, Rinehart and Winston, 1964.

Grombach, John V. *The Saga of Sock: A Complete Story of Boxing.* New York: A. S. Barnes, 1949.

Hart, M. Marie, ed. *Sport in the Socio-Cultural Process.* Dubuque, Iowa: Wm. C. Brown, 1972.

Heimer, Mel. *The Long Count.* New York: Atheneum, 1969.

Heinz, W. C., ed. *The Fireside Book of Boxing.* New York: Simon and Schuster, 1961.

Henderson, Edwin Bancroft. *The Negro in Sports.* Washington, D.C.: Associated Publishing, 1949.

Hicks, John D. *Republican Ascendancy: 1921–1933.* New York: Harper and Row, 1960.

Jacobs, Lewis. *The Rise of the American Film: A Critical History.* New York: Teachers College Press, 1968.

Jacobs, Paul, Saul Landau, and Eve Pell, eds. *To Serve the Devil: Natives and Slaves,* Vol. 1. New York: Random House, 1971.

Johnston, Alexander. *Ten—And Out! The Complete Story of the Prize Ring in America.* 3rd ed. New York: Ives Washburn, 1947.

Kearns, Jack "Doc," and Oscar Fraley. *The Million Dollar Gate.* New York: Macmillan, 1966.

Kirschner, Don S. *City and Country: Rural Responses to Urbanization in the 1920s.* Westport, Conn.: Greenwood Publishing, 1970.

Klapp, Orrin E. *Heroes, Villains, and Fools: The Changing American Character.* Englewood Cliffs, N.J.: Prentice-Hall, 1962.

————. *Symbolic Leaders: Public Dramas and Public Men.* Chicago: Aldine Publishing, 1964.

Lardner, John. *White Hopes and Other Tigers.* Philadelphia: J. B. Lippincott, 1951.

Lardner, Rex. *The Legendary Champions.* New York: American Heritage Press, 1972.

Lardner, Ring, Jr. *The Lardners: My Family Remembered.* New York: Harper and Row, 1976.

Leighton, Isabel, ed. *The Aspirin Age: 1919–1941.* Simon and Schuster, 1949.

Levine, Lawrence, and Robert Middlekauff, eds. New York: Harcourt, Brace and World, 1968.

Liebling, A. J. *The Sweet Science.* New York: Grove Press, 1956.

Loubet, Nat, John Ort, George Girsch, and Dan Daniel, eds. *The 1973 Ring Boxing Encyclopedia and Record Book.* New York: Heath Cote Press, 1973.

Lowenthal, Leo. *Literature, Popular Culture, and Society.* Englewood Cliffs, N.J.: Prentice-Hall, 1961.

Lourie, Joe, Jr. *Vaudeville: From the Honkey-Tonks to the Palace.* New York: Henry Holt, 1953.

Loy, John W., Jr., and Gerald S. Kenyon. *Sport, Culture, and Society: A Reader on the Sociology of Sport.* London: Macmillan, 1969.

Lynch, Bohem. *Knuckles and Gloves.* New York: Henry Holt, 1923.

Mailer, Norman. *Existential Errands.* New York: New American Library, 1973.

McCallum, John D. *The World Heavyweight Boxing Championship: A History.* Radnor, Pa.: Chilton Book, 1974.

McElroy, Walter, ed. *San Francisco: The Bay and Its Cities.* New York: Hastings House, 1940.

Miller, Donna Mae, and Kathryn R. E. Russell. *Sport: A Contemporary View.* Philadelphia: Lea and Febiger, 1971.

Murray, Robert K. *Red Scare: A Study of National Hysteria, 1919–1920.* New York: McGraw-Hill, 1964.

Nash, Roderick. *The Nervous Generation: American Thought, 1917–1930.* Chicago: Rand McNally, 1970.

O'Connor, Richard. *The First Hurrah: A Biography of Alfred E. Smith.* New York: G. P. Putnam's Sons, 1970.

Paxton, Harry T., ed. *Sport U.S.A.: The Best from the Saturday Evening Post.* New York: Thomas Nelson and Sons, 1961.

Plimpton, George. *Shadow Box.* New York: G. P. Putnam's Sons, 1977.

Robinson, David. *Hollywood in the Twenties.* New York: Paperback Library, 1968.

Samuels, Charles. *The Magnificent Rube.* New York: McGraw-Hill, 1957.

Sheeter, Leonard. *The Jocks.* New York: Warner Paperback Library, 1969.

Schulberg, Budd. *Loser and Still Champion: Muhammed Ali.* Garden City, N.Y.: Doubleday, 1972.

Smelser, Marshall. *The Life That Ruth Built: A Biography.* New York: Quadrangle, 1975.

BIBLIOGRAPHY

Somers, Dale. *The Rise of Sports in New Orleans, 1850–1900*. Baton Rouge: Louisiana State University Press, 1972.

Sontag, Raymond J. *A Broken World*. New York: Harper and Row, 1971.

Walker, Mickey, with Joe Reichler. *Mickey Walker: The Toy Bulldog and His Times*. New York: Random House, 1961.

Walker, Mickey. *The Will to Conquer*. Hollywood, California: House-Warven, 1953.

Walsh, George. *Gentleman Jimmy Walker*. New York: Praeger, 1974.

West, Ray B., ed. *Rocky Mountain Cities*. New York: W. W. Norton, 1949.

Weston, Stanley. *The Heavyweight Champions*. New York: Ace Publishing, 1970.

W.P.A. *Colorado: A Guide to the Highest State*. New York: Hastings House, 1941.

Young, A. S. *Negro Firsts in Sports*. Chicago: Johnson Publishing, 1963.

Unpublished Theses and Dissertations

Adams, William H. "New Orleans as the National Center of Boxing." M.A. Thesis, Louisiana State University, 1950.

Betts, John C. "Organized Sports in Industrial America." Ph.D. Dissertation, Columbia University, 1951.

Callaghan, John Lawrence. "An Analysis of the Role of Sport in England and the United States." Ph.D. Dissertation, University of Southern California, 1971.

Flath, Arnold William. "A History of the Relations Between the National Collegiate Athletic Association and the Amateur Athletic Union of the United States, (1905–1963)." Ph.D. Dissertation, University of Michigan, 1963.

Maclen, Ann. "Popular Sports in New Orleans, 1890–1900." M.A. Thesis, Tulane University, 1956.

Stahl, James A. "The Progressive Movement in Toledo, Ohio, 1916–1927." M.A. Thesis, Louisiana State University.

Index